INDEPENDENT FILMMAKING AROUND THE GLOBE

Edited by Doris Baltruschat and Mary P. Erickson

Independent Filmmaking around the Globe calls attention to the significant changes taking place in independent cinema today, as new production and distribution technology and shifting social dynamics make it easier for independent filmmakers to produce films outside both the mainstream global film industry and their own national film systems. Identifying and analysing the many complex forces that shape the production and distribution of feature films, the authors detail how independent filmmakers create work that reflects independent voices and challenges political, economic, and cultural constraints.

With chapters on the under-explored cinemas of Greece, Turkey, Iraq, China, Malaysia, Peru, and West Africa, as well as traditional production centres such as the United States, the United Kingdom, Canada, and Australia, *Independent Filmmaking around the Globe* explores how contemporary independent filmmaking increasingly defines the global cinema of our time.

DORIS BALTRUSCHAT is an SSHRC Research Fellow and instructor in the Department of Theatre and Film and the Centre for Cinema Studies at the University of British Columbia. A former juror for the Canadian Independent Film and Video Fund, she has extensive professional experience in the film and television sectors.

MARY P. ERICKSON is a film/media consultant who specializes in distribution, marketing, research, and writing and founder of the Pacific Northwest Media Research Consortium.

Independent Filmmaking around the Globe

Edited by

Doris Baltruschat and Mary P. Erickson

UNIVERSITY OF TORONTO PRESS
Toronto Buffalo London

ISBN 978-1-4426-4948-4 (cloth)
ISBN 978-1-4426-2683-6 (paper)

Printed on acid-free, 100% post-consumer recycled paper with vegetable-based inks.

Library and Archives Canada Cataloguing in Publication

Independent filmmaking around the globe / edited by Doris Baltruschat and Mary P. Erickson.

Includes bibliographical references and filmography.
ISBN 978-1-4426-4948-4 (bound).   ISBN 978-1-4426-2683-6 (pbk.)

1. Independent films – Production and direction.   2. Independent films – History and criticism.   3. Motion picture producers and directors.
I. Baltruschat, Doris, author, editor   II. Erickson, Mary, 1977–, author, editor

PN1995.9.I457I54 2015   791.4309   C2014-908494-3

University of Toronto Press acknowledges the financial assistance to its publishing program of the Canada Council for the Arts and the Ontario Arts Council, an agency of the government of Ontario.

Canada Council   Conseil des Arts
for the Arts   du Canada

ONTARIO ARTS COUNCIL
CONSEIL DES ARTS DE L'ONTARIO

an Ontario government agency
un organisme du gouvernement de l'Ontario

University of Toronto Press acknowledges the financial support of the Government of Canada through the Canada Book Fund for its publishing activities.

Contents

Foreword

Producing Independently in a Global Industry

DAVID HAMILTON

Filmmaking is often described as a collaborative art and is perhaps the most collaborative of all the arts. Paradoxically, this may explain why so much energy is expended resisting influence or control from any external forces – especially those forces that are not considered to be on the creative side of the collaborative spectrum.

There is a hierarchy of evil where influence is concerned, and at the very top is the studio executive who, looking out from his pala-tial offices, searches the skyline for creative genius over which he can impress his will and thus dilute the genius magic potion to a consist-ency that can be consumed by the largest audience. This image has been promoted and passed on ever since studios came into existence and in some cases by the executives themselves. It is the major reason that the definition of independence has been so often related to inde-pendence from film studios and studio executives. That is not to say that there is no truth in this stereotype. Very, very few directors obtain final cut from the studios, and this is one of the key criteria that filmmakers use in determining their freedom quotient.

Studios are not the only threat to independence, or even the major threat. If we count the number of films made each year throughout the world and calculate the percentage of these that have been made under studio direction, we find that it is very small. If we consider every film director's career over the past fifty years and look at how many direc-tors have ever even spoken to a studio, let alone worked within the confines of a studio production, we would also find this to be a tiny percentage.

The greater threat to independent filmmaking throughout the world, I believe, comes from the exertion of control by governments and by religious, issue-based, and commercial interest groups. There is an increasing awareness of the pervasive intrusions that governments are exercising in our private lives. Much of it appears benign and dormant in Western society, but as more and more information is collected and stored, it provides the fuel for more aggressive interventions in the future. There are many signs of governments' intense desire for greater control even today, but they are somewhat held at bay by the still widely held belief that a democratic and free society is a good thing. As this belief is eroded by the fear of a shift in the world's power balance, it provides a more fertile ground for governments to let loose more increasingly restrictive practices.

There are examples currently throughout the world of governments that find no obstructions of either conscience or public opinion to limit their blatant constrictions on filmmakers and storytelling. There are numerous, well-known examples of attempts on the part of the power elite to control the recording of facts and history and to stifle independent voices that attempt to present an alternative view.

While shooting the film *Water*[1] in India in the year 2000, we were attacked by a crowd of angry Hindu fundamentalists who were apparently outraged by our portrayal of Indian widows. They had no knowledge of the script, and we were perplexed as to the source of their discontent. The Indian Ministry of Information and Broadcasting reviews the scripts of all foreign productions to ensure that there is nothing in the content that could put India in a bad light. We had submitted *Water*, and they had issued full permissions for our shoot and assigned an officer to our set to ensure that we shot the script we had submitted.

When the riots started, the Indian government provided us with three hundred heavily armed troops to move us in convoy to the set every day. When one of the fundamentalists attempted suicide in protest of our film, the ensuing riots convinced the authorities that they could not provide us with adequate protection, and we were shut down.

We subsequently found out that the protestors had been paid and that the so-called suicide attempt was performed by a person who did this as a profession. All of the press knew this, but it was reported as if the issues were real and not the politically motivated charade that it turned out to be. We were told that one of the political parties had

---

1 *Water* (2005) is an internationally acclaimed and Academy Award–nominated film written and directed by Deepa Mehta and produced by David Hamilton.

fomented this pretence in order to gain favour with its electorate and to promote itself as a protector of the Hindu faith. Our meetings with government ministers, religious leaders, and community activists in an attempt to save the situation were always cordial and sympathetic, but, as it turned out, they were all quite aware of the conspiracy and in a collusive relationship with the perpetrators.

I know I am beginning to sound like a fearful, mistrustful, iconoclastic anarchist. But this sort of thinking is an even more dangerous threat to independent filmmaking and storytelling; the concern over what one sounds like or how one might be perceived, or the tendency to follow trends that others have found successful, corrodes our ability or even desire to create original, meaningful content.

How many times have we heard someone say that his or her film is a bit like *My Big Fat Greek Wedding* or, more recently, like *Slumdog Millionaire*. Of course, they are hoping that some buyer will see the similarity and follow the crowd. But even voicing these notions takes away from the originality of the initial creative impulse.

The most profound example of this thinking is in Hollywood itself where over the past five years the majority of films have been based on comic books; here the fan base is built in, and the storyboard is effectively already in place. One can simply assemble the movie by moving the image blocks like a Lego set. Everyone is aware of *Batman, Superman,* and *The Hulk,* but what about *Art School Confidential, Oblivion, Road to Perdition,* and *A History of Violence*? These are also based on comics.

Not that there is anything wrong with comics and not that they cannot be made into compelling films. It is the obsessive servitude to a particular kind of thinking or the desperate clinging to an approach or a genre that creates enormous limitations on the independence of the filmmaking process and has reverberations far beyond the studio lot. It creates a restrictive diet for the potential audience and limits the opportunities for a wide-ranging, luculent cinematic experience. A bit like junk food: delicious but not nourishing or sustaining.

The challenge for independence is not the studios themselves but the limits that their product induces on the audiences' exploratory impulse.

There are many other impediments to independent filmmaking. The focus has been on financing and access to resources and talent, but the issues extend beyond the production process itself to the sale, marketing, and ultimately the exhibition of the film. Not surprisingly, independent filmmaking is most often associated with low-budget art films bereft of marquee acting talent, whose only star is often the director.

Film sales agents and distributors often insist on these attention-getting elements to fuel the launch of a film into the marketplace. Without these aids, independent films have difficulty securing distribution and must hope for recognition from major festivals to gain the momentum that will then garner the interest of companies that can bring the film to market. There are, of course, sales agents and distributors throughout the world who specialize in "art films," but their capacity to absorb new films is limited.

Ultimately the distributor is competing with the Hollywood machine to secure screens and solicit the attention of the media. The barriers to theatrical distribution are increasing, which means that there is greater pressure on independent filmmakers to create movies with a higher quality of execution, and the acting talent must be clearly mind blowing.

At one time there were critics who gave special attention to independent art films, and therefore there was an opportunity to gain audience attention through excellent reviews. Consolidation has eliminated the positions of many newspaper film critics. The ones who are left are syndicated in multiple news outlets, and there is therefore a less diverse landscape of opinion and thus less choice in the theatre. These critics are compelled to give most of their attention to the larger films that already exist in the psyche of their readership, leaving very little room for the smaller films.

Television has also raised the bar for filmmakers and has obstructed the passion of the audience for the theatrical experience. The quality of television production has exploded, the stories that are told are more compelling, and the outlets for viewing are far better and more varied. Binge watching of TV series on a weekend has nudged out the movie night at the cinema hall.

So where is the light at the end of the tunnel? And why are there so many film schools releasing imaginative, passionate, and dedicated storytellers into the world when there appears to be a disappearing venue for the expression of their talent?

The answer appears to be simple, and to that extent somewhat trite, but the landscape for sharing one's creative impulses with a very large audience has altered enormously. The word *viral* has assumed an entirely new meaning in the twenty-first century. Without the instant link to a significant percentage of the world's population how else could you imagine that "Gangnam Style" would become a global phenomenon?

New technologies have affected each and every phase of the life of a film except perhaps the evolution and discovery of new talent, which continues to require the disciplined labour and hungry acquisition of experience by real humans. Financing, production, post-production, sales, marketing, and exhibition have all been impacted by the ability to reach out instantaneously to a constituency that may be interested in what the independent filmmaker is doing.

Crowdfunding has already supported the creation of numerous films (Zach Braff's *Wish I Was Here*, Rob Thomas's *Veronica Mars*, Charlie Kaufman's *Anomalisa*, and Sean and Andrea Fine's *Inocente*). Digital technology has increased immeasurably the ability of independent filmmakers on smaller budgets to create production values that challenge some of the larger films. Much more can be accomplished for far less. Films were exposed to the potential audience long before traditional sales organizations became involved. Outlets for the exhibition of films are expanding and more varied (Netflix; Rogers, Bell, and other big-name providers of on-demand; Hulu; Amazon; Google; Blockbuster On Demand; iTunes). These platforms have become a normal step in the distribution chain. The timing of distribution events is collapsing, and in some cases it can make sense to alter the sequence of distribution and utilize an Internet distributor as the launching platform for a new film if it results in attracting other distribution channels.

Indie directors have even begun to give their movies away for free in order to build up a fan base and get attention. Timo Vuorensola, a Finnish director, released his parody *Star Wreck* for free. He figured it was never going to look attractive to mainstream distributors (it is in Finnish), so he built up an online fan base, and nine million people have since downloaded his movie. He made $430,000 in merchandise on a film that cost him $21,500 to make. These impressive numbers attracted distributors, and Vuorensola has since signed a distribution deal with Revolver Entertainment.

Joss Whedon's *Dr. Horrible's Sing-a-Long Blog* (a three-part short film) was released to the Internet for free viewing. Then it was taken down and sold through regular channels. People had loved it, shared it, told all their friends, and then everyone went out and bought it because they already knew they liked it. I am attracted to this approach and have opened dialogue with distributors to see how this might be implemented in concert with a theatrical release.

American animator Nina Paley released her film *Sita Sings the Blues* directly online for free. Like Vuorensola, Paley also sells merchandise on her site, and she has a donation link. The buyers know that the money is going directly to supporting the filmmaker. To date, Paley has made net profits of $55,000 and secured theatrical distribution in France and the United States.

Filmmakers who release their films for free, or for free for a limited time, start by building interest through social media: blogs, Facebook, YouTube teaser trailers. The goal is to have it go viral and, if it does not go viral, at least to drum up enough interest from the target audience.

The studios are not blind to these incursions into their traditional territories, and as with all entrenched power structures, they are trying to protect their dominance by appropriating the capabilities that this new world offers. There is a gigantic reshuffling of power taking place, however, and the new players have a strong edge springing from their creative initiative that is unbound by traditional distribution channels. Twitter, iTunes, Amazon, Google, Netflix, YouTube, and many others are vying for supremacy. Inevitably there will be greater consolidation and centralization of power, but in the meantime it creates tremendous opportunities for the independent filmmaker and for a revitalization of the autonomous voice.

Acknowledgments

Independent Filmmaking around the Globe is the result of a collaborative effort among researchers and scholars of independent film and cinema. What began as a joint panel discussion at the annual conference of the Society of Cinema and Media Studies in 2010 has been expanded and deepened into a comprehensive study of independent filmmaking practices around the globe. The authors would herewith like to acknowledge the contributions of colleagues, mentors, and friends who made this collaborative achievement possible. We are especially grateful for the constructive feedback we received from colleagues who reviewed the initial manuscript.

We heartily thank our contributors whose work shines a light on an influential and oft-overlooked segment of global cinema. We would also like to thank the filmmakers and other film professionals who are featured in nearly every chapter in this volume. Their participation has deepened the understanding and nuances of filmmaking in unique contexts.

To our editor at University of Toronto Press, Siobhan McMenemy, we express sincere thanks and appreciation for her early and enthusiastic support of this project. The manuscript has improved considerably thanks to the copy-editing skills of Susi Gómez and Angela Inabinett. Scott Forland lent his skills in Photoshop to recreate tables in some of the chapters.

Many thanks go to our families for supporting us while we worked on this book. Mary would like to thank Lucas, Katrine, and Dane Erickson (who came along in the middle of this project) for their love and support. Doris would like to thank her partner, Robin Wylie, for his love, great sense of humour, and occasional proofreading and editorial inputs throughout the project.

INTRODUCTION

Chapter One

The Meaning of Independence: Concepts, Contexts, and Interpretations

DORIS BALTRUSCHAT AND MARY P. ERICKSON

Independent Filmmaking around the Globe calls attention to key developments in independent filmmaking today. It presents independent filmmaking practices in North America, Europe, Africa, Asia, and Australia through a critical analysis of the complex forces that alternately influence and shape the production and distribution of feature films. From historical transitions in countries marked by conflict and change to forces of globalization and the question of identity in cultural works, the volume details the ways in which filmmakers around the world define the "independent voice" in response to, and in spite of, constraints resulting from economic, political, and cultural boundaries.

At the economic level the conventional Hollywood models of film production, distribution, and exhibition have been marked, particularly in the last few decades, by increased corporatization, synergy, hyper-commercialization, and the maximization of revenues. At the same time, co-productions, subcontracting arrangements, and diversification have also become part of the day-to-day operations of major conglomerates, from Disney to Sony to Warner Brothers (Wasko 2003; McDonald and Wasko 2008). The proliferation of American so-called independent films, produced and distributed by specialty divisions of the Hollywood majors, highlights this intricate balancing act between convergence and diversification, while pointing towards the complexity of defining the meaning of *independent film*. Not surprisingly, many film industries around the world have adopted Hollywood modes of production as well as embraced media-conglomerate modes of operation, with the result of flattened cultural content and the emphasis on economic success over cultural, political, or social contributions.

However, the contemporary global film landscape is equally marked by change and diversity with regard to film production and distribution. Today, media-producing communities across the globe are more aware of each other, resulting in widely shared production practices and collaborative activities. Co-financing arrangements and co-productions between European and international partners are increasingly common. Similarly, international film festivals play a significant role in promoting independent films while facilitating networking opportunities for filmmakers and distributors. In addition, digital technology has upended conventional modes of production and distribution. Digital media enable independent filmmakers to produce feature films under difficult environmental conditions – for example, in the Canadian high Arctic – and to circumvent traditional distribution channels by using the Internet as a platform for their work. Digital technology has eliminated the need for expensive cameras and 35 mm film (Cohen 2013). Consequently, independent filmmaking is being facilitated and supported by high-end digital cameras, editing software, Internet distribution sites, and increased ease of home viewing thanks to video on demand and cloud computing. These production and distribution processes unfold and are completed with lower budgets, fewer crew members, and minimal marketing, particularly as more filmmakers rely on social media – from Facebook to Twitter – to connect with audiences.

Digital technologies also force a more nuanced discussion of piracy, specifically the necessity of reconceiving the phenomenon as a mode of distribution. Piracy has long troubled Hollywood because it challenges industry dominance by increasing access to films via DVDs, VCDs (video compact discs), and the Internet, as discussed by Martin Mhando (2009) and Sheila Petty (2008) in their chapters on African cinema.[1] Access has also increased in terms of exhibition via digital technologies, as many more websites are devoted to promoting and screening films across the globe; in turn, these technologies enable diasporic audiences to connect with their native countries. In addition, DVD players and digital projectors enable easier exhibition in the form of microcines in remote regions of Peru and mobile cinemas in Iraq.[2]

As a result, these changes and innovations are beginning to dismantle traditions and conventions. Hollywood's grip on international distribution, for example, is less forceful today, as can be seen when we examine how independent filmmaking communities around the globe challenge traditions and conventions. Driven by technological innovations, along with rapidly changing political, economic, and cultural contexts, spaces have emerged in which independent filmmakers can produce films outside of the dominant global film industry and move beyond the constraints of their own national film systems. These developments have significant implications for a greater variety of feature films circulating through international distribution channels. The objective of *Independent Filmmaking around the Globe* is to provide insights into how independent filmmaking is reshaping and influencing the global production and distribution of films, thus marking a break from past traditions in which Hollywood-type production models dominated the international scene.

Today any country's film industry is one that reflects multiple stories and perspectives. There are the nationally sanctioned films, produced by major studios, such as those in Hollywood or Bollywood, or financed and marketed by government organizations, as in the case of Canada and Australia. There is also the broad scope of small-budgeted films, created by filmmakers who may be largely unknown on the international scene but who are highly respected within their own production communities. Filmmaker and author Erik Knudsen reveals the passion that drives many independent filmmakers to produce features, even under difficult or adverse circumstances that range from lack of funding to stringent government mandates. In his chapter titled "Dependency and Independence" he states that filmmakers' "stories, their character and their family and social upbringing conspire to make them create work that challenges conventions of production, form and content." This passion is shared by many independent filmmakers, who find unique ways to tell their stories on film, be it an Inuit myth as in Zacharias Kunuk and Norman Cohn's *Atanarjuat: The Fast Runner* (2001) or the ways in which Athina Rachel Tsangari tells a story in her Greek film *Attenberg* (2010). These films represent unique contributions to an ever-changing media landscape, where the range of audio-visual media production is vast, but all of it contributes to the overall cultural fabric of a country and of the globe. With the rise of broader participation in and awareness of internationalized film production, we can witness shifts in conventional paradigms of audio-visual media production. The purpose of this book is to study the ways in which the traditional approaches of filmmaking are being transformed and innovative methods and practices are being cultivated and applied in response to a global film industry in transition.

Defining Independence

There are a number of complexities involved in defining *independence* with regard to the production and distribution of feature films (King 2005). Film production inevitably encapsulates the dichotomy of art and commerce, which are not always conterminous. On the contrary, the "dependency" on mainstream financing, production, and distribution channels tends to delimit creative spaces for those filmmakers who seek unique cultural and artistic expressions for their works. This has also led to the standardization of film narratives, predictable generic conventions, and editing formulae, as well as the practice of franchising and serializing popular films (from the *Star Wars* franchise to the *Twilight* saga) in favour of corporate objectives rather than ingenuity and diversity. In stark contrast, independent filmmakers risk to be "different" in their artistic expression and experimentation with storytelling and stylistic novelties and in challenging the status quo. As some countries adopt policies of liberalization and privatization (for example, China), the question arises, how will this have an impact on their locally based and burgeoning independent film movements? Although the removal or scaling back of state regulation opens up the possibilities for enriched independent filmmaking, one has to speculate whether liberalized industry policies will ultimately nurture or hinder the needs and objectives of independent filmmakers.

Independent film does not have one singular definition that applies in all cases. Certainly, work outside the mainstream industry can signal independent filmmaking, but how do we identify that mainstream industry? This might imply Hollywood or Bollywood, or it might imply a government-sanctioned film industry. Several chapters in this volume, including those by Knudsen, Ryan, and Baltruschat, address how governments designate "independent film" for the purpose of cultural policies, funding, and tax incentives. Official subsidies or incentives are issued to counteract the dominance of Hollywood film distribution and exhibition and to develop infrastructures that support the growth of national film industries. Support mechanisms are tied to producers' abiding to criteria and quotas, which may include onscreen representation of characters or cultures, participation of local talent, language, and place of production – all in the name of creating and sustaining national identity.

However, official involvement in local film production may not always lead to desired outcomes. As Mark David Ryan points out,

Australian productions must have a certain level of Australian creative input to qualify for subsidies or incentives. Yet, since the 1990s, official co-production policies – combined with an increasing focus on the global marketplace – have resulted in blurring the lines between Hollywood and local productions, rather than creating a unique Australian cinema. In particular, the mixing and matching of international stars, crews, and creative talent in co-production often lead to films with no distinctive Australian voice or, in some cases, no Australian features, characters, or storylines at all. In the case of Canada's Zacharias Kunuk, his status as an Inuit filmmaker highlighted problems with official cultural policies that were intended to support the country's film industry. In her chapter on filmmaking in Arctic Canada, Baltruschat cites discriminatory practices, in which applicants were required to apply for the smaller Telefilm Canada's Aboriginal production fund (for the film, *Atanarjuat: The Fast Runner*) rather than the more substantial envelope designated for funding Canadian films. In Malaysia, as outlined by Gaik Cheng Khoo, films made in one of the country's numerous local languages are designated as "non-Malay" and are typically considered independent.

We can see that these types of restrictions on how institutional state support is defined are based on fairly exclusive and arbitrary markers. While many of these definitions are intended to promote national filmmaking and industries, they also draw boundaries around the kinds of films that can be made, possibly limiting the range of voices that contribute to the cultural landscape.

Surprisingly, in some cases, a mainstream industry may not even be a factor. Such is the case with filmmaking in Iraq, as discussed by Mary Erickson in this volume. In her chapter "Filmmaking in Iraq: A Rebirth" she describes how the country has only a very small film industry, with no distinction whatsoever between the production of films that are mainstream, government-sanctioned, or independent.

All chapters in *Independent Filmmaking around the Globe* offer a definition of independent filmmaking. They reveal startling congruencies in what it means to create films outside the mainstream industry, and provide evidence of different production practices found in various countries around the world. Tzioumakis's fine-grained analysis describes various phases that have shaped independent filmmaking in the United States, from *independent* to *indie* to *indiewood*, thus pointing towards the importance of the changing political, economic, and cultural contexts, which greatly influence a filmmaker's capacity to be independent at certain points in film history.[3] For this volume, we are predominantly concerned with the practices of filmmaking – those industrial conditions, whether professional, amateur, or somewhere in-between, in which films are produced, distributed, and exhibited. These conditions are dependent on location, historical moments, types of film, their auteurs, and the various stages in a film's production and distribution processes. They are also dependent on the changing nature of feature film development, which is increasingly collaborative across international borders.

An Increasingly Global Cinema

Many of today's filmmakers are global citizens. They are cosmopolitan and media savvy and have been exposed to the world through travel, global pop culture, and attendance at international media venues, such as film festivals and markets. Some have been trained overseas, as is the case with a number of filmmakers in Iraq, while others are self-taught or have been trained by local media organizations. Even though some may produce films on an individual basis, they usually enlist the support of others, through cast and crew, financing, distribution, or exhibition. Filmmaking is at its core a collaborative effort, as noted by David Hamilton in his foreword to this volume. Today, even audiences could be considered part of this collaboration, given the growth and expansion of social media. The question arises then whether filmmaking is inherently *interdependent*. It is collaborative and networked and increasingly spread around the globe. It has typically been dependent on formal institutions such as festivals, investors, or theatres, but the practice has already begun to shift and draw on alternate financing and distribution models, from crowdfunding to new digital and multi-platform distribution channels.

Film funding is increasingly global in nature. International co-productions and co-financing arrangements continue to be on the rise, as budgets are developed according to the incentives presented by governments and partners around the world. Today many independent filmmakers draw on European-based funding sources. Some of these include the World Cinema Fund in France (formerly Fonds Sud), Hivos, the Hubert Bals Fund, the Jan Vrijman Fund, the UK Film Council, TV Española, and other financial or related support from embassies or national cultural ministries. Particularly for filmmakers working in developing countries, these funding sources are tied to development goals and may be linked to colonial roots, as detailed by Mhando in this volume. Certainly, producers still apply for nationally based funds (such as funding from Telefilm Canada or the Greek Film Center), and European filmmakers still access the MEDIA Program for assistance, as Teresa Hoefert de Turégano details in her discussion on European funding mechanisms. Others bypass these formal processes in favour of different models, such as gathering "donations" from interested fans via the process of crowdfunding, or deferring payment to cast and crew, as Lydia Papadimitriou outlines in her chapter on Greek cinema. Increasingly, filmmakers need to cobble together a range of funding sources because single or local sources may be insufficient on their own. The range of sources now extends into the international realm, which contributes to the overall ethos of independent filmmaking as markedly global.

While established filmmakers still participate in the international film festival circuit, screening films at Rotterdam, Cannes, Berlin, Singapore, Dubai, Havana, and elsewhere, many emerging producers are opting to use digital platforms and social media to reach out to audiences for a first glance at their new film. This trend is spreading rapidly in countries with well-developed broadband infrastructures. Yet, Gabriela Martínez rightly points towards a persisting digital divide when she comments on Peruvian filmmakers who had to shoot on traditional film stock in order to qualify for the country's CONACINE grants. Nonetheless, given the fact that Eastman Kodak declared bankruptcy in January 2012, and Panavision and Arriflex halted the production of 35 mm cameras a month later, any filmmakers adamant to shoot on traditional film stock will see their budgets increase significantly, in North America and other parts of the world (Stewart 2013). In other words, digital production and distribution will continue to proliferate and allow for new talent to enter the film industry.

As *Independent Filmmaking around the Globe* highlights, the global dominance of Hollywood is not as totalizing as it would like to believe, nor is it as secure in its foothold. Indeed, in 2013, Steven Spielberg and George Lucas caused shock waves to ripple through the industry when they commented on the "implosion" of Hollywood in the near future. In their view, high-budget and high-risk U.S. blockbuster production is unsustainable in the long run (Iordanova 2010). Yet Hollywood continues to integrate new models of filmmaking into its processes, often usurping or co-opting alternatives to cut costs, eliminate crew positions, reach global audiences, and adapt to, or counter-attack, global movie piracy. Some industries, such as Aussiewood (to use Mark David Ryan's term), welcome Hollywood's traditional financial strength; this professional service industry in Australia partners with Hollywood studios to produce films. But the dominant global force of Hollywood is also being supplanted by major industries elsewhere, such as Bollywood and Nollywood, in addition to many independent filmmakers' innovative uses of digital and social media platforms to create and distribute their works.

Outline of Chapters

Independent Filmmaking around the Globe examines the meaning of independent filmmaking in a contemporary global context. No longer dependent on reproducing formulaic Hollywood production and narrative models, independent filmmakers are charting a new course in creating cultural works that reflect the independent voice and that mark a clear departure from cinematic traditions. This volume offers new insights into contemporary global cinema. At the same time it highlights the importance of studying independent filmmaking as a global initiative for greater media diversity and democracy.

To provide a comprehensive mapping of global cinema, the book's authors address independent filmmaking in the United Kingdom, southern Europe, Iraq, China, North America, Peru, West Africa, Australia, and elsewhere. They reveal how independent filmmaking is characterized in these regions, including the differences between national cinema and the independent voice; the question of identity in cultural works; newly emerging financing models; the impact of international organizations on local production; and the role and meaning of global cinema. The following chapters therefore address a wide range of topics associated with independent filmmaking, including conceptualization, financing, production, co-production, distribution, and exhibition. Several chapters have been written by authors who, in addition to their scholarly activities, are actively involved in the film industry as independent filmmakers, producers, or policy analysts. Their expertise and first-hand experience add another dimension to the study of independent filmmaking in contemporary and global contexts.

In the first section of the book, independent filmmaking practices are examined within the context of national and international financing models, thus highlighting the complexities of film production in the current era of global cinema. Several chapters cover independent film vis-à-vis national and mainstream production practices, which can be either in alignment or in contention with global market dynamics. Accordingly, Yannis Tzioumakis's chapter, titled "An Increasingly Global Presence: Contemporary American Independent Cinema outside the United States," sets the stage for ensuing discussions about the meaning of independence, especially in light of major Hollywood studios' reinventing themselves in the 1990s through launching their own "independent" production film divisions in order to fully exploit their catalogues and to tap into niche audience markets around the world.

Teresa Hoefert de Turégano pursues a similar theme in the following chapter, "European Union Initiatives for Independent Filmmakers across Europe." In her description of funding mechanisms for EU film industries she underlines the importance of building strong infrastructures for national and pan-European cinemas in order to offset the dominance of U.S. movies across European screens. In "Dependency and Independence in British Independent Film" Erik Knudsen also centres his analysis on this enduring cross-Atlantic dynamic. He showcases the way in which Britain's film industry responded to the domination of U.S. film distribution in the United Kingdom through the creation of its own independent funding and distribution channels, with a resulting increase in independent film productions. However, as Knudsen rightly states, although the term *independent* is often used to describe a film that is independent of Hollywood, the institutional structures created to build a sustainable independent film culture in Britain often suffer from hidden aspirations to mimic Hollywood itself.

Mark David Ryan addresses the independent film sector in Australia. Despite geographic distances his chapter addresses surprisingly similar themes to those discussed by Tzioumakis, Knudsen, and others in the first section, namely the struggle to establish an independent Aussiewood outside of the United States's dominance on the international scene while, at the same time, maintaining a reliance on American producers to model Australian films, aesthetically and commercially, along the lines of Hollywood.

Gabriela Martínez provides the final account in this section with her chapter, "Independent Filmmaking in the Peruvian Context: Seeking Meaning." She describes how Peruvian independent filmmakers have historically operated within Latin America, a region that boasts influential and productive film industries in Brazil, Argentina, and Mexico. State support in the form of financial resources and cultural policies have defined Peruvian cinema and have led alternately to the expansion and contraction of independent film success.

In the second section, analyses and case studies from around the world detail the ways in which political, economic, social, and cultural dynamics enable as well as constrain cultural production in search of the independent voice. Authoritarian governments and censorship boards, geopolitical struggles in the Middle East, economic fluctuation in Africa, and increasing financial prosperity in China all have their distinct and unique impact on independent film production. Accordingly, chapters highlight linkages between a country's political, economic, and sociocultural conditions and the ability of its filmmakers and citizens to showcase the varying "realities" – through the medium of film – of current historical developments and strife.

The influence and scope of Hollywood are not the sole concerns for filmmakers around the world. Rather, the achievement of legitimacy and recognition within their own local industries is continually challenging, as dominant film sectors at the national level also define the parameters of independent cinema. Lydia Papadimitriou, in her chapter on independent filmmaking in Greece, describes how the "New Greek cinema" emerged in the 1960s to develop a small but significant independent arthouse film sector, which began to receive additional support through the establishment of the Greek Film Center (GFC) in 1980. Today Greece's filmmakers continue to reveal great ingenuity and creativity in developing movie projects that delight international film festival audiences. Yet, as Greece is at a crossroads and the country's economic deficit has made access to arts funding extremely difficult, the question is raised, how can independent filmmaking be sustained when it gathers the bulk of its financing from private sources, rather than the GFC, which is recognized as the traditional independent film supporter?

In comparison, Murat Akser's account, "Turkish Independent Cinema: Between Bourgeois Auteurism and Political Radicalism," provides guideposts for understanding the dynamics that emerged when independent filmmaking in Turkey, which flourished in the 1960s, was subsequently suppressed by censorship, economics, and a repressive and unstable political climate. The dominant industry that overtook independent filmmaking forced independents to begin championing a politically oriented independent cinema, rather than an aesthetically oriented one. Consequently, contemporary independent filmmaking in Turkey has re-emerged to challenge the authority of the nationally dominant industry.

Mary Erickson provides insights into Iraq's contemporary film industry, which has undergone dramatic changes over the course of its history. Her chapter, "Filmmaking in Iraq: A Rebirth," highlights many of the country's most recent developments and achievements, such as the Independent Film and Television College in Baghdad, the Women Media Initiative of the Institute for War and Peace Reporting, the Iraq Eye project, the Mobile Cinema project, and filmmaking activity in the country's Kurdish region. Erickson's analysis shows how these initiatives have contributed in diverse and significant ways to the regeneration of Iraqi cinema in the years since the fall of Saddam Hussein. This chapter also highlights the ways in which Iraqi filmmakers – often living in exile away from their home country – are forced to work on a global scale, securing funding, distribution, and exhibition support from outside the country.

Hongwei Lu's analysis of China's independent film sector, "The Grassroots Perspective: Sixth Generation Cinema and Independent Filmmaking in China," traces the beginnings of the country's independent film movement to the 1990s when "underground" directors such as Zhuang Yuan and Wang Xiaoshuai began to make films outside the state-controlled studio system. This "Sixth Generation" emerged in an era marked by a gradual weakening of state interference in filmmaking, which coincided with the massive withdrawal of centralized government sponsorship. Market reforms led to the privatization of the film industry, and privatized independent film companies took over where the government had relinquished its interference. Lu asserts that the rise of China's independent-spirited Sixth Generation cinema fits within a larger cultural search for new ways to represent the country's post-reform reality and carries with it social messages – originating from grassroots and underground sources – that are far more comprehensive than overt political dissidence.

Martin Mhando concludes this section with his chapter "Independent Filmmaking in Africa: New Voices and Challenges. In one of two chapters about a continent that has over fifty nations and great cultural and linguistic diversity he provides a comprehensive account of pan-African filmmaking – including francophone, anglophone, and lusophone – and its complex reactions, in narratives and styles, to Hollywood, globalization, and modernity. Yet he argues that the influence of Hollywood is waning, largely owing to the influences of digital media, but also at the cultural level as world cultures are "redefining the structures for articulating cinema's powerful effect on how one sees oneself and the world, as well as the future of human perception." Successes of Nollywood filmmakers as well as the creative appropriation of new digital technologies, from production equipment to the mobile phone, enable new social media networks to develop that go "beyond their initial use, [as] they allow for the transformation of both applied technology and society."

The final section concludes the international overview of independent filmmaking practices by showcasing linkages between independent film and technological innovations, in particular digital and social media platforms. Many authors in this volume comment on the influence of new digital technologies on independent filmmaking practices in their country. This section therefore highlights specific case studies from Malaysia, Arctic Canada, and the African countries of Nigeria, Ghana, and Morocco to illustrate and critically assess the impact of digital means of production and distribution on independent filmmaking, and the implications for greater diversity of expression and social change.

In the opening chapter for the section, "Syiok Sendiri? Independent Filmmaking in Malaysia," Gaik Cheng Khoo raises the question of why independent Malay films seem unable to elicit favourable responses from Malay audiences. Surprisingly, a similar theme comparable to that of the struggles of European filmmakers emerges, namely the necessity of Malay films to compete with the popular American blockbuster films for local screens. Yet the digital distribution of films via the Internet allows Malay filmmakers to gain knowledge of generic conventions and new forms of visual storytelling and reach audiences through the language of film. With these recent developments Khoo hypothesizes that Malay's independent film movement may eventually receive full recognition within its own borders.

In "Independent Filmmaking in the Canadian Arctic" Doris Baltruschat explores independent filmmaking in the Arctic regions of Canada, with a particular emphasis on new digital film production techniques and multi-platform distribution. Until the arrival of digital media, high-quality filmmaking in the Arctic was nearly impossible owing to the vast geographical distances between production and post-production facilities. Today filmmakers are able to access even the most remote locations on earth to create cultural works that reflect a truly independent point of view.

As discussed by Sheila Petty in the final chapter, titled "Digital Video Films as 'Independent' African Cinema," burgeoning film industries in various African nations also take advantage of digital technology to counteract the decline of state-owned film industries, as has been the case in Ghana, or to circumvent government restrictions, as in southern Morocco. With media innovations, a more decentralized and internationalized community of media producers has emerged, both professionals and amateurs, who network across continents to raise money for film projects, share expertise, co-produce, and connect with audiences, the large portion of which are diasporic populations.

Conclusion

Independent Filmmaking around the Globe offers new insight into how independent filmmaking is defined around the world. As discussed in chapters throughout the volume, this independence does not always derive from a film's relationship to the major Hollywood studios; rather, there are a variety of institutions from which filmmakers are independent, such as governments, corporations, financing entities, and traditional production centres. As we address the meaning and characteristics of independent filmmaking in a contemporary global context, we seek to increase an understanding of the ways this independence is being redefined by a shift in geopolitical dynamics, economic reforms, new sociocultural paradigms, and technological innovations. Ultimately, we aim to showcase how independent filmmakers chart a new course in creating cultural works that reflect the independent voice, and thus create new opportunities for media democracy around the globe.

A key theme throughout the volume is the impact of digital technologies on the production, distribution, and reception of independent films. In spite of the vast improvements that these technologies afford with regard to access and opportunities, especially for first-time filmmakers, one needs to caution against an overly optimistic attitude towards these developments. As noted by David Hamilton in his foreword, widespread surveillance and interference in the day-to-day existence of ordinary citizens have become part and parcel of government action around the world, as highlighted by globally reported incidents such WikiLeaks (Khatchadourian 2010) and the more recent National Security Agency surveillance revelations in the United States (Greenwald et al. 2013). It is obvious that digital media provide less of an independence than do analogue media because all digital activities leave "footprints" that can be logged, mapped, documented, and – given national, historical, or political contexts – also lead to the restriction or termination of data flows, especially with regard to social media access (for example, Twitter) (Wikipedia 2013). Thus, in spite of the fact that digital media affords easier access to the means of production, in addition to enabling networks across the globe, unbridled enthusiasm and "technological determinism" are not only misleading but also cloud the threat that these media can pose to personal and collective freedoms.

Each author of *Independent Filmmaking around the Globe* provides a specific definition of what it means to be an independent filmmaker and to create works with a unique vision. Following these analyses, it becomes clear there is no easy or one-fits-all answer to what constitutes independence in media production, because changing circumstances and contexts affect the degree of independent filmmaking that a producer can pursue. Yet, without a doubt, independent filmmaking remains an integral part of any society as it can provide a platform for the expression of diverse ideas and opinions and foster a viable public sphere. Just as art mirrors society, independent filmmaking reflects the degree of freedom that citizens and producers are afforded in a society – thus providing a measure for attitudes and a tolerance for "otherness," including belief and value systems that may diverge from the status quo. This also includes race, gender, abilities, and religion, and the question of who can partake in the cultural production of a country?

With this book we want to highlight the importance of independent filmmaking in a great variety of contexts and national environments. Since the independent voice expressed through independent film remains an important aspect of all democratic societies, we need to understand past and current practices and avoid the pitfall of being too optimistic with regard to the future, especially where digital production is concerned. At the same time, it remains vital to create spaces and opportunities in which independent filmmaking can flourish, because it reflects who we are and what we are capable of producing.

NOTES

1 See also Davis (2003), Lobato (2011), and Miller et al. (2005).
2 Other studies about alternative or marginal film distribution and exhibition include, for example, Lobato (2007) and Himpele (1996).
3 A great many studies have been published on independent film in the American context, with specific attention to the intersection of independent film and Hollywood. For example see Tzioumakis (2006), King (2005), and Molloy (2012).

PART ONE

Independent Film vis-à-vis the Local and Global Mainstream

Chapter Two

An Increasingly Global Presence: Contemporary American Independent Cinema outside the United States

YANNIS TZIOUMAKIS

In the early spring of 2011 the founder and long-term leader of the Sundance Institute, Robert Redford, announced the creation of Sundance London.[1] Taking its name from the best-known U.S. festival dedicated to independent film, Sundance London entailed the organization of a four-day "multi-disciplinary arts festival" in April 2012 that would revolve primarily around the screening of American independent films. At the press conference Redford highlighted his main goal: to "bring to the UK the very best in current American independent cinema, to introduce the artists responsible for it, and in essence help build a picture of [the United States] that [was] broadly reflective of the diversity of voices not always seen in [its] cultural exports" (Knegt 2011). To that end, Redford and the Sundance Institute facilitated the UK premiere, under the auspices of Sundance London, of fourteen of the features originally selected to participate in the 2012 Sundance Film Festival in Park City, Utah (Sundance Institute 2012).

With the well-established independent film festival having been recently celebrated as becoming "relevant" again through its showcasing of "an outstanding crop of hard-hitting documentaries and challenging features" following a long period of hype, "flashy budgets and celebrity parties" (Rocchi 2012, 14–16), Sundance London would also stand to benefit from this shift in the festival culture. The majority of American independent features that had reached theatres around the world in recent years were relatively big-budget indiewood productions, often associated with studio specialty film labels such as Fox Searchlight and Focus Features or diversified stand-alone companies like Lionsgate. In this respect, Sundance London would have the opportunity to be associated with a new dawn of American independent cinema that was in the process of severing many of its ties with the Hollywood majors, specifically after the closure between 2008 and 2010 of specialty divisions such as Warner Independent Pictures, Paramount Vantage, Picturehouse, and, perhaps more important, Miramax Films. Indeed, the fourteen-film program for Sundance London was almost equally divided between dramatic features and documentaries (an eight-six split), with only two dramatic features – *Liberal Arts* (Josh Radnor, 2012) and *2 Days in New York* (Julie Delpy, 2012) – representing filmmaking with elements of obvious commercial appeal (well-established stars, popular generic frameworks, and easy narrative accessibility).

While for a brief period Sundance relocated American independent cinema to London, another established film festival strongly associated with independent film had been leading a different kind of initiative. In 2009 the Tribeca Film Festival, in association with the Qatar Museums Authority, established the Doha Tribeca Film Festival in the state of Qatar. Showcasing films from around the world, including independent films from the United States, the Doha Tribeca Film Festival has used Tribeca Film Festival's established brand of patronage of independent film and media to encourage comparable support of film (and film culture) in the Arab world (Tribeca Film Festival 2012). The Doha Tribeca Film Festival celebrated its fourth successful year in 2012, attracting thousands of visitors and securing high-profile films from around the world.[2]

If nothing else, these two examples reveal clearly the level of internationalization that characterizes American independent *film*, as a distinct category of filmmaking, and American independent *cinema*, as a well-defined institutional apparatus that supports this category of filmmaking. This level of internationalization not only exists in the realm of film festivals but also can be seen in other areas of the film business, including theatrical distribution, with various studio specialty film divisions and diversified stand-alone companies distributing primarily a particular brand of indiewood film product around the world; online distribution, with several Internet companies making independent films available in a variety of markets; and even box office performance, with a variety of films performing well outside the United States, often surpassing the box office receipts achieved in the domestic market.[3]

This degree of internationalization, however, has not always characterized contemporary American independent cinema, which for most scholars covers the period from the late 1970s or early 1980s to the present.[4] Indeed, for most of the 1980s, American independent film had little exposure and only occasional success outside the United States, while the industrial and institutional apparatus supporting it was firmly rooted in organizations, companies, and initiatives that were based in the United States. It was only in the 1990s, when contemporary American independent cinema arguably moved to different phases in its history – phases that I have labelled elsewhere as "indie" and "indiewood" (Tzioumakis 2012a) – that American independent film started circulating globally and on certain occasions with the level of success that is normally associated with major Hollywood film productions.

The present chapter will chart this journey of American independent film and cinema, paying particular attention to numerous factors that encouraged and facilitated their internationalization at particular historical junctures. I will argue that this internationalization has been driven primarily by the rising convergence of independent film with the major Hollywood studios, which, since the early 1990s, and specifically during the 1995–2005 decade, annexed large factions of independent cinema (Schatz 2012, 121), ultimately reshaping it in a way that fitted their corporate structures, their business practices, and their position in the global entertainment market. The main agents in this process were the second and third waves of the studio specialty film divisions (companies such as Miramax, Focus Features, and Paramount Vantage),[5] which became heavily associated with American independent film from the early 1990s and until the late 2000s when some of these divisions were shuttered by their conglomerate parents. In many ways, then, the chronicle of the internationalization of American independent film and cinema is intricately linked with several business decisions taken by these studio specialty film divisions in the face of a changing film marketplace, driven by the rise of what Thomas Schatz (2012, 121) has labelled "Conglomerate Hollywood."

Independent, Indie, Indiewood

In a number of recent studies[6] I have argued for the periodization of contemporary American independent cinema into three relatively distinct historical phases, under the labels "independent," "indie," and "indiewood," particularly as other scholars have also used these labels to account for expressions of independent filmmaking that are arguably distinct from each other.[7] Ranging from the late 1970s to the late 1980s and the runaway success of *sex, lies, and videotape* (Steven Soderbergh) in 1989, the first of these periods – the independent – is characterized by a particular type of film that I called the low-budget, low-key quality film (Tzioumakis 2012a, 32). Produced and distributed primarily by companies with no ties to the Hollywood majors, independent film benefited from an emerging industrial and institutional apparatus that included a variety of initiatives designed to support it, such as the Sundance Institute, the Independent Film Project, Public Broadcasting Service (PBS) and its American Playhouse series, and an increasing number of distribution companies. Some of these distributors set up shop in the late 1970s and early 1980s with the explicit intention of supporting this type of film (First Run Features, the Samuel Goldwyn Company, Cinecom, and a few others), while existing distributors that specialized in genre and exploitation filmmaking also noticed the significant activity in quality independent film production and decided to branch out or intensified their commitment to that kind of business (such as Atlantic Releasing Corporation and New Line Cinema). Independent film also benefited from the introduction of the first wave of the studios' and the mini-majors' "classics" divisions (United Artists Classics, Triumph Films, Universal Classics, Twentieth Century Fox International Classics, and Orion Classics) in the early 1980s, though these companies released only a handful of U.S. films as negative pickup deals (films financed and produced by independent companies without having a distribution deal in place) and steered clear of investing in production as more recently established studio specialty divisions did in later years.

With the majority of these quality independent films during this period being financed, produced, and distributed outside the Hollywood studios, it is not surprising that by and large these films were permeated by a variety of alternative aesthetics that marked them as distinct from their Hollywood counterparts. Furthermore, and given that a lot of the filmmakers in that period received financial support from institutions with a social impact remit such as the National Endowment for the Arts and the National Endowment for the Humanities (NEH) or public service broadcasters such as PBS, it is also not surprising that a large number of these films dealt with strong socio-political themes. These included themes such as unionization; the experience of ethnic, racial, and gender minorities; and little-known histories about under-represented groups in American society (for instance, the 1980 film *Heartland* [Richard Pearce], which dealt with the history of pioneer women in the frontier, received substantial funding from the NEH's

Hidden Histories program [Cornwell 1981, 62]). These "uncommercial" subjects were often accompanied by the use of unusual filmmaking techniques (such as the direct camera address in Spike Lee's *She's Gotta Have It*, 1986, or the exclusive use of long takes in Jim Jarmusch's *Stranger than Paradise*, 1984), which were in contrast to Hollywood's firm return to the rules of classical filmmaking after the creative experiments of the Hollywood Renaissance period in the late 1960s and early 1970s.

Following the great commercial success of *sex, lies, and videotape* in 1989 and other independent films around that time (*Stand and Deliver*, Ramón Menéndez, 1988; *Do the Right Thing*, Spike Lee, 1989; and *Roger and Me*, Michael Moore, 1990), the early 1990s saw an outburst of activity in the high-quality independent sector. Most of this activity took place under the auspices of major studios, which introduced the second wave of specialty film labels, either through the establishment of subsidiaries such as Sony Pictures Classics in 1992 or through the corporate takeover of formerly stand-alone producer-distributors, such as Miramax, which was taken over in 1993 by Disney. While a large number of films continued to be produced and distributed by companies without any ties to the major studios, Miramax, Sony Classics, and New Line Cinema's specialty film division Fine Line Features quickly became the market leaders. Some of these companies also started financing and producing films, which meant that these films were guaranteed distribution. Not surprisingly, these companies started attracting many successful independent filmmakers (Robert Altman, Hal Hartley, and Gus Van Sant at Fine Line; Quentin Tarantino and Kevin Smith at Miramax) and in a way helped to create a two-tiered independent film sector, one under the aegis of the Hollywood majors and one outside it. At the same time, however, the sector that had no ties to the studios continued to grow, creating a progressively more congested marketplace for independent film. Given the strong presence of several major studios on the independent film scene, it became untenable for filmmakers, critics, the trade press, and the film-going public to continue using the label "independent." In this respect, the label "indie" became almost immediately popularized. As many indie films became more expensive to produce and promote, and increasingly featured commercial elements normally associated with Hollywood studio films (stars, genre, accessible narratives), it could be argued that the time following the success of *sex, lies, and videotape*, and until the mid-1990s, represents a distinct period in the history of contemporary American independent cinema – the indie years.

The above changes had a clear impact on the aesthetics of the films. On the one hand, the increasing proximity of some factions of independent filmmaking to Hollywood cinema that was facilitated by the second wave of the studios' specialty film divisions came part and parcel with an increasing use of the conventions that were hitherto associated with Hollywood cinema. These included the presence of stars (Angelica Huston in *The Grifters*, Stephen Frears, 1990; River Phoenix in *My Own Private Idaho*, Gus Van Sant, 1992; and Harvey Keitel in *Reservoir Dogs*, Quentin Tarantino, 1992, for example) and the use of clear-cut generic frameworks (such as the heist movie in *Reservoir Dogs* or the con artist film in *The Grifters*). Adherence to Hollywood conventions prompted the construction of increasingly accessible narratives, despite the playful execution of these narratives in terms of the use of visual style. On the other hand, however, the indie films that continued to be made and distributed away from the Hollywood studios arguably retained stronger links than did their studio-endorsed counterparts with the low-budget, low-key quality films of the 1980s and their often esoteric, challenging, and politically significant subject matter. These included, for instance, the New Queer films of the early 1990s such as *Poison* (Todd Haynes, 1991) and *Swoon* (Tom Kalin, 1992), which were far removed narratively and stylistically from the more mainstream indie titles mentioned above, including Van Sant's *Idaho*, which was also part of the New Queer film cycle. In this respect, and as I argued elsewhere (Tzioumakis 2012a, 35), this second phase of contemporary American independent cinema included a heterogeneity of voices, narratives, styles, ideas, and budgets that were loosely grouped under the catch-all label of indie cinema.

While a large number of indie films did manage to retain their links to the challenging material that characterized many of the films of the earlier independent phase, beginning in the late 1990s American independent film arguably moved to yet another phase, which has been characterized by even greater commercial success than that of the indie period but reveals considerably less overlap with the films of the independent period. Led by Miramax's growing emphasis on big-budget, star-driven, and narratively accessible films, and the introduction of a third wave of specialty film divisions that saw Fox, Paramount, Universal, and Warner Bros. establish companies that would trade in the indie film market, contemporary American independent cinema rapidly moved towards the indiewood era, which was characterized by an intensified convergence with the Hollywood major studios and their films.[8] The establishment of Fox Searchlight, Focus Features, Paramount Classics (later Paramount Vantage), and Warner Independent came with a mandate from their parent companies for a renewed emphasis on film production, with an even greater dependence on elements with commercial appeal (primarily Hollywood stars and popular film genres) that pushed production and marketing costs to new heights. Despite the blockbuster success of several titles (among others, *Good Will Hunting*, Gus Van Sant, 1997; *Traffic*, Steven Soderbergh, 2000; and *No Country for Old Men*, Joel and Ethan Coen, 2007), many indiewood films failed to find an audience, while even the commercial success of many films was often mitigated, especially because by 2007 the average negative and marketing costs of films from the studio specialty film divisions had reached an astounding $74.9 million (Miller 2008, 53–4).

Following the closure of Warner Independent, Paramount Vantage, Picturehouse, and Miramax in the 2008–10 period, American independent cinema underwent a major transformation. While the indiewood model continues to define the sector, the consolidation that followed the closure of studio divisions, in tandem with an escalating success of low-budget films via online delivery platforms, points to a newly emerging era, the parameters of which have yet to be fully defined.

The advent of the indiewood model in the contemporary independent cinema sector brought more far-reaching changes in the aesthetic organization of American independent films. With the studios' third wave of specialty film divisions concentrating primarily on production, often accompanied by substantial financial investment, it is not surprising that more care was taken to enable the commercial elements of indiewood films to shine through. Stardom became even more central in terms of narrative construction than it had in the earlier period, with major Hollywood stars such as Tom Cruise (*Magnolia*, P.T. Anderson, 1999), Michael Douglas (*Traffic*), and Jim Carrey (*Eternal Sunshine of the Spotless Mind*, Michel Gondry, 2004) appearing in high-profile indiewood productions. Equally, genre became a cornerstone of most indiewood films, and a number of generic categories that were formerly almost exclusively associated with Hollywood studio filmmaking became co-opted by indiewood (such as the musical [*Chicago*, Rob Marshall, 2002]; the western [*Brokeback Mountain*, Ang Lee, 2005]; the revenge film [*Kill Bill*, volumes 1 and 2, Quentin Tarantino, 2003–4], and the "teen pic" [*Juno*, Jason Reitman, 2007]). Although many of these films also dealt with political subject matter (the futility of the fight against drug trafficking in *Traffic*) or offered hard-hitting critiques of particular issues (celebrity culture and homophobia in *Chicago* and *Brokeback Mountain*, respectively), which audiences have come to expect of American independent cinema, these efforts were often buried under the films' slick production values, strong stardom, genre expectations, and very high quality entertainment. This prompted Geoff King (2009, 3) to argue that although indiewood combines "some qualities associated with the independent sector, [these tended to be] understood as softened and watered-down, with other qualities and industrial practices more characteristic of the output of the major studios."

The rest of this chapter will chart the internationalization of American independent film, with a focus on development in these three periods: the independent, the indie, and indiewood.

Limited Circulation: The Independent Years

During the first phase of U.S. independent cinema's history, low-budget, low-key, high-quality films were rarely distributed or shown outside of North America. As the vast majority of these films were financed, produced, and distributed outside of Hollywood's influence, their exposure was limited to the festival circuit and, from there and via the services of international sales representatives, potentially to distribution deals with a handful of regional or local distributors. A small number of films were also represented in film fairs and showcases like MIFED (Mercato Internazionale Filme e Documentario) in Milan (1980–) and the Marché du Film, the official film market of the Cannes Film Festival. Overall, though, the number of films from the high-quality independent film sector that "travelled" outside the United States remained low, with only a few titles securing distribution deals in foreign theatrical and ancillary markets, like the home video market, especially in the first half of the 1980s.

The main problem faced by independent film producers in their efforts to secure foreign theatrical and ancillary distribution for their films was the absence of visibly commercial elements that would help international distributors to determine how to market such films. Most of that period's films were produced by small companies, with investments that ranged from a few thousand to a few hundred thousand dollars and without the presence of Hollywood stars and/or popular genre frameworks; the chances of securing distribution both in the United States and in the international markets were limited. In this respect, while obviously focusing primarily on the domestic market, the emerging industrial and institutional infrastructure in the United States also strove to create opportunities for independent films in the international markets. Two of the key early initiatives that targeted both fronts were the American Film Market, established in Los Angeles in 1981, and the International Feature Film Market (later relabelled as the International Film Project Market), set up in New York City around the same time.

Established by the American Film Marketing Association (which later changed its name to the Independent Film and Television Alliance), the American Film Market has been a major destination for independent films. The association has historically consisted of the key stand-alone U.S. distributors as well as a substantial number of non-U.S. financing, production, and distribution companies such as the French Canal Plus. In this respect, independent films showcased at the American Film Market had some exposure to international distributors and therefore the potential for a distribution deal in one or more foreign markets. The International Feature Film Market (IFFM), on the other hand, was set up by the Independent Film Project (IFP), an organization established in 1979 by independent film pioneers (headed by Sandra Schulberg) to support the work of non-commercial filmmakers. The IFFM quickly became a major showcase for films by members of the organization who could use it to screen their work – complete or in progress – for distributors and/or investors. Furthermore, as a member of an inter-national network of partnerships (including the Berlin International Festival and market and, more recently, the Rotterdam Cinemart and the Cannes Producers' Network) the IFP channelled a selection of films made by its members to key international festivals and events, where some of them attracted significant attention and, on some occasions, secured distribution deals with international distributors.[9] For instance, following its participation and success at the Cannes Film Festival in 1984, Jim Jarmusch's *Stranger than Paradise* secured various distribu-tion deals around the world, including in countries such as West Ger-many, Sweden, France, Netherlands, Portugal, Finland, Hungary, and Australia.[10] Rosen and Hamilton (1990, 111, 118) also demonstrate how *Heartland*, one of the key early titles credited with kick-starting con-temporary American independent cinema in the early 1980s, was sold in many European territories following the film's exposure at festivals prior to its theatrical release, especially the Berlin International Film Festival where it was awarded the main prize.

In the 1980s, festival participation represented by far the most important opportunity for international exposure for American independent films. As Marijke de Valck (2007, 87) has argued, film festivals such as Cannes, Berlin, and Venice "are central sites within a global influential film system that both counters and complements the Hollywood hegemony." In this sense, and while films by the Hollywood majors have always been part of the festival scene (often participating in special out-of-competition screenings), the primary emphasis for international and mainly European film festivals has been on non-U.S. titles. As de Valck explains, festivals became popular as they allowed European films to be exhibited "in prestigious international settings without being dependent on intermediate distributors" (93), who were selecting films for distribution on purely commercial criteria and who were often associated with the distribution networks of the major Hollywood studios. This means that the festivals were very receptive to "alternative" forms of filmmaking, with Cannes in particular acquiring a reputation in the late 1970s and early 1980s for promoting a "surge of marginalised and new productions," including horror, instructional video, and pop video (97).

It is within this context that the low-budget, low-key, high-quality independent film of the 1980s found a fertile ground for exposure outside the United States. With their often clear anti-Hollywood stance[11] and their numerous points of contact with films associated with the European art-house cinema,[12] American independent films were added to a variety of festivals from the 1980s onwards. This can be seen clearly in the list of U.S. independent films that participated in the Cannes Film Festival (see table 2.1) between 1980 and 1985. Cannes was an early supporter of American independent film by featuring a selection of now canonical titles. Indeed, in the 1978–84 period three American independent films received the prestigious Caméra d'or award, which was introduced in 1978 for directors' first feature films: *Alambrista!* (Robert M. Young, 1978), *Northern Lights* (John Hanson and Rob Nilsson, 1979, and *Stranger than Paradise* (Jim Jarmusch, 1984). This clearly demonstrates that American independent films were of a quality comparable to that of their European and world art-house cinema counterparts.

The success of these and other films on the European festival scene had a further but less obvious impact on American independent cinema of the time. It led to its increased recognition in the domestic marketplace, which has relied traditionally on profitability as the key criterion for success. This was particularly the case for American cinema in

Table 2.1 American Independent Films at the Cannes Film Festival, 1980–5

Year	Competition	Un Certain Regard	Section Parallèle	Key Independent Titles
1980	0	1	3	*Sitting Ducks*; *Gal Young 'Un*
1981	0	1	5	*Let There Be Light*; *Americana*; *Tell Me a Riddle*
1982	1	1	1	*Smithereens*; *Forty Deuce*; *Too Far to Go*
1983	0	2	2	*Can She Bake a Cherry Cake?*; *Lianna*; *The Haircut*
1984	1	1	4	*Under the Volcano*; *El Norte*; *Stranger than Paradise*; *Variety*
1985	2	1	4	*Mishima*; *Kiss of the Spider Woman*; *Latino*; *A Flash of Green*

Source: Collated from the Cannes Film Archives, http://festivalcannes.fr, 2012.

the early 1980s, which privileged increasingly blockbuster and high-concept films, while it was still recovering from the indulgence and excess that had characterized a number of the Hollywood Renaissance films of the late 1960s and 1970s, culminating with the staggering box-office failure of *Heaven's Gate* (Michael Cimino) in 1980. Given that low-budget, low-key, high-quality American independent films could not live up to the commercial success of the majority of Hollywood studio films, the European festival scene provided the former with an ideal basis to garner attention, occasionally win awards, and highlight their (generally limited) potential for profitability. On many occasions this translated into a distribution deal with a U.S. company – since most of the films had been produced with no such deal in place – and the opportunity for a limited theatrical run. Even though large box-office successes were extremely rare in the 1980s, festival participation did provide American independent films with the credentials that they would otherwise be lacking. This was especially important to the small but loyal art-house film audience for which Hollywood studio films tended to lack sophistication and challenging subject matter.[13]

Despite exposure on the festival scene, theatrical and non-theatrical distribution outside the United States remained a dream for most of these films. On the one hand, theatrical distributors were reluctant to acquire the rights for films that had no clear commercial appeal. On the other hand, video and cable distributors were hesitant to release them in ancillary markets because video and cable penetration in Europe and the rest of the world lagged behind that of the United States.[14] As a result, despite a fairly good representation of American independent films in U.S. ancillary markets,[15] their numbers were substantially fewer in comparable international markets. One could argue that American independent film in the 1980s, during the independent years, had few opportunities for international circulation and success.

The Makings of an International Distribution Network: The Indie Period

For most scholarly accounts of American independent cinema, including this chapter, the critical and commercial success of *sex, lies, and videotape* represents a major turning point in the development of the independent film sector.[16] Steven Soderbergh's film was selected for the official program of the 1989 Cannes Film Festival and competed against other U.S. independent film productions such as *Do the Right Thing* and *Mystery Train* (Jim Jarmusch). The film won the Palme d'Or that year, amidst great media hype. Following a successful theatrical release by Miramax, *sex, lies, and videotape* recorded an impressive U.S. theatrical box-office gross of approximately $25 million. It also performed particularly well on the international theatrical market, grossing a total of $12 million (Nash Information Services 2013). The film was released in, among other countries, France, Sweden, Germany, Australia, Japan, and the Netherlands (Internet Movie Database 2012), which, together with the United Kingdom and Spain, made up 85 per cent of American foreign sales, including home video and television, in the early 1990s (Wiese 1992, 94).

The success of *sex, lies, and videotape* in the key international markets for American films helped set in motion numerous developments that would make the circulation of American independent films much smoother outside the United States. This became evident when independent films continued to win acclaim at international film festivals, such as *Wild at Heart* (David Lynch) and *Barton Fink* (Joel and Ethan Coen) which won the Palme d'Or in 1990 and 1991, respectively, underscoring in the most affirmative of ways the endorsement of American independent film by the international film and critic community. These developments included the proliferation of foreign sales companies willing to represent U.S. independent productions in the international markets; the distribution of independent films by American companies with established distribution networks in key international markets; and the emergence of a multitude of funding sources in the form of terrestrial, cable, and satellite television channels and networks, following the deregulation of television in many European markets. Indeed, the European television industries, hungry for programming, became one of the most prominent supporters of American independent cinema in the first half of the 1990s.

Central to all these developments was an increase of commercial elements in many of the films that characterized this phase of contemporary American independent cinema, especially the presence of stars and the use of genre. These elements, in addition to higher budgets and production values, made American independent films more marketable, both inside and outside the United States. This, in turn, prompted foreign film sales companies that were based in the United States to take these films more seriously and to start scouting festivals and commercial showcases such as the American Film Market (AFM) for clients. According to Wiese (1992), the sixty or so foreign film sales companies that were operating in major film markets were typically handling the distribution of American independent films outside the United States, not just for the theatrical market but also for home video and television (278).

While in many ways this kind of approach was similar to the manner in which business was conducted in the previous period, new distribution channels started to emerge for independent film outside the United States. In 1990 successful stand-alone producer and distributor New Line Cinema established Fine Line Features as a subsidiary with a mandate to focus exclusively on low-budget films in English, and in particular American independent film titles. With such (now) canonical titles like *My Own Private Idaho*, *Trust* (Hal Hartley), and *A Night on Earth* (Jim Jarmusch) in its first line-up in 1991, Fine Line became quickly a major force in the sector. Unlike its competitors, Fine Line could rely on its films being distributed outside the United States through New Line International, the foreign sales and distribution arm of its parent company, while also occasionally using foreign sales agents for markets in which New Line did not have direct representation (Carver 1998, 18). This arrangement allowed Fine Line to operate successfully in the 1990s, despite the fact that many of its titles underperformed at the U.S. theatrical box office.[17]

Fine Line's successful utilization of foreign film distribution as a cushion that mediated box-office disappointments in the domestic market clearly shows the growing importance of the international markets for a film's profitability. In this respect, it seems that companies with even more established and extensive foreign distribution networks, such as the Hollywood majors, would be in a more advantageous position than stand-alone companies to push the independent film product, not only in the key markets for American films but also in smaller markets, where companies such as New Line International might not have access. During the indie years, between the late 1980s and mid-1990s, there were two Hollywood studios involved with independent film distribution: Sony Pictures and Disney. The former entered the American independent film market through the establishment of a subsidiary, Sony Pictures Classics in 1992, and the latter through the corporate takeover of the stand-alone company Miramax Films in 1993.

While Sony Pictures Classics focused predominantly on the U.S. theatrical market, Disney-backed Miramax gained immediate access to its parent company's international distribution network, Buena Vista International, and consequently a large number of international markets. With this kind of access, it is not surprising that Miramax moved immediately into production and reaped the benefits of this approach with its record-breaking production *Pulp Fiction* (Quentin Tarantino, 1994). Distributed by Buena Vista International, the film recorded a staggering international box-office gross of $106 million, one-sixth of which ($18 million) came from the United Kingdom alone (Internet Movie Database 2012). In this respect, a major studio and its specialty film subsidiary followed Fine Line's approach: the use of the parent company's established international distribution network in tandem with the sale of a film's rights to several distributors through the help of foreign sales representative and agents.

By the mid-1990s, however, only a small number of films like *Pulp Fiction* were being financed and produced by a studio subsidiary and had a distribution deal in place right from the beginning. The majority were still funded and produced by independent production companies that had no ties to the major Hollywood studios. Financial sources included limited partnerships, personal loans, private investors, and pre-sales (Levy 1999, 496). A major new source of financing came through pre-sales to foreign television networks, which proved to be important backers of American independent film production throughout the 1990s. Following the deregulation of many European countries' television markets in the late 1980s and the concomitant launch of countless new terrestrial, cable, and satellite television channels, the demands for programming became particularly pronounced. With contemporary American independent cinema's increased emphasis on elements with commercial appeal, and with the television rights of these increasingly popular films available for a relatively small amount compared to that of Hollywood studio films, it was no surprise that they represented an attractive option in terms of programming. As a result, the early and mid-1990s saw European broadcasters investing en masse in American independent film production as a cheap and effective way to acquire commercial U.S. product without having to pay the exorbitant prices that the major Hollywood studios were asking for their expensive blockbuster films. According to Levy (1999), overseas sales of American independent films peaked in 1996 at $1.65 billion, aided above all by the still expanding television market. Fifty-six per cent of these revenues came from European markets alone (25–6).

This boom came to an end in the late 1990s as a result of factors that included "intensified competition in European countries' cable and satellite television sectors which forced pay TV rates to plummet" (Molloy 2010, 12) and the inability of a large number of independent films to attract a significant television audience. In addition, the slowdown of the German economy caused a downturn in one of Europe's biggest markets for American independent films and foreign television pre-sales (King 2005, 37). However, by that time, contemporary American independent cinema had already entered into its next phase, the indiewood years, which brought with them new models for the circulation of American independent film outside the United States.

Studio Specialty Film Divisions and Digital Delivery Systems: The Indiewood Years

The global commercial success of *Pulp Fiction* demonstrated – with even greater emphasis than did *sex, lies, and videotape* – that niche film production and distribution in general, and American independent film in particular, had the potential for excellent profits when handled properly. In this respect, if Soderbergh's film had become one of the catalysts for the establishment of specialty film divisions by major Hollywood studios such as Sony Pictures and Disney, Tarantino's film became an even stronger motivator for the rest of the studios to start trade in independent film. Sony and Disney were soon joined by others who focused on the distribution of independently produced films: Fox, with Fox Searchlight, started in late 1995; Paramount, with Paramount Classics, in 1998; Universal, with Focus Features, in 2002; and Warner Bros. with Warner Independent Pictures, in 2004. In addition, Sony added Screen Gems in 1999 as a specialty division, as did Warner

Bros. with Picturehouse in 2005. Furthermore, the early 2000s also witnessed the emergence of a number of "mini-majors" – well-capitalized producer-distributors that were either divisions of media conglomerates other than the Hollywood studios (USA Films, which was a division of the USA Network) or stand-alone companies (Artisan, Newmarket, and Lionsgate). These companies squeezed out of the market a large number of the smaller, less financially secure, independent companies of the 1990s such as October, IRS Media, and Triton Pictures.

The gradual entrance of these mini-majors into the independent sector inevitably changed the rules of the game. Supported by the deep pockets of their parent companies, the studios' specialty film divisions turned to film production with a greater focus on commercial elements and higher production and marketing costs (Tzioumakis 2012b, 10–12). Although many of the productions were financed by corporate capital provided by the parent company, the specialty divisions also started progressively to exploit opportunities for partnerships and collaborations on a global scale, effectively through co-financing arrangements and co-production. For instance, Fox Searchlight benefited from an agreement with the British company DNA Films, which was partly funded by UK Lottery Funds (Tzioumakis 2012b, 147). The companies co-financed an assortment of commercially appealing films, including *28 Days Later...* (Danny Boyle, 2004) and *The Last King of Scotland* (Kevin Macdonald, 2006), which became great box-office successes in Fox Searchlight's theatrical and home entertainment markets. This trend reached a critical point in the late 2000s when various Hollywood studios closed their U.S. film–focused studio divisions and established new subsidiaries in order to exploit opportunities for the financing, production, and distribution of niche filmmaking around the world. For instance, following the closure of Paramount Vantage in 2008, Viacom established the Paramount Worldwide Acquisitions Group in July 2008 as "a centralized acquisitions and local productions arm that [would] feed pics into the pipelines of Paramount Pictures [International] and Paramount Vantage" (quoted in Tzioumakis 2012b, 170). Notwithstanding the closure of Paramount Vantage's physical distribution facilities, the name was retained as a marketing brand.

Despite this new emphasis on commercially appealing world cinema films in the 2000s, U.S. indiewood remained important for studio divisions and key stand-alone distributors. Stars, genre, niche marketing, exploitation of authorship, accessible narratives, and the presence of often gratuitous sex and violence became particularly pronounced characteristics of a large number of films from the sector. According to Geoff King (2009), the growing emphasis of these divisions on production led to "an increasing tendency to favour more conservative or star-led properties" that often blurred previously well-established distinctions between the independent and major studio sectors (110).

Not surprisingly, this convergence between independent and Hollywood cinema – eventually known as indiewood – had dramatic repercussions on the ways in which American independent film travelled around the world. With the specialty film subsidiaries of major studios controlling production and worldwide distribution rights, the studios' distribution networks became prominent conduits for the circulation of an increasing number of American indiewood films, which were perceived as products with a distinct marketing identity. As the major Hollywood studios were producing a small number of mostly expensive films per year, their global distribution networks were in great need of additional product, which their specialty film divisions started to supply in substantial numbers. In this respect, from the late 1990s onwards, Buena Vista International, Twentieth Century Fox International, and other distribution networks that belonged to major studios with a global reach started to include large numbers of independent titles in their catalogues.

Arguably, more than any other major Hollywood studio, it was Universal that took steps to maximize its profits from the films produced by its specialty labels. Although Universal had invested in many independent companies in the 1990s (for instance, Gramercy and October Films), it was only in 2002 that it established its wholly owned subsidiary Focus Features, a company that was the product of a large number of complex mergers and takeovers.[18] Despite having merged a number of companies, Universal did not feel that it had the complete package needed to be able to compete with established forces such as Miramax and Fox Searchlight. Therefore, it acquired the stand-alone company Good Machine, together with its successful foreign sales division under the name Good Machine International. Under the new banner of Focus Features International, the division pursued the sale of foreign rights for approximately fifteen to sixteen films per year – which were all Focus Features films, including titles from producers who had established a relationship with Good Machine International before its takeover from Universal ("Universal's Independent Movie Operation" 2003, 10).

At the same time, new types of independent filmmaking emerged, which complemented the global presence of indiewood. Exploiting the presence of constantly improving digital production and delivery systems, low-budget – often "do-it-yourself" – independent filmmaking started growing exponentially. Since then, multi-platform access of content on laptops, mobile phones, and tablets, in addition to social media (from YouTube to Facebook to Twitter), has allowed independent film to become visible and, perhaps more important, easily accessible on a global scale. Part of these initiatives involves the teaming up of independent filmmakers with film festival organizers and non-theatrical distributors (such as pay cable and other on-demand services) as well as social media (YouTube, in particular) to make available the low-budget films that no commercial theatrical distributor would represent (Hernandez 2010). All these developments have created an unpredictable global distribution landscape for American independent film, especially as this landscape continues to feel the aftershock of the closure of over half of the studios' specialty film divisions between 2008 and 2010.

Conclusion

Within the space of approximately thirty years, from the early 1980s to the early 2010s, American independent film outside the United States changed dramatically, influenced by its movement through the independent years to the indie and indiewood" phases. In addition to growing commercialization, this evolution brought about the gradual shift of a large part of independent film production from outside of Hollywood into the fold of major film studios. This movement became especially significant once the studio specialty film divisions – during the indie and indiewood phases – began to finance and produce independent films, thus creating an independent cinema category as part of their commercial mandates. As producers of independent films, the studio specialty film divisions used their parent companies' established international theatrical and non-theatrical distribution networks. As a result, their titles became available globally and often achieved great commercial success. Such practices, however, were far removed from those associated with the independent phase of contemporary American independent cinema, during which only a small number of films had attracted foreign distribution deals after their successful reception at international film festivals and venues.

These developments have changed the fabric of contemporary American independent cinema. Independent film has been reconfigured – from the outside to the inside – and consequently has come closer to the horizontally and vertically integrated corporate Hollywood. However, while clear signs of co-optation by Hollywood can be seen in more commercialized productions and in the designation of indiewood, this does not mark the end of independent cinema and film. Today, more and more American independent films are digitally distributed and consequently migrate across mobile media platforms to be enjoyed by global audiences.

NOTES

1 This announcement was made in association with AEG Europe, the company that owns and operates the O2 arena, one of London's prime venues for cultural events.

2 The Doha Tribeca Film Festival ended its run in 2012, when the head of the festival, Amanda Palmer, departed the organization (now known as the Doha Film Institute). The DFI will continue to operate a festival, albeit with leadership firmly planted in the Middle East (Vivarelli 2013).

3 For instance, the film *Lost in Translation* (Sofia Coppola, 2003) recorded a U.S. theatrical box office gross of US$44.6 million, while its international box office receipts stood at US$61.9 million, approximately 30 per cent more than its domestic take (Box Office Guru 2012).

4 See, for instance, Levy (1999), King (2005), and Newman (2011), who focus either primarily or exclusively on the post-1980s era.

5 For more on the distinctions between the different waves of studio specialty divisions see Tzioumakis (2012b).

6 See in particular Tzioumakis (2012a) and Tzioumakis (2012b).

7 See, for instance, King (2009, 268–9), who uses *independent* and *indie* interchangeably and distinguishes them from *indiewood*.

8 I use the term *convergence* here following the work of Henry Jenkins (2006), who argued that its manifestation can be seen in the media industries in terms of "the concentration of ownership" (in the case of American independent cinema this involves the corporate takeover of several previously independent companies by the conglomerated majors) and the increasing presence of "extensions," "synergies," and "franchises" (19), which were strictly characteristics of filmmaking under the aegis of the majors until recently (see, for instance, the franchising of the "Viewaskew universe" created by well-known independent filmmaker Kevin Smith).

9 For more details see IFP's website (Independent Filmmaker Project).

10 The film won the Caméra d'or at Cannes, and the Pardo d'oro at the Locarno International Film Festival.

11 Peter Biskind (2005, 19) describes the early 1980s high-quality independent film productions as "anything that Hollywood was not."

12 In a scene-setting account of independent film production in the early 1980s Annette Insdorf (1981, 57–60) identified the "European style" that permeated these films.

13 I would like to thank the editors of this volume for pointing out this issue to me.

14 In the United States the number of households with videocassette recorders (VCRs) jumped from 1,850,000 in 1980 to 23,500,000 in 1985, and the number of pay cable subscriptions increased from 8,900,000 in 1980 to 31,700,000 during the same period (Motion Picture Association of America 1991, 86–7).

15 Several video companies (such as Vestron), desperate for product, had financed American independent films in exchange for their home video rights.

16 See for instance Levy (1999, 94), Biskind (2005, 40), and King (2005, 261).

17 For more on Fine Line see Tzioumakis (2012b, 99).

18 On the establishment of Focus Features see Tzioumakis (2012b, 179–83).

Chapter Three

European Union Initiatives for Independent Filmmakers across Europe

TERESA HOEFERT DE TURÉGANO

Public policies implemented at European, national, and sub-national levels, combined, serve to sustain and enhance the film and audio-visual sector in Europe. Within the European filmmaking industry there is strong consensus that the film and audio-visual policies of the European Union (EU) are a crucial motor in the flourishing of independent filmmaking on the continent. No other region in the world has such an elaborate implementation of film and audio-visual policy, and the offer of films available in Europe, even in spite of the market domination of the U.S. industry, is impressive. Alongside a long history of national film policies, that of the audio-visual policy in the European Union is one of constant struggle between European and national interests, and between economic integration and cultural diversity, and has entailed a perennial contextual discourse that tries to reconcile industry and culture in the audio-visual sector.

Approaches to the subject generally tend towards two directions. First, European film is set in opposition to the Hollywood monolith and U.S. industry and as such is under threat. This introductory position can be found in sources ranging from academic journals to professional trade magazines and is discussed in great detail by Tzioumakis with respect to so-called indie films and by Ryan on Aussiewood in this volume. Film professionals acknowledge that the two industries cannot actually be compared; one, regarding the United States, is an industry, and the other, in relation to Europe, is not really an industry per se. Second, there are more complex approaches, which analyse the intertwined nature of the European and American audio-visual industries, through, for example, the flow of European funding in the direction of Hollywood and/or the interdependent positions of Euro-American art-house cinema. A glimpse at the literature on the subject shows above all a long-standing concern and debate that hinges mostly on the contradictions between the EU's objective of economic integration (to counter the existing fragmentation of the market, which is essentially constituted through small and medium-sized companies (SMEs), in order to have a stronger competitive international position) and the objective of cultural diversity (to maintain and nurture the construction of European identities and of Europe as a whole).[1]

This chapter situates independent filmmaking in Europe within this dual perspective of the European public policy balancing act, between furthering economic integration in favour of the greater Europe and pursuing cultural diversity within. In spite of the apparent pressure to achieve European integration and greater industry competitiveness, I would argue that in recent years the results of policy tend towards the increasing success of the audio-visual sector as a locus of cultural diversity. While the process of cultural diversity in Europe surely could be more inclusive, the success of the EU's policy, from an industry perspective, lies more in the area of diversity than of a traditionally cohesive, integrated industry.

Two recent debates within EU audio-visual policy suggest that for the time being cultural factors have momentarily gained an upper hand. The first debate revolves around the challenge to the audio-visual industry caused by the EU competition policies that placed the dual policy objectives at the centre of direct discussion – by challenging state aid and territorialization practices as a distortion to competition – and resulted in rather massive and rapid mobilization of the professionals in the European film industry. The second debate revolves around the extension and renewal of the current MEDIA 2007 program and the creation of the new Creative Europe program. Each of the debates will be examined in this chapter in greater detail, following an overview of the development of European film and audio-visual policy.

From the outset it should be noted that the line between commercial and independent filmmaking in Europe is really very difficult to define. The means of production are predominantly independent, even in what classically constitutes more commercial and mainstream work. Some of the larger European companies, such as Constantin or Senator in Germany, or Gaumont in France, certainly also produce films that, by international and American standards, would be considered independent, at least in terms of their narrative form. It is often the case throughout Europe that national commercial successes remain national events and do not travel easily across intra-European borders. For example, the films of Tilman (Til) Schweiger are often German national box-office hits, but they barely travel outside of the country. The French have been more successful with some of their national box-office hits such as *The Untouchables*, *Welcome to the Sticks*, or *Amelie Poulin* in terms of their ability to travel. These films also enjoyed considerable box-office success in various European countries in addition to France.

Inversely, more mainstream narrative cinema is produced by smaller independent companies. For example, the German actor and director Til Schweiger produces films via his production company, Barefoot Films. His films are mostly romantic comedies in the Hollywood style and are generally hugely successful box-office hits in Germany. They constitute by various definitions the more commercial end of filmmaking. Indeed most of his productions are distributed by Warner Bros. Germany, an American major well known for its mainstream cinema. However, Schweiger's films can be defined as independent productions, certainly in comparison to the U.S. commercial productions circulating in the European market. Barefoot is owned by two individuals, of which Til Schweiger is one. The budgets of his films are comparatively small, in a range of around €6 million. Compared to many U.S. productions, this would really be considered an indie budget. Their mode of production is similar to that of other independent film production companies. In addition, his productions frequently benefit from public subsidies, which he often pays back to the funding institutions. In this case, the term *independent* is still appropriate even if the films themselves are more akin to commercial cinema, from formal and aesthetic perspectives.

At the same time, *Das weisse Band / The White Ribbon* (Michael Haneke, 2009, Austria/France/Germany), *Waltz with Bashir* (Ari Folman, 2008, Israel/Germany/France), *Le Quattro volte / The Four Times* (Michelangelo Frammartino, 2010, Italy/Switzerland/Germany), and *The Turin Horse* (Bela Tarr, 2011, Hungary/France/Germany) are examples of films that are clearly familiar as typical art-house and independent productions. The budgets of these films range from €800,000 to over €10,000,000. In general, one could argue that in Europe the term *art house* is of far greater currency than the term *independent*. As already mentioned above, but worth reiterating, most of the European film industry consists of SMEs, and these are small independent companies making small independent films.

The term *independent* is clearly defined on paper by both the European Union and the Council of Europe (COE). In both cases it is determined by the extent of the share of broadcaster ownership of a company. For example, Eurimages of the Council of Europe defines independent in the following manner:

1.2.1. Financial support may only be awarded to European natural or legal persons governed by the legislation of one of the Fund's member states, whose principal activity consists in producing cinematographic works, and whose origins are independent of public or private broadcasting organisations or telecom companies.

1.2.2. A company is considered European if it is majority owned and continues to be majority owned, either directly or indirectly, by nationals of the member states.

1.2.3. A production company is considered independent when less than 25% of its share capital is held by a single broadcaster or less than 50% where several broadcasters are involved (Council of Europe 2009, 1).

Overview of the General European Film and Audio-Visual Policy Context

European public film and audio-visual policy is implemented through two major pan-European institutions – the European Union and the Council of Europe. Both institutions were created to further the idea of a common Europe. The former is rooted in the basis of economic integration while the latter in the ideals of democracy, the rule of law, and human rights issues.[2] While the EU and its policies in the film and audio-visual domain are clearly the heavyweights, the COE and in particular Eurimages and the European Convention on Cinematographic Co-production also play a non-negligible role in the world of independent European filmmaking. The policies of the two pan-European institutions are indeed complementary and in turn are also designed to complement national and sub-national policies.

Council of Europe

The Council of Europe was established in 1949 with the aim of a common Europe, but from the beginning the objectives of the institution also prioritized cultural, social, and human rights issues. In 1978 the COE published its first report on state aid for the European film industry (Symposium on the Cinema and the State 1978). In 1988 it created a European support fund for co-production and distribution of creative cinematographic and audio-visual works, called Eurimages. "Eurimages aims to promote the European film industry by encouraging the production and distribution of films and fostering co-operation between professionals. Eurimages' first objective is cultural, in that it endeavours to support works which reflect the multiple facets of a European society whose common roots are evidence of a single culture. The second one is economic, in that the Fund invests in an industry which, while concerned with commercial success, is interested in demonstrating that cinema is one of the arts and should be treated as such" (Council of Europe 2012). Eurimages can be considered as the "prestige fund" for independent European filmmaking, in spite of having an annual budget of slightly over €20 million (€21.3 million in 2010), 90 per cent of which is allocated for production activities.

The second major instrument of the COE with respect to the European film and audio-visual industry is the European Convention on Cinematographic Co-production, which entered into force in 1994. A recent study, which is intended to serve as a basis for revising the convention after its seventeen years of existence, concluded that the convention provides a platform to make co-productions more systematic and easier to construct and thereby contributes to European cinema as a whole and is fundamental to its success (Olsberg, SPI 2007). The growing importance of co-productions within the European market is an important signal in terms of cultural diversity and the diversity of cinema available, as is discussed below in the next section (European Audiovisual Observatory 2008a). As outlined by Papadimitriou in this volume, co-productions between film producers and partners in Europe and the United States also play a significant role in promoting a country's film industry on the international market.

The Council of Europe is extremely active in supporting the cultural sector in Europe through various programs, policies, initiatives, declarations, and recommendations. Even though the Council does not come close to having the budget of the European Union in terms of its input in the cinema and audio-visual sector, its role cannot be overlooked. In addition, the cooperation between the COE and the EU particularly in the film and audio-visual sector has benefited from closer and more cooperative relations in the past few years.

The European Union

The 1957 Treaty of Rome established the European Community (Treaty Establishing the European Community, TEC) with the aim of fostering European economic integration by establishing a set of rules to help create a common internal market. This market is based on the idea of free competition and prohibits restrictive agreements and state aid that affect trade between member states and whose objectives are to prevent, restrict, or distort free competition. It did, however, include an "industrial state aid derogation" (Psychogiopoulou 2010, 274). Through the Treaty on European Union (TEU; known as the Maastricht Treaty) of 1992 the European Community became the European Union and for the first time included a cultural dimension to its objectives. It stipulates in article 3(3) that the internal market and economic growth must be accompanied by respect for the EU's cultural and linguistic diversity. A new derogation called "the cultural state aid derogation," which is also part of the Treaty on the Functioning of the European Union (TFEU), entered into force in 2009 through the Lisbon Treaty (European Commission 2013b). This new provision specifies under point 3(d) that "aid to promote culture and heritage conservation where such aid does not affect trading conditions and competition in the Community to an extent that is contrary to the common interest" may be considered compatible with the internal market (European Commission 2013b). EU action vis-à-vis the film and audio-visual sector is primarily based on articles 167 and 107 of the TFEU.

Historically, EU film and audio-visual policy has been implemented through two main strategies: legislative instruments and expenditure programs (otherwise known as state aid). The first MEDIA program was established in 1991 on the basis of EU industrial policy. This measure was part of an overall strategy in the cinema and audio-visual sector, which included a regulatory structure and which was intended to create a common market in broadcasting (the Television Without Frontiers Directive), later replaced by the Audio-Visual and Media Services Directive (AVMS). The MEDIA program focuses on supporting measures related to pre-production (development, training) and post-production (distribution, promotion) in the film and audio-visual sector. This has largely remained constant, as one can see from the table below.[3] In this sense it is really complementary with Eurimages, which focuses mainly on production support.

The overall objectives of the MEDIA 2007 program are preserving and enhancing European cultural diversity and its cinematographic

Table 3.1 History of European Union Programs in the Audio-Visual Sector

Period	Program(s)	Budget	Key Areas of Support
1991–1995	MEDIA I	€200 million	Transnational collaboration
1996–2000	MEDIA II	€310 million	Training, development, and distribution
2001–2006	MEDIA Plus	€454 million	Development, distribution, and promotion
	MEDIA Training	€59 million	Networking between training partners
2007–2013	MEDIA 2007	€755 million	Distribution, development, promotion, and training
2008–2010	MEDIA International	€8 million	Cooperation with third countries
2011–2013	MEDIA Mundus	€15 million	Cooperation with third countries
2014–2020	Creative Europe – MEDIA strand	€1.46 billion	At least 56% of the budget will be allocated to the MEDIA sub-program

and audio-visual heritage, guaranteeing its accessibility to European citizens, and promoting intercultural dialogue; increasing the circulation of European audio-visual works inside and outside the European Union; and strengthening the competitiveness of the European audio-visual sector in the framework of an open and competitive market (European Commission 2007). As is the case with Eurimages, the eligibility criteria focus support on independent European producers, distributors, and exhibitors and are clearly aimed at SMEs. The definition of *independent* as used by the European Union and the MEDIA program[4] is the same as the one applied by Eurimages.

In addition to the film and audio-visual policies directly supporting the European film industry, the EU has implemented a number of programs through its development policy to support the film and audio-visual sectors beyond Europe. For example, since 1986 the African, Caribbean, and Pacific (ACP) countries have had the opportunity of obtaining direct support for their film and audio-visual sectors. This was enabled through the addition of a cultural chapter to the Lomé Accords, which at that time regulated EU-ACP relations, later replaced by the Cotonou Agreement (European Commission 2013a). More recently, Euromed Audiovisual (Council of Europe 2003) and Mercosur Audiovisual have also opened doors for Europe's Mediterranean neighbours and Latin American countries respectively. These programs are also designed to support independent filmmakers and the audio-visual industries within the participating countries.[5] In contrast, MEDIA Mundus, which has functioned alongside the MEDIA structure, is intended to support international cooperation and partnership building rather than developing external local industries as is the case with the ACP, Euromed, and Mercosur programs.

While the aim of this chapter is not to engage in a detailed evaluation of the successive MEDIA programs, it is useful to look at a few of the twenty conclusions in the final report of the evaluation of MEDIA 2007 because we can see where some of its strengths lie. For example, in conclusion 1, "the integrated logic of the programme (i.e., covering the entire value chain, including MEDIA Training), its anchorage on the European audio-visual scene, and the fact that it is designed to support change in the sector enable MEDIA 2007, inter alia, to provide an appropriate response to the needs of the sector" (Euréval and Media Consulting Group 2010, 8). The proximity of the institution (EU) and program (MEDIA) to the industry, which is referred to here, is crucial to the working of the MEDIA program because it enables its continual redesigning to meet the needs of the sector. Conclusion 4 also attests to the crucial role that the MEDIA program plays for the professionals in the sector: "The steep increase in the number of applications for the various forms of support offered by the programme attests to the fact that it corresponds to the needs of the sector. However, this entails an increasingly selective process leading to the exclusion of primo-participants and very small businesses, increasing management costs, and discouragement among potential participants" (ibid., 9). Conclusion 11 notes: "MEDIA 2007 support for Distribution is effective on the whole; it contributes significantly to improving conditions of distribution (automatic support) and to strengthening professional networks (selective support)" (ibid.). Finally, conclusions 16 and 17 are also worth highlighting: "By supporting training for professionals, the structuring of projects and the networking of actors, MEDIA contributes to making the European audio-visual sector more competitive" (ibid., 10); "In the continuity of MEDIA Plus, MEDIA 2007 support probably contributes to better circulation of European works" (ibid.). The use of the term *competitive* is noteworthy given the reference to training and networking. In contrast, conclusion 17 refers in a hesitant manner to the improved circulation of European works, although this is certainly one of the true strengths of the program. In terms of validity, these reports are completed by independent consulting companies, which compete for the tender, and they are mostly very comprehensive studies that are the result of research, interviews, and so forth, at the very least, across the industry.

The European Audiovisual Observatory (2008a) published a study on the circulation of European co-production, based on a sample of over five thousand theatrical releases in Europe between 2001 and 2007. Not surprisingly, the conclusions stated that European co-productions travel better than their wholly national counterparts and are released in twice as many markets. In addition, European co-productions attract on average 2.7 times as many admissions as do national productions. These types of results are to a large extent the consequence of various European support policies, including Eurimages and MEDIA distribution support. One would actually have to analyse each film's production credits to see exactly which program was involved. In many cases, one finds within a single film the traces of multiple European support measures from various programs, as described in detail by Papadimitriou in her chapter on independent filmmaking in Greece. This is common practice in independent filmmaking in Europe. There is little doubt that the MEDIA program has become a strong label and is visibly present throughout the European film and audio-visual sector.

As mentioned above, there have been two periods of massive mobilization of the European film and audio-visual industry. Both of these are integrally linked to the role of the EU in the independent filmmaking sector, and both attest to the importance of the role of the EU for this sector. The first pertains to the mobilization that resulted from the call for a review by the EU Directorate General of Competition on the free trade and competition practices within the European film and audio-visual sector, in particular the question of whether existing territorialization practices were contrary to competition practices. The second period is linked to the renewal of the MEDIA program and its amalgamation into the proposed Creative Europe program.

Territorialization in the EU and the Challenge to Competition Practices

After entry into force of the new cultural state aid derogation, the European Commission began to examine national film support schemes with regard to their compatability and adherence to the rules on competition in the TEC from 1997. As a result, in 2001 a "communication on certain legal aspects relating to cinematographic and other audiovisual works," otherwise known as the Cinema Communication, was published (European Commission 2001). The criteria for determining whether state support for cinema is compatible with EU competition law are defined in the 2001 Cinema Communication. This general approach to state aid for the cinema and audio-visual production sector was extended to 30 June 2007 by a further Communication (the Cinema Communication of 2004), which also announced the Commission's intention to study the effects of state aid systems and in particular the economic and cultural impact of territorialization requirements and their impact on co-productions (European Commission, 2008). Because the study had not been completed by the expiration date of the Communication in 2007, it was again extended, until 31 December 2009.

The Commission stated in the 2004 Communication that its main concerns were not related to the volume of the aid, which, being aimed at supporting culture, was compatible with the treaty, but to the territorialization clauses of certain aid schemes. Such territorialization clauses impose on producers an obligation to spend a certain amount of the film budget in a particular member state as an eligibility condition for receiving the full aid amount. Territorialization clauses may therefore constitute a barrier to the free circulation of workers, goods, and services across the European Community. They may, therefore, fragment the internal market for the provision of goods and services for audio-visual production and hinder its development. However, the Commission considers that these clauses may be justified under certain circumstances in order to ensure the continued presence of the human skills and technical expertise required for cultural creation (European Commission 2001, 6).

As a result of this announcement by the Commission there was a massive mobilization of the European film and audio-visual sector at all levels, ranging from film agency directors to the public in a hearing in Brussels in July 2007. Statements, letters, and comments were submitted from across the sector, for example, from the European Film Agency Directors (EFAD) network, from Cine-Regio, and from Capital Regions for Cinema (CRC), in support of the existing state aid structures including territorialization requirements. Further liberalization of the sector and dismantling of the existing support were not seen as options and certainly not as ones that would benefit the industry.

In February 2009 the Commission communicated the results of the independent study: "[T]he current State aid assessment criteria can continue for the time being to promote cultural creation and will ensure that the aid granted to film and audiovisual production does not affect competition and trading conditions to an extent contrary to the common interest. However, a number of different trends have emerged since the 2001 Cinema Communication, which will require some refinement of these criteria in due course."

Those trends include support for aspects other than film and television production (such as film distribution and digital projection), and more regional film support schemes, as well as competition among some member states to use state aid to attract inward investment from large-scale, mainly U.S., film production companies. These are complex issues that require reflection by the member states and national and regional film support bodies to develop appropriate criteria. Consequently, the Commission decided to continue to apply the current criteria until such time as new rules on state aid to cinematographic and other audio-visual works came into effect (European Commission 2009, 4).

Indeed, professionals from all areas of the film and audio-visual sector in Europe, in particular the national and regional agencies, are working on input for a new and updated Cinema Communication. In sum, this territorialization saga was an instance in which the entire film and audio-visual sector joined forces to counter the threat of greater deregulation in the face of the EU competition policies' working to the detriment of this cultural sector.

Creative Europe and MEDIA

Another example of the European film sector's joining forces in support of public policy and state support for the industry manifest through the expiry of MEDIA 2007 in 2013. The possibility of a major change in EU policy and a rumour of the disappearance of the MEDIA program caused rapid mobilization again and, one might even say, panic in the film and audio-visual sector. A quick glimpse into some of the professional trade magazines, such as *Screen Daily* or *Blickpunkt: Film*, shows the magnitude of concern on the subject (Blaney, 2011b). The rumours about the end of MEDIA were ultimately unfounded although in reality there is much unease at the idea that the major European program to support the film and audio-visual sector will henceforth be subordinated within the greater program of Creative Europe.

It seems that the Commission has recently discovered the importance of the creative industries and has fully adopted its discourse. There does appear to be a return to the economic rationale on which the EU was based in spite of, or in addition to, the overtures made to culture over the years. With reference to the film and audio-visual industry, Androulla Vassiliou (EU Commissioner for Education, Culture, Multilingualism, Sport, Media, and Youth) recently noted: "3%–4% of the GDP of the EU is a very, very important contribution. It's more than the car industry, the plastic industry, the chemical industry" (quoted in Blaney, 2011b). Vassiliou has argued that bringing MEDIA into the Creative Europe program could "create more synergy in all of our actions in the field of culture and creativity," "cut down on red-tape," and "mean more funding will be directed where it's need[ed] most" (ibid.). Furthermore: "Our support for film distribution, development and digitisation fills a funding gap ... and it's good for cultural diversity, competitiveness and jobs. Without it, audiences would see fewer European films" (quoted in Blaney, 2011a). Many of Vassiliou's interventions regarding the film and audio-visual sector emphasize the importance of the sector for its contribution to the GDP and job growth.

The budget available for MEDIA will possibly be increased to €900 million, although the exact final budget must still be approved by the Council and Parliament.[6] The Commission document gives an indication of how the new program will look. Existing actions that have proven their effectiveness in the past, such as support to distribution, will be maintained, as will the complementarities with national schemes, and there will be a focus on structuring actions with a maximum systemic impact, for example, by increasing the use of financial instruments and having an integrating approach across the value chain. In sum, the report suggests increasing resources for distribution on all distribution platforms; expanding and structuring audience-building measures; increasing the use of financial instruments; expanding to include video games; supporting co-productions; and addressing the problem of insufficient data collection (European Commission 2011, 83–5).

The main notable difference from preceding programs is a clear emphasis on expanding a new financial instrument, which provides state guarantees for obtaining bank loans. "Given the leverage effect of financial instruments and their structuring effect on the industry, direct support in the form of subsidies could be progressively shifted to financial instruments for some types of supports and beneficiaries. This would entail an increase in size and scope of the existing guarantee fund or the creation of a new Cultural and Creative Sectors (CCS) financial instrument (subject to a separate Impact Assessment)" (ibid., 85). This clear shift attempting to stimulate private funding for SMEs in the culture and creative industries is entirely in line with the liberalizing competitiveness discourse of the EU. It will be extremely interesting to see how the process evolves and how the facilitation of access to private loans will change the nature of the European film and audio-visual sector.

The subject of territorialization measures is again a major issue with respect to any new EU policy and the new draft of the Cinema Communication. During the Cannes Film Festival in May 2012, at the annual European Audiovisual Observatory Workshop, which was focused on the new proposed film-funding rules in Europe, there was clear resistance shown on the part of many interlocutors, in particular with respect to the reduction of territorialization measures.[7]

In spite of the pressure on the EU to counter the fragmentation of the European film and audio-visual sector through its policies, its real success seems to lie in the greater circulation of European films, and in particular the increasing circulation of co-productions within Europe. This clearly underpins the positive factor of there being a greater diversity of films available and thus a stronger cultural diversity. In addition, the manner in which the professionals of the sector have reacted to the challenges of the EU policy indicates that the priorities are placed on nurturing the film sector above all for its cultural importance to Europe and that the success of the EU policy, from an industry perspective, lies more in the area of diversity and of legitimately supporting local, regional, and national interests, than in the area of an economically integrated industry.

Subsidies and public policies alone cannot make an integrated industry when the predominant idea of cinema and audio-visual production is based on other priorities, as it is in Europe. Certainly there are also drawbacks to the processes of public funding and public policies, and these processes are not the only panacea for the independent filmmaking sector in Europe. However, the European subsidies and policies in place are, without a doubt, crucial to the idea of a cinema that furthers independent voices and cultural diversity. This is a priority for the filmmaking sector in Europe.[8]

NOTES

1 For example, Toby Miller et al. (2005); Herold (2004).
2 The primary aim of the Council of Europe is to create a common democratic and legal area throughout the whole of the continent, ensuring respect for its fundamental values: human rights, democracy, and the rule of law. Its objectives are to protect human rights, pluralist democracy, and the rule of law; to promote awareness and encourage the development of Europe's cultural identity and diversity; to find common solutions to the challenges

facing European society; and to consolidate democratic stability in Europe by backing political, legislative, and constitutional reform.

3 With respect to the opportunities available for newcomers in accessing MEDIA funding, one could say that, for example, training measures, and also perhaps professional networking, are clearly domains in which newcomers are quite present. By contrast, in certain other MEDIA domains it is more difficult for newcomers, but this is then balanced out, ideally, through support programs implemented at national and regional levels (European Commission 2011, 61).

4 "An independent production company is an audiovisual production company which does not have majority control by a television broadcaster, either in shareholding or commercial terms. Majority control is considered to occur when more than 25% of the share capital of a production company is held by a single broadcaster (50% when several broadcasters are involved) or when, over a three-year period, more than 90% of a production company's revenue is generated in co-operation with a single broadcaster. The following are not eligible: foundations, institutes, universities, associations and other legal bodies acting in the public interest; applications from groups of companies; private individuals." See Media Production Guarantee Fund, *Eligibility Criteria for the MPGF Guarantee*, accessed 19 November 2013, http://www.ifcic.eu/media-production-guarantee-fund/eligibility-criteria-for-the-mpgf-guarantee.html.

5 See, for example, Hoefert de Turégano 2004.

6 Aviva Silver, *European Film Academy - MEDIA lunch* (Berlin, 6 December 2011).

7 Observations made by the author.

8 Thanks go to Roberto Olla (Eurimages) for discussion on this subject.

Chapter Four

Dependency and Independence in British Independent Film

ERIK KNUDSEN

The future of cinematography belongs to a new race of young solitaries who will shoot films by putting their last cent into it and not let themselves be taken in by the material routines of the trade.

(Bresson 1975, 62)

Independence must necessarily be relative, for no one is wholly independent of their biological, family, and cultural contexts. Somehow independence is set against the structures of dependencies that in part give shape to our lives. Yet there seems to be, like the child growing into adulthood, a perpetual tension between the desire for the comfort, stability, and consistency offered by a world built around dependency on the familiar, the established, or the official and the desire for the freedom that independent action allows. There is a close connection between independence and freedom, which is characterized by an underlying tendency of independent filmmakers to break free of "the material routines of the trade" (Bresson 1975, 62) in a bid to free themselves from the constraints of established processes, content, and form. Perhaps these disparate acts of independent action share the same underlying urge found in many of us – an urge to seek freedom from many different types of imprisonment that bind us to the conventions and forms imposed on us by others.

This urge for freedom through independent action is actually critical for our survival. In cinematic terms, without the – at times defiant – independent film, the mainstream would wither away and die, existing only, like a dead star, on its own clichés and burned-out ideas. As in other sectors, the software industry being a good example, innovations and new ideas are generated on the fringes of the mainstream and eventually brought into this mainstream as part of a process of renewal and rejuvenation. Although there is consequently a symbiotic relationship between the mainstream and its fringe, this fringe is characterized by individuals and smaller groups of people – sometimes, in the case of those operating largely on the Internet, large communities – who have acted independently to create works that could never have originated within the mainstream. Many of the significant innovations coming out of Microsoft and Apple, for example, have resulted directly from these large companies buying start-ups or picking up ideas that they have spotted being developed by independent individuals and communities via the Internet. Likewise, the entire history of Hollywood is littered with examples of fringe directors being brought in. Rodriguez,[1] Coppola,[2] and Lynch[3] were once independent filmmakers operating on the fringe; not to speak of such foreign imports as Ophuls, Polanski, and Besson. In Britain, equivalent examples might be Davies,[4] Meadows,[5] and McQueen.[6]

If the mainstream is dependent on the fringe and independent sectors for its renewal and survival, then, of course, the independent sector is equally dependent on having a mainstream from which to be independent. Both interact in a process of osmosis with each other. It is in the interest of the mainstream to have a healthy and vibrant independent sector; just as it is important for the independent sector to exist in contrast from a vibrant mainstream.

In the context of Britain, there is confusion about what independent means. The term *independent* is often used to denote a film that has been produced independently of Hollywood. The annual British Independent Film Awards awarded its 2010 Best British Independent Film to *The King's Speech* (Tom Hooper, 2010, United Kingdom), and the popular press refers to many UK-produced films, including *Harry Potter and the Deathly Hallows, Part 2* (David Yates, 2011, UK), and *The Inbetweeners* (Ben Palmer, 2011), as independent films.[7] However, these are films that were produced by some of the biggest and most established mainstream production companies that in many cases are not even British. The Weinstein Company, Warner Bros., Pathé, Channel Four's Film Four, and BBC Films are pillars of the British film industry establishment and are either American companies with offshoots in the UK or UK companies with significant interest in the U.S. market. Their so-called independent films are heavily promoted as potential Golden Globe winners or serious Academy Award contenders. Notwithstanding this understanding of the term *independent*, it is hard to claim that these films are anything but mainstream in their form, content, and production processes. The term *independent* is, therefore, often used as a marketing tool and a political tool: marketing, in the sense that using the term *independent* is geared to appeal to the David-and-Goliath complex that perhaps exists in all of us here in the UK; political, in the sense that the policy debates that dominate discussions about maintaining a viable UK film industry relate to dependency and independence from Hollywood. This is not unlike the U.S. independent sector that Yannis Tzioumakis discusses in his chapter, "An Increasingly Global Presence: Contemporary American Independent Cinema outside the United States," where we see significant companies such as Miramax Films and Lionsgate creating types of films marketed within a highly marketable concept that Tzioumakis terms *indiewood*. Similar issues and questions arise about the term *independent*.

The debate about creating a sustainable indigenous UK film industry is a long-standing policy preoccupation dating back to the 1950s when the Eady Levy was introduced to help support the British film industry. This levy, which continued to operate until 1985, was effectively a tax on every cinema ticket sold in the UK, which was then reinvested into British-based production. Running alongside the Eady Levy was the National Film Finance Corporation, whose role was to pump prime British production. Maintaining an independent indigenous production industry has therefore been part of the British policy agenda for more than half a century and continues to this day. More recently, the UK Film Council (UKFC), created in 1999 and disbanded and subsumed into the British Film Institute in 2010, was the lead agency for film production funding in the UK. Tasked with investing in production of commercial and cultural film by distributing government grants and National Lottery monies, the UKFC operated predominantly centrally but did distribute some of its funding through regional screen agencies, such as North West Vision, East Midlands Media, and Yorkshire Screen, which covered the NorthWest, the East Midlands, and the north of England. The UKFC was also involved in supporting a network of regional cinemas. Its focus was production funding, and though its remit was to cover both cultural production and commercial production, its preoccupation was with commercial film financing.

The scale of the task of maintaining an independent indigenous film industry in the UK is considerable. In 2010, just 5.4 per cent of the UK box-office revenue was deemed to have been generated by "independent" British films (British Film Institute 2012, 14). This share came from 108 titles, which constituted 19.4 per cent of the films released that year. Only one of these films, *StreetDance 3D* (Max Giwa and Dania Pasquini, 2010, UK), made it into the top twenty grossing films. Faced with this task, it is perhaps understandable that the term *independent* is used so extensively to describe what are essentially mainstream British films trying to survive in a marketplace that is completely dominated by the Goliath of Hollywood. However, in terms of development, production, distribution, form, and content, the vast majority of these films that are created within the context of the British mainstream are striving to compete with American products. As Adams (2011) points out, "this over-reaching ambition to compete with American product on a global basis resulted in a conservative approach to scripts and excessive emphasis on international production values (stars, locations, technologies), representing the United Kingdom through a narrow prism of 'British' story genre: bleak social realism, bland heritage film, blackish comedy" (113).

The creation of the production arm of the British Film Institute in 1964 recognized the need to foster and encourage alternatives to the UK mainstream in content, form, and process. This ambition was further boosted by the arrival of Channel Four Television in 1982. Within Channel Four, a specific department, Independent Film and Video, led by Alan Fountain between 1982 and 1995, clearly indicated the channel's commitment to the idea of encouraging an independent film sector within the UK. Channel Four, mainly through its film arm Film Four, was, and continues to be, an important contributor to indigenous UK film production. The publisher-only model of Channel Four allowed it to develop a broad set of relationships with production companies, production workshops, and individual filmmakers. Indeed, the Independent Film and Video Department is widely credited as being a prime force in the revival of the Film Workshop movement, originally set up by the British Film Institute, which supports independent filmmakers across the country through direct funding of workshops and collectives and the commissioning of films through these workshops. Amber Films in Newcastle, Four Corners in London, and Sheffield Independent Film are examples of workshops that thrived during the 1980s with direct support from Channel Four and to this day are still in operation, even if their funding from the channel has been greatly reduced or has ceased altogether.

Focused very much at the youth end of the television market, Channel Four, through Film Four, part-financed a string of films that straddled the mainstream and what we may call the art market, such as *My Beautiful Laundrette* (Frears, 1985) and *This Is England* (Meadows, 2006). Despite its early engagement with independent film, Channel Four changed in 1995 when it took over responsibility from Independent Television (ITV) for selling its own advertising. The change in leadership and approach within the Independent Film and Video Department at that time is an indication of the broader change that occurred. Stuart Cosgrove replaced Alan Fountain as commissioning editor for the department, and the change in philosophy was immediate. Where Alan Fountain sought to listen to what filmmakers across the country were interested in making and would then sprinkle his funding as a catalyst to grow a diverse offering, Stuart Cosgrove' drove very much from the centre in his approach. Independent Film and Video moved towards the more mainstream television approach of tightly defining briefs for slots and strands to which filmmakers would have to adhere. Terminology such as *cutting edge, underbelly of society,* and *innovative* crept into the language of commissioning briefs set entirely in London. The inevitable consequence of this change was the near demise of the Channel Four–funded regional workshop.

The UK Film Council set up regional agencies. Dependent largely on funding from the parent body, these agencies tended to focus on inward investment into regions for commercially driven films, with token investment in limited short-film production under the banner of talent development. Since the dismantlement of the UKFC these agencies have largely disappeared or radically transformed. Creative England and Film London, new bodies overseeing the development of film culture across the country, are now the only effective bodies, in collaboration with the BFI, with a remit to develop a film production culture in England.[8] Non-territorial in its structure, Creative England has yet to establish itself, and its effect and influence have yet to be seen. This development is set within the context of a film policy review commissioned by the UK government's Department for Culture, Media, and Sport and headed by Lord Chris Smith. He published his report in January 2012, and a consultation about its findings ensued.[9]

Britain does not have an underlying independent culture comparable to that of the United States. There is no comparable culture of private investment and philanthropy that provide a strong hinterland of film financing beyond the more formal and established studio and co-production routes that underpin the mainstream. Apart from the major multiplex cinemas, which are largely owned by US studios, almost all cinemas, such as the regional film theatres initially set up by the BFI in the 1960s and 1970s, are dependent on funding from a government-funded agency, such as the UKFC/BFI. The major UK broadcaster and the producer of a number of UK films, the BBC, is funded effectively by a special tax – the Licence Fee – and the major UK production companies have become dependent on government subsidies that flow through the UKFC/BFI. Some tax incentives are in place to encourage a broader investment base, but this does not form the mainstay of wholly UK-financed productions. In addition, all the government-driven agencies, and consequently all the decision makers, are based in London. As is clear from Lydia Papadimitriou's chapter, "In the Shadow of the Studios, the State, and the Multiplexes: Independent Filmmaking in Greece," other European countries have similar tendencies for the decision making and funding of independent films to concentrate around key state institutions. Indeed, as Papadimitriou points out, in many continental European countries, such concentrations are closely aligned to political power and control, and the history of European cinema is, in many cases, also the history of political power and its counter forces.

If we consider independent film to mean independence from the mainstream British film, as opposed to the British film's independence from the Hollywood film, then indeed what does independence mean in the British context? Independence from what? In the British context, the meaning of independence must include not only a sense of independence from the mainstream form, content, and production process but also independence from policy-driven agendas articulated through quasi-governmental funding bodies. There is, of course, a close connection between content, form, process, and film policy, and we shall look briefly at how these are connected and relate to independence. Can independence thrive as an outcome of policy, particularly if that policy is set by a relatively small elite based in London who control key funding sources?

Aesthetic Dependencies

The British establishment and institutions have always had an ambivalent relationship with film; they cannot work out if it is an industry or an art. While French artists immediately embraced film in its early years as an equal to other more established art forms, which in turn had a significant impact on how subsequent French film policy viewed the role of film in French society and the French economy, the British tended to look at film as part of an entertainment industry, leading to a completely different view of why and how government policy should engage with film. For example, prior to government film policy being set within the Department of Culture, Media, and Sport, as is currently the case, the former Department for Trade and Industry was responsible for film. The British establishment – politicians, opinion leaders, and actual leaders of key cultural institutions – tended to be educated in educational environments in which the theatrical and literary traditions dominated. This is, indeed, still the case today: the theatrical and literary heritage of British culture dominates approaches to content and form in British film. Almost all contemporary British films are based on an adaptation of a novel, a theatrical work, or a play. If not, key British gatekeepers will often insist on employing a novelist, a playwright, or a television dramatist to write the screenplay. British television drama – a halfway house between cinema and theatre, essentially filmed theatre – with its strong roots in the dramaturgy of theatre and in the story sources in literature – dominates the aesthetic of the contemporary British mainstream cinematic film, and it is therefore no coincidence that writers such as Frank Cottrell Boyce (*Welcome to Sarajevo*, Michael Winterbottom, 1997, UK; *24 Hour Party People*, Michael Winterbottom, 2002, UK; *Millions*, Danny Boyle, 2004, UK), Hanif Kureishi (*My Beautiful Laundrette*, Stephen Frears, 1985, UK; *Venus*, Roger Mitchell, 2006, UK), and Alex Garland (*28 Days Later*, Danny Boyle, 2002, UK; *Sunshine*, Danny Boyle, 2007, UK), whose backgrounds are based in theatre, television drama or literature, are often employed to write screenplays.

With the combination of a contemporary-film funding environment dominated by a few gatekeepers whose aesthetic values are dominated by a literary and theatrical tradition, and the constant battle with the powerful wake of the mighty Hollywood, it is perhaps inevitable that the British contemporary mainstream output is dominated by certain types of films. As John Adams (2011) points out about the legacy of the UKFC, the "mainstream commercial production is not the game in which to stake a public investment in film: commodity logic shapes the ideas and values of films that aspire to the global market and, despite the occasional high-profile success, there is little public benefit or justification for support from the Lottery shilling" (113).

The classic upper-class period drama, the classic Dickensian working-class period drama, the contemporary cosmopolitan middle-class romantic drama, and the gritty working-class "kitchen sink" or "post-industrial" urban drama all have a number of common features: they are usually based on an established literary or theatrical work; their main narrative mode is the dramaturgy of dramatic conflict; they are usually dominated by dialogue; the aesthetic values of the performances in the films are largely based on performers who have been theatrically trained; heritage, and particularly the relationship to nineteenth-century heritage, features strongly; and class consciousness and class conflict underpin almost every story. Whether or not they are independent films, the body of largely mainstream work produced in the UK tends to be created around something quintessentially British, a narrative commodity that speaks of heritage and class easily recognizable in external markets, particularly the United States. Is there a connection between this approach to content and form and the poor commercial presence of wholly UK-produced films at the UK box office?

In exploring what independent British film is, one finds excellent examples of filmmakers who over the past forty years or so have sought to be independent of the content, form, and processes of the dominant tendencies described above. Have they also managed to be independent of UK film policy and the values of the key gatekeepers?

When looking at the works of Bill Douglas,[10] Terence Davies,[11] Sally Potter,[12] Derek Jarman,[13] Peter Greenaway,[14] Andrew Kötting,[15] Isaac Julien,[16] Mike Leigh,[17] and Gideon Koppel,[18] we start to see a cluster of filmmakers whose work seems to have an inherent sense of independence from the dominant preoccupations of the mainstream British film. The language of film departs from the reliance on dramaturgy and conflict as the central tool of expression, and the exploration of film form reveals a diversity of vision and cinematic engagement that helps reveal the unique qualities of the film form. The cultural influences seen in the works usually go well beyond literature and drama, embracing other influences such as painting, photography, poetry, music, dance, conceptual art, and philosophy. Bill Douglas's use of evocative black-and-white photography, Terence Davies's gentle play with "time present and time past,"[19] Sally Potter's exploration of dance and movement, Derek Jarman's incorporation of fine art into his works, Peter Greenaway's strong connection to conceptual art, Andrew Kötting's exploration of the visually idiosyncratic, and Gideon Koppel's documentary poetry – all explore the cinematic form in ways that the mainstream does not or can not. The cinematic works of these filmmakers go beyond merely filming drama, by utilizing the full spectrum of cinematic tools to tell stories in which all aspects of the film form are creatively and evocatively used to shape narratives. Even a filmmaker like Mike Leigh, whose works could be said to be based predominantly on dramaturgy, explores different approaches to this dramaturgy, for example through his deployment of improvisation and the telling of stories by focusing on the non-dramatic components of character interaction.

Almost without exception, for a significant number of their key works these filmmakers have been dependent on funding their films through one single organization, the BFI. Between 1967 and 1999 the BFI was effectively the primary source of feature-length-film funding for those filmmakers seeking to be independent of the dominant approaches to form and content. Between 1982 and 1995, there was, as mentioned earlier, some collaboration between the BFI and Channel Four, which saw some co-funding, but on the whole Channel Four would never have entered into the funding of many of the works by a number of these filmmakers without the proactive presence of the BFI. One could say that, coupled with the work of the Independent Film and Video Department at Channel Four, the independent film production from a nation of 60 million people has been dominated by, if not dependent on, the decision making of less than a handful of people within two or three institutions based in London.

What is the effect of such a heavy concentration of gatekeeping on the independence of filmmakers? To answer this question would require a closer textual analysis of key works, but there is a lingering sense that while the exploration of the film form has been relatively diverse, a traditional perspective on content around class and heritage still dominates the subject matter of the supported films. In "Eyes of the Beholder" (Knudsen 2005, 181–6), I argue, in the context of the UKFC development of screenplays, that the UK films eventually seen on the screen by audiences do not reflect the quality and diversity of the available talent across the nation but rather reflect the values and aspirations of the gatekeepers who select, commission, and steer the development and production of the works. The values and aesthetic appreciation of various ethnic minorities, for example, are not seen on the British screen, nor are the spiritual and religious interests that occupy many people's thoughts, nor are certain perspectives on a number of moral dilemmas that challenge the values of the media-political elite.

The challenge for independent film in the UK has been, and continues to be, twofold. First, there is a need to transcend the notion that independent British film is concerned with independence from Hollywood.

Much policy and support infrastructure – including the infrastructure around supporting short-film production primarily as a "stepping stone" to producing *independent* British films that will make it in the U.S. market – has been concerned with developing a mainstream indigenous British film industry with the focus very much on commerce and commerciality. This near obsession with matching indigenous British film with, and emulating, U.S. conventions, as well as successfully accessing the U.S. market, seems more about dependency than independence. Second, for the independent filmmaker whose concern is not so much with maintaining independence from Hollywood and its values and conventions but with maintaining an independence from the British establishment institutions in relation to the values and conventions around form and content – in particular, those institutions whose aim is to support cultural filmmaking – the challenge is more insidious and complex. There is a chance that to be a truly independent filmmaker in the UK means to be invisible. But being invisible to the key decision makers of two or three film institutions in the UK is, as will be touched on later, the same as being invisible to British audiences.

Technology and Independence

Britain does not have a culture of philanthropy comparable to that of the United States. The United States has an active philanthropic culture and an entrepreneurial economy; this culture has combined with formal funding models, such as investment and co-production, to engage a home market that is large enough to support a lively filmmaking scene that is independent of government or other institutional grants. In fact, the success of the Sundance Film Festival is a recognition of the importance of a philanthropically driven film production culture in American cinema.[20] Indeed, the many successes of independent films at the box office even led Paramount Pictures to set up a separate company in 2011, Insurge Pictures, to develop and produce a slate of films with a budget of just under US$100,000, recognizing the potential of low-budget independent films in the marketplace. Although the idea of majors investing in independent film as part of their research and development is not new, as Tzioumakis points out in his chapter, "An Increasingly Global Presence," what has traditionally been considered independent never dealt with budgets as low as those proposed by Insurge Pictures. This is as a direct result of the digital revolution, in terms of both production and dissemination. Their bet is that the strike rate of significant successes will see substantial profits generated from relatively low investment and low-risk ventures in which new ideas and approaches can be explored. The culture of maverick independent filmmakers bucking the system to produce their independent films is not as prevalent in the UK as it is in the United States. It is relatively rare to see a British independent film readily available in the marketplace that was produced outside the established structures of funding. Nor does Britain have heavy government intervention in cultural film production, distribution, and exhibition on a scale that can transform a nation's engagement with the medium, such as in France. The French government's direct intervention in the market, and overtly nationalistic investment policies, has ensured that French cinema is not grappling with the same scale of issues in relation to the country's audiences engaging with indigenous film, as is the case in Britain. Somehow, Britain hovers unconfidently between these two great cinematic nations and their contrasting approaches to the cinematic art and cinematic business.

However, developments and changes in technology are changing the picture in the UK. The commercially driven low-budget movie *Monsters* (Gareth Edwards, 2010) and the issue-driven feature documentary *The Age of Stupid* (Franny Armstrong, 2009) are two varied examples of British independent filmmaking utilizing new technologies in ways that aid independence. Gareth Edwards utilized very accessible production and post-production technology to make an epic science-fiction thriller on a minuscule and essentially self-funded budget that was, in terms of production values, able to match much higher budgeted movies in the same genre. In contrast, Franny Armstrong utilized the Internet to build a funding model based on crowdfunding[21] to engage an audience in the process of the filmmaking, which enabled her to remain independent of traditional funding sources. Neither film was unique in terms of form and content, working as it did within an established genre, but both films demonstrate well the opportunities that changing technology in the moving image offer the independent filmmaker. This is indeed a revolution that has led to YouTube, Vimeo, Amazon Video on Demand, and an explosion of film festivals across the globe. Several tens of thousands of feature films are made around the world every year, and the new kind of online film distributors such as Netflix and Amazon report that the vast majority of their moving image turnover is based on the sale of films that have never been shown in a cinema (Anderson 2006).

The United States, of course, leads the way in these developments. While Amazon in the United States is able to make a service like CreateSpace available for independent filmmakers to distribute their films free of charge, using print on demand and download technologies, the regulatory framework in the UK prevents the company from providing a similar service there. How many independent UK-produced films that are available in the United States on this service are unavailable in the UK? We might never know the answer. When quantifying the number of feature films made in the UK, the BFI has only recently started including films with a budget of less than £500,000.[22] They counted 397 feature films made between 2008 and 2010 that were produced on budgets of less than £500,000, 130 of which were produced on budgets between £10,000[23] and £100,000,[24] and 54 made for less than £10,000 (British Film Institute 2012, 157). By way of example, the North West of England, probably the most active film production region outside of London, which was serviced by the UKFC-funded agency North West Vision (NWV) until 2010, saw a total of eighteen indigenous[25] feature films produced between 2003 and 2005.[26] A further six feature films were inward-bound[27] productions that were largely shot and produced outside the region. The majority of the inward-bound productions would have received some sweetener funding from NWV and substantial funding from the UKFC. Of the eighteen indigenous films produced during this period, fifteen were produced without any public funding and without support from NWV (Murray 2006, 7–8). In fact, it is highly likely that NWV knew nothing about them being produced. Their development, production, and distribution were independent of the very policy-directed public infrastructure that was designed to promote, encourage, and support regional independent filmmaking. While the public funding infrastructure is not necessarily designed to accommodate all independent production, the scale of the circumvention suggests that policymakers may be out of touch with the reality of what happens on the ground, particularly as new technologies enable independent filmmakers to cost-effectively circumvent the very structures that, from a policy perspective, are meant to support them. One or two public-funded agencies are responding to the new micro-budget opportunities for independent film, particularly Film London, and have created a film fund with pots of money for feature film projects budgeted at under £50,000.

Distribution remains the single largest problem for independent filmmakers, in particular theatrical distribution. While a number of independent films may obtain a very limited run in a handful of cinemas, online distribution, including DVD sales and downloads, provides the most realistic route to an audience. Nevertheless, where independent films do have a very limited, independently organized theatrical exposure, *Sight and Sound*, arguably the UK's leading film journal, has a policy that is indicative of the film establishment's attitude towards independent filmmaking. *Sight and Sound* lists and reviews monthly "every film released in the UK," according to its introduction to this section of the journal. Yet, the list is drawn exclusively from films released by the twenty-three members of the Film Distributors Association. There is no such organization to accommodate lower-budget independent film distributors. Compare this to the Independent Publishers Association, which has a membership of over 480 independent book publishers accounting for £500 million turnover,[28] or the Association of Independent Music, whose over 850 members account for 25 per cent of the UK music market.[29]

Understanding the complex issues around film distribution requires a separate enquiry, but suffice to say that in an age of abundance brought about, in the cinematic sphere, by the proliferation of digital technologies,[30] the independent UK filmmaker and film entrepreneur still have some way to go in gaining the equivalent recognition and status afforded by their independent counterparts in music and book publishing. In these two sectors the independent artist and entrepreneur form an important and fully recognized component of the overall industry, and the engagement with the established institutions appears more mature. Although authors may bemoan the deals that are sealed between the major publishers and the main retail outlets, the fact remains that it is still possible to go into a major bookshop chain such as Waterstones and find books – even if in an obscure corner on the third floor – published by truly independent book publishers. Live performances of music, combined with a plethora of download opportunities and high-street[31] outlets, give the independent musician considerable access to audiences.

Yet, in film there is still a legacy of an old business model that dominates policy developments and the attitudes of those who have influence within the film establishment. That old business model was built around heavy gatekeeping, protectionism, and the control of limited screens (essentially a handful of cinema chains and four television stations controlled largely by economic interests outside the UK). This was a model that encouraged nepotism, elitism, and the notion of the professional. Two film schools – the National Film and Television School and the London Film School – provided two new gateways into the industry during the 1970s and 1980s, though since the 1990s other film schools and universities have opened. We now have a multitude of educational establishments in the UK – both private and public – which provide education and training in predominantly digital film production. While large parts of the film industry, perhaps inadvertently, seek to preserve the old business model, independent filmmakers – as suggested by the figures for the North West of England mentioned earlier – are subverting and circumventing the policy-driven frameworks and infrastructure.

Can one talk of independence in the same way in this emerging context? Do we need to re-evaluate what we mean by a film industry? What is the distinction between an amateur and a professional (a distinction encouraged by the notion of being either in the film industry or out of it)? Would authors who make a living by supplementing their income (as do the vast majority of published authors) by doing a range of – sometimes related – activities other than writing think of themselves as independent authors? Would musicians who likewise supplement their income from a variety of sources other than the release of music recordings call themselves independent musicians? Perhaps there will come a time when the term *independent* will become as redundant as the term *digital*. When the effects of technological change fully embed themselves in the culture of filmmaking, with the consequent effects on business models, convergence, and processes, perhaps we will see a situation in which filmmakers working outside the parameters of globally scaled companies will have a larger and more seamless impact on the film economy as a whole. To a great extent, this is likely to be driven by the evolving relationship between the independent filmmaker's engagement of enabling technologies, such as the Internet, and the audiences' ability to develop a more sophisticated relationship to accessing content. Given the evidence that Amazon and Netflix have found in the online purchasing patterns of movies (Anderson 2006), it would seem that audiences are getting a taste for exercising their interest in diverse content. We have certainly seen this to be the case in music, and to some extent in film too, where niche and genre interests drive audiences to particular websites; these sites then see substantial turnover from content that, for the mass marketeer, seems marginal. While most people will have their clear interest in the popular product that is produced explicitly for mass market consumption, which in terms of cinema releases increasingly focuses on a narrower demographic, they will also from time to time demonstrate an interest in something more niched or specialized. New business models, seen already in book publishing, will need to evolve around diversity of content, and it is perhaps in such a scenario that the term *independent* will start to change its meaning, if not actually become obsolete.

The Outsider and Independence

Most filmmakers make films because they cannot help it. Necessity drives them, and they seem to have no control over this impulse. The films will out, and the filmmakers use whatever tools and circumstances are around them to give their stories form and shape. Even though, increasingly, they are educated and trained in film, they cannot help but use the medium in particular ways that are shaped by inexplicable tastes and experiences. Filmmakers do not choose to be independent on purpose: their stories, character, family, and social upbringing conspire to make them create work that challenges the conventions of production, form, and content. A filmmaker's independence is not necessarily a cause; it is more often a consequence, a consequence of having a voice that instinctively speaks from the outside. Who would deliberately put themselves into a position of hardship and struggle if it were not because some kind of inner necessity took them there?

It is therefore important, when trying to understand what independent film is, to factor in what some might describe as an idealistic or romantic notion of a film artist. Being an independent filmmaker does not make financial sense; it does not make sense if you hope to reach a large audience; it does not make sense whatsoever if you intend to raise a family. Why do it then? Why not simply learn how to make films that make lots of money, or join a production company that has a successful formula? When we talk about independence, we must therefore also talk about the deeper motivations that drive individuals and communities to be outsiders, in some cases lone voices, wanting to say something that they think is critically important. We know, too, that these are the same forces that often drive the "independent" scientist, the "independent" poet, or the "independent" shoemaker for example – the outsiders who make things that are often created in the shadows of the noisy mainstream.[32] Who knew much about Blake in his lifetime? What about Kepler? Copernicus wrote one book that took him ten years to publish because he was too shy or embarrassed about it. Joyce had to self-publish. Van Gogh did not sell a single painting outside his family during his lifetime. All these outsiders were driven by the nature of their character, their heritage, and their circumstances to be *independent*, and their works have subsequently had a profound effect on our lives.

We are quite happy to talk about poets, painters, and composers in this way, yet when we talk about filmmaking, we somehow are drawn back to the industrial model. Everything that filmmakers do is part of an industry of some kind, everything has the potential to make them a living, and there is always the chance that they will strike it lucky and that something that started on the fringe will become incredibly successful. Filmmakers might also become lucky if they fall into a situation where their inner calling coincides with an industrial situation that allows the artist in them to flourish. There are very few filmmakers who would not want their work to be successful, but an independent artist – an independent filmmaker – is forced, by inner necessity, to take the risk that it might never be so. The mainstream of culture needs these artists to take the risk, because if there were not some people taking the risk of remaining invisible or remaining outsiders or rejected, where would the new ideas, the fresh or refreshed perspectives, the opening up to seeing the sublime or the profound, or the new talent come from? Do we have a Blake, a Copernicus, or a Joyce in our midst? A characteristic of the British independent scene is that it is filled with filmmakers who are largely invisible. It is therefore important for any culture to enable structures, infrastructures, and contexts to encourage independence, diversity, and subversion.[33]

It is interesting that Robert Bresson (1975) talked about the "future of cinematography [that] belongs to a new race of young solitaries who will shoot films by putting their last cent into it and not let themselves be taken in by the material routines of the trade" (62), at a time that everything in film was analogue. He could surely not have known about the digital revolution that would transform the "divine" (ibid.) machines, as he called them, of the camera and tape recorder. He could not have known, either, that the Internet would explode our way of distributing and watching films. He did not need to, for, irrespective of technology, at the heart of any future there are people who will sacrifice the comforts of "material routines" (ibid.) in order to create a better world through a medium that they love.

NOTES

1   From *El Mariachi* (Robert Rodriguez, 1992, United States) to *Sin City* (Robert Rodriguez, 2005, United States).
2   From *The Bellboy and the Playgirls* (Francis Ford Coppola, 1962, United States) to *Twixt* (Francis Ford Coppola, 2011, United States).
3   From *Eraserhead* (David Lynch, 1980, United States) to *Inland Empire* (David Lynch, 2006, United States).
4   From *The Terence Davies Trilogy* (Terence Davies, 1983, United Kingdom) to *The Deep Blue Sea* (Terence Davies, 2011, UK).
5   From *Small Time* (Shane Meadows, 1996, UK) to *This Is England* (Shane Meadows, 2006, UK).
6   From *Being a Fine Artist* to *Shame* (Steve McQueen, UK, 2012).
7   See *The Guardian*, http://www.guardian.co.uk/film/2012/feb/01/uk-box-office-1bn-harry-potter.
8   Scotland has Scottish Screen as its main film policy and funding agency.
9   See the UK Government, Web Portal, http://www.culture.gov.uk/news/media_releases/8779.aspx.
10 *My Childhood* (Bill Douglas, 1972, United Kingdom), *My Ain Folk* (Bill Douglas, 1973, UK), and *My Way Home* (Bill Douglas, 1978, UK) occupy a prominent place in the history of British independent film.
11 *Distant Voices, Still Lives* (Terence Davies, 1988, UK) and *The Long Day Closes* (Terence Davies, 1992, UK) are some of his most evocative works.
12 *The Gold Diggers* (Sally Potter, 1983, UK) and *The Tango Lesson* (Sally Potter, 1997, UK) illustrate her long-time attachment to dance.
13 *Jubilee* (Derek Jarman, 1978, UK) and *Caravaggio* (Derek Jarman, 1986, UK).
14 *The Cook, the Thief, His Wife, and Her Lover* (Peter Greenaway, 1989, UK) and *Prospero's Books* (Peter Greenaway, 1991, UK).
15 *Gallivant* (Andrew Kötting, 1996, UK) and *This Filthy Earth* (Andrew Kötting, 2001, UK).
16 *Young Soul Rebels* (Isaac Julien, 1991, UK) and *Ten Thousand Waves* (Isaac Julien, 2010, UK).
17 *High Hopes* (Mike Leigh, 1988, UK) and *Secrets and Lies* (Mike Leigh, 1996, UK).
18 *A Sketchbook for the Library Van* (Gideon Koppel, 2005, UK) and *Sleep Furiously* (Gideon Koppel, 2008, UK).
19 T.S. Eliot, *Burnt Norton in Four Quartets* (London: Faber and Faber, 1959). Terence Davies once told me that he never leaves home without this collection of Eliot's poems.

20 Some may argue, however, that its original philosophy has been somewhat eroded over recent years by the influx of studio product into the festival.

21 A fund-raising technique in which the filmmaker engages directly with his or her audience through a website interface and invites micro-investment in the project in exchange for privileged access to, and engagement with, the filmmaking process. There is usually no financial gain on the part of the investor; it is effectively a donation.

22 Approximately C$868,699 or US$818,450 in 2012.

23 Approximately C$17,374 or US$16,389.

24 Approximately C$173,708 or US $163,890.

25 In other words, where the main production company and key talent are based within the region.

26 Examples include *Revengers Tragedy* (Alex Cox, 2003) and *Sea of Madness* (Erik Knudsen, 2005).

27 In other words, films whose main production company, leading talent, and, in many cases, the vast majority of the production crew emanate from outside the region; thereby they primarily use location and periphery services, usually in order to "unlock" funding.

28 See Independent Publishers Association, http://www.ipg.uk.com/home.

29 See Association of Independent Music, http://www.musicindie.com/home.

30 See Knudsen (2010).

31 Or *main street* in the United States.

32 For further reflection on this see Stanley Burnshaw (1991) and Arthur Koestler (1989).

33 This in itself creates the paradox of how well institutions and their structures sit with the notion of independence.

Chapter Five

From Aussiewood Movies to Guerrilla Filmmaking: Independent Filmmaking and Contemporary Australian Cinema

MARK DAVID RYAN

The prominence of Australian cinema as a distinct and recognizable national cinematic style in the international marketplace has waned to some extent in recent years in comparison to the 1990s (albeit with a few individual exceptions). In terms of productivity and the commercial success of local titles, Australian cinema has always been characterized by periods of boom and bust. The 1990s in particular was a vibrant period in Australian cinema history, one that forged a global reputation for Australian film as a distinct and creative style of independent filmmaking. Titles such as *The Piano* (1993), *Shine* (1996), *Muriel's Wedding* (1994), *The Adventures of Priscilla, Queen of the Desert* (1994), *Strictly Ballroom* (1992), and *Babe* (1995) achieved both critical acclaim and worldwide commercial success and, for many, became synonymous with a quirky Australian screen sensibility. Throughout the 2000s and so far during the second decade of the twenty-first century Australian cinema has remained a seedbed for independent breakout titles. Yet the structure of Australian feature filmmaking, and the government subvention models that support them, have undergone significant change in recent years.

Since the 1990s – and even in the decade prior in critical discussion – there has been acknowledgment within Australian film studies that the term *national cinema* is becoming more and more problematic as a way to describe Australian film (Sabine 1995; Goldsmith 2007). Such debate has emerged in recognition of the declining influence of the national identity agenda (strongly advocated by government screen agencies in the 1970s and 1980s) and the increasing internationalization of the industry. By 2012 it could be argued that Australian cinema was a post-national cinema experiencing somewhat of an identity crisis – learning to move beyond a nationally contained and defined cinema but unable to fully embrace the possibilities of transnational cinema. Furthermore, since the late 2000s, there has been a marked shift in government policy rationales away from the subsidy of cultural production without commercial imperatives towards developing larger and more commercially successful production. At the core of this strategy has been the pursuit of internationalization in an attempt to foster local production. The government's push for a more commercial filmmaking culture, however, has arguably led to the dilution of a recognizably Australian style or brand of filmmaking (trading upon distinctly Australian settings, character types, themes, and vernacular) that has defined Aussie filmmaking since the 1970s and, in some cases, has resulted in an increasingly blurred line between Hollywood and local production. In contrast to the aforementioned quirky films typical in the 1990s – even though there have been smaller independent films such as *Red Dog* (2011) and *The Sapphires* (2012) that were successful domestically – a large number of the most prominent and internationally successful Australian movies in recent years have been high-end, culturally nonspecific titles such as *The Great Gatsby* (2013), *Knowing* (2009), *Legend of the Guardians: The Owls of Ga'Hoole* (2010), *Happy Feet* (2006), and *Happy Feet Two 3D* (2011).

As such, independent filmmaking within the context of Australian cinema is a multifaceted subject. In comparison to the United States, where production can be characterized as bifurcated between major studio production and so-called indie or independent production without the backing of the majors,[1] since the 1970s and until recently the vast majority of Australian feature film production has been independent. Like most so-called national cinemas, most Australian movies are supported by both direct and indirect public subvention administered by state- and federal-government funding bodies (Canadian movies, as discussed by Doris Baltruschat in this volume, are another example), and it could be argued that filmmakers are, to a certain degree, "dependent" on official mandates. As this chapter demonstrates, national production slates are subjected to budget restraints and cutbacks, official cultural policies (for example, pursuing international co-productions and local content quotas), and shifts in policy directions, among others. Therefore, within the context of Australian cinema, feature film production that is operating outside the public funding system could be understood as independent. However, as is the case for most English-language national cinemas, independence has long been defined in terms of autonomy from Hollywood, and – as alluded to above – as Australia becomes more dependent upon international inputs into production, higher-budget movies are becoming less independent from Hollywood. As such, this chapter argues that independence in Australian cinema can be viewed as having two poles: independence from direct government funding and independence from Hollywood studios.

With a specific focus on industry and policy contexts, this chapter explores key issues that constitute independence for Australian cinema. It begins with an analysis of the defining features of independence in North American and Australian cinema. The following discussion examines independent filmmaking in the 1990s and some of the market and policy forces that have shaped the Australian film industry's direction since the mid- to late 2000s. The chapter's focus then turns towards the broad production characteristics of four primary domains of contemporary independent filmmaking in Australia: "Aussiewood" production; government-backed, low- to mid-budget production; co-productions; and guerrilla filmmaking.

Independence and Australian film is a complex and evolving issue, and as such this chapter is by no means an exhaustive account of the subject. In terms of definitions, in Australia, the term *indie* is rarely used by industry, nor is it commonly used in policy discourse or screen studies to describe local filmmaking; it is widely regarded as a term associated with North American independent filmmaking. The term *independent* is generally used to refer to local feature film production. Another key point of clarification concerns production budgets. As a guide, informed where possible by data from Screen Australia and the Screen Producers Association of Australia (SPAA), low-budget filmmaking typically accounts for movies budgeted at AU$0.5 million to AU$7 million (Screen Australia 2013a, 8), mid-range films at AU$8 million to AU$30 million (SPAA 2012, 5), while big-budget Aussiewood movies can cost between AU$50 million and AU$150 million. Guerrilla films generally have budgets of less than AU$500,000 and often less than AU$150,000. (The gap between mid- and high-budget films reflects the fact that, at this point in time, production rarely occurs within this range.)

Independence and Australian Cinema

In *American Independent Cinema*, Geoff King (2005, 2–3) identifies three key characteristics that shape the independence of U.S. indie filmmaking: "(1) industrial location, (2) the kinds of formal/aesthetic strategies they adopt, and (3) their relationship to the broader social, cultural, political or ideological landscape." To summarize, independent filmmaking requires some degree of geographical distance from the Hollywood studio system "for substantial formal or socio-political departure from the dominant norms" (ibid, 2). Moreover, independent filmmaking can attempt to oppose the aesthetic style of mainstream cinema through experimentation, often in the form of "artistic" or "avant-garde" approaches to production. Indie film can also address politically and socially difficult issues in an attempt to challenge dominant social or cultural discourses. In the United States some indie films "operate at a distance from Hollywood in all three respects. Others exist in a closer, sometimes symbiotic relationship with ... Hollywood" (King 2009, 2).

Until the mid-2000s the independence of most Australian feature filmmaking – with the exception of the occasional Hollywood-backed local title – was characterized by its distinction from Hollywood in all three regards. However, as touched upon previously, Australian cinema's independence from Hollywood is to an extent eroding. Furthermore, as suggested above, "independence" can also be shaped by government subsidies and official policy mandates within national borders.

Australian cinema is a small English-language industry geographically isolated from the Western world. Since the 1970s, it has largely been developed and sustained by cultural policies and public subsidy to foster Australian stories and the "representation and preservation of Australian culture, character, and identity" (Maher 1999, 13). As Reid (1999, 11) argued in the late 1990s, "the cultural and economic rationale for government subsidy of a local film industry" has been "about assisting talented Australians to bring the stories they most passionately want to tell to the big screen, not the stories overseas studio executives want them to tell."

Until quite recently an issue critical to Australian cinema's attempt to achieve independence from Hollywood filmmaking has been the production of "peculiarly Australian genres" (Routt 1999) or the "Australianisation" of international genres (Rayner 2000). Between the 1970s and 2000 local genres included the "AFC genre," the "male ensemble film," and "new glamour," while Australianised genres encapsulated "Australian gothic" and "ocker comedy" (Rayner 2000; Dermody and Jacka 1988). However, the production of popular genre movies such as action-adventure, science-fiction, fantasy, and horror – long associated by some in the Australian film industry and government film agencies with Hollywood filmmaking – has occupied a tenuous position within Australian cinema (Ryan 2009). The Australian film industry's long-standing refusal to "recognise ... generic status," which has been strongly advocated by government policy at various times since the 1970s, has been an attempt to differentiate "itself from Hollywood, which has always been interested in refining and developing specific film genres" (Mayer 1999, 178). Nevertheless, Australian cinema has always produced an undercurrent of generic-based film popularly referred to as "Ozploitation" (Martin 2010). Classic titles include *Razorback* (1984), *Turkey Shoot* (1982), and *The Chain Reaction* (1980); more contemporary titles consist of *Wolf Creek* (2005), *Daybreakers* (2009), and *Red Hill* (2010).

Notwithstanding the national policy agenda that has shaped aesthetics and production strategies, there are parallels between North American indie filmmaking and the lion's share of independent Australian feature film production. Australian movies, like their North American indie counterparts (especially Canada's), compete for audiences on cinema screens dominated by Hollywood movies (Australian titles captured between 2 and 5 per cent of the local box office between 2005 and 2010; see Screen Australia [2012a] and Screen Australia [2009]). The average low-budget Australian feature film is released with limited to no marketing budget alongside the Hollywood movies, which are led by A-list stars, are supported by multimillion-dollar marketing campaigns, and have expensive production values.

Like North American indie filmmaking, there is also overlap between domestic independent filmmaking and the Hollywood majors. Even though many films are produced without initial backing from Hollywood, various titles secure distribution deals with the majors or their subsidiaries as negative pickups upon completion (Tzioumakis's chapter herein examines this issue from the perspective of distribution and the internationalization of North American independent cinema). Furthermore, many of Australia's most successful filmmakers, from Peter Weir and Baz Luhrmann to Alex Proyas, go on to develop successful careers directing Hollywood titles.

The following section explores trends in Australian independent filmmaking during the 1990s, structural changes in the global film industry, and the impact on local release strategies.

On the Risky Fringes: Australian Cinema in the Late 1990s and Early to Mid-2000s

At the end of the 1990s, according to Mary Anne Reid (1999, 11), Australian cinema was comfortably "perched, in commercial and creative terms, on the risky fringe surrounding mainstream global film production [a reference principally to Hollywood filmmaking]." While Reid acknowledges that this was a "tenuous position," it was also potentially "a viable one, given that the global environment is signalling to Australia and other minority players that diversity, or difference, has an inherent economic value which can work as a natural armour against the dominant culture." Throughout the decade Australian cinema was focused, by and large, on generating value through the "prestige economy" (such as festival awards, prominent festival screenings, and critical prestige) and cultural returns (such as the development of cultural capital and cultural identity, and the promotion of a nation's image overseas). As I argued in 2009, "domestic cinema release and national and international critical acclaim [have] long been regarded as a measure of a film's success and prestige within Australian cinema" (Ryan 2009, 48). Profits, international sales, and international box-office returns have been secondary concerns.

Throughout the 1990s Australian cinema developed a global reputation as a unique style of independent cinema, often characterized by critics as being quirky and difficult to fit into generic categories. In particular, the decade was defined by several influential independent titles. Two key movies include the drama *Shine* (1996), starring Geoffrey Rush, about the life of the eccentric pianist David Helfgott; and the hauntingly beautiful period drama, *The Piano* (1993), directed by Jane Campion about a mute woman who is sent to New Zealand in the 1850s with her daughter and her piano in an arranged marriage. Other outstanding films include the quirky comedy *Muriel's Wedding* (1994) directed by P.J. Hogan, which celebrates the socially awkward Muriel Heslop and her pursuit of love and happiness; and the visually striking *The Adventures of Priscilla, Queen of the Desert* (1994), which follows the journey of three drag queens across the harsh Australian outback.

The 1990s saw an explosion in the diversity of Australian cinema. Much has been written about the emergence of post–New Wave cinema in the 1990s and the break with the aesthetic tendencies popularized by the government-sanctioned Australian Film Commission (AFC) genre[2] in the 1970s and 1980s (see Craven 2001 and Martin 2010), which actively sought to project a "middlebrow cultural worthiness to the world" (Dermody and Jacka 1988, 32). The AFC genre is exemplified by films such as *Picnic at Hanging Rock* (1975), *Breaker Morant* (1980), and *Sunday Too Far Away* (1975). In particular, 1990s cinema challenged the AFC genre's portrayal of a rural-centric view of the Australian way of life in which women's stories, issues regarding contemporary domestic life, and a more critical picture of Australian history were at times neglected (McFarlane 1988; Craven 2001). *The Adventures of Priscilla, Queen of the Desert* and *Strictly Ballroom*, among other titles, challenged stereotypical representations of masculinity and the idea of the Australian landscape or outback as being a man's country. *Shine* and *Proof* (1991) presented a softer, more complex side of Australian masculinity. An increasing number of films were set in urban and suburban settings, rather than in the iconic outback settings that were common in the 1970s and 1980s. In parallel, there was a burgeoning of narratives, which explored gender relations, such as *The Sum of Us* (1994) and *Love Serenade* (1995) (Craven 2001), and the perspectives of women, through iconic films such as *Muriel's Wedding* and *The Piano*.

However, following the dawn of the twenty-first century, Australian cinema's position on the risky fringes of mainstream cinema became untenable. There are arguably numerous reasons for this (only some of which can be examined here owing to scope limitations). By the end of the 1990s, and becoming more widespread by the mid-2000s, the global market for independent filmmaking experienced a sharp contraction. At the heart of the issue were fundamental structural changes in the global market for the theatrical release of feature films and a decline in pre-sales. Stacey Parks (2007, 2) summarizes:

> By the late nineties, distribution deals became harder and harder to come by. Previously, the pre-sale market had guaranteed distribution in the territory of the pre-sale. Now that market dried up, filmmakers could no longer rely on foreign sales to finance their budgets. Once upon a time, two or three foreign sales could finance an entire independent-film budget, and the rest was profit. By the late nineties and early 2000, that was no longer the case at all. At this point in distribution history, the market turned upside down. By the years 2001 and 2002, independent films were a commodity. They were sold by the pound to foreign buyers, for a thousand bucks here and there. Now filmmakers had to rely on getting a U.S. distribution deal to recoup their budget.

In addition to the contraction of pre-sales, upon which the Australian film industry and public finance structures were heavily dependent (Zion 2005), there was a narrowing in the duration of release windows for theatrical exhibition, with greater emphasis being placed on movies earning box-office revenue in an opening weekend (Iordanova 2012). For Australian films, with limited marketing budgets, the mounting pressure for success in an opening week minimized the effectiveness of the "grey dollar" – a low-budget marketing approach that relies heavily upon generating audience awareness through reviews and word-of-mouth promotion over a long release period. Similarly, the increasing dominance of mainstream cinema markets by a smaller number of tent-pole Hollywood productions (Elberse and Oberholzer-Gee 2008) meant that small local films without A-list stars, multimillion-dollar marketing campaigns, and slick production values struggled to secure theatrical release. In addition to structural changes in the international marketplace, tensions arose from domestic challenges.

The Contemporary Policy and Genre Movie Turn

By the mid-2000s the Australian feature film industry had reached a crisis point. In 2004 the local share of the box office dropped to a dismal 1.3 per cent, its lowest level in recorded history. This was followed by 2.8 per cent in 2005, a far cry from the 7.9 per cent captured in 2000 (Screen Australia 2012d). Following the release of these figures, the Australian film industry and government funding agencies were heavily criticized in the media. They were accused of producing dark, depressing, and self-indulgent movies with little regard for the audience (Nowra 2009; Bodey 2009; and Schembri 2008, among many others). Examples were *Candy* (2006), a tragic love story about two heroin addicts; *Somersault* (2004), an art-house cinema film revolving around a young woman who is confused by the difference between sex and love; and *Little Fish* (2005), a drama about a reformed heroin junky and her struggle to start her own business.

For Verhoeven (2006), at the core of the issue was a divide between the national policy agenda and audience consumption practices. While the funding of Australian movies had been largely driven, since the 1970s, by policies attempting to foster a sense of national identity and the telling of authentic local stories with little concern for entertainment value and commercial returns, Australian audiences "are inclined to watch films in a way that has almost no relationship to the national agenda or the general quest for a national cultural identity in the cinema" (158).

In 2007, as part of the 2007–8 federal budget, the then Howard government announced a suite of new incentives to develop a more commercially sustainable screen industry (Brandis 2007). The centrepiece for the local production sector was the "Producer Offset," which provided Australian producers with a 40 per cent rebate on eligible film expenditure (assessed on whether a film met the criteria defining Australian content, an issue discussed in more depth below). The reforms also included the creation of the superagency Screen Australia in 2008 – an amalgamation of the Australian Film Commission,[3] Film Finance Corporation,[4] and Film Australia.[5] Collectively these changes constituted the most significant overhaul of public finance structures for the screen industry in almost three decades. Following the announcement the Minister for the Arts, the Honourable Peter Garrett, MP (under the newly elected Rudd government), and the chief executive of Screen Australia, Ruth Harley, began championing a new era for Australian screen industries. Harley (2009, 6), in particular, outlined a future in which "better business and bigger audiences have taken centre stage." The transition in policy rationales marked a shift from cultural to industry policy and, by implication, a greater emphasis on growth and commercial returns.

As a direct consequence, in comparison to the 1990s there has been marked growth in the production of genre movies and large-scale Australian movies intended for wide release. Between 1994 and 2000, according to Screen Australia statistics, an astounding 76 per cent of Australian feature films were classified as either drama (40 per cent) or comedy (36 per cent); thrillers accounted for 11 per cent, action-adventure 5 per cent, and horror and science fiction a combined 3 per cent (Screen Australia 2013d). In other words, over three-quarters of all Australian feature films released over a six-year period were either drama or comedy, albeit the titles classified as "drama" may have arguably included some "art-house cinema" or "quirky Australian" films that did not fit into other generic categories. In stark contrast, following the implementation of the Producer Offset, between July 2010 and June 2012 drama and comedy accounted for 55 per cent of national production, thrillers comprised 20 per cent, action-adventure 8 per cent, horror 8 per cent, and science fiction 6 per cent (Screen Australia 2013d). The 2010 feature film slate in particular produced a diverse range of genre movies, including the musical *Bran Nue Dae* (2009); comedies *I Love You*

Too (2010) and *The Kings of Mykonos: Wog Boy 2* (2010); horror movies *Daybreakers* and *The Loved Ones* (2009); the action-adventure film *Tomorrow When the War Began* (2010); the war movie *Beneath Hill 60* (2010); the crime drama *Animal Kingdom* (2010); and the western *Red Hill*. Since 2006 – although the 1990s produced a handful of high-budget local films with some Hollywood backing – there has been a surge in high-end "local" blockbusters released worldwide. Titles include *Happy Feet*, *Australia* (2008), *Knowing*, *Legend of the Guardians: The Owls of Ga'Hoole*, *Killer Elite* (2011), *Happy Feet Two 3D*, and *The Great Gatsby*. (A similar trend can be observed in contemporary Greek filmmaking; see Lydia Papadimitriou's chapter in this volume.) As this suggests, the Australian film industry's pursuit of aesthetic and generic difference from Hollywood has become less important in the current phase of industry development than at some points in previous decades since the 1970s.

Independent Australian Cinema and the Sectors of Independence

To reiterate, this chapter contends that there are two key defining characteristics of independence in Australian filmmaking: independence from public subvention and from Hollywood. Contemporary independent filmmaking can be characterized by four key domains of filmmaking with varying degrees of independence and interdependence: Aussiewood production; government-backed, low- to mid-budget production; co-productions; and guerrilla filmmaking.

Aussiewood Production

Aussiewood is a term that has been used interchangeably in the national media in recent years to refer to the country's elite acting and film production talent (including directors and cinematographers) working in Hollywood and, although less commonly, to signify Australian studio facilities servicing Hollywood "runaway" films. In this essay I use the term *Aussiewood* to denote high-end Australian blockbusters or mini-blockbusters released into cinema markets worldwide with strong creative and financial input from Hollywood majors. There is a distinction to make between Aussiewood movies, like *Happy Feet* and *Legend of the Guardians*, and Hollywood runaway movies, such as *The Matrix* (1999), *X-Men Origins: Wolverine* (2009), and *Inspector Gadget* (1999). The latter are produced in Australia and draw upon local technical crew, sometimes heads of department and supporting cast, but – as Miller et al. (2005)

observe in relation to the function of global Hollywood – Hollywood studios control the intellectual property, finance, and creative input. Such films are also recognized by government screen agencies as *foreign films*, and although runaway movies qualify for tax breaks developed to lure foreign production to Australian shores, they do not qualify for *local* production subsidies.

As the term *runaway* suggests, despite the fact that Australian production companies generally have a greater level of control over and creative input into Aussiewood productions than runaway films, there is perhaps a fine line of distinction between what could be regarded as home-grown Australian content and Hollywood movies looking to gain access to local production incentives. Films such as *Knowing* and *Legend of the Guardians* received a significant amount of government investment under the 40 per cent Producer Offset rebate (as much as AU$20 million in the case of *Knowing* [Bodey 2010]). As the Producer Offset is designed to lever non-government market investment, finance secured through this incentive is distinguished from "direct" government subsidy (Screen Australia 2012a, 7). Nevertheless, Aussiewood movies could be seen as providing Hollywood studios with access to the lucrative production incentives that are only available to local film production, and therefore offering the majors far greater financial benefit (40 per cent) than they would have otherwise attained from "foreign production" incentives such as the Location Offset (a 16.5 per cent refundable tax offset on eligible production expenditure) (Screen Australia 2013c).

Aussiewood films can also be distinguished from 1980s Australian blockbusters such as *Crocodile Dundee* (1986), *Crocodile Dundee 2* (1988), *Mad Max 2* (1981), and *The Man from Snowy River* (1982), which were largely independent titles and drew primarily upon private rather than public finance. At the heart of the issue is the question of what constitutes Australian content. In the 1970s and 1980s an Australian feature film was defined as a movie produced in Australia, by an Australian crew, with a local cast, drawing upon domestic finance, and, importantly, achieving an Australian look and feel (a film that is distinctly Australian onscreen). The latter often translates into narratives revolving around authentic representations of cultural identity and featuring Australia's unique flora and fauna. Australian blockbusters in the 1980s met all of these criteria (with the exceptions of cast and authentic cultural representations, but all were recognizably Australian stories). However, in a global era of film production, Aussiewood movies have a mix of financial and creative input (as do many contemporary Australian films).

To qualify for the Producer Offset, projects must satisfy what is known as Screen Australia's Significant Australian Content (SAC) test. The test considers the following criteria: subject matter of the film; production location; "the nationalities and residences of the persons who take part in the making of the film (including producers, directors, writers, actors, composers, editors, etc.)"; production expenditure occurring in Australia; and "any other matters" deemed relevant (AusFilm 2012).

In undertaking a joint venture, Hollywood studios and Australian production companies looking to secure finance through the Producer Offset attempt to develop a project that has enough Australian creative input to qualify as a local production. A common formula adopted by producers is an Australian director (though not always), a combination of Australian and international screenwriters, and a cast comprising both A-list Australian (such as Nicole Kidman and Hugh Jackman) and Hollywood actors. The films generally have a mixed crew, though usually dominated by local technicians, and are largely filmed and post-produced in Australia. In practice, "subject matter" rarely determines which films qualify for the offset. In some cases, the definition of Australian content can be reduced to the location of production, expenditure occurring in Australia, an Australian film crew, and *some* "above-the-line" creative input. For example, *Legend of the Guardians: The Owls of Ga'Hoole* (2010) was directed by American Zack Snyder, was based on a series of books by American author Kathryn Lasky, and was written by American screenwriters John Orloff and Emil Stern. The film was, however, a co-venture between Warner Bros. and Australia's leading animation studio, Animal Logic, and had a cast dominated by Australian actors.

In the vein of Hollywood film, Aussiewood movies have large budgets of between AU$50 million and AU$150 million, are supported by substantial marketing campaigns, and are released theatrically around the world. Most Aussiewood titles are a combination of finance deals and co-ventures and generally have greater production scale and Hollywood input than do official co-productions (discussed below). Aussiewood movies have sophisticated visual styles. In terms of storytelling, their narrative structure and textual content can vary from quirky and original to typical Hollywood formulas and conventions. George Miller's *Happy Feet*, for example, is "a familiar story about [an] outsider forced to struggle against the usual odds ... to discover his inner penguin" (Dargis 2006), before it "turns into an environmental cautionary tale of serious bleakness, capped off with a spectacular Busby Berkley song and dance number" (Arendt 2006). As this suggests, *Happy Feet* avoids a three-act structure, contains darker themes than does a standard animated children's feature, has very little plot, and revolves around a mix of quirky anthropomorphic characters and extravagant dance sequences. In the words of the British Broadcasting Corporation's Paul Arendt (2006), "[*Happy Feet*] is one of the oddest computer animated tales ever made ... At first glance, this looks like your regulation kiddie fare ... What you actually get is ... environmental polemic, all scored to cheesy pop hits."

Baz Luhrmann's *Australia* (2008) is another example. An attempt to create an Australian version of *Gone with the Wind* (1939), the film has more in common with a classical Hollywood epic driven by melodrama and a character-based plot, while showcasing numerous Australian clichés and stereotypes, than it does with a contemporary blockbuster driven by an action-based or comedy-dominant plot and "culture-neutral subjects and contents" to appeal to the broadest possible audience (De Propris and Hypponen 2008, 275). Alex Proyas's *Knowing*, a conventional science-fiction-based disaster movie, and Zack Snyder's *Legend of the Guardians*, an epic adventure movie, however, have narrative forms typical of Hollywood films.

With the exception of *Australia* – which traded upon a distinctively Australian identity in the marketplace (containing Australian character types, vernacular, and unique cultural themes) – such films are generally consumed around the world as Hollywood fare. Nevertheless, some filmmakers have paid homage to their movie's Australian origins in the film text. An example is a scene featuring the late Steve Irwin's voice as that of an elephant seal in *Happy Feet*, which includes a barrage of "G-day, mates" and Australian vernacular (though there are few other distinctly Australian story elements). In the case of *Legend of the Guardians*, though the story unfolds in a fantasy world of warring owls, most of the characters have Australian accents, and the flora and fauna are subtly Australian: from Tasmanian Devils lurking upon forest floors to eucalyptus bush settings reminiscent of the "Australiana" animated television series *The Adventures of Blinky Bill* (1993).

Government-Backed, Low- to Mid-Budget Independent Cinema

Low-budget feature films are the staple of Australian filmmaking. Most titles in this category are independent from Hollywood (although breakout titles sometimes receive release via a major) but are highly dependent upon direct public investment from government agencies. Most low-budget feature films have budgets of between AU$0.5 million and AU$7 million and are financed by a combination of direct and indirect public funding, and private and international sources of finance (pre-sales in particular). Such films draw upon a combination of Australian and marquee international actors (in similar vein to U.S. indie films). *The Hunter* (2011), for example, starred both Sam Neill and Willem Dafoe. Although such films are increasingly released on various platforms – including straight to video and some via pay-per-download services – the lion's share receive a limited domestic and international theatrical release.

The output from this domain has been extremely diverse over the last five to ten years. Unsurprisingly, then, the narrative forms of low-budget titles have also been wide ranging: from art-house cinema attempting to subvert Hollywood modes of storytelling, to local generic traditions (such as the "ocker" comedy), to more formulaic genre movies (for example, horror and crime). While there has been growth in the latter in recent years, art-house cinema titles comprise a significant proportion of the titles.

In terms of broad aesthetic trends, these independent films often trade upon social realism owing to lower budgets (*Animal Kingdom* is one of many examples) and usually have lower production values than do mid- to higher-budget films (though again there are exceptions). A stream of titles, which can be labelled as distinctively Australian storytelling, is still identifiable but is less dominant than it was in the 1970s, 1980s, and 1990s. A standout title is the ocker comedy *Kenny* (2006), a film that celebrates the Australian vernacular and is about a simple larrikin (a person who rarely takes anything seriously, likes a joke, and has little respect for authority figures) working as a plumber in the toilet industry. Moreover, Indigenous Australian stories have been a major feature of production trends in recent years; for example, *Samson and Delilah* (2009), about love between two Indigenous Australian youths in a remote outback community; and the musical *Bran Nue Dae*, following the homeward journey of an Indigenous schoolboy who flees a religious mission.

Although there has been a spate of mid-budget movies in recent years, the production of such films has been relatively rare over the last decade. While the Producer Offset has been successful in fostering high-budget Aussiewood movies, the production of mid-budget movies – which are less likely to attract the attention of Hollywood studios – has been less prolific under the scheme. As the Screen Producers Association of Australia (SPAA), the peak professional organization for national screen producers, has argued, it is the films of "the 'medium budget' range of AU$7 million–AU$30 million, which are proving the most problematic to finance with a combination of Producer Offset and Screen Australia funding [direct public funding]" (SPAA 2012, 5). In 2011 and 2012 both SPAA and Screen Australia lobbied the federal government for a commercial film fund and a AU$30 million film fund respectively to bankroll mid-budget films and address this deficit; both proposals were rejected.

As the budgets for these movies are generally too high for direct public investment alone, mid-budget independent films often have higher levels of international finance and market investment than those of low-budget titles. Nevertheless, they still rely to a greater or lesser extent upon *some* public investment. For example, close to AU$20 million of *Daybreakers'* budget was bankrolled by the international distributor Lionsgate Films, while the remaining AU$5 million came from direct public investment (Ryan 2008, 150). Conversely, the AU$25 million film *Tomorrow When the War Began*, financed largely by the Australian entertainment company Omnilab Media, received AU$3.5 million from Screen Australia (Screen Australia 2010, 90).

Since the late 2000s some of the industry's more commercially successful breakout titles in theatrical markets – without backing from Hollywood – have been mid-budget titles. The AU$25 million futurist vampire movie *Daybreakers* went on to earn over US$50 million at the global box office and was ranked among the top fifty highest-grossing worldwide independent films of 2010 (Dallas 2011). *Sanctum* (2011), the AU$30 million cave-diving action-adventure movie backed by *Avatar's* (2009) James Cameron, went on to earn over US$110 million internationally.

Mid-budget films tend to embrace popular genres, have higher production values than do low-budget titles, receive theatrical release, and often attempt to emulate Hollywood's visual styles.

Co-productions

The Australian Official Co-production Program was first established in 1986 and is currently known as the International Co-production Program. A co-production in its simplest form is a movie produced by filmmakers from two or more countries, having split creative control, creative and technical input, and resources. Producers who intend to undertake a co-production and, as a consequence, secure public investment for the Australian proportion of their budget must officially qualify for, and comply with, Screen Australia's International Co-production Program Guidelines (Screen Australia 2013b).

As Hammett-Jamart (2005, 123) argues, even though the guidelines have been altered on numerous occasions (for both political and practical reasons), "the core procedure of assessing Australian contribution through a three-tiered barometer of 'participation levels' has remained consistent": namely, (1) "Australian financial investment as a proportion of the budget"; (2) "the percentage of Australian 'down-the-line' crew must likewise equal the percentage of Australian investment in the production"; and (3) "there is a minimum requirement level of Australian involvement in 'key creative' roles as defined by a points system." As this suggests, formal co-productions are highly regulated and controlled by official checks and balances.

Examples of official co-productions include Jane Campion's *Bright Star* (2009, United Kingdom/Australia/France), *Death Defying Acts* (2007, United Kingdom/Australia), and *The Children of the Silk Road* (2008, Australia/China/Germany). However, as a result of the restrictions of the aforementioned points system (Hammett-Jamart 2005), some local producers opt for unofficial co-productions that operate outside the official program. The most well-known example is *The King's Speech* (2010), an Academy Award–winning movie produced by See-Saw Films based in Sydney and London, and headed by Australian producer Emile Sherman and UK producer Iain Canning. As one observer has explained, "the formula for being Australian [to qualify as a co-production] is a complicated mix of local financing, production and/or post-production and talent. It is a technical distinction that exists – and rightly so – for the purposes of film funding analysis ... Sadly for those keeping score, *The King's Speech* is merely a Clayton's Australian Film – the Australian film you have when you're not having an Australian film. For despite the film's Aussie characters, Australian producer, executive producer and the dual nationality that both its production company and director maintain, it does not fulfil the technical requirements to make it an official co-production" (Hardie 2011).

A key issue was that *The King's Speech* appeared to be a natural co-production, and it would have accrued various benefits for the Australian film industry if the film had been classified as an official co-production (box-office returns, prestige, follow-on effect for industry, and so on). The movie's story revolved around the speech impediment of Prince Albert – a member of the British royal family – and his treatment by the unorthodox Australian specialist Lionel Logue. The film was directed by Tom Hooper, a dual Australian-UK citizen. Emile Sherman and See-Saw Films have Australian roots, and Australian actors Geoffrey Rush and Guy Pearce played the leading roles (Robinson 2011, 25). Therefore, the movie had strong Australian creative input, but it is officially recognized as a UK film and an un-official Australian co-production. As such, an unofficial co-production can result in independence from government screen agencies and public finance. However, within the context of Australian cinema, this is not always viewed as a positive outcome for the industry (especially by government screen agencies), although in this case the film itself – earning over US$400 million at the box office worldwide – was an outstanding success. Therefore, this raises the question of whether the program's rules and guidelines may in some cases dissuade formal co-productions and act as an impediment to production activity occurring within the Australian production system.

Working mostly with mid-range budgets, co-productions generally have higher production values and more sophisticated visual styles than those of low-budget, government-backed films. Co-productions generally receive both domestic and international theatrical release. The stories of co-productions are sometimes international rather than local (in terms of settings, characters, and so on) and do not always have a distinctively Australian voice or style (though some, like the UK-Australian film *The Proposition* [2005], do). An example is *Green Card* (1990), an official co-production between Australia, France, and the United States, directed by Australian Peter Weir, and starring American actress Andie MacDowell and French actor Gérard Depardieu. Set in New York, the film tells the story of the French national George Faure and the New Yorker Bronte Parrish who enter a marriage of convenience; George needs a work permit, and Bronte wants the ideal flat, which is available for married couples only. There is little, if anything, onscreen to suggest to an audience that this is an Australian film.

Guerrilla Filmmaking

Local guerrilla filmmaking is arguably the most independent segment of contemporary Australian cinema. Like guerrilla filmmaking anywhere in the world, guerrilla production in Australia is an ultra-low-budget domain of filmmaking. Guerrilla filmmaking rarely receives direct public funding (though there are exceptions) or the backing of Hollywood majors. At the time of writing, there were few government incentives targeting such production.

The vast majority of guerrilla filmmaking draws upon small, privately financed budgets of typically less than AU$150,000. This film culture "is characterised by filmmakers who self-finance movies, shooting guerrilla style and working with crews drawn from a combination of film-school dropouts, enthusiastic amateurs and professionals honing their trade between gigs" (Sargeant 2011, 90). Such films are almost always shot on digital video and edited on home-editing equipment. While most titles are negative pick-up deals and released straight to video or through online mail-order services, there are exceptions that secure theatrical release. The mockumentary *The Magician* (2005), following the story of a Melbourne hit man, was written, directed, and produced by Scott Ryan and filmed for just AU$3,000; it secured theatrical release in Australia, the United Kingdom, and the United States. The line between professional and amateur production is often blurred, the quality of individual titles can vary greatly from production to production, and the visual style can range from sophisticated to low grade.

The ground-breaking horror movie *The Tunnel* (2011) is a prime example of guerrilla production. The first feature film to be officially released via the free-download website BitTorrent, the movie was co-written by first-time filmmakers Enzo Tedeschi and Julian Harvey and directed by Carlo Ledesma. *The Tunnel* is a mockumentary about journalists who venture into tunnels beneath Sydney to expose a government cover-up over an abandoned plan to use a subterranean reservoir to solve the city's water crisis. They soon discover that something monstrous lives underground, and their only escape is back through the tunnels.

The Tunnel is one of a growing number of independent Australian films (across the lower- to guerrilla-budget range) harnessing digital distribution and crowdfunding. After the launch of thetunnelmovie.net, 135,000 individual movie frames were made available for purchase for AU$1 each to generate a production budget of AU$135,000. Although crowdfunding raised just AU$36,000, well short of the intended budget, the movie still went into production. On 19 May 2011 the movie was released simultaneously on BitTorrent, Australian pay-TV, and DVD (distributed by Paramount and Transmission). Paramount's decision to release the movie in parallel with its free release online was based on the belief that BitTorrent distribution would only appeal to a specific market segment that was unlikely to purchase the film, and would not undermine the movie's "legitimate" market. By the end of January 2012 the movie had achieved over one million downloads via BitTorrent, the website's fourth-most-downloaded title. By popular demand the movie received a limited theatrical release in Australia and Canada in 2011.

To summarize, in the face of technological changes and globalization Australian cinema is undergoing a process of redefinition and is attempting to reposition itself after the tightening of markets for independent film and structural changes within the industry. Independent filmmaking in Australia is characterized and defined by its relationships with public subsidy – which is administered by federal and state government-funded screen development agencies – international distributors, and Hollywood. At this juncture, Australian cinema is increasingly integrated into a global production sector, and Australian cinema's independence is challenged by Hollywood and other international forces more than ever before.

NOTES

1 Paramount Motion Pictures Group (Paramount Pictures Corporation), Warner Bros. Entertainment (Warner Bros. Pictures), Sony Pictures Entertainment (Columbia Pictures), The Walt Disney Studios (Walt Disney Pictures), NBC/Universal (Universal Pictures), and Fox Entertainment Group (20th Century Fox).
2 The Australian Film Commission was superseded by Screen Australia.
3 The Australian Film Commission (1975–2008) was a federal development agency responsible for financing the professional development of filmmakers and script development for feature films, although it was also responsible for funding actual production between 1975 and 1981.
4 The Film Finance Corporation (1988–2008) was a film bank and the principal financier of Australian film and television during its tenure.
5 Film Australia (1973–2008) was a government-owned company commissioned to create an audio-visual record of Australian life through the production and commissioning of television documentaries and educational programs.

Chapter Six

Independent Filmmaking in the Peruvian Context: Seeking Meaning

GABRIELA MARTÍNEZ

Since the early twentieth century several Peruvians have documented local events and produced fictional films. Indeed, Peru has a long history of filmmaking. However, the country's film development has remained "one of Latin America's most impoverished" (da Gama, 2007). Peruvian filmmaker Luis Figueroa once said, "El cine peruano es cine hecho a mano" (Peruvian cinema is handmade cinema).[1] His comment explains the manner in which filmmakers struggle to produce and distribute their movies. It also speaks to the fact that Peru's filmmaking development has never achieved industrial production levels; compared to some neighbouring countries like Brazil or Argentina, Peru has rarely produced more than ten feature films per year and has never developed a studio system or large film companies with significant annual production.

Figueroa complains, as have many other filmmakers during the course of Peru's film history, about the fact that Peru's film development has no real prospect to grow as an industry, either independent or otherwise. It is indeed surprising that Peru has not managed to develop a film industry or to solidify a buoyant independent cinema environment, despite many talented and aspiring filmmakers and a good number of films produced throughout the twentieth century.

Looking at Ricardo Bedoya's (1997) *Diccionario ilustrado de películas peruanas* (*Dictionary of Peruvian Films*), it is clear that filmmaking in this country has been around for over a hundred years, and filmmakers have produced for local companies, for the state, and also on their own (23). Nevertheless, there is resilience on the part of some filmmakers who have been working for several decades, like Francisco Lombardi and the Grupo Chaski; the newer generations who aspire to contribute to this national cinema, such as Josué Méndez and Claudia Llosa; and those recently self-defined as independent filmmakers, like Fernando Montenegro.

This chapter focuses on four decades: the 1970s, 1980s, 1990s, and 2000s. These forty years are a good example of the overall promises and perils of filmmaking in Peru. I am approaching the subject of independent filmmaking or independent cinema (terms used interchangeably in this chapter) from a historical and political economic perspective. I will also touch upon some aesthetic discussion when necessary, but this will not be the core of the discussion.

What Does It Mean to Be an Independent Filmmaker in the Peruvian Context?

Unlike the United States, or other countries like Mexico, Argentina, and Brazil, where a studio system and large film companies developed early, setting particular genres, specific modes of production, and aesthetic approaches, Peru has never managed to have a dominant film system or well-established large companies. Hence, independent filmmaking as a mode of production in opposition to the mainstream domestic film structure or outside a dominant film trend is basically non-existent. For the most part, filmmaking in Peru has developed organically. Some periods have been more intense than others in terms of the number of productions distributed; however, it has never approached industrial levels, nor has it anchored the development of large numbers of individual (or independent) feature films.

It is important to note also that discussions of independent cinema are new and unusual in Peru, and there is not yet any literature addressing the topic in the context of this country. However, some local film scholars and filmmakers such as Ricardo Bedoya, Joel Calero, and Alberto Durant are beginning to take an interest in this discussion because of the increasing use of new technologies such as digital video and digital film production, as well as a variety of alternative distribution circuits for the works that are produced digitally. Most of these works are being produced with low budgets and, in some cases, in opposition to the meagre number of bigger budget films made for theatrical release and the international circuit of film festivals; such works include *Dioses* (Josué Méndez, 2008) and *La Teta Asustada* (Claudia Llosa, 2009).

Thanks to these low-budget productions, the notion of independent filmmaking is beginning to have a certain currency in Peru's small film circles where digital production is achieving similar technical and visual quality to that of traditional celluloid-based film production. However, because of their digital nature, these films are not necessarily exhibited in traditional film theatres. The final version of the majority of these digital movies is directly cut for DVD distribution. They are exhibited in alternative venues like universities, in museums, or in other small theatres equipped with projectors for digital works.

A first step towards a better understanding of what constitutes independent filmmaking took place in March 2010 when the University of Lima's *Revista de Cine Ventana Indiscreta* (*Film Magazine Rear Window*) organized a *conversatorio* (forum). This forum was important because of the participation of well-known local film scholar Ricardo Bedoya as moderator; film critic and journalist Rodrigo Portales and film critic and filmmaker Joel Calero as panelists; veteran filmmaker Alberto "Chicho" Durant; and young, independent filmmaker Fernando Montenegro. The forum's main discussion focused on the mode of production and budgeting for independent filmmaking; additionally, it focused on modes of distribution (theatrical release versus alternative theatre screenings or venues, web streaming, and street sales of DVDs). For the past forty years or more Peruvian filmmakers have been discussing these two general points – modes of production and distribution; however, the present-day discussions are helping us to elucidate the meaning of what constitutes an independent filmmaker in Peru's contemporary filmmaking scenario.

Filmmaker Alberto "Chicho" Durant (2010b) concurs with the definition of independent filmmaking made by most scholars, explaining that independent films are those produced in opposition to or outside of a dominant paradigm. In the United States this consists of working outside of the Hollywood system and making movies that do not follow Hollywood formulas. In Europe, independent cinema is produced outside of major state sponsorship or mixed private-public media systems (such as BBC's commercial branch Channel Four, Spain's TV Española, Germany's ZDF, and Italy's RAI).

In Peru, independent filmmaking currently consists of producing without the sponsorship of the Consejo Nacional de Cinematografía (CONACINE, National Council for Cinema),[2] which since the mid-1990s has provided two grants annually for film productions. During the 1970s and 1980s independent filmmakers would have produced and distributed outside of the Film Law, which, as will be addressed later in the chapter, was created for the promotion and protection of national cinema.

Being an independent filmmaker in Peru may also involve working outside the financial model of international co-production agreements with major private or state institutions such as TV Española, Channel Four, and lately Ibermedia.

Peruvian filmmakers Durant (2010a) and Montenegro (2010) agree that it is quite difficult to define independent filmmaking in general, and even more challenging in the Peruvian context. During the forum Durant explained that there are various manners in which one could be an independent filmmaker – financially, aesthetically, and with regards to distribution.

However, in Peru it has been and remains quite difficult to be completely independent in all three of these aspects owing to the many challenges facing most filmmakers. During the economic and political crises from the 1970s into the 1990s all Peruvian filmmakers struggled to make their movies. Many borrowed money to produce, others ended up in total bankruptcy and unable to produce a second feature film, and some opted for pre-selling the rights of their films to local or foreign distributors in order to finance their film productions.

The Role of the State

The two main difficulties for the development of Peruvian cinema in general, and independent filmmaking in particular, have always been finances and distribution. Throughout the twentieth century and the first decade of the twenty-first century, film production in Peru has had a very uneven path. Dozens of filmmakers as well as small film companies have appeared and then disappeared from the filmmaking scene. A look at the history of Peru's national cinema would shed light on the conflicting efforts in the development of a local film industry and the distribution and exhibition of foreign films. The preference for distributing foreign movies has been the prime threat to local production for decades, and remains so today.

As film production and distribution require much infrastructure and capital, the Peruvian state, for good or bad, has always played a role in the development of filmmaking, with varying degrees of involvement. During the first half of the twentieth century its role was limited, but, with major social and political changes occurring in the second half of the century, the state took a more active role in promoting filmmaking; towards the end of the century, however, the state became more active in hindering such production. In other words, filmmaking is always in a pendulum-like state controlled by the whims of different governments, some of which understand the importance of investing in culture and some of which do not care about it.

As Barrow (2005, 41–2) suggests, the film technology and film culture in the first half of the twentieth century in Peru, especially in Lima, are seen as an intrinsic part of modernity. Some governments of that time used first film, and later television, to aid the country's modernization plans as well as to consolidate nation building. The goals of modernization significantly merged with the goals of strengthening national identity (Martínez 2008, 1), and film had a role. However, the role of film in this context is understood more as a tool for the advancement of particular agendas and not as a form of expression.

President Augusto Leguia's government (1919–30) supported the production of documentaries commemorating the one-hundredth anniversary in 1921 of Peru's independence from Spain. The goal of these documentaries was to portray a cohesive nation by bringing together images from different parts of the country. Nonetheless, the nation was portrayed from a Lima-centric, oligarchic, and even racist point of view. Rural Peru was rarely represented, and the presence of a great majority of Indigenous peoples was either totally romanticized or simply non-existent. For those in the capital, Indigenous people represented a backward and an ancient way of living that was stalling the country's modernization.

Similarly, other governments after Leguia's have hired filmmakers to advance their own agendas. However, the different governments of the first half of the twentieth century never elevated filmmaking as an art or a form of expression or as a cultural force supported by clear cultural policies promoting further development of a film industry.

The great majority of filmmakers invested their own funds either individually or in association with other filmmakers or business people who were willing to invest in film companies. The first feature fiction film, *Negocio al agua / Business Down the Drain*, was made in 1913.[3] The Empresa del Cine Teatro, a film company that also owned a movie theatre, produced this silent feature (Bedoya 1997, 23). In 1934 Alberto Santana directed *Resaca/Hangover*, the first sound film (86). Bedoya (2009, 33) suggests that the most important film company during the 1930s until the early 1940s was Amauta Films. It came to be the most prolific of its time with ten feature films that, to some extent, emulated the genres and styles of the Mexican and Argentinean cinema of that era – family dramas, popular comedy, and folk stories.

With the advent of sound cinema in Peru in the 1930s, audiences showed a preference for films in Spanish; thus, during the 1940s and 1950s Mexican and Argentinean movies competed with Hollywood films in the Peruvian market. These imported films hindered the distribution of local films as they occupied most of the national screens. Despite the production of a good number of domestic films, Peruvian cinema did not achieve the output number (and, in some cases, quality) that could compete with the studio systems of Hollywood, Mexico, and Argentina.

As the state did not regulate the film market share, Peruvian filmmakers had a tougher time distributing their films and recovering their investments. Distributors and exhibitors made agreements with foreign film companies far in advance, using the booking system (as they continue to do today), thereby leaving much of the domestic production out of the exhibition circuit. Some filmmakers lobbied different Peruvian governments prior to the government of General Juan Velasco Alvarado (1968–75) to gain better access to film distribution and to gain state support for the promotion of filmmaking as a cultural asset of the nation. However, it was not until the populist and nationalist regime of Velasco Alvarado that a government would seriously listen to this request from filmmakers for assistance.

In fact, a profound socio-political shift took place in 1968. The democratic government of President Fernando Belaúnde Terry (1963–8) was deposed by a military coup d'état carried out by Velasco Alvarado, who went on to rule until 1975. In 1972 Velasco Alvarado's populist and nationalist military regime passed Decree no. 19327 for the Promotion of the Film Industry. This legislation is simply known as Ley de Cine (Film Law).

Velasco Alvarado's Film Law must be understood within the context of an overarching nationalistic reform of various aspects of the economic, political, social, and cultural life of the country. His military regime launched various sweeping reform programs in, for example, agriculture, education, and oil and mining. Furthermore, these reforms should be contextualized within the broader Latin American political and economic paradigm shift of the 1960s and 1970s, in which various countries moved towards the left and adopted import substitution industrialization (ISI) as part of their economic model. The adoption of ISI was aimed at promoting the development of domestic industries and local production and replacing imported goods.

In terms of film production, the two main objectives within the ISI political and economic paradigm were, first, to stimulate the development of a film industry, which eventually could supply the internal demand for entertainment and could replace, at least in part, foreign films. Second, it aimed to develop a national cinema, which could represent Peru internationally while also creating an internal national dialogue about Peruvians living in urban areas and those living in the highlands and other rural places.

Under the Film Law the government created the Comisión de Promoción Cinematográfica (COPROCI, Commission for the Promotion of Cinema), which worked under the Oficina Central de Información (OCI, Central Office for Information). The COPROCI oversaw all issues relating to production, exhibition, and distribution of films. One of its roles was to reorganize the film market share through a quota system in which different world regions could be represented on the screens, such as Latin America, North America, and Europe (Carbone 2007, 21). In addition, this system would give priority to the exhibition of domestic productions, since the Film Law guaranteed compulsory exhibition of locally produced short and feature-length films, thus securing a market share for Peruvian filmmakers. The COPROCI attempted to diminish the overwhelming presence of foreign, namely Hollywood, films from the local market (Carbone 2007, 22–3; Martínez 2008, 4; Bedoya 2009, 164).

Another aspect of the law guaranteed certain tax breaks and incentives to filmmakers and distributors of national cinema (Bedoya 2009, 163; Carbone 2007, 32–3). The admission ticket for a feature film included a tax, which was allocated to pay for the short movie shown before the feature presentation. This ensured, for the most part, that filmmakers or their companies would recover their investments; in some cases, they even made some extra money to capitalize or to use for salaries. Another initiative, as part of the law, ensured that the Banco Industrial, a state-owned bank, provided loans at low interest to filmmakers with well-defined film proposals (Martínez 2008, 4).

The Film Law mandated that exhibitors screen Peruvian films, displacing in some cases foreign films that had already been booked (Bedoya 2009, 164). This was one of the major complaints by exhibitors who claimed that the law was against free trade. The law mandated that short films be exhibited for at least three weeks in each theatre of the distribution circuit, while feature films should be shown for a minimum of one week. Under the Film Law, which was in place for roughly twenty years (1972–92), the bulk of the domestic film production was short films, and most of these were documentaries. The law was rescinded by the neoliberal regime of President Alberto Fujimori.

I would dare to say that the period of 1972 to 1992 was, at least in terms of output, a sort of mini golden age of Peruvian cinema. Filmmakers managed to finally produce and distribute a substantial number of films, anchoring the existence of a national cinema. However, this mini golden age had its problems. First of all, not even with this supportive law were Peruvian filmmakers able to build infrastructures capable of creating a dominant film culture or developing genre films, much less compete with the international film flow. Nor could independent cinema develop, because filmmakers who wanted to take advantage of the Film Law, especially the access to exhibition, needed to formally establish a film company approved by COPROCI. In addition, in that twenty-year period there were no marked alternative channels of distribution.

During that time, filmmakers were not thinking in terms of being independent producers but rather in terms of whether or not they could at least produce, exhibit, and recoup their investment and cover some living expenses (Durant 2010b). In other words, most filmmakers worked in subsistence mode with no time to theorize or engage in discussion of whether their films were part of a dominant trend or the filmmakers were working outside or within a particular paradigm (much of this is similar to the way in which filmmakers are working today in Iraq, as discussed in Mary Erickson's chapter in this volume). Most filmmakers were in support of the Film Law and state support, taking advantage of working within the framework of the Film Law because it was one of the very few ways to survive as a filmmaker. Today most filmmakers from that generation, and even younger ones, see this period as the best moment in the history of Peruvian film development, despite criticisms of the Film Law. Indeed, the new generation of filmmakers, as those before them, is urging the current government for state support.

Distributors and exhibitors never warmed up to the law and its implications. The mandatory exhibition was seen as a dictatorial imposition and absolutely against free trade. Also, the majority of the domestic audiences, especially the middle and upper classes, tended to think of most domestic productions as bad – technically and aesthetically. They also disliked the films' narratives. Of course, the point of reference for comparing the quality of Peruvian cinema was foreign films, particularly Hollywood ones. Audiences resented the imposition of having to watch bad films when they could be watching what they considered to be better films. It was not easy to generate sufficient revenue from local feature-length productions, and many times the feature films plunged at the box office. Short films were somewhat more protected from economic failure because of the taxed ticket.

The production of short documentaries helped to advance the careers of many filmmakers during that time, including Francisco Lombardi, Alberto "Chicho" Durant, Nora de Izcue, José Carlos Huayhuaca, and Kurt and Christine Rosenthal, as well as the members of the Grupo Chaski. Some of these filmmakers later produced feature-length movies that have become part of the Peruvian canon. Furthermore, it was during the life of the Film Law that some people managed to develop their careers as actors, like Gustavo Bueno and Antonio Vega; some made crossovers from theatre to film, like Delfina Paredes and Orlando Sacha, and from television to film, like Tulio Loza.

Looking for the Meaning of Independence under the Film Law

Despite Peru's lack of a dominant film structure and its unclear independent filmmaking activity, we can broaden our view of what constitutes independent cinema to take into account not only internal factors but also external ones. Then we begin to see more clearly that, even during the existence of the Film Law, there was independent film activity. Furthermore, I would like to suggest that the passing of the Film Law was an act of independence for Peruvian filmmaking in general. During that time, the production and exhibition of all films – short and feature length – with all of their technical or acting defects, represents first and foremost a reclamation of Peruvian screens for the circulation of Peruvian images. Peru's filmmaking activity developed the most within a political economic environment of import substitution, and the law that supported such development was part of a radical reform program in opposition to the U.S. influence in the region. Thus, the Film Law stands in opposition to Hollywood and other foreign film industries.

Many forgotten filmmakers who made shorts for the mandatory exhibition provision, and even some feature filmmakers, financed their movies by accessing bank loans or by investing personal capital. In this sense, we can think of them as independent. Many filmmakers chose to engage in international co-productions or pre-sales because of the difficulties in financing and the need to get advanced monies for production. Some of the filmmakers who implemented these practices have become the most well-known and canonic in the contemporary history of Peruvian cinema. Engaging in international co-production or pre-sales not only gave these filmmakers financial backing but also provided them an almost secure distribution in the European film and television market. It also opened the doors for their entrance into the European film festivals, where many have won awards over the years.

The Cases of Francisco Lombardi and the Grupo Chaski

Francisco Lombardi is one of the most established and respected film directors in Peru. He has had a long and steady career, despite the ups and downs of filmmaking in the country. Lombardi is not an independent filmmaker in the economic sense, but he is independent in the ideological or political sense. All of his works have been produced within the international system of co-production. He is one of the directors of his generation who have secured financial backing from mainstream European private and state media institutions such as TV Española. His career has been built using this model, making some concessions to fit into the international market in which his financial sponsors operate (similar to the practice of other independent filmmakers in Greece, Malaysia, and elsewhere).

Lombardi's films touch upon social and political issues without pushing a specific ideological agenda. Lombardi has remained thematically, intellectually, and artistically independent from the strong militant and socialist Latin American ideas of the 1960s and 1970s, in which film became a site for social struggle and a tool to denounce the evils of capitalism and U.S. imperialism against poor nations and, in particular, Latin American countries. Lombardi's films, although part of Latin America's canonic cinema of the 1980s, do not fit into the dominant trend of militant cinema of that period.[4] Lombardi studied film in Santa Fe, Argentina, with Fernando Birri, one of the most influential filmmakers of the militant cinema and the New Latin American Cinema movement,[5] but Lombardi has always produced outside of this movement's politics and themes. His films do not side evidently with a particular sector of society, but they are reflective and subtly critical of Peru's different social classes and of significant political and economic moments. Many critics and even audiences may define his films as commercial or mainstream because the release of most of his films has been accompanied by well-designed and well-funded (compared to others) publicity campaigns. The films have been shown primarily in commercial theatres, rarely making it to alternative venues or cine clubs.

Lombardi started his career, as did many others, by producing short movies in 1974. In 1977 he made his first feature film, *Muerte al amanecer / Death at Dawn*, funded by José Zavala Rey de Castro, who owned the Peruvian company Inca Films. This movie was co-produced by Inca Films and Cine Film 71 from Venezuela. It is a fictional recreation, based on true events that occurred in 1956, about the last hours of a man on death row who was to be executed at dawn for his crime of raping and killing a boy. The film was a domestic success and launched Lombardi's career.

Thanks to this film and some of Lombardi's subsequent work in the 1980s, Peruvian audiences became more appreciative of domestic productions. The growing audience, that anticipated the next Lombardi film, also became interested in paying to see other Peruvian productions. Of the top ten most successful Peruvian feature films from the 1980s to the early 1990s, four of them were Lombardi's films: *Muerte de un magnate / Death of a Magnate* (1980); *La ciudad y los perros / The City and the Dogs* (1985), which also launched his international career in the Spanish-speaking world market; *La boca del lobo / The Lion's Den* (1988); and *Caidos del cielo / Fallen from Heaven* (1990). These movies received multiple awards from key European international film festivals, including San Sebastián, Huesca, Trieste, and Moscow. Lombardi also won awards in Havana, which is considered the most important Latin American film festival.

Lombardi consolidated his film career during the 1980s, and his body of work includes thirteen feature films, seven of which are adaptations of literary works. Of these seven, two are based on books by Nobel Laureate Mario Vargas Llosa – *La ciudad y los perros / The City and the Dogs* (1985) and *Pantaleón y las visitadoras / Captain Pantoja and the Special Service* (1999). Both the books and the films are critical of the military. Although government support allowed Lombardi to start his career, his success later allowed him to become independent enough to criticize the military.

Grupo Chaski

Grupo Chaski is a film collective that flourished under the support of the Film Law in 1982. Its original members – María Barea, Susana Pastor, Fernando Barreto, Fernando Espinoza, Stefan Kaspar, and Alejandro Legaspi – worked individually or in partnership with other filmmakers prior to founding the Grupo Chaski. This collective has been committed to providing a voice for those who traditionally have been marginalized in Peruvian society. Its work focuses primarily on significant social issues, tracing the lives of the poor living in urban areas. The first documentary produced by Grupo Chaski as a collective was *Miss Universo en el Perú / Miss Universe in Peru* (1982). It interweaves the story of the world pageant Miss Universe, which took place in Lima in 1982, with the lives of lower-class women in the capital.

Like Lombardi, Grupo Chaski has been successful at securing international funding, mainly drawing on support from European private and state media institutions. However, unlike the more conventional Lombardi, who was not committed to a militant cinema, the collective produces films that are socially and politically ideological. The collective's production approach may be considered to some extent independent. Its first main objective is to work in collaboration with its subjects and outside of the commercial or mainstream cinema produced in or imported into Peru. Their second objective is to avoid replicating hierarchical labour structures such as those that exist in mainstream film production. The collective aims at a horizontal and collaborative workflow between the members of the group as well as between the group and its film subjects. We can see that the collective's approach in its films draws on the influences of European neo-realism and Latin American Third Cinema.[6]

Grupo Chaski's most successful feature films to date are *Gregorio* (1984) and *Juliana* (1989), both of which are among the top ten films of the 1980s in Peru. Both films deal with poor children whose parents have migrated from rural Peru to the capital, seeking a better life, only to find discrimination and urban misery. *Gregorio* and *Juliana* combine documentary techniques with dramatic storytelling; the main actors are embedded among real people in their natural environment who perform their daily life to the extent that fits the screenplay.

Considering the constraints of distribution and exhibition in the country, what has made Grupo Chaski unique, especially during the 1980s and early 1990s, is that the collective has "consistently worked on creating alternative modes of exhibition at the same time that they have sought to make their films available to the public via commercial releases, television screenings, videos, and other more mainstream distribution outlets" (McClennen 2008, 1). They are perhaps the only filmmakers of their generation who took distribution into their hands; while they made use of the Film Law for the release of their films in the mainstream theatrical circuit, they also engaged in their own alternative distribution. They have been taking their movies outside of Lima, including into some rural areas, and they have been making use of alternative exhibition venues. In addition, they have managed to assist other Peruvian filmmakers of their generation by managing the Peruvian commercial releases of those films, such as Lombardi's *La ciudad y los perros* and Alberto "Chicho" Durant's *Malabrigo* (1986).

The activities of Grupo Chaski, as those of other film companies and filmmakers, came to a halt when the Film Law was dismantled in the early 1990s. However, the group reunited in the early 2000s, and currently they are fairly active in the alternative distribution and exhibition of domestic and Latin American films. Grupo Chaski, taking advantage of digital and new technologies, has created what it calls "microcines" (Ross 2008, 4). These microcines are small theatres with a digital projector, a DVD player, and a portable or permanent screen. It is through microcines that a diversity of audiences without access to regular or mainstream film theatres can now enjoy movies. (Alternative exhibition options have been operating in Iraq as well, with mobile cinema bringing films to remote locations.) Without microcines, hundreds of thousands of Peruvians would not have access to any type of movie theatre; for example, the city of Cuzco, with over 200,000 inhabitants, does not even have one movie theatre. All the movie theatres in Cuzco, as well as in other cities of the country, were closed down with the arrival and growth of home movie consumption (in VHS and later DVD), which coincided with the internal war that engulfed the country in the 1980s, affecting all kinds of businesses.

The End of the Film Law and the Birth of the "New Law"

In 1990, Peru was involved in an internal war, a staggering economic recession, and absolute social and economic chaos. The election of Alberto Fujimori brought a major shift in economics and politics. His regime adopted neoliberal policies and moved the country towards the global economy, liberating trade and lifting previous restrictions in industries that had been affected by nationalist and protectionist laws. In addition, Fujimori sold more than two hundred major national industrial assets such as telecommunications and oil on the international market. Although film was not really important in the economic scheme of things, Fujimori sided with the distributors and exhibitors and dismantled the Film Law and the organizations created to oversee and apply the law, giving way to a free film market.

In October 1994 a new law was passed, no. 26370, which created the Consejo Nacional de Cinematografía Peruana (CONACINE, National Council of Peruvian Cinema). The law established that the CONACINE should organize a twice-yearly competition of screenplays and give financial support to the winners for the production of their films. It stipulated that there were to be three prizes for each competition and that the money should be dispersed in three payments: at the beginning of the production, at the end of the shooting schedule, and once the film had been completed and was ready for distribution. However, throughout the 1990s, and even now, the CONACINE has not been able to fully comply with its legal mandate because the state is not providing enough funds. In 2010, Congress approved a law that allocated 3 per cent of all box office proceeds to promote production, distribution, and exhibition of national cinema ("Nueva Ley de Cine Aprobada" 2010).

These new laws have not generated enough revenue to support the development of Peruvian filmmaking. Since the CONACINE's creation only about twenty movies have been completed, and not all of these had CONACINE's support. According to Bedoya (2009), beginning in the 1990s the estimated number of foreign films populating the screens of the country each year has been over two hundred (218). It is in this uncertain new terrain that the growth of independent filmmaking is taking place.

Several filmmakers of the newer generation, such as Josué Méndez (the director of *Días de Santiago / Days of Santiago*, 2004, and *Dioses*/Gods, 2008) and Claudia Llosa (the director of *Madeinusa*, 2006, and *La teta asustada / The Milk of Sorrow*, 2009), are establishing a successful commercial model and strengthening their ties to major international media organizations such as Ibermedia, TV Española, and Channel Four.

There are also many other filmmakers working outside of this system, opting not to participate in the production of films for the international film festival circuit or for exhibition in mainstream theatres. These filmmakers are defining themselves, for the first time in Peru, as independent filmmakers.

The Self-Defined Independent Filmmakers of the Twenty-First Century

The advent of digital and new technologies during the first decade of the 2000s has been a blessing for the dire situation of Peruvian filmmaking. Younger generations of filmmakers are developing a new

Peruvian cinema that is not constrained by conventional modes of production or by specific technical support that requires big budgets, large crews, and an expensive post-production process. These film-makers are creating "digital films," that is, films produced without using celluloid; rather, they are shooting on digital video cameras or digital film cameras. Most are using low-cost digital video cameras, editing with "prosumer" software, and distributing by streaming online or releasing direct to DVD.

Producing films in material other than celluloid, as an alternative to the high costs of filmmaking, is not new, but certainly it is now more common. In 1985 filmmaker Juan Carlos Torrico Méndez made use of three-quarter-inch analogue video to produce a low-budget movie that was shot in video, *Los Shapis en el mundo de los pobres / The Shapis in the World of the Poor* (1985). This movie was blown up to 35 mm film for the-atrical distribution. The film is about the Shapis, a popular 1980s music group, whose popularity resided mainly with the lower classes because the band members came from a similar social background. They repre-sented all those migrants from the interior of the country who were try-ing to survive in the capital. Although the transfer from analogue video to film did not provide a perfect picture, the movie still had success among the target audience: the Shapis's fans and followers. This mild success allowed director Torrico to produce a second film, *El rey / The King* (1987), this time shot in celluloid.

In 1991, I produced a feature movie in Super VHS, *El despertar de Adriana / The Awakening of Adriana* (1991). It is the story of a young man dealing with his sexuality and, in the process, struggling with his transgender identity in an intolerant society. The movie was exhibited at the National Cultural Institute (INC) and the Bartolomé de Las Casas Centre in Cuzco; later, it was exhibited in the Cine Club El Cinemató-grafo in Barranco, Lima. It was produced, screened, and distributed as an alternative to the high production costs of film and in response to the dismantling of the Film Law. The movie was projected onto a normal silver screen using a Super VHS deck connected to a video projector. I distributed the movie on VHS through word of mouth, which was the social network of the day. However, the experiment of shooting movies in analogue video did not catch on at the time with most other filmmak-ers, mainly because analogue video was perceived as being suitable only for television and being of lower quality, which technically it was. However, producing in analogue video requires the same amount of time and effort in constructing sets, lighting, and filming in order to tell a story. At that time those of us who began shooting in video had been actually trained first in film.

In the 1980s filmmakers in Peru marked a clear division and difference between their work and that of video-makers. Now those lines are blurring because of digital technologies; the use of "digital video" and "digital film" to make "digital movies" is becoming commonplace, especially in various developing countries. After 2005 there has been an explosion of digital cinema in Peru, flying under the radar of the film critics and film scholars who continue to focus primarily on films produced in celluloid or with big budgets.

Most of these new producers and directors have declared themselves independent filmmakers because they receive no support whatsoever from state or other institutions for their productions. Until recently, CONACINE did not prioritize screenplays that were to be shot digitally. Today, this has changed (yet, some independent producers still opt not to compete for a CONACINE grant). In terms of distribution and exhibition, independent filmmakers tend to choose alternative platforms and venues. Many distribute by selling their DVDs directly to stores and street vendors and on the web, though the latter is still less common. Their movies are exhibited in art houses, community centres, university cultural centres, and other small places interested in supporting this independent film trend.

The number of these independent filmmakers is such that they are now forming regional organizations of independent filmmakers who produce in digital formats. In June 2011 the first annual Festival Lima Independiente was held. This film festival is dedicated to the work of independent filmmakers producing with digital technologies and low budgets. There were entries to the festival from various neighbouring Latin American countries. One of the guests of honour was Geraldine Chaplin,[7] who attended in support of this new generation of filmmakers ("Lima se prepara" 2011). In February 2012 the Ministry of Culture, the Municipality of Lima, and the Cultural Centre of the Spanish Embassy sponsored the Primer Festival Iberoamericano de Cine Digital (First Latin American Digital Film Festival) in Lima. Many of the participants defined themselves as independent filmmakers.

The presence of self-defined independent Peruvian filmmakers is not centralized in Lima, as was the case for celluloid filmmakers in the past. There are independent filmmakers in different regions of the country, and they have formed an association named Asociación de Cineastas Regionales e Independientes del Peru (ACRIP, Association of Regional and

Independent Filmmakers of Peru). The most active regions are Ayacucho, Puno, Huancayo, Arequipa, and the peripheries of Lima. Most of these filmmakers are committed to making films that reflect their regional realities, and they focus on the social issues affecting their localities. Some are somewhat more experimental than others who follow a more conventional mainstream trend in the stories they bring to the alternative screens.

Currently the most well-known independent filmmakers working in digital formats in Lima are Fernando Montenegro, Raúl del Busto, Rafael Arevalo, Javier Bellido, and Juan Daniel Fernández, all of whom have at least one feature-length movie. Three of the best-known filmmakers from other regions are Jaime Nilo Inga from Huancayo, Luis Berrocal from Ayacucho, and Roger Acosta from Arequipa. The independent regional filmmakers have also begun their own festivals, and they are demanding the decentralization of media in Peru in order to provide adequate help to the national development of the film industry across the country.

The Approach to Aesthetics

Latin America has produced three major film aesthetic manifestos: "An Aesthetic of Hunger" by Brazilian filmmaker Glauber Rocha in 1965; "For an Imperfect Cinema" by Cuban filmmaker Julio García Espinosa in 1969; and *Towards a Third Cinema* by Argentinean filmmakers Octavio Getino and Fernando Solanas, also in 1969. The ideas presented in these three manifestos have been highly influential throughout Latin America and other world regions, especially Africa and parts of Asia. Many Peruvian filmmakers from the 1970s, the 1980s, and even the 1990s produced their films, consciously or not, expressing the ideology embedded in these manifestos, which concerned not only art but also politics and resistance.

The common thread of these three manifestos is the framing of cinema as an artistic expression and as a profound social and political tool for filmmakers. The manifestos underpin Latin American aesthetic and thematic approaches that do not replicate or emulate the cinema of Hollywood or of Europe. Another important aspect to point out is that, owing to economic and technical constraints, many films could not have high production values. Yet filmmakers have found ways to articulate this lack as part of their aesthetic approach. For example, if one were only able to shoot in 16 mm, resulting in a grainy quality to the final 35 mm print, then that graininess would become part of the story or the essential look of the film.

Furthermore, almost in anticipation of what we are now experiencing in the twenty-first century thanks to digital technologies, the call is for the subjects and spectators of movies to play an active role and show their own agency by becoming co-authors with the filmmakers. This activity thus breaks the cycle of having an artistic elite mediating people's stories and instead has the people produce and tell their own stories. We can say today that the sprouting of independent producers and directors across Peru is thanks to digital technologies, and these technologies are allowing the fulfilment of the manifestos that anticipated this new era of independent cinema.

Conclusion

It is a challenge to have a concrete definition of what independent filmmaking is in general, and even harder in the context of a country that has struggled so long to build a filmmaking industry. There is a definite need for further study on the topic in the context of Peru, as well as in other developing countries. I consider this a first step in that direction. It is also important to pay attention to the possible convergence that may exist between those producing in celluloid and those producing in digital video or digital film. These technical differences are beginning to blur, and, certainly in a country with no infrastructure or major financial resources for large-budget films, digital technologies are the answer. Furthermore, it would be worth exploring what constitutes a "film," given the technological changes and the evolution of distribution systems.

Some members of the newer generation of filmmakers are digital natives, and thus it is natural for them to adopt digital technologies to tell the stories they want to share with the public. It is important for future study of the Peruvian film industry to look at this shift in technological use, and also to study it in the context of this generation. As was the case when 16 mm film appeared, which helped to liberate filmmakers from the studio system and create many independent filmmakers, digital video and digital film are liberating this new generation of filmmakers from the constraints of expensive technology and expensive modes of production. We need as well to study further the different channels of distribution that are being invented and used. Deeper analysis of the microcines of Grupo Chaski will shed light on whether or not the independent digital filmmakers are part of the pool that will be selected for this alternative distribution. The twenty-first century in

Peru will likely bring an evolution in filmmaking that we cannot even begin to imagine. However, we can look at the locally organized film festivals and home-grown microcines and be certain that the Peruvian definition of an independent filmmaker will continue to evolve and present new complexities.

NOTES

1 Luis Figueroa is one of the producers and directors of the Peruvian film *Kukuli* (1961), which has become a classic example of Andean cinema. Other titles to his name are *Toro Pucllay* (1998), *Yawar Fiesta* (1982), *Los Perros Hambrientos* (1976), and several video documentaries that he produced during the 1990s with the sponsorship of Pontificia Universidad Católica del Perú and other institutions.

2 Since 2011 CONACINE has operated under the Ministry of Culture as a consulting body, and its functions as CONACINE have been dissolved; it is now the Cultural Industries and Arts unit of the Ministry of Culture (Peruvian Minister of Culture 2012).

3 There is no director listed for *Negocio al Agua* (*Business Down to the Water*). The screenplay was co-written by Federico Blume and Jorge Goitizolo. This information is taken from the list of credits in Ricardo Bedoya's book *Un cine reencontrado: Diccionario ilustrado de las películas peruanas* (1997) and from Mario Lucioni Guerra's website *Celebrando el cine mudo peruano* (http://www.archivoperuano.com/cinemudo.htm).

4 Political militant cinema was part of the Latin American film scene from the 1950s and had a stronger presence in the 1960s, 1970s, and part of the 1980s.

5 The New Latin American Cinema movement is a cinematic movement that organically took hold in the Latin American continent during the 1960s, 1970s, and part of the 1980s. During this period there was tremendous film production despite, and perhaps thanks to, an environment of underdevelopment and dependency. The New Latin American Cinema movement was political in nature and sought to liberate filmmakers and films from economic and cultural dependency. It worked in opposition to Hollywood cultural products.

6 Third Cinema is a Latin American movement of the 1960s and 1970s that began with a manifesto entitled *Towards a Third Cinema*, written by filmmakers Fernando Solanas and Octavio Getino. Its philosophy is to make films in opposition to colonialism, imperialism, and capitalism. It urges filmmakers to work against the Hollywood model (First Cinema) and the

European model (Second Cinema) and to create an indigenous model that is born from the people and for the people of the Third World. Third Cinema has been fairly influential not only in Latin American filmmakers but also among African filmmakers (Solanas and Getino 1971, 16–30).

7 Actress Geraldine Chaplin, daughter of Charles Chaplin, attended the festival to learn more about Peruvian and Latin American cinema. Owing to her fame, her presence enhances the growing importance of independent filmmaking and the festivals for independent film productions.

PART TWO

The Meaning of Independence in Regions of Conflict and Change

Chapter Seven

In the Shadow of the Studios, the State, and the Multiplexes: Independent Filmmaking in Greece

LYDIA PAPADIMITRIOU

For the first time in thirty-four years, in 2011, a Greek film was nominated in the Best Foreign Language Category of the Academy Awards. The film was Yorgos Lanthimos's *Dogtooth*,[1] which was co-financed by the state-owned Greek Film Center (GFC) and the privately owned, independent Boo Productions. The nomination was the culmination of a very successful run for the film in the European and international film festival circuit (during which it had been awarded a number of prizes, such as "Un certain regard" at the Cannes Film Festival in 2009, as well as very positive reviews). Most important, however, this event marks the starting point from which to consider the international relevance of contemporary Greek cinema – a type of cinema that can be seen as artistically and, to a certain degree, institutionally independent.

Dogtooth is an excellent example, if not the frontrunner, of the latest version of independence in Greek cinema. It was hybrid in terms of financing (made with both state and private funds) and highly dependent on the international film festival circuit for critical recognition (first outside and then within Greece). Authorial vision and control were combined with new sources of funding and modes of production and met a new audience, both within Greece and abroad. Some of the infrastructural changes that have contributed to the creation of this new independent cinema in Greece include the involvement of advertising companies in film financing and production, the increasingly global orientation of some new independent producers eager to appeal to international audiences, and the practice of working on productions on a "deferral" basis. This chapter will offer a historical overview of the changing versions of independence in Greek cinema, before spotlighting and then concluding with some of the most recent developments in Greek independent cinema.

There is nothing self-evident in the concept of independence in cinema. By definition, *independence* is understood as the opposite of *dependence*, as poignantly noted by Erik Knudsen in his chapter on independent filmmaking in the United Kingdom. In the context of cinema this usually refers to films produced and distributed outside the network of major studios or the state. Nonetheless, in practice, independence might be understood better in relation to and with reference to such networks, rather than in opposition to them (Kleinhans 1998, 308). In this sense, as independence is not an absolute concept, it is important to define its use and to explore degrees and varieties of interdependence, as outlined by Baltruschat and Erickson in the introduction to this book.

A small digression to explorations of independence in American cinema would be helpful here, mainly because it is in this context that research around the concept and set of practices has been mostly conducted so far. In their respective studies of independent American cinema, both Yannis Tzioumakis (2006) and Geoff King (2005) have shown the extent to which the term has been fraught with contradictions and inconsistencies. In his highly illuminating overview of American independent cinema from the studio era onwards, Tzioumakis demonstrates the changing meaning of the term with regard to different industrial, critical, and historical contexts. He convincingly argues that the most effective way of conceptualizing *independent cinema* is as a discourse whose meaning depends on a variety of contexts. The flexibility of this approach provides a very appropriate framework in which to explore independence in Greek cinema.

King (2005, 2) highlights that independent films may be recognized on the basis of such diverse criteria as "(1) their industrial location, (2) the kinds of formal/aesthetic strategies they adopt, and (3) their relationship to the broader social, cultural, political or ideological landscape," as discussed by Baltruschat and Erickson in the introduction. Such criteria are clearly applicable to different contexts. Again, they prove to be useful for an exploration into Greek cinema. King also indicates that films designated as independent – according to all or some of these criteria – vary with respect to how different they are from the so-called Hollywood-styled independent films (as addressed in Tzioumakis's chapter in this volume). While such variety is certainly key to understanding independent cinema, what makes the picture more complex is the case of a smaller national cinema. In Greece, for example, Greek films have always competed for the attention of the audience with regard to foreign imports, which, since the post-war era, have been predominantly American. In order to survive in this highly competitive context, Greek cinema has adopted different approaches at different stages in its history: it used a commercial model of genres and stars (1950s and 1960s); it became increasingly dependent on state funds and embraced art-house cinema (1970s and 1980s); or it opened up to European and transnational co-productions (1990s and 2000s, as detailed by Hoefert de Turégano in this volume). In each of these contexts the meaning of an *independent Greek cinema* varies significantly.

This leads to the following questions: is a Greek film independent when it is financed and produced by a small company but follows narrative and aesthetic conventions akin to Hollywood and/or Greek popular genres? Can a politically controversial, aesthetically experimental film be called independent if it is financed through state funds? Is it possible for films that follow the strict quotas of European co-productions to be considered independent? This chapter will try to address these questions in all their complexities. While locating Greece within a wider European and international context, and drawing some parallels between other European cinemas and Greece, the following analysis will focus on Greek cinema, addressing it first through a historical lens and then via contemporary case studies.

Independent Cinema in Greece: A Historical Account

Independent film practices have existed throughout the history of Greek cinema, but the extent to which they have been identified as such has varied significantly. In the history of American cinema the first so-called independents were, paradoxically, the burgeoning studio moguls who, in their desire to flee Edison's control on the east coast in the early 1910s, decided to move west and set up what was to become Hollywood, the single most influential industry globally, at least in the twentieth century (Lewis 2008, 20–3). No use of the term *independent* can be found in the history of early Greek cinema, but, as Delveroudi (2011, 115–28) indicates, there is still a lot to be discovered about this period. The activities of filmmakers and cameramen of the era suggest that they may have worked independently, but it is possible (albeit still unproven) that foreign (possibly European) companies, as well as Greece's royal family, were hiring filmmakers for their services. Apart from very few exceptions, early Greek film culture was dominated by imports, predominantly European films (Tsitsopoulou 2011, 73–95), and it was only after the Second World War that systematic film production began in Greece. The sites of exhibition (open-air cinemas as well as fully equipped film theatres) were owned by businessmen, who often had binding agreements with Europe-based distributors – mostly Pathé and Gaumont – for the provision of the films screened in these cinemas (Delveroudi 2011, 391). The brothers Gaziadi's film company Dag Films, which produced and directed seven feature-length films, represents the most sustained filmmaking activity in Greece in the 1920s. With the exception of the government funding they received to film an uncompleted documentary of the Asia Minor campaign, it appears that the Gaziadi brothers were acting as independent producers and trying to develop a distinctively Greek style of filmmaking (Karalis 2012, 15–20). Following King's criteria noted above, we could argue that the Gaziadi brothers were independent with respect to both their industrial location and their aesthetic strategies.

Apart from the challenging political and economic circumstances facing Greece in the 1920s and 1930s, one of the greatest problems of its nascent film industry was the imposition of heavy tax duties on all public events. During the Metaxas dictatorship of the 1930s such duties were as high as 70 per cent (Karalis 2012, 31). This established a system – only reversed in the 1980s – which profited the state and effectively turned the film industry into a cash cow, thus, undermining any serious attempts at developing a stable and long-term industry (Delveroudi 2011, 371).

The culture of adversity has characterized filmmaking in Greece throughout its history. It could be argued that the overly melodramatic statement by director Orestis Laskos that "all films made in Greece [in the early 1930s] were made with blood" (quoted in Delveroudi 2011, 371–2) reflects a rather widespread perception of filmmaking as a heroic pioneering enterprise of cultural modernization during a period plagued by political and economic problems, which was further compromised by the arrival of the "talkies."

Defining independent film of the pre-war era is challenging. The post-war era presents a different set of issues. It marks the period in which Greece's commercial film industry began to take shape. While the term *commercial* attached to *industry* might seem to be a tautology, it is worth using it in this context as it has often been seen to represent the antithesis of an independent, art cinema.[2] The post-war film industry developed owing to initiatives by producers such as Filopimin Finos. In spite of the difficult times during the Greek civil war (1945–9) he enabled the production of Greek films that slowly, but steadily, were becoming noticed. In the period of national reconstruction of the 1950s more producers entered the scene, initiating healthy competition and a significant increase in box-office revenues. The transformation of producers such as Finos, and its main competitor, Anzervos, from small, effectively independent companies to large studios began in the late 1950s and lasted to the early 1960s. By then, Finos Films and its major competitors – Anzervos and Damaskinos-Mihailidis in the 1950s, Karagiannis-Karatzopoulos and Klak (and Damaskinos-Mihailidis) in the 1960s – dominated the market. They mass-produced films and controlled distribution during what we might call the Greek studio system of the 1950s and 1960s. In order to survive amidst increasing competition – from each other as well as incoming independent producers – these companies increased their output dramatically. For example, Finos increased film production from two or three films a year in the 1950s to an average of nine features a year in the 1960s (Papadimitriou 2006, 168–9). For a market that had no potential for expansion, as Greek films were only shown within Greece (as well as in Greek diasporic communities in Canada, Australia, and Germany), such overproduction led to the overall lowering of production standards and investments per film and contributed to the eventual implosion of commercial modes of production by the 1970s (Karalis 2012; Papadimitriou 2009).

The extent to which Greek films from this period were simply copies of Hollywood or significantly different in style, content, and tone has often been debated, and critics of the time were often quick to dismiss Greek genre films as second-rate imitations. However, closer examination of popular Greek films from the 1950s and 1960s shows a mixture of indigenous elements drawn from local theatrical traditions, combined with a range of cinematic influences, not only from Hollywood but also from European and Indian films. Depending on the genre (folk costume films, comedy, melodrama, musical), the degree and kind of foreign influences varied, but, overall, Greek popular cinema was a stylistically hybrid cinema in which local elements mixed with attempts to emulate and imitate foreign norms (Papadimitriou 2006; Eleftheriotis 1995).

While directors and other creative and technical personnel were often contracted by studios on a long-term basis (for example, Yannis Dalianidis at Finos Films), sometimes they worked independently by making separate film-by-film arrangements with different commercially oriented small to medium-sized production companies (for example, Grigoris Grigoriou). This suggests that the studio system did not have total control and that there was a degree of flexibility in the working terms and conditions for people in the industry. In fact, from a purely industrial perspective, the large number of smaller production companies that entered the market for a quick profit (and were not affiliated with Greek studios) were independent. These companies had no artistic aspirations. Their films were shot within days, on small budgets, and exhibited in rural and suburban second-run (*B Provoli*) theatres. They represent a version of independence akin to the films of the Poverty Row companies in the 1930s and 1940s and the exploitation film companies of the 1950s and 1960s in the United States (Sotiropoulou 1989).

The meaning of independence during this period, however, is mostly associated with a different phenomenon: the emergence of a few individual investors or small companies that financed some films *in the name of art*, not profit, and that helped to establish a tradition of a high-quality art cinema. It is worth noting that this tradition, which developed further in the 1970s, was also supported to a limited extent by some studios, such as Finos. This fact suggests that art cinema was not always financed independently (Chalkou 2009, 103–20).

To exemplify, the work of director Nikos Koundouros reveals the funding options that are available to art-cinema directors. It also highlights the complexities of using the term *independence* in this context. Koundouros's first film, *Magic City / Magiki Polis* (1952), a neo-realist and expressionist exploration of the underside of the capital, was both financially and artistically independent. It was funded by a private investor, Despina Skalotheou, and by a small production company, Athens Film Company, which later went on to finance Koundouros's second film, *The Ogre of Athens / O Drakos* (1956). The film's politically oppositional stance is highlighted by the controversy it caused when censors banned it from representing Greece at foreign festivals; it was seen to portray an unfavourable view of Athens, populated by destitute refugees and petty criminals. Critically acclaimed, though, his first two films put Koundouros on the map as a director with a distinct and powerful vision. By the time he had completed his third and fourth features, *The Outlaws / I Paranomi* (1958) and *The River / To Potami* (1960), Finos Films had become an investor in his films, despite the fact that both films involved only thinly disguised references to the taboo (and banned) topic of Greek cinema at the time: the Greek civil war. However, Finos's willingness to support such artistically and politically daring films only went so far. For most of the 1960s and early 1970s the company invested in popular genres (mainly comedies, melodramas, and musicals) and stars. The company achieved the reputation of producing commercial films of "quality," in other words, of having the highest technical and production standards for Greek films at the time. Nevertheless, the significantly lower budgets and less streamlined mode of production of Greek films meant that – compared to Hollywood – even the most expensive productions (for example, the musicals) appeared to be of lower quality. In the context of Greek cinema, the standards of Finos Films were consistently the highest, a fact that resulted in the company's high box-office yields, both in relation to other studios and to the "exploitation independents" (the small companies that entered the market for a quick profit as mentioned above and whose films resembled the cheapest versions of Poverty Row studio films).

Despite a number of synergies between the established studios and the artistically minded independents (including the apprenticeships of several emerging independent directors in the studios), the polarization between commercial and art or independent cinema intensified during the 1960s, both by a lowering of the quality of mass-produced films and by the emergence of an oppositional discourse expressed by some left-inclined film journals (for example, *Ellinikos Kinimatografos*, *Sinhronos Kinimatografos*, *Othoni*, and *Film*). Cinephile audiences could see international art films in various clubs around Greece, which in turn helped the development of future filmmakers (Chalkou 2009, 64–99).

Alongside a handful of politically and artistically aware films that emerged in the 1960s, funded either independently (such as *The Roundup* / *To Bloko*, 1965, directed by Adonis Kyrou and produced by Griff Films) or by a larger company or studio (such as *Treason* / *Prodosia*, 1964, directed by Kostas Manousakis and produced by Klearhos Konitsiotis), it is worth noting the distinctive case of Takis Kanellopoulos, a "lonely auteur from Thessaloniki" (Karalis 2012, 114). All his feature films from the 1960s were financed independently: his modernist anti-war exploration *Sky* / *Ouranos* (1962) was privately financed by Vasilia Drakaki, while his next two films were funded by the director's brother (*Excursio/Ekdromi*, 1966) and by the director himself (*Interlude/Parenthesi*, 1968).[3] Interestingly, his first film of the 1970s, *The Last Spring* / *I Teleftea Anixi* (1972), was funded by Finos Films production, while his next two, *The Chronicle of Sunday* / *To Hroniko tis Kiriakis* (1975) and *Romantic Note* / *Romantiko Simioma* (1978), were among the first films supported by the newly established Greek Film Center, which would dominate financing options for Greek filmmakers for at least two decades. However,

Kanellopoulos was never assimilated by an artistic movement or a critical narrative, such as that of New Greek Cinema, and as a result he later struggled to find both financing and (until very recently) critical recognition. His last film, *Sonia* (1980), was, once again, self-financed, placing him firmly within the context of industrial independence (Mini 2011, 239–54).

The 1970s were characterized by the gradual decline of the studios (Finos Films closed in 1977 with the death of its founder) and by the establishment of New Greek Cinema. This new cinema represents the oppositional, politically aware, and artistically innovative films that emerged during the dictatorship (1967–74). It established what was to become the dominant mode of filmmaking in Greece up until (and, according to some critics, throughout) the 1980s: a director-centred art cinema, initially independently funded, later financially supported by the state (Papadimitriou 2009, 66–70). These were films that bore no resemblance to Hollywood and that drew their inspiration predominantly from European art-house films and movements.

At first, New Greek Cinema was a purely independent enterprise. Theo Angelopoulos's *Reconstruction/Anaparastasi* (1970), the film that has often been seen as marking the beginning of New Greek cinema, was financed by Yorgos Samiotis, an independent producer who had already funded two shorts (but afterwards would only be peripherally involved in New Greek Cinema). The other milestone of the early 1970s, Alexis Damianos's film *Evdokia* (1971), was also produced privately by two small companies, Katamor and Poria. Financing by the directors or their families and friends, and/or by private investors and sponsors such as Yorgos Papalios was the norm in early 1970s New Greek Cinema. During that time, art filmmaking became implicitly associated with an act of resistance against the junta, and it was far removed from the nationalistically driven, often propaganda-oriented, commercial enterprise of the declining studios. Distribution was similarly ad hoc and depended, as Karalis (2012, 154) notes, "on personal connections and affiliations."

The fall of the dictatorship in 1974 and the subsequent return to democracy – the *metapolitefsi*, as it is known in Greek – had significant repercussions. First, censorship gradually declined and, eventually, disappeared altogether. Second, new support mechanisms for filmmakers were introduced. Paradoxically, even though financial and political conditions improved, Greek cinema went through a period of intense crisis. On the one hand, the commercial film industry effectively collapsed by the mid to late 1970s (but not before a significant rise and decline of a different form of exploitation cinema, the soft porn industry). This can be partly attributed to the rise of television, introduced in Greece in 1966. On the other hand, the conditions of adversity that marked the rise of New Greek Cinema led to fragmentations among filmmakers and an overall loss of direction, both reflected in and arguably caused by a significant decline in audiences for Greek art films.

Two institutions were central in supporting New Greek Cinema up until the late 1980s: the Thessaloniki Film Festival (established as Week of Greek Cinema in 1960, renamed the Thessaloniki Film Festival in 1966, and transformed into the Thessaloniki International Film Festival in 1992), where the vast majority of Greek art films were shown; and the Greek Film Center, which started funding films in 1975 and became effectively the sole financier of cinema in Greece after 1981 and until the early 1990s. It is worth noting the significant changes in the political climate after 1981 when a socialist government came to power. It not only lifted the remaining censorship restrictions but also actively privileged director-driven art cinema as a way of highlighting the new regime's different ideology. Proposals were generously financed at the scriptwriting stage, and, provided they broadly satisfied the ideological premises of the governing party, projects were funded (Karalis 2012 195). The impetus for politically driven films gradually subsided, and throughout the 1980s mostly introverted, existentially themed films were produced. Most of these films were only screened at the Thessaloniki Film Festival and never released theatrically. Despite the fact that films produced during the state-supported period reflected the artistic identity of their respective authors – and as such marked independent filmmaking practices that privilege artistic control and creativity – the almost total dependence of these films on state funds makes it difficult to discuss them as fully independent.

The 1990s signalled a gradual transformation of the Greek Film Center. On the one hand, it placed more emphasis on funding the work of young directors. On the other hand, it began to co-produce films with other Greek partners (state or private) and European and international companies. Theo Angelopoulos was one of the first directors to systematically embrace the practice of co-producing with European partners. This was matched by an increasing thematic emphasis in his films on less nationally specific issues and by a more transnational direction, with topics that transcended borders and opened questions regarding identities (Papadimitriou 2011, 496–7). As discussed by Teresa Hoefert de Turégano in her chapter on EU initiatives, co-productions remain a key production technology for European producers to proliferate production and to increase profitability. She points out that co-productions "travel well," an indication that they tend to be profitable on the international market. Some Greek filmmakers therefore follow a global trend, combining international financing and talent to guarantee higher budgets and international distribution. In some cases (for example, Yannis Smaragdis's *God Loves Caviar* / *O theos agapaei to haviari*, 2012), there is little to distinguish these films stylistically from American or other globally orientated productions.

Despite the critical success and major international recognition that Angelopoulos's films found in the 1990s,[4] Greek productions failed to attract audiences. The proliferation of free television channels after the deregulation of 1988, and the reputation of Greek films as being downbeat and depressive, compounded the problem. However, the unprecedented box-office success of the comedy *Safe Sex* (directed by Mihalis Reppas and Vangelis Papathanasiou, 1999) changed these perceptions.[5] *Safe Sex* inaugurated a new era in Greek film production, and Greek cinema was once again seen as commercially viable. Formally, this signalled a return to popular genres, especially comedies. It also marked a renewed focus on the values of older Greek films from the 1950s and 1960s, with which audiences were familiar owing to television repeats. It also foregrounded a "televisual aesthetic" in the form of scripts, stars, and style. From an economic perspective, it encouraged television channels to finance more films. This, in turn, paved the way for the involvement of theatrical distributors in production, as exemplified by the financing of Tassos Boulmetis's *A Touch of Spice* / *Politiki Kouzina* (2002) by Village Roadshow, the production branch of an Australian-based distributor with investments in Greece's theatrical exhibition sector.

The predominance of the Greek Film Center as effectively the only financing option for Greek films in the 1980s and most of the 1990s had created a kind of state monopoly, despite the gradual increase in co-productions. But the re-emergence of a commercial sector resulting from the involvement of private television channels and distribution or exhibition companies in financing changed the landscape in the 2000s. This was also the decade of a greater number of box-office successes for Greek films in Greece (Papadimitriou 2011). The strong links between new funding sources and large media sectors (such as the Lambrakis Press Group, owner of television channel Mega), as well as influential distributors and multiplex owners Odeon and Village, preclude any discussion of such productions as independent. The motivation for film production in these cases is almost exclusively profit. Furthermore, the films financed by these producers are mainly star vehicles and comedies designed to appeal to the widest possible national audience, one familiar with the featured stars through television. In other words, these films do not fit any of King's criteria of independence, as outlined above, as they are industrially, aesthetically, and politically mainstream.

The deregulation of Greek television, which resulted in the significant increase of freely available audio-visual material on television, seems to have initially kept audiences away from the cinema. However, even if film production itself was not flourishing, the opportunities offered by the television industry to young directors, scriptwriters, and other creative personnel allowed them to hone their professional skills. It also led to the emergence of a number of small to medium-sized companies specializing in the production of commercials and/or providing specialist services for digital effects. This new media landscape has influenced and provided the basis for reviving Greek cinema since the late 2000s. Despite its often hybrid financing nature, it represents a new version of an independent Greek cinema that been successful in putting Greek films on the international map.

Dogtooth and *Attenberg*: Towards an Internationally Oriented Independence

The nomination of *Dogtooth* for the 2011 Oscars was of great symbolic significance to Greek cinema, as it represented an international recognition that had not been enjoyed for over three decades. The fact that the nomination was preceded by an award at the Cannes Film Festival, where the film premiered in 2009, was also significant because the film's qualities were recognized on both sides of the Atlantic. This suggested that the film could appeal to international audiences with diverse cultural backgrounds and cinematic traditions. The film's success is undoubtedly due to its aesthetic and thematic dimensions: its powerfully claustrophobic and humorous script; its consistent and distinctive visual style; its openness to varied interpretations; and its un-naturalistic acting. The creative vision of the director, Yorgos Lanthimos, is evident behind all these aspects, rendering him unambiguously the auteur of the film. Despite its intrinsic qualities, however, it is important to highlight that the film's success is also to a large extent

7.1 Film still from *Dogtooth/Kynodontas* (2009), directed by Yorgos Lanthimos. Image courtesy of Yorgos Lanthimos.

the result of a strategy recently adopted by a number of Greek art films: they are meant to appeal to a transnational, global, art-cinema audience, and they premiere at international film festivals to increase interest in Greek cinema.

Apart from being shot in Greek and set in an affluent villa that is flooded by the Mediterranean sunlight, there is little else to suggest that the action in *Dogtooth* takes place in Greece and relates to a specifically Greek experience. In fact, the film's premise – the confinement of three "adult" children within their family home, controlled by their authoritarian and overprotective father and compliant mother – could have taken place anywhere. The referential openness of the film makes it accessible to international art-cinema audiences that are not necessarily interested in or attuned to Greek social realities. It also makes it able to uphold a number of allegorical interpretations, some of which may bring it back to specific Greek sensibilities.[6] But apart from the film's formal dimensions, the international visibility and success of *Dogtooth* had a lot to do with the release strategy chosen by Boo Productions, its main producer. As Angelos Venetis, co-owner of Boo Productions, has noted, "our philosophy has been this from the start: from outside to inside [Greece]. Better for *Dogtooth* to open at Cannes and then get the reception back in Greece. If you open in Thessaloniki [Film Festival], it is difficult to even get to Cannes then" (Angelos Venetis, personal communication 2012).

This approach was also adopted for *Attenberg*, a film written, directed, and produced by Athina Rachel Tsangari, a close collaborator of Yorgos Lanthimos (who also appears as an actor in Tsangari's film). *Attenberg* premiered at the Venice Film Festival in September 2010, where it won awards for both its director and the key actress.[7] It also competed successfully at the Thessaloniki Film Festival later that same year, before it was released theatrically in Athens and Thessaloniki.[8] Just like *Dogtooth*, despite being set in Greece – in a semi-abandoned modernist seaside village designed in the 1960s in order to house workers at the nearby factory – it bears few signs of Greekness. The location is significant not only as a semi-abstract backdrop to the action but also in narrative terms because it signifies the life project of the protagonist's dying father, an architect who believed in a modernist vision of progress but experienced its failure. Mechanistic actions, ritualistic dances, and references to animal behaviour (which explain the film's title, a corrupted version of David Attenborough's surname) are used to explore the central character's concerns – the impending death of her father and her sexual inexperience – and the film's key themes. In its multilayered reflexivity, as it indirectly references a number of cinematic traditions, the film's allusions to Greekness are finely distilled through the film's self-aware style.

Dogtooth and *Attenberg* are two of the most critically acclaimed examples of the recent artistic renaissance of Greek cinema, an aesthetic and thematic revival of Greek cinema brought about by a new generation of directors (mostly in their thirties and forties) and their vision, coined by some critics as the "New Greek Current," or the "Weird Wave" of Greek cinema (Demopoulos 2011, 52; Rose 2011). While not all recent films have followed the "from the outside to the inside" (and out again) trajectory (meaning they received critical acclaim abroad first), this is certainly the case for Lanthimos's and Tsangari's films. *Attenberg*'s well-documented Facebook pages trace very effectively the international scope of the film's critical acclaim, thus indicating the success resulting from the maximization of international exposure at film festivals and related events.

Apart from their similar release strategies, these two films are also representative of a changing attitude of Greek filmmakers towards

7.2 Film still from *Attenberg* (2010), directed by Athina Rachel Tsangari. Image courtesy of Haos Film.

funding options. While neither of these films is purely independent – in the sense of being totally financed by the directors themselves (or their families or generous sponsors) – they represent a form of independence whereby their makers do not compromise their creativity because of lack of funding. Instead they devise different ways of getting the job done, including exchanging creative services and working on deferral – a key practice among American independent filmmakers who assist each other in the absence of a larger budget. Looking at the films' production credits, it becomes clear that a range of sources from within Greece, including the Greek Film Center, financed these two films. But rather than exclude them from a definition of *independence* (because they received some state money), it is more useful to explore the specific financing and working practices that were applied. This will help to explain the type of independence they represent.

The mode of production and the manner of financing of the two films is not identical. *Dogtooth* lists Boo Productions as its main producers, and the Greek Film Center and Horsefly Productions as co-producers. *Attenberg* cites Haos Films, Faliro House Productions, Boo Productions, and

Stefi S.A. as producers and lists the support of the Greek Film Center and the European MEDIA program, which is discussed in detail by Teresa Hoefert de Turégano in chapter 3 of this volume. The different status of the Greek Film Center in the credits results from the fact that *Attenberg* went into production *after* Greece's current financial crisis began; therefore, the producers were unable to use the funds previously allocated for completion of the film. This uncertainty as to whether the funds would ever be released led Tsangari to raise the capital by involving new independent producer Christos V. Konstantakopoulos's Faliro House Productions, which covered the costs that should have been met by the Greek Film Center. As an independent producer, Faliro House has no partnerships with other production or distribution companies in Greece or abroad but is increasingly becoming involved in international (mainly American-based) co-productions, which, on the one hand, render the company financially viable and, on the other, create a platform for the international visibility of its films. The company's business (and aesthetic) strategy is to finance projects that are "relevant to an international audience" (Christos V. Konstantakopoulos, personal communication 2012).

A closer look at the financing of the two films within the context of independence reveals that the companies – Boo Productions and Haos Film – represent very different types of independent producers. Boo is a small to medium-sized company that produces mostly commercials for television, while Haos is, as the company's co-founder and main representative Athina Rachel Tsangari calls it, a small "filmmaker's company" whose capital is mainly the "know-how" of its partners (Athena Rachel Tsangari, personal communication 2012).

Boo Productions was established in 2007 to produce commercials for television, but it soon developed a reputation as a company that encouraged creativity and consequently attracted directors with a unique vision. It is in this context that Yorgos Lanthimos initially worked with Boo and became one of its regular directors for commercials. The involvement of Boo in the financing and production of *Dogtooth* happened, as Venetis pointed out, ad hoc: Lanthimos mentioned that he was preparing a funding bid for a script he was working on for the Greek Film Center and that he was looking for co-producers; the owners of Boo read the script in development, liked it, and, as they believed in Lanthimos's directorial abilities, decided to support it (Angelos Venetis, personal communication 2012). It was Boo's first involvement in feature-film production. What becomes evident from this example is that, despite the commercial identity of the company, its involvement with *Dogtooth* was not driven by profit motives but was a gesture towards supporting an artistic project that was not expected to yield financial returns. The film's critical success and international visibility will probably bring some profit to its producers in due time. However, according to Venetis, almost three years after *Dogtooth*'s premiere the company has yet to recoup its investment.[9]

Making films without expecting too much profit also characterizes the work of Athina Rachel Tsangari at Haos Film (Tsangari, personal communication 2012). Originally a student production company while Tsangari and writer and editor Matt Johnson, Haos's co-founder, studied at the University of Texas in the 1990s, Haos was formally established as a limited partnership company in Greece in 2005. It produced Lanthimos's first feature film, *Kinetta* (2005). As Tsangari notes, Haos's company ethos is that of a cooperative, in which its members and partners do not have fixed roles but contribute to production in multiple and flexible ways. The company's name was chosen in order to reflect this ethos, as the word *Haos* alludes both to "chaos" and "house," suggesting a relatively unstructured, small-scale, and hands-on way of working. It is a model of production akin to that of small American independent companies, and, to a certain extent, similar to an older European model of filmmaking, as exemplified by Godard. As opposed to the established ways of working in Greece since the 1980s, whereby the running costs of a film were met by state funds, Haos adopted the American model of independent production of working on deferral, whereby crew and cast become co-producers. Those who do not get paid in advance receive a percentage of the film's profits, if any. Tsangari's experience at the University of Texas in Austin, which involved, among other roles, her being artistic director of the Cinematexas Short Film Festival, was crucial in familiarizing her with such working practices, which are particularly associated with the independent film scene in Austin.[10] Haos's productions all involve co-producers, which supply part of the capital and offer some services on deferral. It is this emphasis on the *artistic dimension of filmmaking*, on investing work and funds not with the expectation of profit but because of the belief in the intrinsic value of the films – as well as the desire to actually make the films rather than spend years waiting for funds – that renders these productions independent, even if to a certain degree they both had some support from the state.

The distribution company Feelgood Entertainment contributed to the promotion of these two films (and to a number of other recent Greek productions). Established in 2008, it covers theatrical distribution and the DVD release of films and supports independent productions by providing a "minimum guarantee." This means that producers receive an advance on their future profits, thus enabling films to be completed. Feelgood has emerged as one of the main distributors of independent films in Greece and Cyprus. It rapidly developed into a medium-sized company amidst the greatest financial crisis facing Greece since the Second World War. As of March 2012, the company employs forty-eight people and has offices and real estate in both Athens and Thessaloniki. The decisions about which films to support are led by the company's "president and directing adviser," Irini Souganidou (personal communication 2012), with the consultation of a team of collaborators. Feelgood, however, is not purely an independent company; its main profits are derived from being the exclusive theatrical distributor (in Greece and Cyprus) for Walt Disney and Sony Pictures Releasing International. It also oversees Sony Pictures Home Entertainment Hellas, a DVD-distribution subsidiary, whose portfolio includes films released by Sony, Disney, and Universal. Feelgood's profile as a for-profit company with a strong commercial identity, which has nonetheless significant investment in independent cinema, is unique in the context of Greece. While commercial distributors, such as Odeon, occasionally promote independent films, their choices are usually geared towards relatively mainstream options. Feelgood, however, has released a number of thematically and aesthetically challenging films apart from *Dogtooth* and *Attenberg*, such as Panos Koutras's *Strella* (2009); Lanthimos's *Alps* (2011), which it also co-produced; and Babis Makridis's *L* (2012). It should be noted that there are also several more purely independent distributors operating in Greece, such as Nutopia Entertainment. These represent a number of recent Greek independent films. However, their marketing and promotional strategies are limited by comparison.

The question of independence in Greek cinema has not been exhausted with the above analysis. There are many varieties and variations of independence and interdependence, some of which require further research, while others are still unfolding. Despite the elusive nature of the term, the concrete perception by filmmakers, audiences, and critics, at different historical junctures, that some films are independent (while others implicitly are not) renders it a fascinating area of study. In this sense, the strong belief among filmmakers, producers, distributors, critics, and international audiences that something significant is happening in Greece's film production – from the development of a different cinematic language to a novel way of representing the country – allows us to discuss several recent films as examples of a new independent Greek cinema.

NOTES

1 *Kynodontas* (2009), translated as *Dogtooth*, directed by Giorgos Lanthimos.
2 This perceived polarity between commerce and art was underpinned by a political polarization between the dominant right and the repressed left, as it was experienced throughout the post–civil war era, which was for the most part dominated by more or less repressive right-wing regimes. The election of a socialist party in 1981 reversed the terms, although the perceived polarities remained for at least one more decade. (For more on the political history of Greece, see Gallant 2001).
3 Thanks to Panayiota Mini who brought to my attention a note by Vasilia Drakaki, which explains that her motivation to finance *Sky* was to prove that it was possible for Greece to make films of high quality. The critical success of the film, as well as the very positive reception at international festivals, validated, as she notes, her project.
4 *Ulysses' Gaze / To Vlemma tou Odissea* (1995) won the Grand Prix at the Cannes Film Festival; *Eternity and a Day / Eoniotita ke mia mera* (1998) won the Palme d'Or at the same festival.
5 The film was mainly funded by one of the largest private television channels, Mega Channel, without any state involvement in financing.
6 See Celik (2013); Lykidis (2014).
7 There was a significant Greek presence at the 2010 Venice Film Festival, widely reported in the Greek media. Apart from *Attenberg*, Syllas Tzoumerkas's *Homecoming / Hora Proelefsis* (2010) and Yorgos Zois's short *Casus Belli* (2010) also opened in different sections of the festival, while Filippos Tsitos's *Plato's Academy / Akadimia Platonos* (2010) had premiered over a year earlier at the Locarno Film Festival and was shown in Venice out of competition (see *To Vima*, 29 August 2010, B2, 2–3).
8 According to data provided by Feelgood Entertainment, *Attenberg* opened in Athens on three screens on 9 December 2010 and had 11,000 admissions.
9 *Dogtooth* opened theatrically in Greece on 22 October 2009 on two screens and had a total of 40,000 admissions (information from Feelgood Entertainment). The expected returns for Boo Productions, however, also include international sales on all platforms.
10 The practice of working on deferral is closely related to the "mumblecore" films, an independent American film movement associated with Austin (Texas) and SXSW Festival. See Van Couvering (2007).

Chapter Eight

Turkish Independent Cinema: Between Bourgeois Auteurism and Political Radicalism

MURAT AKSER

This chapter provides an overview and analysis of the key periods, directors, feature films, and aesthetic styles in Turkish independent cinema. Without financial backing and with little public interest and an authoritarian censorship board – curtailing individualistic and political forms of expression – Turkish independent cinema developed, against all odds, in the 1960s. Since that time independent filmmaking has evolved as a result of different movements led by urban and well-educated directors. Yet, many of these cinematic movements never made it past their fringe existence, because Turkey's mainstream film industry has always relied on the commercial and entertainment aspects of film production. Consequently, these movements played a minor role in the country's overall cinema history; nevertheless, their influence and importance with respect to inspiring new generations of filmmakers continues to this day.

Introduction

As in many countries across Europe, audiences in Turkey saw the screenings of Lumière and Pathé shorts in 1896. During that period, film crews also documented city life in Istanbul and exhibited these films in major European centres (Scognamillo 2003). For their first dramatic features, in the 1920s, Turkish filmmakers adopted the Hollywood model of using genre films and star vehicles to entice the public's interest (Arslan 2011). It would be decades before Turkish film directors developed their own style and focused on the more personal, political, and aesthetic aspects of film. One of the key reasons that independent filmmaking would not proliferate until the 1960s was the lack of support by Yeşilçam – as Turkey's film industry is known – of local film movements. In addition, the political establishment tended to ban or censor the social ideals and opposing political convictions reflected in independent films.

Aesthetically, Turkey's independent filmmakers followed the style of Europe's art-house cinema. Their works reflected an anti-Hollywood stance and, to a certain degree, envy of a prosperous European way of life. The results were films that focused on personal introspection and a critical take on life as seen through the lens of a Western-educated intellectual and filmmaker. As international funding became available in the 1980s, Turkish filmmakers began to showcase their works on the international film festival circuit as well.

An increasing spotlight on political themes brought filmmakers into conflict with the censorship board. As early as 1919, Turkey's review board and censors had banned films in the name of decency. Ahmet Fehim's *Mürebbiye / The Tudor* (1919) was banned because it insulted the French occupying forces in Istanbul after the First World World (Scognamillo 2003). In the following years other films were censored by local police forces, but Metin Erksan's *Karanlık Dünya / Dark World* (1952) was the first to be banned for political reasons. Other independent films were banned over the next two decades. The most infamous ban occurred in the 1980s and involved the destruction of all of Yılmaz Güney's films. When film censorship was finally lifted in 1992, the doors were opened for indie directors to address sensitive political themes in films like *Sonbahar / Autumn* (directed by Özcan Alper, 2008), *Bahoz / The Storm* (Kazım Öz, 2008) and *Press* (Sedat Yılmaz, 2010).

The early independents of the 1960s (such as Halit Refiğ and Erksan) were in favour of a social realist and national cinema, but their efforts were met with little interest from audiences and the general public. Consequently they returned to mainstream cinema. During the 1970s directors who were trained in France, like Ali Zeki Heper, made some films, as did a few documentary producers focusing on short films. Yet this era of relative political freedom for filmmakers was short lived. A brutal military coup crushed dissidents in 1980; independent filmmakers with an opposing political stance were sent to prison or into exile, their films were banned, and in some cases all their film negatives were destroyed.

In the post-1980s era indie films were created by several new directors, such as Ömer Kavur, Ali Özgentürk, and Yusuf Kurçenli. Unfortunantely their films held little appeal for larger audiences. Nevertheless, they were the first to receive foreign funding and recognition at international festivals. A decade later, Turkey's commercial cinema lost its place to television and Hollywood film imports. At the same time new filmmakers – like Yeni Sinemacılar, Serdar Akar, Kudret Sabancı, and Önder Çakar – emerged, gathering a cult following for their directorial style of depicting harsh urban realities. Soon these directors were absorbed into what was left of Turkey's commercial film and television industries.

As described by other authors in this volume – Lydia Papadimitriou with respect to Greece, and Sheila Petty with regard to film production in Africa – increased access to digital cameras and editing equipment provided a boost for independent filmmakers in Turkey as well. In the 2000s directors like Nuri Bilge Ceylan, Semih Kaplanoğlu, Zeki Demirkubuz, and Derviş Zaim offered intimate portraits of life in the city (especially of urban alienation) and created a unique cinema for the modern age. Their films gained recognition at European film festivals, as illustrated by Nuri Bilge Ceylan who won awards at Cannes for every one of his films. Their success provided the basis for a New Cinema Movement (with directors like Yeni Sinema Hareketi), which probably constitutes the best-organized group of independent filmmakers in Turkey. They collaborate on films and assist each other in obtaining development or project funding, consequently achieving international acclaim from critics and scholars alike. Today they even operate their own film theatre (Feriye Sineması) where they regularly gather for panel discussions and screen their favourite films.

In spite of aesthetic and stylistics differences, Turkey's independent cinema movements share many elements with other independent cinemas of the world. From an aesthetic point of view, Turkish independent cinema shares various qualities with American independent cinema; for example, working within a commercial system, but stepping out in order to create new styles and content, is common to both. As for differences between Turkish and Hollywood films, Turkish crews, from directors, actors, and technical crews, are trained on the job rather than obtaining their professional credentials at a film school. Funding is mostly based on private or "personal" investments, especially by producers. Sometimes exhibition chains pre-buy film rights as well.

From a stylistic point of view, Turkish filmmakers aspire to what Erdogan (1998) refers to as a two-dimensionality of the frame rather than the creation of a three-dimensional perspective. Also, films are shot using non-synchronous audio systems and are dubbed later

(Erdogan 2002). Although Turkey's film industry has its own stars and genres, its fast and cheap approach to productions targets the domestic market, which is in direct competition with Hollywood (Akser 2013).

Turkey's independent filmmakers progressively acquired know-how with respect to the funding mechanism and distribution channels for their films. They learned to cope with a stringent censorship board by avoiding explicit political themes in their films and choosing to portray personal angles instead. Yet each movement operated from its own set of ideas and values. They were, and still are, recognized and celebrated by international film festival communities, while their home-grown audiences remain mostly unaware of their existence and their importance.

Declarations of Independence in Turkish Cinema

Independent cinema can be interpreted in many ways, as highlighted in Yannis Tzioumakis's definitions of *independent, indie, indiewood* or Martin Mhando's notion of African independent filmmaking and its complex reactions to Hollywood, globalization, and modernity. Yet there also exist commonalities in the way critics and audiences receive these films. Independent films often win awards at film festivals for their unique representation and interpretation of human existence. At the same time they tend to appeal to niche audiences only and therefore can be box-office failures. In other words, independent films tend to gain prestige but not necessarily widespread popularity. According to Chris Holmlund (Holmlund and Wyatt 2005, 2), independent films suggest "social engagement and/or aesthetic experimentation – a distinctive visual look, an unusual narrative pattern, a self-reflexive style." Indie films are characterized by the personal and indelible imprints that directors impart on narrative, focuses, style, and aesthetics during production. From a broader perspective, auteur films and avant-garde works, as well as identity-based and socially conscious films, all fall under the umbrella of independent cinema. They also tend to reflect the filmmakers unique take on life, human existence, and the status quo. As Emanuel Levy (1999, 2) points out, "ideally, an indie is a fresh, low-budget movie with a gritty style and offbeat subject matter that express the filmmaker's personal vision." It is also a mode of production, as Yannis Tzioumakis (2006, 1) notes: "independent filmmaking consists of low-budget projects made by (mostly) young filmmakers with a strong personal vision away from influence and pressures from the few major conglomerates." Turkish independent cinema is characterized by groups of artists who temporarily coalesce around similar values and ideas that culminate in a "manifesto" about their vision for independent film. These movements form, create a variety of unique works, achieve international acclaim and success with niche audiences at film festivals, and then disperse.

Throughout its history and across its various movements Turkish independent cinema has been an alternative to the country's commercial film industry, the Yeşilçam. Especially in the 1960s, it presented a counterpoint to the national-populist entertainment cinema. With an increase in the number of films produced during that time, the stage was set for the first independent filmmakers to arrive on the scene. Many of these filmmakers were well educated and shared an urban background. Their works focused on the alienation of modern life, class differences, gender issues, and ethnic conflict. They openly expressed political viewpoints in spite of state censorship. In most cases, their films were government funded (or sourced from international funding streams), not for profit, and only enjoyed a limited theatrical run. Overall, production was small scale with no guarantees of distribution.

In the early days of the 1960s, independent-film financing relied on voluntary contributions from cast and crew. At times, producers like Hürrem Erman and Türker İnanoğlu set up special deals with successful directors (for example, Metin Erksan and Halit Refiğ) who agreed to direct a more commercially oriented film in exchange for an independent film the following year. Crews were also compensated accordingly. This practice was popular until the 1990s when indie directors could access grants issued by the Ministry of Culture or by pan-European initiatives like Eurimages (for a detailed discussion about Eurimages, see Teresa Hoefert de Turégano's chapter, "European Union Initiatives for Independent Filmmakers across Europe," in this volume). Some directors set up their own production companies that focused on commercial films such as Memduh Ün's Uğur Film and Ömer Kavur's Alfa Film, in addition to independent productions. However, overall, Turkish indie directors tended to be more interested in developing a unique style that would set them apart from their contemporaries than in accumulating profits at the box office.

Auteurs and Independents of the 1960s

In the 1960s a group of young intellectuals formed a group that envisioned a "cinema for the people" (Refiğ 2009).[1] It would portray "real" people and their everyday problems, underscored by a new aesthetic and formal experimentation that had not been seen in mainstream cinema before. The group was active from 1961 until its peak in 1965, when it became a predominantly social-realist movement, refocused on national cinema production, and then disappeared in 1969. The young directors followed the lead of Kemal Tahir, a leftist author and intellectual known for his socialist interpretation of Turkish history. He inspired the group's films with an anti-capitalist stance, portrayals of alienation in modern society, and the loss of human values. A "cinema for the people' also necessitated films that depicted common social or political incidents, such as a strike, civil disobedience, or rural migration to the big city. Members like Halit Refiğ, Metin Erksan, Memduh Ün, Lütfü Akad, Duygu Sağıroğlu, and Ertem Göreç organized meetings in each other's homes as early as 1959 to discuss the direction they envisioned for Turkish cinema. The turning point for the group came when one of them, Metin Erksan, suddenly won the coveted Berlin Golden Bear Prize in 1962 with *Susuz Yaz / Dry Summer* (1963). Some of their most memorable films include Metin Erksan's *Gecelerin Ötesi / Beyond the Nights* (1960), *Yılanların Öcü / Wrath of the Snakes* (1962), and *Suçlular Aramızda / Criminals Are Among Us* (1964); and Duygu Sağıroğlu's *Bitmeyen Yol / Never-Ending Road* (1965) (Refiğ 2003).[2]

After 1965 and the general election, which resulted in the right-wing Justice Party taking power, Turkey's filmmakers turned increasingly to commercial film production. The National Cinema Movement, which superseded the previous group of indie filmmakers, was linked to the release of two influential films by Metin Erksan, *Sevmek Zamanı / Time to Love* (1965) and *Kuyu / The Well* (1967). The films received neither critical acclaim nor widespread interest from audiences. In addition, distributors refused to distribute *Time to Love*, which was shot and financed entirely by its director. Nonetheless, the film remains a masterpiece of Turkey's cinema owing to its contemplative treatment of fundamental questions: What is the meaning of love? And what is the nature of reality versus illusions? It is reminiscent of the works of Antonioni and Visconti, two directors that Erksan greatly admired. One can sum up the National Cinema Movement as a group of filmmakers who aimed for a unique aesthetic in their films, in particular with regard to embracing Turkey's dramatic arts and traditions. It was a cinema about Turkey's people and the stark contrasts they experience in their daily lives. Thus, it departed from the ideas and aesthetics found in other European films of that time.

8.1 The arrival of the rural family to Istanbul in Halit Refiğ's *Birds of Exile /
Gurbet Kuşları* (1965). Migration was a major issue for the independents of the
1960s. Image courtesy of Gülper Refiğ.

8.2 A man in love with the image of a woman, which was hard for the audience of the 1960s to understand. Metin Erksan's *Time to Love / Sevmek Zamanı* (1965). Image courtesy of Özlem Havuzlu.

An Anomaly: Alp Zeki Heper

One of the most visually original and truly independent Turkish directors was Alp Zeki Heper. Born in 1939, Heper attended film school in France and made experimental shorts that were comparable to Roman Polanski's works from the 1950s. Heper financed most of his films himself, all of which were censored by the authorities. His feature film *Love Stories of the Pale Night / Soluk Gecenin Aşk Hikayeleri* (1966) was banned by the Turkish Film Commission and later the Turkish Supreme Court. It is still unavailable even today. His two short films, *Le parfum de la dame en noir* (1962) and *Dawn* (1963), became accessible online (Vimeo and YouTube) in 2011. These shorts reveal Heper's surrealist tendencies in the tradition of Luis Buñuel. He chose psychoanalytic elements and sexually explicit materials for his films, which conservative audiences found difficult to tolerate. Yet Heper was outside any political movement and pursued arts like poetry and painting away from the spotlight. Frustrated by a society and government that curtailed his sense of creative freedom, Heper gathered all of his creative works and burned them in front of his apartment in 1975. In many ways Heper's career is a tragic example of how a Western-educated, independent Turkish filmmaker with a European aesthetic never received the proper support from Turkey's mainstream industry and, in addition, suffered extensive negative press that lead to the ban of his films (Scognamillo 2003). Heper died of cancer in 1984. In his will he forbade his family from ever screening any of his films in public again.[3]

The 1970s Manifesto of a Group of Young Rebels

When Turkey's National Cinema Movement came to an end, several young directors found new inspiration in Paris's uprisings of May 1968. The Young Filmmakers Group (Genç Sinema Topluluğu) screened their short films at the Hisar Film Festival in Istanbul, the first of its kind to embrace and screen shorts. They were not afraid to take a political stance; in their view, cinema needed to be political and deal with social issues. They protested against Shell Oil Company and the exclusion of Ali Tara's anti-American short film from the Hisar Film Festival (Gevgilili 1989). In their view, cinema was more than entertainment; it represented culture. Therefore, to work as a filmmaker meant to aim for creating a better world, including workers' rights (Paneli 2005). Members of the Young Filmmakers Group such as Artun Yeres, Ahmet Soner, and Veysel Atayman went on to become successful documentary filmmakers and eventually established Turkey's Documentary Filmmakers Association.

Yılmaz Güney's Political Independence

Yılmaz Güney was active in Turkish commercial cinema as an actor, screenwriter, and assistant director before he became an independent filmmaker. Between 1963 and 1972 Güney played the lead role in adventure thrillers, portraying the rugged, crime-fighting, dark hero. In an interview he referred to himself as the "ugly king," a nickname that stuck with producers and audiences alike (Akser 2009). Gradually Güney turned to directing films, where he expressed his socialist convictions, especially with regard to the exploitation of labour. He wrote, directed, acted, and funded his films, which were mostly critical portrayals of

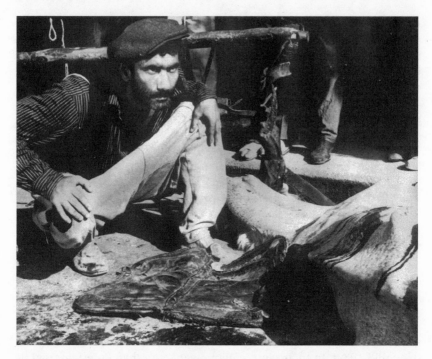

8.3 The stark reality of the poverty of the people in Yılmaz Güney's *Hope/ Umut* (1970). Image courtesy of Fatoş Güney.

Turkey's ruthless capitalist society. Some of his films include *Seyyit Han* (1968), *Hungry Wolves / Aç Kurtlar* (1969), *Hope/Umut* (1970), *Pain/Acı* (1971), *Comrade/Arkadaş* (1974), *The Poor Ones / Zavallılar* (1974), and *The Herd / Sürü* (1978).

In *Hope*, Güney follows the lives of three treasure hunters in contemporary Turkey. His realistic portrayal of the characters and their living conditions was celebrated by film critics as a masterful example of independent cinema. As others before him, Güney eventually came in conflict with the state's censorship board because his films depicted class and ethnic differences and Kurdish culture. He was also imprisoned for accidentally killing a judge during a brawl. Güney directed his last films from prison by proxy. Eventually he escaped from prison, took refuge in France, and completed the last two films, *The Way / Yol* (1982) and *The Wall / Duvar* (1984). Güney won numerous awards at European film festivals.

His political convictions and independent stance inspired future generations of Turkish filmmakers, especially his two assistants, Şerif Gören
and Zeki Ökten, who continued on his artistic path until the mid-1980s.

The Elite Independence of the 1980s

In 1982 Yılmaz Güney was awarded the Palme d'Or at the Cannes Film
Festival for his film *Yol*. Even though *Yol* was banned from being exhibited in Turkey until the 1990s, it opened the way for other independent
filmmakers in Turkey. Europe had taken notice, but, since it was dangerous to make openly political films, Turkish filmmakers channelled
the political through the personal in the form of stories and character
portrayals. They were inspired by the aesthetic and narrative conventions of French cinema and auteurs like Visconti, Antonioni, and Bergman.
They emulated the use of long takes to depict urban alienation and the
psychological complexity of their characters.

The most notable among these directors was Ömer Kavur. He
received his training at a French film school and consequently worked
in France with Alain Robbe-Grillet. Kavur revolutionized Turkish indie
filmmaking by starting his own production company, securing international film funding, attending film festivals worldwide, and having an
uncompromising aesthetic that defied box-office demands. He inspired
other filmmakers like Erden Kıral, Yavuz Özkan, Zülfü Livaneli, Ali
Özgentürk, and Yusuf Kurçenli to follow his artistic path. Their films
focused on personal stories, alienation, and loss of traditions. Like
Kavur, they sought international funding for their films, followed the
global festival circuit, and showed little concern with respect to their
film's profitability or impact on Turkish audiences.

The New Filmmakers Movement (Yeni Sinemacılar), 1997

Film production in Turkey declined dramatically between 1990 and
1996. Yet, strangely enough, a new idealism could be felt among those
who still made independent works. Similar to the earlier indie movement,
filmmakers organized in a cooperative that shared joint authorship of
the works they produced. The New Filmmakers included directors
like Serdar Akar, Önder Çakar, and Kudret Sabancı, all of whom had
received formal training in film schools. The first film associated with
this movement was the critically acclaimed *On Board / Gemide* (1998),
with a screenplay written by Serdar Akar. Set on a merchant ship, it

portrayed the harsh realities of working-class life. *On Board* was followed by the sequel *A Saint in Laleli / Laleli'de Bir Azize* (1998), which focused on a similar storyline (the kidnapping and rape of a young girl) but presented it from a different point of view.

Serdar Akar wrote the script for *Off-Site / Dar Alanda Kısa Paslaşmalar* (2001) and *Maruf* (2001). He made his directorial debut in 2006 with *A Man's Fear of God / Takva* (2006), a film about the inner workings of a religious sect. This was followed by *Valley of the Wolves: Iraq* (2005) and the debut of Akar, together with his friend Kudret Sabancı, as a director for television. Akar became one of the most financially successful directors of his time.

The New Filmmakers Movement flourished with the end of state censorship in 1992 and the emergence of new funding streams for independent directors (for example, Eurimages). Turkey's filmmakers also began to use co-production as a means to develop new films with partners in Europe. Between 1991 and 2002 Turkey's social-democratic Ministry of Culture created a climate for innovative and progressive films with edgy and politically charged topics. Even today, under the more right-wing conservative Adalet ve Kalkınma Partisi (AKP) government, filmmakers continue to tackle socially and politically challenging themes, which have won awards at many European film festivals.

The Festival Auteurs of the 2000s

Turkey's decline in commercial film production between 1990 and 1996 provided an opportunity for independent filmmakers to flourish. The Festival Auteurs released their first features between 1993 and 1994 but only rose to international prominence in the 2000s. They included indie directors like Nuri Bilge Ceylan, Zeki Demirkubuz, Semih Kaplanoğlu, Derviş Zaim, Reha Erdem, and Yeşim Ustaoğlu, also known in the scholarly literature as the founding fathers of the New Turkish Cinema (for example, Atam 2011; Suner 2010; Dönmez-Colin 2008; Arslan 2009). They successfully accessed international development funding and the international film festival circuit. Like their counterparts in other countries, they were celebrated abroad; yet only select audiences, numbering a few thousand, viewed their films at home. Nonetheless, they were respected as artists and for their own non-traditional visual style.

In the 2000s Turkey's commercial cinema and film production recovered, aided greatly by locally controlled theatre chains in support of Turkish film. Beginning in 1997, audiences also began to show a growing

8.4 The lonely individuals of the 2000s indie directors in Zeki Demirkubuz's *Underground/Yeralti* (2012). Image courtesy of Zeki Demirkubuz.

interest in blockbuster films as well as Turkish mainstream productions. Both the television and the advertising industries were responsible for this growth as they encouraged young professionals to enter the field. Art-house-film audiences also increased during this period,[4] and the Turkish media commented favourably on new independent production (Akser 2010). Indeed, SİYAD, the Turkish Association of Film Critics, has presented an award for best director at every film festival since 2000.

The Festival Auteurs of the 2000s developed and honed their unique style for over a decade. They preferred themes that portrayed the past through a lens of nostalgia, such as small-town life and the yearning for a lost childhood. They found inspiration in the works of Dostoevsky and Andrei Tarkovsky. They were independent from Turkey's commercial film industry Yeşilçam and showed no interest in the blockbuster boom of the late 1990s. Yet they benefited from the theatre proprietors' fostering of Turkey's film talent and consequently found a welcoming exhibition space for their films. Noteworthy examples of the movement's films include *Somersault in a Coffin / Tabutta Rövaşata* (Derviş Zaim, 1996), *Innocence/Masumiyet* (Zeki Demirkubuz, 1997), *Journey to the Sun / Güneşe Yolculuk* (Yeşim Ustaoğlu, 1999), *Distant/Uzak* (Nuri Bilge Ceylan, 2002), *Times and Winds / Beş Vakit* (Reha Erdem, 2006), and *Honey/Bal* (Semih Kaplanoğlu, 2010).

8.5 A man alone. Ahmet Uluçay reinvented the way in which one man, by himself, can make film. Image courtesy of Ezel Akay.

Ahmet Uluçay: Standing All Alone

Ahmet Uluçay is unequivocally the most impressive of all independent filmmakers in Turkish cinema. His humble origins in a village in mid-Anatolia never posed a hurdle to his forging a career that began with underground films in the 1990s and led to critical success with feature films such as *Boats out of Watermelon Rinds / Karpuz Kabuğundan Gemiler Yapmak* (2004). With no formal education or training, Uluçay mastered the art of filmmaking by meeting members of a travelling cinema show in his village and by building his own camera. His style and vision were unique in Turkish film. Uluçay died from a brain tumour in 2009. His films remain as expressions of the most distinctively independent filmmaking practices in Turkish cinema.

New Cinema Movement (Yeni Sinema Hareketi), 2007

Turkey's independent film movements tend to reinvent themselves decade after decade. The more organized of these movements acquire a designated theatre and multi-purpose space for exhibiting their films. They share this space with production companies, film festivals, and industry training workshops. The latest group of filmmakers coalescing around the New Cinema Movement made their initial mark with the following films: Özcan Alper's *Autumn / Sonbahar* (2008), Seyfi Teoman's *Summer Book | Tatil Kitabı* (2008), and Hüseyin Karabey's *My Marlon and Brando | Gitmek* (2008).

In 2008 Alper, Teoman, and Karabey formed a union in support of first-time film directors. The following year, Seren Yüce's film *Majority/Çoğunluk* (2010) firmly established the reputation of Turkey's new independent film movement when Yüce received the Lion of the Future award at the Venice Film Festival. Unlike previous movements, members of the New Cinema Movement never disbanded but continue to collaborate on film. Their common themes and styles are exemplified in two masterpieces, the films *Majority* and *Autumn*.

Majority tells the story of a typical middle-class Turkish family living in Istanbul. The father, a patriarch and a building contractor, embodies the country's unbridled capitalism; the mother silently preserves the domestic order. But their son is a lost, clueless teenager who has given up on his dreams. He and his Kurdish girlfriend are unlikely to fulfil their parents' expectations of settling into a stable home life in the near future.

The film reveals its alliance to the New Cinema Movement right from the start when the movement's official logo is displayed as part of the opening credits. Erkan Can (the captain from *On Board*), a member of the previous indie movement, assumes a brief role as a taxi driver, thus showing a connection between the New Filmmakers Movement and the New Cinema Movement.

Majority also focuses on the post-2000 "shopping mall generation" who are clueless of the ideological and political frameworks underpinning their lives. Mertkan, the son, is raised to become a typical consumer, someone who follows an impulse to satisfy his material needs. He eats at fast-food restaurants, hangs out with his friends, and shows off an expensive new car. His relationships with women are insincere as he exploits them mostly for sex. As such, the film is a powerful critique of capitalist consumer society, legitimized by law and state, as well as the patriarchal, nuclear family. Race is also an important issue in *Majority*. Mertkan's father hates his girlfriend, Gül, because she is of Kurdish descent.

Another quintessential film of the New Cinema Movement is Özcan Alper's *Autumn/Sonbahar* (2008). *Autumn* is the story of the final days of

Yusuf, a political prisoner, who has just been released from prison for health reasons. He returns to his hometown, Artvin, a city bordering on Georgia. Yusuf is greeted by his only living relative, his elderly mother. He goes downtown and meets Eka, a young Georgian prostitute. Eka is moved by his story: Yusuf has lost his father and his love while in prison. He tries to talk Eka into going to Batumi with him. However, Eka leaves him before he can arrange a trip to Georgia for both of them.

Like *Majority*, *Autumn* reflects a loss of idealism and the isolation felt by members of a minority group living amidst a different ethnic community. Ethnic, social, class, and gender differences therefore lie at the core of the film. Alper accentuates this sense of loss, alienation, and the internal conflict of a man at the end of his life, by choosing the gloomy northeastern Black Sea region of Turkey as a backdrop. Yusuf and his family speak Hemsin, a version of Armenian. The Armenians have long left Turkey, during and after the First World War. There is only a small population left in Hemşin, unnoticed by the rest of the world.

Alper chose to depict Yusuf's alienation through the metaphors of nature. His lens captured a landscape that was equally isolated and alienating. It framed the lost battle of an aspiring society, the languished ideals of socialist reform, and personal sacrifices. In *Autumn*, Yusuf's existence continues to resemble that of a prisoner; his home feels like a jail cell, cut off from the outside where there is life, vegetation, and people. Yusuf is mostly shown from behind, which emphasizes his loneliness and loss. Alper contrasted the psychological stagnation of his main character by juxtaposing images of isolation and distance, achieved through a vast landscape, from the deep blue sky and sea to snow-capped mountain ranges to the endless horizon. In one scene Yusuf stands on a pier and stares at the sea. His inner conflicts are echoed by the giant waves crashing against the shore, as if they could wash away all his sorrows.

The founding directors of the New Cinema Movement remain active filmmakers to this day. Özcan Alper made *Future Lasts Forever / Gelecek Uzun Sürer* (2011), and Pelin Esmer directed *Watchtower / Gözetleme Kulesi* (2012). One of the group's members, Seyfi Teoman, passed away in 2012; he leaves behind a legacy of award-winning films like *Our Grand Despair / Bizim Büyük Çaresizliğimiz* (2011), which was nominated for the Berlin Golden Bear Award in 2011. New filmmakers like Tolga Karaçelik (*Toll Booth / Gişe Memuru*, 2010) and Tayfur Aydın (*Trace / İz-Reç*, 2011) have joined the movement. With films that highlight the alienation of modern life and personal loss, the New Cinema

8.6 The dying revolutionary experiences loss in its depth in Özcan Alper's
Autumn/Sonbahar (2008). Image courtesy of Özcan Alper.

Movement continues to shine at international festivals. Films like
Beyond the Hill / Tepenin Ardı and *Mold/Küf* (2012) count as their most
recent achievements.

Conclusion

Independent filmmakers in Turkey have had to face many challenges,
from lack of funding to censorship and persecution. Eventually their
unique oeuvre and contribution to the cultural life of the country was recognized. In spite of influences from their European counterparts, they
followed a unique vision of Turkey's independent cinema. The directors
came mostly from elite and urban backgrounds. They included theorists
like Halit Refiğ, great stylists like Metin Erksan, and odd mavericks like
Alp Zeki Heper, who dared to take on the establishment but tragically
lost. In every decade new and talented directors emerged who labelled
their movement as ground-breaking and unique; yet each of Turkey's
independent film movements has dealt with similar themes. Even today,

filmmakers like Ahmet Uluçay set out to shoot feature films in remote villages with minimal input from collaborators and all by themselves. At the same time, many indie filmmakers embrace the growing internationalization of the film community. They show their films at festivals and enjoy the devotion of their niche audiences. While some filmmakers like horror director Tan Tolga Demirci (*Gomeda*, 2007) are ignored by critics, Turkish independent filmmaking continues to thrive and will most likely leave its indelible mark on cinema history.

NOTES

1 *Halk Sineması* in Turkish.
2 Additonal titles include Halit Refiğ's *Şehirdeki Yabancı* / *Stranger in the City* (1963), *Gurbet Kuşları* / *Birds of Exile* (1964), and *Haremde Dört Kadın* / *Four Women in the Harem* (1964); Ertem Göreç's *Otobüs Yolcuları* / *Bus Riders* (1961), and *Karanlıkta Uyananlar* / *Awaking in the Dark* (1965).
3 A similar victim of independence was Atilla Tokatlı, another Institut des Hautes Etudes Cinématographiques (IDHEC) graduate who made *The Street That Led to the Sea* / *Denize İnen Sokak* in 1960. The film was shown at the Karlovy-Vary, Locarno, and Venice film festivals and won the best film award in İzmir Film Festival. Tokatlı produced his second feature in 1964 and then left filmmaking forever. Both directors were interested in the psychology of the alienated individual and the surreal-abstract esthetics of European cinema (Sivas 2011).
4 According to *boxofficeturkiye.com*, the number of viewers who came to see a typical Nuri Bilge Ceylan film increased from a few thousand to 300,000 with his film *Three Monkeys* (2008).

Chapter Nine

Filmmaking in Iraq: A Rebirth

MARY P. ERICKSON

In 2003, U.S. forces bombed the National Film Archives in Iraq, obliterating its collection of celluloid almost completely. A journalist came through the archives and discovered eight remnants of celluloid, which amounted to 14.3 seconds of film. This destruction is a physical manifestation of the way in which the Iraqi film industry contracted and nearly vanished under the regime of Saddam Hussein and as a result of wars with Iran, Kuwait, and the United States.

Yet within a dangerous and difficult environment a nascent film industry has begun to re-emerge, complete with passionate and skilled filmmakers and other film professionals devoted to reclaiming Iraq's cinematic culture. Despite the country's risky security situation, particularly from 2003 to 2007, multiple filmmakers have endeavoured to tell Iraqi stories, to rebuild Iraqi culture, and to participate in the global film industry. Many of these filmmakers are exiles or part of the Iraqi diaspora, and they work to draw attention to the burgeoning filmmaking movement within their native country.

A consideration of independent film in the Iraqi context requires an understanding of the full picture of filmmaking in the country. To many working Iraqi filmmakers today, the articulation of *independent* versus *dependent* filmmaking is a moot point, given the condition of the industry today. Independent film is the only one that exists.

Iraqi cinema has had business relationships with a number of institutions (including Egyptian film studios, governmental cultural agencies, and Hollywood) that have, alternatively, contributed to and detracted from its development. Filmmakers operating outside of these institutions have shaped the Iraqi film industry nearly as equally. With so little consistent support from any one source as to constitute a dominant institution, Iraqi filmmakers generally have had to cobble together resources wherever and from whomever they have been able; they often work with funding sources from Europe (for example, France's World Cinema Fund, the Dutch embassy, or the UK Film Council) or the Middle East (for example, Al Jazeera or the Al Sumaria satellite television network in Iraq). As a result, the nature of Iraqi cinema can be characterized historically as one of transnationality. Certainly, characteristics of Iraqi cinema today reflect an internationally collaborative dynamism that permits its growth. We see these characteristics in modes of production, distribution, marketing, and exhibition.

This chapter explores the conditions and realities of filmmaking in Iraq and for Iraqis in a country marked by war, occupation, infrastructural collapse, and cultural stifling. It focuses on the nature of filmmaking in Iraq, the conditions under which filmmaking is happening roughly ten years after the start of the war, and some of the individuals creating and supporting the national film industry. This requires an understanding of the history of Iraqi cinema, from the early days of exhibition-only exposure to filmmaking, to a so-called golden age starting in the mid-1940s, to the repressive and propagandistic influence on cinema during Saddam Hussein's reign. I will then turn to the contemporary era, describing the climate of filmmaking at the start of the war in 2003 and the development of current infrastructures and resources for filmmakers.

At the core of this research are questions relating to the way that cinema develops and survives, the role of exiled filmmakers – and the global film community – in sustaining that cinema, and ultimately how culture endures despite repression and destruction.

Considering "Iraqi" Cinema

As noted by Terri Ginsberg (2009), there is a considerable lack of academic reflection and analysis on the condition of the media landscape in Iraq in the era of war and occupation in the 2000s. While the study of Arab and Middle Eastern cinema has enjoyed increased attention in the past several years, the research has focused much more closely on other countries in the region such as Iran, Egypt, and Palestine (for example, Shafik, 2007; Khatib, 2006). Iraq has received only limited attention in the literature; Italian scholar Lucia Sorbera (2009) is one who has examined to some degree the nature of Iraqi cinema in the mid- to late 2000s. It is likely that Iraq has been omitted from in-depth analysis of cinema in the region because there has, at least in the last two to three decades, been very little filmmaking activity. But, as this chapter shows, the rapid and dedicated re-emergence of film production in Iraq warrants close attention. In particular, it is necessary to highlight the ways in which filmmaking activity has overcome the obstacles presented by war and occupation.

It must be noted too that the very notion of "Iraqi" cinema is complex and subject to interpretation. We can note at least four different types of film production that is in some way tied to Iraq cinema. These include Iraqi filmmakers working within the country, many of whom graduated from or now attend film programs in Iraq. Others have gained film-making skills and now work in satellite television, while others have non-film-related jobs and produce films as time and finances allow.

Kurdish filmmakers can be considered another – and in many ways separate – group of filmmakers working in Iraq. The Kurdistan region in the northern part of the country was established as an autonomous federal region in 2005. Kurdish cinema, according to many, must be recognized separately from Iraqi cinema. Iraqi-Kurd filmmaker Adnan Osman (*Death Triangle*, 2012) champions Kurdish cinema, and increasingly there is strong support for this cinema in many festivals around the world, including the London Kurdish Film Festival, the Montreal Kurdish Film Festival, and the Köln First Kurdish Film Festival ("Iraqi Film Fails" 2012).

Third, we can acknowledge the contribution of exiled filmmakers who left Iraq for political and security reasons and who settled in Europe, the United States, Canada, and elsewhere. These filmmakers include, among many others, Jano Rosebiani (now based in the United States), Koutaiba al-Janabi (UK), Ja'far Abd al-Hamid (UK), Hineer Saleem (France), Abbas Fahdel (France), Mohamed al-Daradji (UK), Ahmed Kamal (Netherlands), Baz Shamoun (Canada), and Maysoon Pachachi (UK).

Fourth, there are also foreign filmmakers who have filmed in Iraq especially since the beginning of the war with the United States in 2003. These include filmmakers, frequently Americans, who seek to capture stories of average Iraqi citizens and bring them to the rest of the world: for example, individuals like Mike Shiley, a filmmaker based in Portland, Oregon, who fabricated journalist credentials to gain entry into Iraq in December 2003 to shoot his documentary *Inside Iraq: The Untold Story* (2004). Seattle-based James Longley focused on various individuals in his documentary *Iraq in Fragments* (2006). Both films received significant attention in the United States; Longley's film was even nominated for an Academy Award in 2007. These filmmakers, along with others, have helped draw attention to the political and social situation in Iraq.

This chapter focuses primarily on the first three groups of filmmakers: Iraqis in Iraq, Kurds in Kurdistan in northern Iraq, and exiled Iraqis and Kurds who still very much identify as Iraqi or Kurdish filmmakers despite their foreign residences.

Question of Independence

The definition of *independent film*, as demonstrated throughout this book, can vacillate from independence from Hollywood to independence from the state to independence from regionally dominant industries. In the case of Iraq, independent filmmaking might be described by all three of these definitions, albeit rather scantly in each form.

Some of the more common indicators of independence in filmmaking might include the manner of financing, production, or distribution; many scholars even apply the definition of American independent filmmaking to the international context (Tzioumakis 2006). We see this evidenced in several chapters of this book (for example, Lydia Papadimitriou's study of Greek cinema or Mark David Ryan's discussion of Australian cinema). Other indicators might include a film's narrative or stylistic content. However, as is the case with many of the national case studies in this book, it may not be overly productive in comparing ways in which filmmakers produce films to differentiate between filmmakers who are *more* independent than others. There is a general consensus that the conditions of Iraqi film production, distribution, and exhibition are by definition independent. As filmmaker Mohamed al-Daradji notes, "there is nothing but 'independent' filmmaking" in Iraqi cinema (email to author, 2 December 2011). Filmmaker Koutaiba al-Janabi concurs: "I think there is only independent filmmaking. There are many independent filmmakers who studied in Europe for example and came back to make films" (email to author, 16 February 2013).

No matter the skill level or source of funding, Iraqi filmmakers are independent because they all initiate their own projects with their (often limited) connections. There are no film studios, and there is extremely limited government involvement. Equipment, resources, and infrastructure are also limited or non-existent. Film production is generally financed by many partners – or sometimes only the filmmaker. Larger productions have secured the support of funding sources that include the Kurdistan Regional Government, the UK Film Council, the

Sundance Institute, and Al Jazeera. Distribution is typically limited and coordinated by the filmmaker. There is no formal film distribution in Iraq, and most filmmakers rely on the festival circuit to disseminate their films. Some distribution may be secured in foreign territories, particularly for films that may have achieved some level of critical acclaim at a major festival, such as the festivals in Dubai, Rotterdam, Singapore, and Munich. Exhibition is also limited in Iraq, with few cinemas in operation in the country (as discussed later in this chapter).

The low level of financial resources, coupled with the lack of professional resources and equipment within the country, has had an impact on the types of films that are made. Isabelle Stead, a producer who works with Iraqi filmmaker Mohamed al-Daradji, says, "Production for documentaries is easier in Iraq than [for] fiction as we needed less resources" (email to author, 2 January 2013).

Indeed, there is still little consideration about the marketability of Iraqi films, as is the case in more commercially oriented filmmaking in the United States and other more stable filmmaking markets. The Iraqi film industry is slowly rebuilding itself by first addressing the painful recent histories that mark and define its relationships. Many Iraqi filmmakers emphasize the cathartic experience of delving into the difficulties presented by living in a war-torn country, particularly after the fall of Saddam in 2003. Some films that explore these themes include *Return to the Land of Wonders* (Maysoon Pachachi, 2004), in which Pachachi accompanies her father on his return to Iraq after two decades of exile; *16 Hours in Baghdad* (Tariq Hashim, 2004), documenting Hashim's own return to Iraq after years of exile; *Leaving Baghdad* (Koutaiba al-Janabi, 2010), about a cameraman working for Saddam Hussein, and his struggle to reconcile the horrific activities he filmed in that position (the film intercuts actual footage of torture and killings); and *In My Mother's Arms* (Mohamed al-Daradji, 2011), a film about thirty-two boys at a Baghdad orphanage. As filmmaker Ja'afar Abd Al-Hamid notes, "it is going to be hard for Iraqi filmmakers to get out from this cloud of chaos ... The next generation of filmmakers might focus on other aspects" (Vettath 2012).

This subject matter tends to overshadow most of the aesthetic shortcomings of these films. For example, one American film review of *In My Mother's Arms* was rather forgiving of the film's technical and aesthetic problems, noting that "raw emotional content trumps rough filmmaking style" (Simon 2011). Al-Janabi's film *Leaving Baghdad*, according to another critic, "isn't glossy, stylistic or even edited well but it needn't be because when a victim appears before you, tied up, gagged and teary eyed with fear – you take this very seriously" (Kayastha 2012).

So little unfiltered video footage emerged from Iraq in the first few years of the Iraq war that films – both narrative and documentary – function as a window into how Iraq "really" looked and felt in this period. The everyday existence of the Iraqi people was often missing from the international narrative of the war, dominated instead by imagery of American military prowess and the installation of democracy. There were nearly 26 million people living in Iraq in 2003 whose stories were not widely told on the global stage; soon, there was a burgeoning global hunger for those stories, particularly in the art world (of which the film festival circuit is part). Iraqi filmmaking has been lauded for what it gives the outside world: a view into the lives of regular citizens. Film critic Deborah Young (2010) writes about Oday Rasheed's film *Qarantina* (2010): "Clearly, the film intends to hold up a mirror to Iraqi society at large, but its metaphoric quality is really the least interesting thing about it. More intriguing are the realistic glimpses of life outside the house, where director Rasheed is adept at conveying the anguishing atmosphere of occupied Baghdad." For film critic Alissa Simon (2011), the immediacy of the camerawork brings the viewer closer to the experience of living in Iraq during this time. In *In My Mother's Arms*, Mohamed al-Daradji's documentary about war orphans, "the camera does provide a you-are-there feeling, even reeling, like the boys, from an explosion close to the safe house."

On-location, guerilla-style filming marks most contemporary films shot in Iraq, particularly those filmed in the mid-2000s, as filming itself was a dangerous activity. Many non-actors are used in these films, although Iraq has a fairly strong tradition in theatre and therefore experienced actors who move into film acting. The technical quality of many films is relatively poor, especially for Western audiences accustomed to a certain level of technical achievement. As will be discussed later in this chapter, professional experience in cinematography, editing, and other filmmaking functions is low for many Iraqi filmmakers, with few mentors to assist new filmmakers in developing their skills. The more experienced filmmakers are those who reside in Europe or the United States and who have more ready access to professional development and quality equipment.

International partnerships and resources have been most influential in the contemporary era in shaping the viability of the Iraq film industry. As will be discussed, filmmakers who fled Iraq – no matter in the 1970s or the 2000s – have called upon foreign connections to finance, produce, and distribute their films. Today there seems to be international recognition – at least within the global film community – of the adversity that Iraqi filmmakers undergo to make films. The global visibility of Iraqi work has increased, and more partnerships have developed to bring Iraqi stories to the screen. Film festival organizers in Hamburg and Milan in 2007, for example, were "convinced of the necessity to promote the work of courageous Iraqi filmmakers. Thus, while some young Iraqis are fighting to produce their films, their European counterparts are engaged in their distribution" (Sorbera 2009, 321). This international collaboration is the central marker that identifies the condition of Iraqi filmmaking today.

A Brief History of Iraqi Cinema

It is important to trace the history of Iraqi cinema, particularly in light of the question of independence and transnational participation, because this history has only been documented to a limited extent elsewhere.[1] The history recognizes the development of the industry and the factors that led to its current condition.

The first feature film to be produced in Iraq was an Iraqi-Egyptian co-production; the Egyptian Misr Studio filmed *Cairo-Baghdad* (Ahmed Bader Khan, 1946) in Iraq, using an Egyptian crew and an Iraqi cast. The same year, *Son of the East* was produced by another Iraqi-Egyptian company, Al-Rashid Film Company; this film also used Iraqi actors, as well as Sudanese and Egyptian ones, and was directed by an Egyptian (Allawi 1983, 191). A handful of other films in the subsequent decade were produced – some by international collaborations (such as *Alia and Ossam*, 1948, which was financed by and starred Iraqis and was directed by Frenchman André Shatan) and some by fully Iraqi groups (such as *Fetneh and Hassan*, 1953, which used an entirely Iraqi crew) (Allawi 1983, 191). The private sector became more closely involved, as did increased international partnerships through the film production units of the British-run Iraqi Petroleum Company and the United States Information Agency (ibid., 194). Filmmakers enjoyed increased access to professional equipment and more skilled crew, while others travelled abroad to study filmmaking. These individuals returned with new-found skills and artistic sensibilities to cultivate the national industry. Films produced during this era included *Who Is Responsible?* (1956) and *Said Effendy* (1957), both of which tackled the political and social realities of Iraq of this period.

It is important to note that while there may have been some level of increased filmmaking activity during this time, it was still quite limited. According to Roy Armes (2010, 15), there were only fourteen feature films made between 1945 and 1959, and only one filmmaker, Hyder al-Omer, made more than one film (he made two). This period of productivity initiated by the private sector was short lived, however, as the political landscape underwent significant changes with the country's 1958 revolution. The private sector and its corollary financing allowed for a basic infrastructure to be put in place, but soon the state involved itself in filmmaking because it recognized the potential of the film industry as an economic, political, and social vehicle. As George Sadoul noted, many Arab governments moved towards integrating cinema into their national aims because they considered cinema "the best and most influential means of propagating culture and national ideas among the people" (Sadoul 1966, 135).

The first governmental subsidies of the industry were instituted in 1959 with the establishment of the General Organization of Cinema and Theatre (GOCT) under the Ministry of Culture and National Guidance.[2] This organization's objectives were to encourage the growth of a film industry, supporting infrastructural and professional development. As well, the GOCT dispensed subsidies and prizes to artists and writers to "assure successful artistic and literary production in the spheres of the Cinema and the Theater" (Chebli 1966, 119).

Over the next decade the General Organization of Cinema and Theatre grew in size and doubled its capital. However, only three feature films were produced under the GOCT in the 1960s, including *The Collector* (1966), *Good Omen* (1967), and *The Liberal's Bridge* (1969). These films could be construed as the beginnings of a national cinema, with themes of social justice and freedom resonating throughout (Allawi 1983, 196). One of the GOCT's artistic divisions, the Cinema Service, produced over fifty documentaries and short films on topics ranging from art to labour to the military; it also co-produced numerous feature-length films with the United Arab Republic (Egypt and Syria) and other Arab countries ("The Iraqi Cinema in 1964" 1966, 185–6). In addition, a number of cinematographic units operated within various governmental ministries, including the ministries of Health, Defence, Education, Agriculture, and Transport (Nouri 1986, 64).

The GOCT went through a few iterations before it was restructured under the Ministry of Culture and Information in 1975. Under the GOCT, filmmaking in Iraq needed to actively support the country's cultural, political, and economic development. As such, films were overtly political in tone, but they still lacked professional quality and expertise. They did, however, continue to participate to some degree on the international stage; many Iraqi films were screened – and some honoured with prizes – at film festivals around the world, including Moscow, Locarno, Berlin, Tashkent, Damascus, and Leipzig (Allawi 1983, 203).

The private sector continued to operate during this period as well, producing more commercial films rooted in genres such as musical comedies and melodramas, including *Autumn Leaves* (Hikmat Labib, 1963) and *The Night Watchman* (Khalil Chawqi, 1967).

It soon became apparent, however, that public financing and priorities would turn filmmaking into a primarily political tool, marking the evolution of propagandistic cinema in Iraq. Documentaries such as *Houses in That Alley* (Qassim Hawal, 1977) and *The Experiment* (Fuad El-Tohami, 1978) were produced, emphasizing conditions for Iraqi peasants and labourers. This move intensified as Saddam Hussein rose to power in the late 1970s. The GOCT financed Iraq's most expensive production, *Al-Qadisiyya* (Salah Abou Sayf), released in 1981 at a cost of $15 million; it was an international collaboration with a director from Egypt and cast members from Iraq, Lebanon, Syria, and elsewhere in the Middle East. Although it reportedly played at every movie theatre in the country and was Iraq's official submission to the Cannes Film Festival that year, it failed miserably at the box office (Allawi 1983, 204, 238; Bengio 1998, 174). The film was a move to reinforce messages of Arab unity and to inflame popular support for Saddam Hussein (rooted in historical mythology) at the beginning of the Iran-Iraq war.

During Saddam Hussein's regime nearly all filmmaking served propaganda purposes, containing a "coherent and often blunt political message" that reflected the "revolution and developments in ancient and modern Iraqi history" (McCarthy 2002). Yet still, the internationally collaborative nature of Iraqi filmmaking continued even for the most overtly nationalistic films. Saddam Hussein's rise to the presidency was retold – allegedly with much artistic licence – in *The Long Days* (1980), a six-hour epic directed by the Egyptian Tawfiq Saleh; the production was rumoured to have employed British editor Terence Young (Aburish 2000, 48). Another epic, the three-hour *Al-Mas'ala Al-Kubra / The Clash of Loyalties* and *The Great Question* (Mohamed Shukri Jamil), was produced in 1983 and financed by Saddam himself. This film also employed international cast and crew members, featuring British actor

Oliver Reed in a key role, the noted British cinematographer Jack Hild-yard, the Royal Philharmonic Orchestra of London playing the musical score, and an additional eighty-eight foreign crew (out of a total crew of one hundred) and forty-four foreign actors (nearly half of the cast) (Nouri 1986, 153).[3]

As the lengthy and devastating Iran-Iraq war continued for nearly a decade, film production was practically non-existent. Many filmmakers left the country in order to continue producing, while others ceased film work altogether. Soon thereafter, in 1990, Saddam Hussein invaded Kuwait, and the resulting United Nations sanctions on Iraq severely affected the film industry. As Rory McCarthy notes, "new equipment, film stock, and chemicals for film laboratories were forbidden under new import rules designed to curb Saddam's chemical, biological, and nuclear weapons programme" (McCarthy 2002). Government financing of the film industry dried up, as did domestic film production itself.

Within Iraq the political and economic climate in the 1990s and early 2000s did not support much filmmaking. A handful of filmmakers, including Oday Rasheed, produced some films or videos. Rasheed briefly attended the Academy of Fine Arts in Baghdad in the late 1990s but was allegedly expelled. He produced a number of experimental videos, including *Mud Whiteness* (1997), *Another Introduction* (1998), and *Gilgamesh: The Epic ... The Place* (2002), but underground films "only circulated among friends" (New York University 2006; Kettelhake 2005).

Others also studied filmmaking at the Academy of Fine Arts and were challenged to change their film production processes because of a dearth of film equipment and film stock. Those who had graduated from film school did not even have access to film cameras, according to filmmaker Maysoon Pachachi. "There weren't any during sanctions," she said. "If a camera fell into disrepair, you couldn't fix it. There was no digital equipment" (Clarke 2009). Yet video cameras circulated, and, according to Rory McCarthy (2002), the students "continue[d] to direct their own movies, relying now on video rather than celluloid." We can see this type of technical and stylistic accommodation – moving from film to video – for a number of independent filmmakers, such as those working in Peru (see the chapter by Gabriela Martínez), and, indeed, this trend has continued to include digital video in the past decade, as illustrated by numerous contributors to this volume.

Especially after the American invasion of Iraq in 2003, filmmaking became a highly dangerous activity in Iraq. Bombings, kidnappings, and violence were very real threats for filmmakers. Many Iraqi filmmakers, particularly those living abroad, were only able to shoot their films quickly and surreptitiously in order to not attract much attention.

Oday Rasheed was the first filmmaker to shoot a feature-length film in Iraq after the war had started in 2003. He assembled a crew in November that year, and, although production lasted until the following April, they only spent about thirty days on set because of the extremely dangerous security conditions (Sorbera 2009). Because the UN sanctions on the country continued during this period, film equipment was nearly non-existent within the country; nor was it easy for filmmakers to bring equipment with them as they entered the country. For his film, *Underexposure* (2005), Rasheed used thirty-year-old Kodak film stock from Saddam's archives that he had somehow obtained from the black market. As the story goes (promoted heavily by *Underexposure*'s marketing), Rasheed did not even know if the film stock was usable; he later consulted with Kodak, which recommended he "underexpose" the film, and thus the name of the film was born (Kettelhake 2005). He and some members of the crew funded the project by selling some of their possessions and through local fund-raising (Deasy 2010). The film soon secured international attention from, among others, X-Filme Creative Pool, a German production company co-founded by Tom Twyker (*Run Lola Run*, 1998). It was then brought to the international film festival circuit in 2005 and screened at festivals such as Rotterdam, Singapore, Durban, and Munich. The timeliness of "the first feature film shot in the country since the fall of Saddam Hussein" played to the sensibilities and concerns of an international art audience that was suddenly aware of the cinema of Iraq (Deasy 2010).

Mohamed Al-Daradji is another filmmaker who ventured to Iraq from his home in Europe to shoot a feature-length film in the early days of the Iraq–United States war. A Dutch-Iraqi national, Al-Daradji returned to Baghdad in 2004 to film *Ahlaam/Dreams* (2006), despite the warnings by his parents (who still resided in Baghdad) that the security situation in the country was extremely dangerous. He chronicled his experiences of filming in Iraq in his documentary *Iraq: War, Love, God, and Madness* (2008). Having smuggled some equipment across the border with him, he also acquired one of the few cameras still available in the country. He began the project with a certain level of naivety about the state of security in Baghdad. During principal photography the production was targeted by insurgents, and his sound engineer was shot in the leg, members of his crew were abducted, and his make-up person was beaten. Al-Daradji seriously questioned the purpose of finishing the film, but his crew, who were deeply invested in the film and what it would mean to complete any film in Iraq, persuaded him to continue.

The history of filmmaking in Iraq has been intertwined with the history of global cinema because there has been a much stronger tendency towards international partnership than strictly Iraqi involvement. Historically, assistance with financing, production, and distribution has involved Egyptian, Syrian, and British sources. Today many film productions use European-based film funds such as France's World Cinema Fund and the Hubert Bals Fund (also used to finance independent films in Malaysia and parts of Africa; see the corresponding chapters in this volume for further discussion). This history indicates that heavy reliance on international collaborations only goes so far, however, because the Iraqi film industry's vitality has suffered from a lack of infrastructure, investment, and resources.

As the film industry here has entered the twenty-first century, and as another decade of war has ended, Iraqi filmmakers are finding new opportunities to instate an Iraqi role in the process of global film production, distribution, and exhibition. Threaded through many interactions between Iraqi filmmakers, however, are themes of exile, which significantly influence the approach both to filmmaking, in process and content, and to building an industry at home.

Filmmakers in Exile

Themes of exile have permeated Iraqi filmmaking over the last thirty or more years. Many filmmakers, writers, and other artists went into exile in the late 1970s or thereafter. Many left just prior to the start of the Iran-Iraq war, while others left the country during the war. These include filmmakers Maysoon Pachachi (who went to the UK) and Baz Shamoun (to Canada), and actress Nahida al-Rammah (to the UK). Others were children when they left Iraq with their parents, such as Dena Al-Adeeb and Usama Alshaibi, and many of these individuals became filmmakers or media artists in adulthood.[4]

A number of the more prolific or well-known Iraqi filmmakers of the past several years can be considered what Hamid Naficy (2001) calls "exilic filmmakers." They are individuals or groups "who voluntarily or involuntarily have left their country of origin and who maintain an ambivalent relationship with their previous and current places and cultures. Although they do not return to their homelands, they maintain an intense desire to do so" (Naficy 2001, 12). When many of these filmmakers do in fact return to Iraq to reconnect with a country no longer controlled by Saddam Hussein and the Ba'ath Party, they bring with them filmmaking practices and sensibilities acquired overseas. This, in turn, has directed the landscape of Iraqi filmmaking to accommodate a more globally appreciated aesthetic as well as stories of global citizens who find themselves immersed in multiple cultures, similar to many filmmakers based in Malaysia (discussed in Gaik Cheng Khoo's chapter in this volume).

Some of the films produced by these exiled filmmakers address themes of exile, documenting where people of Iraq have gone and how they live in the diaspora. For example, Koutaiba al-Janabi produced *Wasteland: Between Baghdad and London* in 1998; this documentary focused on well-known Iraqi theatrical and cinematic actress Nahida al-Rammah, who was forced into exile in 1979 because of her political leanings. Maysoon Pachachi, an exiled Iraqi filmmaker living in Britain, shot the documentary *Iraqi Women: Voices from Exile* (2004), which features interviews with exiled Iraqi women also living in Britain.

Many films produced by exilic filmmakers have also addressed the filmmaker's return to his or her home country (Iraq or Kurdistan). Baz Shamoun arrived in Iraq, after twenty-seven years of living in exile in Canada, to film *Where Is Iraq?* in 2003. The next year Tariq Hashim returned to Baghdad after twenty-three years of exile to film *16 Hours in Baghdad* (Karroum 2006). Iraqi-American filmmaker Usama Alshaibi returned to his birth country after twenty-five years and filmed *Nice Bombs* (Koziarski 2010).

Films about exiles or about the return to one's homeland have functioned to bring the story of Iraq to the global stage. By the same measure, they re-emphasize Iraqi filmmakers' connections to their home countries even as these filmmakers utilize the post-production, distribution, and exhibition infrastructures of their adopted countries and beyond. In essence, these films enable Iraq to participate in the global film community, where it cannot compete on equal footing in terms of financing, production facilities, or distribution infrastructure.

For most of its history the Iraqi film industry has been enabled by international collaborations that contribute financing and professional expertise. Historically there has been particular cooperation with the much more active film industry in Egypt, and these collaborations have expanded in recent years to include many more European partners.

As the film industry regrows and strengthens in the years after the U.S. invasion, it faces a number of challenges, some of which are faced by any and all independent film industries, while others are very specific to the context of Iraq and film production. I turn now to a discussion of these challenges, which include financing, professionalization and training, exhibition, and cinema appreciation.

Challenges in Building an Infrastructure

The contemporary filmmaking environment in Iraq is marked by many of the same challenges that face independent filmmakers the world over. These include the lack of financing, the dearth of professional opportunities and training, few venues for exhibition, and a general lack of appreciation of cinema. These challenges, however, are intensified in Iraq because of the decades of Saddam Hussein's regime, war, sanctions, and security threats.

Financing

As is the case for virtually any independent filmmaker, obtaining financing is perennially challenging, and Iraqi filmmakers are no exception. Funding for films is most often cobbled together and, more often than not, self-funded. Filmmakers may work in other sectors to gather enough money to finance their films, often waiting a long time to secure that money. Taher Alwan, the director of the Baghdad International Film Festival, notes that funding is the number one issue that hinders the growth of Iraqi cinema (interview, 28 December 2011). State-sponsored filmmaking is rare although growing, but filmmakers tend to focus more on pursuing a range of financing options, since few sources can fund an entire production.

STATE SUPPORT
In the early 2000s the Iraqi government kept its involvement in filmmaking at arm's length, hesitant to direct its limited funding to the rejuvenation and stabilization of this cultural industry. According to some, including Taher Alwan, the government is not yet confident in the potential of the film industry to be a viable contributor to the country's overall economy. In other words, it has not expected a sizeable return on its investment and therefore has not been forthcoming with support or even much interest in the potential of the film industry. Indeed, the government only allocated 40 million dinars to the film industry from 2004 to 2012, or approximately US$35,000 (Kami 2012).

In 2012 the Arab League chose Baghdad to be the 2013 Arab Capital of Culture under UNESCO's Capitals of Culture Program. As part of this initiative, the Iraqi Ministry of Culture announced that it would invest at least 5.0 billion dinars (US$4.2 million) in the industry to produce nineteen films, allocating up to 1.25 billion dinars for a feature-length film and up to 74.0 million dinars for a short film (Kami 2012).[5] A number of films have been selected to receive this funding (see table 9.1), including Mohamed Shukri Jameel's *Pleasures and Pains* and Raed Meshatat's *The Silence of the Shepherd*, *A Man's Tear* (Dunya al-Kabany) and *From the Bottom of the City* (Jamal Abed Jassem) ("Iraq Invests" 2012; Kami 2012). It is not clear, however, how these film projects were chosen to receive funding from the ministry; furthermore, it is interesting to note that Mohamed Shukri Jameel was also the director of *Clash of Loyalties*, the historical epic produced and financed by Saddam Hussein in 1983.

Many filmmakers, particularly those who are recipients of the ministry's funding, are optimistic about state involvement in filmmaking. "I feel they want to support us," says Saad Abdullah, production manager of *A Man's Tear*. "They have only given us a little but we will take what we can get" (Kami 2012). In the world of independent film financing, every little bit counts, and state funding can bring a film's budget closer to its desired level. Another filmmaker, Koutaiba al-Janabi, is also cautiously optimistic: "[It is] a good starting point [and] gives hope to the filmmakers. We need to wait and see what kind of films this process produces" (email to author, 16 February 2013).

The Ministry of Culture is not the only state organization to contribute to filmmaking. The Iraqi Kurdistan Regional Government (KRG)

Table 9.1 Films chosen to receive funding from the Iraqi Ministry of Culture under increased arts funding for the selection of Baghdad as the 2013 Arab Capital of Culture.

Film	Director
Pleasures and Pains	Mohammad Shukri Jameel
The Rosy Dream	Faisal al-Yassery
The Shepherd's Silence	Raad Mushatat
Farewell to Ninawa	Emanuel Tomi
A Man's Tear	Dunya al-Kabany
From the Bottom of the City	Jamal Abed Jassem
Suspended Assassination	Farouk al-Qaisi
Imposers of Security	Hashem Abu Iraq

9.1 Film still from *Jiyan/Life* (2009), directed by Jano Rosebiani. Image courtesy of Evini Films.

has also been a strong supporter of film projects in recent years, providing up to $200,000 to films through its Ministry of Culture and Youth. These funds help to finance seven or eight feature films, as well as a handful of shorts and documentaries, every year ("Iraqi Film Fails" 2012). Films that have received support from the KRG include *Jiyan/Life* (Jano Rosebiani, 2002), *Kilometre Zero* (Hineer Saleem, 2005), *Niwemang / Half Moon* (Bahman Ghobadi, 2006),[6] *Sirta la gal ba / Whisper with the Wind* (Shahram Alidi, 2009), and *Death Triangle* (Adnan Osman, 2012).

Despite warm relationships between some individuals and state funding agencies, there are also a number of criticisms about the funding relationships between the state and the film industry. Kasim Abid, an Iraqi cinematographer based in London, returned to Iraq and started the Independent Film and Television College in Baghdad in 2004. He feels that the Ministry of Culture's five-billion-dinar initiative is "for political propaganda, not for culture" (Kami 2012). Jano Rosebiani, a Kurdish filmmaker living in the United States, says, "There is a lack of competence and understanding of cinema" within the Ministry of Culture, which assumes 75 per cent ownership over films that receive its funding (email to author, 9 January 2013). The funds are low enough that filmmakers must work in other jobs in order to make a living.

For others, there is a sense that the model of seeking government support for the industry will not yield the best results. In other words, the industry should develop as an industry, with investors and commercial opportunities, rather than relying on ministries to finance filmmaking. Developing business acumen in the industry will, according to some, provide sustainability for the growing yet weak industry. Nizar Al-Rawi, the director of the Iraqi Short Film Festival, comments, "So far, filmmakers are begging for money from the ministries [such as Iraq's Ministry of Culture], and this error will lead the industry to a halt immediately" (interview, 2012).

ALTERNATIVE SOURCES OF FINANCIAL SUPPORT

Many Iraqi filmmakers are not waiting for the government to become financially involved at a sustainable level. Rather, like many of their international counterparts, they finance themselves or enter into partnerships with various organizations, such as the former UK Film Council and the Hubert Bals Fund. As many of the more visible Iraqi filmmakers live outside of Iraq, they have been able to tap into non-Iraqi funding sources. These are often tied to co-production partnerships with other countries like the United Kingdom and France, as well as with film festivals.

Mohamed al-Daradji is arguably the most visible Iraqi filmmaker living outside the country, and his international reputation has helped him secure some decent financing for his films. *Son of Babylon* (2009) was a $1.5 million co-production among seven countries (Iraq, UK, France, Netherlands, United Arab Emirates, Egypt, and Palestine) and secured funding from over twenty sources, including the UK Film Council, Screen Yorkshire (UK), Fonds Sud Cinema (France; now called the World Cinema Fund), and the Sundance Institute (United States).[7] The Iraqi Ministry of Culture was initially planning to support this film but declined in view of al-Daradji's decision to cast a Kurd instead of an Arab actor, which the ministry viewed as divisive. Al-Daradji defended his decision, however, saying, "It was an important aspect of the film, a way to make Iraq united" (Connolly 2011). *In My Mother's Arms*, Al-Daradji's 2011 film about life in an Iraqi orphanage, was a co-production with the UK, the Netherlands, and Iraq; Al Jazeera English also joined this film as co-producer.

Jano Rosebiani, a Kurdish filmmaker based in Los Angeles and Erbil, Kurdistan, garnered support for his film *Jiyan* from the Kurdistan Regional Government (KRG) and "a few European entitles, among them Rotterdam, Gutenberg, and Locarno film festivals"

9.2 Film still from *Son of Babylon* (2010), directed by Mohamed al-Daradji. Image courtesy of Human Film.

(email to author, 9 January 2013). Kurdish filmmaker Hineer Saleem secured participation for his film *Kilometre Zero* (2005) from the KRG and Kurdistan TV (Kurdistan); Fonds Sud Cinema, Centre National de la Cinematographie, and TV5 Monde (France); and Yleisradio (Finland).

Independent filmmakers, no matter their location worldwide, usually struggle to find adequate financing for their productions, so it should not be inferred that Iraqi filmmakers living abroad have a number of guaranteed financing options for their films. It seems, however, that many Iraqi filmmakers living abroad may have more access to potential financing sources than do those living in Iraq. Filmmakers based in the country have fairly scant funding options. Without a history of a strong cinema industry in Iraq, there is also little recognition that film production can be an industry capable of contributing substantial economic benefit; therefore, investors are less willing to invest, or aware of investing, in film production. Most of the support, both financial and infrastructural, arrives from international sources – from Iraqis now living abroad or sources that support "developing world" cinema (such as France's World Cinema Fund). For example, Oday Rasheed, based in Baghdad, was awarded a €385,000 (C$517,000) post-production grant from the Hubert Bals Fund of the International Film Festival Rotterdam for his 2010 film, *Qarantina* (Saray 2010). Koutaiba al-Janabi's film *Night Train* also received script and project development funds from the Hubert Bals Fund in 2009 (Bruno 2009).

According to some filmmakers in Iraq, the influx and attention from international funding sources has not done enough to support the construction and sustainability of cinema's infrastructure in Iraq. According to Hussam al-Saray (2010), "the acclaim for foreign-funded movies made by mostly western-educated Iraqis is likely to do little to affect immediate improvements for aspiring actors and directors working in Iraq, where there's practically no funding available for the film industry." Bashir al-Majid, an actor and director working in Iraq, concurs: "Let's face it: there are only a handful of directors who happen to be working abroad because of foreign support. This is not going to shake up the situation of cinema in Iraq, and we shouldn't dare to call it a comeback of Iraqi film or any kind of New Iraqi Cinema" (al-Saray 2010).

Professionalization and Training

The availability of adequate professional training options in Iraq has been problematic, not just in the years since the start of the Iraq war but since the production of the first film in the country in the late 1940s. There has never been a really strong tradition of filmmaker training, in large part because there were few filmmakers available who could act as model practitioners and mentors to aspiring filmmakers. According to Iraq Short Film Festival director Nizar Al-Rawi, "there is no good history of this industry, [so] this makes access to experts difficult" (interview, 2012).

The acquisition of filmmaker training has relied historically on international producers, cinematographers, and other crew – Egyptian, French, British, and so on – who held lead crew positions and provided on-the-job training to Iraqi filmmakers and other crew. Even in the 1940s, actors and crew were recruited from theatre to work on film productions headed by Egyptian and French producers, for example. Yahya Fa'ik was a theatre actor in Iraq and participated in some of the country's first film productions, including acting in the role of Theyab in the 1948 film *Alia wa Isam / Alia and Ossam*, directed by Frenchman Andrea Chotan. Fa'ik went on to direct some films, including *Warda* in 1956.

For the bulk of film training and hands-on experience, many filmmakers, driven abroad in political or security exile, have studied abroad, most often in European locations like the UK, France, and the Netherlands, and have returned to Iraq with skills in film production. In fact, there is an expectation that as students become more skilled at filmmaking, they will want to study outside of Iraq, making professional connections with other filmmakers as well as funders (Pachachi 2004).

Training in film production (and in media production, especially television broadcasting) is available at a handful of institutions around the country, such as Baghdad University's Department of Cinematic Arts and Television, which was established in 1973. However, the majority of these programs have suffered from a lack of equipment and hands-on experience for their students. Filmmaker Ahmed Kamal, who studied in the University of Baghdad's College of Fine Arts, recalled, "The problem was that I learned everything from the books very well; it was all theoretical, but I didn't have any chance to [gain] practical [skills]" (email to author, 9 March 2013). Another student reflected, "Sanctions destroyed education. All our cameras were stolen during the looting" (Pachachi 2004). Furthermore, as will be discussed later in this chapter, younger generations of filmmakers who grew up under Saddam's reign were not exposed much to cinema appreciation and did not have much opportunity to attend movie theatres. As filmmaker Mohamed al-Daradji states, "even the students of film academies have never been to the cinema" (Heemstra 2009).

Many of those who trained in Iraqi college programs have gone to work in television in Iraq. According to Taher Alwan, who was also formerly professor of Cinema at Baghdad University, approximately seventy to eighty film graduates come out of Baghdad's university-level film programs; most prefer to work for the rapidly proliferating satellite television companies based in Iraq because they are guaranteed steady work and a monthly salary, unlike the tenuous circumstances, financial and otherwise, that filmmakers endure. Ahmed Kawal, for example, studied at Baghdad University's Department of Cinematic Arts and Television from 2000 to 2004 and began working as an assistant director for Al-Rasheed, one of Iraq's satellite television channels. Kamal gained further experience as coordinator of the Iraq Short Film Festival and as a cameraman on a number of productions. He eventually moved to the Netherlands in 2006 because his film www.gilgamesh.21 was highly critical of the Iraqi government, and it was too dangerous for him to stay in Iraq (email to author, 9 March 2013).

The Independent Film and Television College (IFTVC) was established in 2004 by Maysoon Pachachi and Kasim Abid, two Iraqi filmmakers based in London, as a way to offer short courses without charge, thereby contributing to the professional development of filmmakers in Iraq. The first documentary course offered at the college was originally planned to take three months, but it took a year to complete because of security risks. "Students would come to shoot, only to find that things had changed; it was now too dangerous to film that particular story or in that particular neighbourhood, and they would have to start again," said Pachachi (2006).

Exhibition and Cinema Appreciation

With the resurgence of interest in filmmaking within the country, there are several organizations that are committed to fostering an infrastructure for cinema exhibition and appreciation. According to Taher Alwan, it is imperative to promote a culture of cinema appreciation, particularly because the public, worn from decades of war, has not been exposed to cinema-going as a communal experience. Indeed, only recently have Iraqis felt safe enough to congregate in any public space, let alone a movie theatre.

The number of movie theatres in Iraq has fluctuated over the decades, reducing to nearly zero in the early 2000s. Sadoul noted that there were eighty-six cinemas with 35 mm projection capabilities in the country in 1964, at the height of Iraqi cinematic production; nearly half were in Baghdad, with ten each in Basra and Mosul. Some mobile cinema units, called cinebuses, operated in rural regions of the country, projecting 16 mm films ("The Iraqi Cinema in 1964" 1966, 185). Later there were more than 275 cinemas in the country (Heemstra 2009).

When the war with the United States began, audiences were unwilling or unable to gather in a public place to watch movies. Theatres were destroyed, closed, or repurposed, and in the mid- to late 2000s there were only a handful of theatres operating in the country. Saleem al-Qaisie, who used to frequent movie theatres when he was young, described the movie theatre landscape in 2010: "The sign for the [now-closed] Babel Cinema has vanished. Baydha is now a department store. Nujoom is still open but it looks like an abandoned building. I heard Semiramis is being repaired but old posters and ticket prices are still posted outside" (Saray 2010). The owner of the Atlas theatre in Baghdad lamented in 2009 that the theatres also faced challenges in terms of the clientele who frequented the cinemas that had remained open after the U.S. invasion in 2003; the audience was comprised of "uneducated people. They know nothing about cinema. They don't care for a film's theme. They want to pass the time and see some shots of women's bodies" (Salman 2009).

More movie theatres opened in the early 2010s as a result of concentrated investment and the reintroduction of film product both imported from abroad and produced within the country. A new fourteen-screen multiplex was proposed by the Lebanese distribution and exhibition company Empire Cinema in Erbil, Kurdistan, in 2011, and an entrepreneur invested $800,000 to open two small-scale cinemas in Baghdad (Empire Cinema n.d.; Ansary 2011).

Despite this growth there are still few theatres. However, filmmakers such as Mohamed al-Daradji and Oday Rasheed are changing the way that people can access movies. Al-Daradji and Iraq-based filmmaker Rasheed began the Iraqi Mobile Cinema Project in 2007. This travelling program of films has toured the country a number of times since its beginning, visiting various cities and screening short and feature-length films that celebrate Iraqi history and culture. The cinema unit screens films in parks, hospitals, army barracks, and elsewhere (Connolly 2011). The Mobile Cinema Project, operating under the auspices of al-Daradji's production company, Human Film, developed into the Iraqi Mobile Cinema Festival, which was established two years later in 2009. Today the festival enjoys multinational funding, including Iraqi funding from the Council of Baghdad, the Ministry of Culture, the Iraqi Film Foundation, and Al Sumaria TV; and Dutch funders such as the Dutch embassy, Doen, and Hivos (Human Film 2013). According to Human Film's Isabelle Stead, Mobile Cinema "always draws big audiences and is a clear indication there is a hunger for cinemas and film exhibition across Iraq" (email to author, 2 January 2013). There is, too, the necessity to rely on international financing to make this possible, as exclusive Iraqi funding is not a reality.

The concern over the lack of film appreciation has been an undercurrent driving various cinema exhibition initiatives in the country, particularly those that celebrate the burgeoning Iraqi film industry. A number of film festivals, in addition to the Iraqi Mobile Cinema Festival, have started in Iraq and have been able to promote and support the local film industry. These festivals include the Baghdad International Film Festival (BIFF), the Iraq Short Film Festival, and the Baghdad Eye Human Rights Film Festival. Film festivals in the country have been more sporadic, operating in some years and not operating in others. This intermittent activity is indicative, however, of the tenacity of festival organizers and filmmakers.

The Baghdad International Film Festival began in 2005 and has since operated several times (including 2007, and annually 2011–14). The 2011 festival hosted 150 films from thirty-two countries, and the 2012 festival doubled in size, screening 300 films from sixty countries over a five-day

9.3 The Iraqi Mobile Cinema Project was started by Iraqi filmmakers
Mohamed al-Daradji and Oday Rasheed in 2007. Image courtesy of Human Film.

period. However, the festival has suffered harsh criticisms, in part
owing to the severe lack of funding – and resulting unprofessionalism –
of the festival. Director Taher Alwan said that many governmental,
private, and non-profit organizations declined to support the festival
in 2011 because the general sense was that it would not be successful
and would be subjected to numerous security difficulties (interview,
28 December 2011). Yet the festival was extremely well attended and
did not have any security incidents. The 2012 festival enjoyed a higher
profile but endured a number of criticisms about its funding – about
$50,000 for the entire festival – and insufficient organization. One jour-
nalist commented that the festival "lacked the basic conditions to make
it look like a real film festival," while a cinema critic complained that it
was "illogical to organize a film festival in a country whose capital does
not have a single functioning cinema" (Reuters 2012).

The Iraq Short Film Festival (ISFF), organized by Iraq's non-
governmental Contemporary Visual Arts Society, was established in
2005 with several interrelated goals in mind. It would connect filmmakers with production companies, provide venues for film exhibition and

9.4 Iraqi movie stars arrive on the red carpet at the 2011 Iraq Short Film Festival in Baghdad. Image courtesy of Nizar al-Rawi.

film appreciation, encourage audiences to support and value cinema, and function as "an instrument to create a global network between filmmakers, production companies and lending bodies," according to the ISFF website. The ISFF is another example of an organization that utilizes foreign involvement to facilitate its operations, which in turn contributes to the development of cinema infrastructure in Iraq. The ISFF partnered with a European consultancy firm to arrange the 2005 festival and secured a number of international sponsors, including Germany's Ministry of Foreign Affairs, AG Kurzfilm, and the Goethe Institute. Its second festival was held in 2011, with the third edition planned for October 2013.

Conclusion

There is dedication and passion emanating from the fledgling film industry in Iraq and from the exiled and diasporic filmmakers who share a common nationality. There is excitement and a desire to rebuild the culture of a country that has for a long time been restrained in its ability to express and share its culture. Over the past several years the film industry in Iraq has experienced increased interest both within and beyond its borders, and it stands to enjoy even more support, particularly when diasporic and exilic Iraqi filmmakers become more involved with that industry in Iraq.

There is much scepticism from Iraqi filmmakers as to the opportunities for the film industry within the country. For some, these opportunities hinge on filmmakers' abilities to secure global support. Koutaiba al-Janabi says that Iraqi cinema will have a future "if we can find a new cinema style and get the attention of the world. But there are no big plans, I don't think, and no cinemas" (email to author, 16 February 2013). For many others, however, the optimism surrounding the potential for the Iraqi film industry outweighs this scepticism. Perhaps too, their optimism arises from the recognition of the reality of the filmmaking modes of production and distribution; in the contemporary landscape they are such that geographic place is less important than the connection that shared identity provides. While the physical location of Iraq can only boast limited infrastructural film resources right now, the Iraqi film industry can boast more expansive and supportive infrastructures based all over the world, particularly elsewhere in the Middle East and Europe but also increasingly in the United States (for example, the Sundance Institute) and Asia (the Singapore Film Festival). These in turn bolster those internal infrastructures and help grow networks.

As scholar Lucia Sorbera (2009) notes, Iraqi filmmaking – and cultural production more broadly – faces a number of challenges, many of which have been outlined in this chapter. To overcome these challenges, networks have to be created and nurtured, often across international boundaries. "Iraqis have not renounced producing culture, the only antidote to the violence of the present," wrote Sorbera in 2009. "Cinema is a dream factory, but the Iraq of today is not the right place for dreamers. If the network between European and Iraqi artists improves, new dreams will find their place in cinema, and if it is true that artists can create another world, they will take part in this new creation" (Sorbera 2009, 329). While the Iraqi film industry has the potential to grow on its own, we must also recognize the support that the global film industry can contribute, for it is the interconnectedness of global cinema networks today that enables filmmaking to flourish around the world.

ACKNOWLEDGMENTS

I would like to thank the many individuals who shared their perspectives about filmmaking in Iraq, including Mohamed al-Daradji, Koutaiba al-Janabi, Nizar Al-Rawi, Taher Alwan, Ala Fa'ik, Ahmed Kawal, Jano Rosebiani, and Isabelle Stead. I would also like to extend thanks to Peter Laufer and George Papagiannis, who helped me to connect with other individuals working in filmmaking in Iraq.

NOTES

1 The most comprehensive histories of cinema in Iraq were both published in the 1980s: Jabar Audah Allawi's 1983 dissertation, *Television and Film in Iraq: Socio-political and Cultural Study, 1946–1980*, and Shakir Nouri's 1986 book, *A la recherché du cinema irakien: Histoire, infrastructure, filmographie (1945–1985) [Searching for Iraqi Cinema: History, Infrastructure, Filmographie (1945–1985)]*.
2 This iteration of the General Organization of Cinema and Theatre has also been called the Cinema and Theatre General Organization and the Administration of Cinema and Theatre.
3 Two cast members, Nicholas Young and Marc Sindon, recollected that they knew the film was propaganda. Sindon said, "We sat there [watching the film] and howled with laughter. I took the money and ran" (BBC Radio Four, 2011).
4 Dena Al-Adeeb is a multimedia artist residing in the United States. Born in Baghdad, she emigrated to Kuwait in 1980 and then to San Francisco in 1991 with her family. Usama Alshaibi was born in Baghdad in 1969 and spent his childhood living in Iraq, Saudi Arabia, Jordan, Abu Dhabi, and Iowa.
5 There are conflicting reports on the total investment that the Ministry of Culture would make. Some reports cite 5.0 billion dinars, while another cites 10.0 billion dinars (Taie 2012).
6 *Niwemang* is a story about an Iranian Kurd who travels to Iraqi Kurdistan to give one last musical performance. Director Bahman Ghobadi is Iranian, and the film was a co-production between Austria, France, Iran, and Iraq.
7 *Son of Babylon* was Iraq's official entry to the 2011 Academy Awards for Best Foreign Language Film. It was not chosen to be among the films nominated for an Oscar.

Chapter Ten

The Grassroots Perspective: Sixth Generation Cinema and Independent Filmmaking in China

HONGWEI LU

"The crow solves the crow's problems.
I solve mine."

– Director Jia Zhangke quoting poet Xi Chuan, in asserting
his stance on independent filmmaking

China's independent filmmaking started with the so-called Sixth Generation in the post-socialist years of the 1990s. It was an era of massive withdrawal of the centralized government sponsorship of filmmaking with the bankruptcy of the state-owned studio system. The post-Mao shift to a market economy led to the privatization of the film industry and affected every level of that industry, from its basic infrastructure to production, financing, and promotion. Privatized independent film companies took over where the government had left off, and privatized financial support enabled filmmakers to confront the intimidation of state censorship.

In this context it is necessary that we understand the notion of independent filmmaking in relative terms. If in America independent filmmaking refers to a level of independence from the Hollywood system, in China independent filmmaking should be understood as independent in relation to the state studio system rather than as a totally self-supporting practice. Furthermore, not only does the independent movement consist in an independence from the state system of production, distribution, and exhibition, but, more important, it consists in an alternative cultural vision of engaging with taboos on contemporary social reality through exploring new artistic ways to represent them. The Sixth Generation cinema presents a "grassroots" perspective through an unglamorous docudrama mode of filmmaking aiming at contemporary social engagement.

Cinematic periodization is often determined by historical events, socio-political criteria, or stylistic orientations. The generational concept of Chinese film history evolved with the emergence of the Fifth Generation in the mid-1980s when a group of filmmakers was discovered by critics who also proceeded to retrospectively divide Chinese filmography into roughly defined generations. The Fifth Generation is known as the class of 1982 from the Beijing Film Academy, and as a group it also includes directors who share philosophical affinities and cultural convictions. At the core of the Fifth Generation's creed are critical examinations of historical and cultural heritage and national and personal memory and trauma. The designation of the Sixth Generation is thus defined within and against previous generations of Chinese filmmakers.

While it is increasingly complicated to nail down and categorize the new generation of directors who emerged in the post–Fifth Generation and the post-socialist period, and although it is also an imperfect science to set chronological borders, it is not an exaggeration to claim that a new, profoundly different Chinese cinema has emerged since the early 1990s. With implications for marketing strategy, cultural distinction, and artistic division, the term *Sixth Generation* comprises changes in economic, social, and technological norms within China in the post-socialist era. Films focusing on immediate social issues and the drab everyday reality have replaced the historical and costume melodramas that dealt with concerns of historical experiences and cataclysms of Maoism and that aimed at paying tribute to or rediscovering cultural heritage. Characterized by an underclass perspective and underground status, independent filmmaking in China in the Sixth Generation era offers a cinematic window onto the seedy underbelly of Chinese society.

Adopting the "slice of life" or "stream of life" approach, independent films in China are a reactive and correctional response to the traditional socialist approach of a "grand theme" style, which downplays human elements in social life. Establishing and maintaining a cinematic tradition has been an intrinsic part of state building in socialist China. The film industry in Maoist China was nationalized and politicized, with the socialist state taking serious interest in the propaganda potential of this mass medium. The "grand theme" cultural policy was part of the subordination of cinema to the authority of institutions. It began during the Great Leap Forward movement in the 1950s and has always generated role models, heroes, and epics in post-revolution films (Lau 2002, 26).[1] The common stable of socialist-realist genres, aesthetics, and themes were predetermined by political constraints.

When the Sixth Generation directors entered the film force around 1993, they took leave of the melodrama of Chinese history and politics, which had been the central preoccupation of the filmmakers of the earlier generations. The Fifth Generation, for example, is known for dissecting the ills of the past. Zhang Yimou's signature films, such as *Judou* (1990) and *Raise the Red Lantern / Dahong denglong gaogao gua* (1991), clearly highlight the "nature of feudal exploitation, the dynamics of a patriarchal society, and the tragedy of the victimization of women" (Tam and Dissanayake 1998, 27). Chen Kaige's major films, such as *Farewell My Concubine / Bawang bieji* (1993) and *Temptress Moon / Fengyue* (1996), are concerned mainly with a discourse of historical reflection and cultural introspection, among other themes. Fifth Generation films highlight the repressive traditions of historical social and cultural systems.

While the Fifth Generation shows continuous interests in historical topics, often as allegories, the Sixth Generation directors demonstrate an indifference to the Fifth Generation's folk, native, and historical Chineseness. No longer set in China's dynasties or Stalinist-socialist past, the films made by these directors break further away from the "mass catharsis," melodramatic tradition of previous generations. Unlike the Fifth Generation filmmakers whose historical melodramas present grandiose critical engagement with tradition and culture, which results in a form of "cultural exhibitionism" (Zhang 2002, 203),[2] the Sixth Generation uses individual stories to illustrate social and political themes. Jia Zhangke, one of the leading figures of the Sixth Generation, accounts in his own words for the difference: "In the '80s, the Fifth Generation filmmakers were real heroes: they managed to break Chinese cinema out of its closed little mould and try something new. But they've changed a lot: in their current films, you're no longer seeing the experience of life in China … My way of filming allows me to describe Chinese reality without distortion" (quoted in Douhaire 2002).

The subject matter and stylistic orientations of the Sixth Generation directors are inseparable from the deep social and cultural transformation occurring in China today. Growing up in post-Mao China, their lives are affected by many realities that were not present in previous generations. The directors lived their formative years in the midst of China's dislocation from an enclosed Stalinist socialist state with a simple and unified ideology. Chinese politics have stepped away from strong ideology in favour of practical decisions as China joins the trends of globalization that spread throughout the world.

According to Sixth Generation director Lou Ye, who was among one of the first to set up his privately funded film studio, "we have a different attitude to the previous generation of directors. They have a strong idea of Chineseness, and always try to make their films conform to that. It's very different to my approach" (Havis 2000).[3] Lou Ye himself prefers to call the new group of filmmakers the "386 Mhz Generation – three for over 30, eight for educated in the 80s, six because we're born in the 60s" (quoted in Stephens 2000). The term *386 Mhz Generation* bespeaks the youthful experimental nature of their film style. In addition, if situated in the social-cultural context, being born in the 1960s also means that the majority of the Sixth Generation film directors were too young to experience pre-Mao China, which is one of the central concerns of the Fifth Generation.

Much of the inspiration for the Sixth Generation's films comes from their experiences growing up in the dystopian moment of post-Mao, urban China. Many of their films are about the disillusionment and dejection of underclass urban youth in a world without heroes or clearly defined ideals. If major Fifth Generation films were shot at nationally protected key cultural relics and remote mountainous areas replete with ethnographic details, the mise en scène in Sixth Generation films reveals the daily life spaces of urban commoners. Their artistic preoccupation with the cinema-vérité style of filmmaking conveys a patient loyalty to ordinary experiences and silent changes. They aspire to present a raw picture of the cultural conditions and social realities of post-socialist China, addressing existential anxieties and interrogating shifting cultural assumptions and socio-economic changes. Whether as a reaction against the "elaborate allegories" of the Fifth Generation or as reflection of the times, the rise of the Sixth Generation cinema fits within a larger cultural search for new ways to represent the post-reform reality through their direct engagement with the private, lived experience of the underclass individual (Kuoshu 2002, 13). Shooting outside the official studio system allows independent filmmakers some opportunities to deny the state's forty-year control over the definition of reality. It makes it possible for them to film the underground culture and the gloomy and grotesque images of existential struggles and dilemmas experienced by the social underclass, comprising mainly migrant workers, insignificant salesmen, con artists, jobless drifters, prostitutes, social vagrants, and underworld schemers. As an autonomous aesthetic movement with expansive engagement of social issues and of "views from the bottom, not of the light above but of the surrounding murk" (Corliss 2001), independent filmmaking takes shape as a prominent cultural force in turn-of-the-century, post-socialist China, despite the fact that many obstacles were still in the way for these filmmakers: political pressures, financial difficulties, competitions from Hollywood, and even direct police interventions. As director Jia Zhangke recalled in an interview, "whenever I heard a police siren, I'd jump out of bed to check if the film rolls were hidden" (quoted in Pickowicz 2012, 326).

The new generation of filmmakers grew up in the post-Mao era; in their lifetime they experienced the convulsive social and cultural changes that accompanied the nation; they were influenced by ever-evolving technology and global cultural influences to an unprecedented degree; and they created a film culture anchored in a documentary conscience. Starting from the early 1990s and at the turn of the twenty-first century, there were over sixty young film directors working outside the state-owned studio system. Scholars have categorized these directors in a number of ways. Harry H. Kuoshu's (2002) overview of China's filmmaking generations attributed the beginning of independent filmmaking to Zhang Yuan, who "started a trend among the younger film directors of making films outside the state studio system" (19). A few other filmmakers, such as Wang Xiaoshuai, He Jianjun, and Wang Quanan, also ventured into underground filmmaking. Chinese scholar Dai Jinhua linked the Sixth Generation more broadly to include the turn-of-the-century documentary filmmakers closely connected with the artists' village at the Yuanmingyuan Summer Palace (Dai 2002, 75). The Sixth Generation directors themselves, however, resist being branded under a general category, although they have not been against being labelled "independent," a generalization that has "gained more currency in Chinese media and scholarship" (Pickowicz and Yingjin 2006, ix).

Early Sixth Generation films were more preoccupied with contemporary underground culture. Its pioneer director, Zhang Yuan, claimed, "I am not interested in the grand fable narratives. I hope my works can penetrate into people's lives" (quoted in Yu 2002). Zhang Yuan's landmark works focused on Beijing rock and gay cultures in *Beijing Bastard / Beijing zhazhong* (1993) and *East Palace West Palace / Donggong xigong* (1996). Wang Xiaoshuai's early films focused on avant-garde artists in *Frozen* (1997) and *The Days* (1994), and He Jianjun's psychoanalytic work on youth dissidence in *Red Beads / Hong zhuzi* (1994). Towards the mid- to late 1990s, class divisions and underclass youth started to take a central position in Sixth Generation films. China's new under-class emerged as market-oriented reforms took effect. Sociologists have noted that the "net effect" of the introduction of market-oriented reforms has been the unprecedented increase in population mobility across China. Many migrants are forced to occupy marginal spaces in housing and labour markets, which creates a new underclass popula-tion (Smith 2000, 351).

Critics have recognized the Sixth Generation directors' filmic fixation on "the socially powerless group" (*ruoshi qunti*) and "the hidden real-ity" (*bei zhebi de xianshi*) (Yu 2002). The Sixth Generation "grew up with a high degree of cynicism toward politics in general and Communist Party in particular ... they have a profound need to talk about society as they experience it, so most of their work has been absolutely grounded in the day-to-day realities around them" (Said 2002). Their films are committed to exposing dishonesty by magnifying the day-to-day expe-rience: "We don't want to lie anymore ... It used to be during the collec-tive period that there was no difference between the individual and the collective point of view ... But after so much propaganda – when dur-ing the Cultural Revolution we were reduced to seeing 10 movies over and over again and never seeing one true image – we said we don't want to lie anymore. The chance to express myself ... that is a revolu-tion" (Wang Xiaoshuai, quoted in Olesen 2001). Their films could not be legally distributed in China and were not widely seen by Chinese audiences. Take, for example, Wang Xiaoshuai, the director of *Beijing Bicycle / Shiqisui de dance* (2000*), Frozen / Jidu hanleng* (1997)*, So Close to Paradise / Biandan guniang* (1998), and *The Days / Dongchun de rizi* (1993). His first film was banned by the China Film Bureau; his second was released under a pseudonym (Wu Ming, meaning "No Name"); and his third film went through three years of editing before it reached the screen (Sterrit 2002).

A definitive Sixth Generation figure would be a composite of per-sonalities from the everyday underclass. The aimlessness, ennui, and disillusionment of the disadvantaged and disoriented "hopeless loser" populate small-scale and low-budgeted independent films (Beijing Scene 1999). The main characters in Jia Zhangke's *Xiao Wu* (1997)*, Zhantai* (2000), *Unknown Pleasures / Ren xiaoyao* (2002), and *World/Shi-jie* (2004) are featured as con artists, self-employed entertainers, unem-ployed youths, and migrant workers; Wang Xiaoshuai's *So Close to Paradise* and Beijing Bicycle feature migrant workers; Lou Ye's *Suzhou River / Suzhou He* (2000) features a courier and a bar worker; Wang Chao's *The Orphan of Anyang / Anyang yinger* (2001) features a laid-off worker and a prostitute; Li Yang's *Blind Shaft / Mangjing* (2003) features migrant workers; and Zhang Ming's *Rainclouds over Wushan / Wushan yunyu* (1996) features an ordinary signal worker, a hotel receptionist, and a prostitute. These characters personify the social character of underclass China, explicitly connected neither to the feudal or revolutionary past nor to the politically radical years of the Cultural Revolution. Instead, they are mostly lonely, directionless, wandering, and disaffected, social-outsider urban youths. Focus on the underrepresented social underground, and the disenfranchised social underclass, has become a hallmark of the Sixth Generation filmmakers. Furthermore, their aesthetic preference for the existential idiom and ambiguous naturalism conveys a cultural repositioning – for example, the "grassroots perspective" (*dicing shidian*) and "grassroots concern" (*diceng guanzhu*). As Jia Zhangke claims, "I am not imagining the grassroots. My life experience and background predetermine my positioning in the grassroots. And I hate to use melodrama to express life, because it won't exhibit the complex nature of life" (quoted in Feng 2004). He identifies himself as a "movie migrant worker" (*dianying mingong*) (Yu 2007). Director Wang Xiaoshuai distinguishes his grassroots vision of filmmaking from the official discourse: "Chinese audiences do not trust the reality of films approved by censorship precisely because they don't reflect Chinese people's lives" (quoted in Kochan 2003).

Both Jia's and Wang's visions of the grassroots representation of reality coincide with the contemporary search for alternative visions of reality and the search for new ways to present the visions. Compared with the Fifth Generation's "epic shot" (Jameson 1995, 118),[4] a wide range of Sixth Generation films is characterized by a slice-of-life approach, with characteristics of cinéma-verité, long-take temporality, and film noir elements, and a preference for low-key lighting, off-centre compositions, hand-held shots, offhand plots, narrative austerity, and global cultural references.

The whole philosophy of cinema-vérité, which is a way of filming real-life scenes without elaborate equipment and technical means of production (such as a script and special lighting), revolves around the concept of "seizing the event as it actually happens" (Issari and Paul 1979, 7–8; 44–5).[5] This philosophy is found in major Sixth Generation films, which manifest the desire to get closer to real life and aim for a raw sense of reality. The films reject dramatically or melodramatically charged materials in favour of "natural" situations of everyday life. All other artistic concerns are "subsidiary to the bold statement, to the down and docu-dirty, the raw, the real" (Corliss 2001). Their recognition of the value of little moments and ordinary people is a breakthrough from "the 'realism' of the classic Chinese cinema which aims for typicality rather than naturalism" (Berry 1988, 77). These aesthetics serve the subject of the urban underclass particularly well. Their concentration on the natural, quotidian, emotional, and psycho-physiological realities out of which normal individual human life essentially takes shape aligns well with the artistic and intellectual tradition of cinéma-vérité aesthetics, which aim at "capturing life as it is lived rather than as it is re-enacted or re-invented in the old traditional way" (Issari and Paul 1979, 5). Directors such as Lou Ye, Jia Zhangke, Wang Xiaoshuai, and Zhang Ming focus on contemporary subjects and the mundane everyday of urban or sub-urban subalterns. Their naturalistic docudrama mode is a reactionary response to the aesthetic forms and styles of the political sublime, which feature the "spectacles of the non-everyday" with larger than life figures.

The birth of the Sixth Generation was also part of a larger drive towards social documentation in a period of transformation. Independent filmmaking was inseparable from the significant presence of documentary filmmakers in contemporary China. This New Documentary Movement (*Xin jilu yundong*) emerged during the same period as did the Sixth Generation. Both represent contemporary calls for alternative social articulation and social documentation. Chinese official media had long enjoyed the dominance of "hard-news" reporting that dealt only with chronicling events and encasing them within the perspective of assured consensus. This perspective was subservient to government policy and silenced the public voice. According to Kirk Denton (2004), writing for the Modern Chinese Literature and Culture Resource Center listserv,

> it is not until late 1980s when documentary filmmaking in China started to realize the medium's major raison d'être as social expression and critique in the most grassroots way possible. The appearance of such new documentaries – termed as the 'New Documentary Movement' in China – is the combined result of a number of factors: a general mixed sense of hope and loss amidst an era of dramatic change; greater freedom in the economic sector plus technological advancement in digital media that makes independent and amateur filmmaking increasingly possible, etc. This is a movement that does not have a conscious manifesto but has doubtless grown out of the collective psyche of China around the turn of the century.

Chinese documentaries evolved from grand official narratives to more auteur-style personal films about ordinary people. This change of orientation happened in 1993, the same year that *Beijing Bastard* was released; the film was generally considered to be the debut work of the Sixth Generation. Its "telling [of] common people's own stories" became the raison d'être of the movement (Lu 2003, 23). The New Documentary Movement in China "established a new way of looking at the world from the grassroots up; a way of clearly understanding what drives different classes to survive and what feelings they have" (ibid).

Sixth Generation films reflect a range of individualized responses to the unprecedented changes that are now taking place in Chinese culture and society. Their auteur perspectives evidence the Sixth Generation's political and artistic positioning and distinguish them from the former generations. The emphasis on individual auteur style is a reflection of a new positioning that shifts focus from preoccupation with the social macro to the individual micro, and to the valuing of individual expression above other considerations. Ah Nian, the director of the 2000 film *Call Me* (a story about a villager who is struggling for a new life in the city, sells his own blood, and ends up contracting AIDS), argues that "now we have to portray a society by looking at the individual. We can no longer try to know individuals by taking a macro view of society" (quoted in Olesen 2001). In a published interview Wang Xiaoshuai critiques what he calls the "lack of subjectivity in Chinese film" and specifies the nature of the individual perspective of the new cinema: "The main thing was that I felt that China was really missing realistic films that expressed an individual's point of view. There were films expressing what society thought or what the general population thought, what the Chinese Communist Party wanted people to think, and there were some that showed what traditional life was like, these big period films. I wanted to show real thoughts and feelings as they existed, and emotions as they really are" (quoted in ibid).

According to Wang Xiaoshuai, the new cinema is about filming an average individual's very "simple mundane existence, daily life, and through that understanding them" (quoted in Olesen 1999). To the Sixth Generation directors, individual experience is valuable because the Cultural Revolution and Maoism did not support expression of the individual personality. Marxist theoretical works that are predominant in the cultural scene of China's immediate past critique individualism as bourgeois ideology and place group interests ahead of individual expression and agency.

With the slogan "Get onto the streets with a camera on the shoulder," the new documentarists aimed at "cutting directly into life and into a person" and maintaining a "time-sculpting"[6] naturalistic perception of silent but drastic social-cultural transformations (Tarkovsky 1987, 62–3). Their "my-camera-doesn't-lie" naturalistic style closely resembles the filmic expressions of the Sixth Generation; both base their approach on the belief that everyday life itself is honestly significant, capable of offering "an astutely observed and meticulously detailed vision of life's material surfaces and social transactions in order to intimate what's happening beneath those surfaces" (Rayns 2000).

The emergence of digital video technology was one of the major factors attributed to the contemporary drive for the documentary mode. Affordable digital video (DV) cameras made it possible for filmmakers to get high-quality images with a relatively small investment of time, money, and people – a phenomenon also discussed in the chapters about independent filmmaking in Peru, Arctic Canada, and elsewhere. Increased access to DV technology also meant liberation for young directors who worked outside institutions. The DV camera's portability has made it possible for filmmakers to get nearer to subjects and the everyday life. Moreover, DV technology has enlarged prospects for cinema to become a more individualistic means of expression in comparison with the more traditional studio-setting and collaborative style of filmmaking, thus enabling a more personal cinema and a highly "cinematic" film practice. As director Jia Zhangke claimed, the use of the DV camera was a conscious "aesthetic choice" (quoted in Frodon 2002). To Jia and many Sixth Generation directors, DV cameras opened up possibilities for "on location" naturalism that might present the complexities of life and society as they were truly experienced. Lou Ye's *Suzhou River* (2000), for example, showed how videography has become a new means of mass cultural expression. Its ubiquity and availability have supplied means for documenting everyday mass cultural practices such as weddings and birthdays.

DV technology also lowered the professional barrier for filmmakers by reducing costs and bypassing the normal production, processing, and even distribution routes. Electronic media "is not just a random collection of tools for making pictures, but a system interlocking artistic, technological, and commercial interests that are coming together in new cultural and social formations" (Wright 1995, 77). DV technology enabled filming in "guerrilla-style," such as that employed by director Li Yang in his filming of the officially banned *Blind Shaft*, a film that exposes the horrendous underground working practices in China's privatized coal mines, the equally atrocious widespread corruption in local and provincial governance, and the appalling social conditions of the migrant labourers. Wang Chao's *The Orphan of Anyang* was another such example.

The slice-of-life approach combined with long-take temporality magnifies the minute and intimate moments of the lives of the socially deprived, which enables images and voices of the social underclass in China to be seen and heard. Jia Zhang Ke's *Xiao Wu* and *Unknown Pleasures*, Li Yang's *Blind Shaft*, Wang Xiaoshuai's *So Close to Paradise* and *Beijing Bicycle*, Zhang Ming's *Rainclouds over Wushan* (1996), and Lou Ye's *Suzhou River* are all characterized by a compelling feel for the way of life of marginal communities.

Moreover, the penetration of pop cultural influences and multimedia applications into everyday life has made all ephemeral imagery more palpable and actual. There is no longer an absolute assumption that visual reality is one thing and visual art another. The youthful age of the Sixth Generation guarantees their ability to address the new audiovisual sensibility of an audience who, like themselves, grew up watching television and listening to pop music. As China has undergone drastic transformation, and as new ways of living and new values are spread by the mass media, the Sixth Generation films have allowed us to discover that there are ways to represent a China that was never presented before. These directors experiment with filmic techniques that correspond to the new conceptions they have of themselves and their world. The rise of the Sixth Generation cinema fits within a larger search for new modes of representation for a new generation.

Jia Zhangke's *Platform* (2000), to give an example, uses pop-culture references masterfully as a "context-providing '80s chronicle" that "maps an epochal period of sociocultural transition as experienced by the members of a small-town performance troupe" (Lim 2001). In this film Jia's microscopic-fashioned camera faithfully represents the macrocultural and macroeconomic transformations as experienced by a group of state cultural workers in the city of Fenyang throughout the 1980s. In the film, popular music plays the twin roles of epoch marker and memory storehouse in its "casual, real-time" depiction of "the displacement of Maoist culture by popular culture in everyday life" (Said 2002). The gradual social and cultural transitions are manifested through the film's popular songs, as well as through the status change of the cultural troupe. We witness the cultural transition from ideologically appropriated folk songs to Deng Lijun's love tunes and disco music; we also witness the cultural troupe switching its identity from a group of state-run cultural propaganda workers to privately owned entertainers. By placing popular music in its own social contexts and original forms, *Platform* not only presents the cultural metamorphoses that China experienced in the decade after Mao died but also articulates an alternative historical and social documentation. Its pop-culture references are as much a cinematic survey of the entertainment that surrounds a group of ordinary youngsters growing up post-Mao as they are an index to the organization and discursive formation of post-Mao culture.

The Sixth Generation cinema is aesthetically engaged with the social reality and the state of mind of the contemporary Chinese underclass existence. Its independent stance is politically, aesthetically, and socially loaded with a humanist grassroots perspective. The predominant use of DV technology facilitates a departure from studio-minded conventions, encourages the search for fresh filmic language, introduces electronic media into daily life, and becomes a contemporary means of expression. The application of digital video in filmmaking allows the directors a greater degree of improvisational freedom for capturing slice-of-life scenes. The Sixth Generation's association with "independent" or "underground" filmmaking is partially a result of this new trend.

Sixth Generation cinema's central concern with the impacts of post-socialist de-collectivization and privatization on the peripheral urban and suburban underclass heightens the focus on their plights and struggles; it also emphasizes their social disorientation and displacement amidst China's convulsive changes in the wake of the bankruptcy of socialism. This leads to a bifurcated grassroots perspective on independent flimmaking in China. On one level there is an alternative cinematic language and style, while on the other level there is the need to explore alternative ways of understanding and addressing the new realities of the post-socialist condition from multiple perspectives. The latter is what independent filmmaking in China is truly about.

NOTES

1 The "grand themes" policy is "题材决定论" in Chinese. The notion of "stream of life" art is described by Maria Galikowski, author of *Art and Politics in China*, according to Lau (2003, 19).

2 Zhang attributes the concept to Esther Yau and defines it as "the repackaging of what is generally believed to be Chinese national culture and its redistribution to the international film market" (Zhang 2002, 203).

3 Lou Ye uses the symbol of a mermaid in his well-acclaimed *Suzhou River*, which is not a traditional part of the Chinese folklore. Although his latest film, *Purple Butterfly*, is about historical experience involving the Japanese occupation of Manchuria, it is more concerned with stylistic orientation and clever narrative than with history.

4 Fredric Jameson uses the term *epic shot* to define the stylistic signature of the Fifth Generation cinema in its affirmation of epic narrativity, which "claims to constitute some new way of appropriating tradition" (Jameson 1995, 118).

5 The use of the term *cinéma-vérité* covered diverse approaches to filmmaking, and there were many ways of understanding the cinéma-vérité style: living camera, direct cinema, mobile cinema, realistic cinema, film inquiry, synchronous cinema, cinema of common sense, cinema of behaviour, personal documentary, tele-vérité, film journalism, truth film, direct shooting, candid-eye, and free cinema, etc. The three terms that have proven to be most hardy are the first three mentioned: cinéma-vérité, living cinema, and direct cinema. Cinéma-vérité has remained the subject of sharp controversy, since it meant different things to different people.

6 Time-sculpting is a filmic principle proposed by the genius of modern Russian cinema, Andrey Tarkovsky, who suggests that what comes into being with the birth of film is a new aesthetic principle, an aesthetic principle that enlarges and concentrates the living experience.

Chapter Eleven

Independent Filmmaking in Africa: New Voices and Challenges

MARTIN MHANDO

In the context of African independent filmmaking, it is conceptually advisable to look at Africa as a continental whole, even though Africa is not a homogenous entity and one can discern regional and linguistic groupings developing their own independent structures in the continent. Moreover, I believe this to be a valuable feature in the discussion of independent filmmaking at the global level, given that the diversity Africa brings to the study poses an interesting phenomenon to contrast with independent production cultures elsewhere in the world.

My perspective will be based on the perennial African cinematic production groupings – francophone, anglophone, and lusophone. While I dislike their colonial insinuations, they conveniently help to focus the past and the present and possibly even help to define the future. In addition, there are such groupings as Nollywood and Swahiliwood,[1] as well as other inter-sectionalities across the diverse groupings (including those discussed by Sheila Petty in this volume). The aim here is to show how current industry developments function in depth, by articulating complex reactions to Hollywood in the continent, and how film expresses the many important features of geopolitical and fiscal order, power, and influence.

To discuss this growing aesthetic of independent filmmaking, I would like to begin by looking at an illustrative framework of film production in the continent in order to position this particular view, and the study of the formal and discursive filmic innovations, within their historical and theoretical contexts. This, I hope, will assist us in developing an understanding of the issues of identity in African cinema and the way in which historical and social experiences help to define their "independent voice." This will be followed by an overview of the conditions of production prevailing in the continent, taking the linguistic anglophone, francophone, and lusophone bastions into the conversation. Viewed as complex reactions towards the dominant cinematic paradigm, African filmic texts reveal how the "mutating corpus ... stretches beyond social challenges, dualities and cultural essentialism" (Tcheuyap 2011, 14). They are presented here as a response to the innumerable historical, political, and cultural constraints traversing geopolitical boundaries.

A short discussion of two of the most independent of African filmmakers, Jean-Pierre Bekolo and Abderamanne Sissako, will be presented to exemplify the growth of the independent voice in the continent. The final section will portray distribution as the circulation of the independent voice, looking at whether it is primarily successful or curtailed through the palpable visibility of the product. Through this I hope to provide an insight into African independent film practices as reflections of new conditions of production and distribution, which have enabled filmmakers to challenge the stranglehold of the dominant global film industry.

There has always been an implied ideological premise to African film and production. Often this particular perception is substantiated by "idealism" about Africa that is then reflected in the polemics of African filmmakers. This ideological view is often based on stereotypical attitudes towards Africa, and this alone gives rise to the need to re-question the aesthetics and praxis of African cinema narration.

Although tradition and history are heavily inflected in the enunciation of African cinema, there are many incongruities brought about by both "modernity" and Africa's position in the globalized social, political, and economic conditions. In this discussion these influences must necessarily be seen as part of the conscious motivation of African filmmakers because they articulate responses to the specific conditions of their existence while remaining constrained by the formal structures associated with African cinema history. Further, it is increasingly claimed that this cinema culture, erected under colonial paradigms, continues to embed attitudes linked to "national" cinemas.

I would like to argue that, on the contrary, contemporary African social structures are deeply reflective of the globalized industrial society and that this is what continues to be communicated through African film. As Jonathan Haynes (2012, 14) puts it, "African film criticism and the Nigerian videos are not well suited to one another; the videos are not what is wanted by the criticism, and the criticism lacks many of the tools necessary to make sense of the videos."

Could this be the ultimate purpose of African film? Is its aim to express the experience of this contradiction as the response of a dynamic culture? Is African cinema a potential instigator of social change through its promotion of conflicting interpretations?

In this discussion of African independent filmmaking I would like to pose a number of questions, including whether the current associated structuring processes of global cinema may serve to further magnify the role of digital media, networks, and filmic productivity or even accelerate the decline of the dominance of Hollywood as a global production centre.

The dominance of Hollywood is waning, primarily owing to the influences of the digital world, but even at the cultural level we see world cultures redefining the structures for articulating cinema's powerful effect on how one sees oneself and the world, as well as the future of human perception. As the saying goes, films are not so important for what they say as for what they make one think. This attitude to film has informed many African filmmakers.

In certain parts of Africa the concept of independent filmmaking is, to put it mildly, a misnomer. Depending on the definition of independent filmmaking to which one subscribes, most African filmmaking has been seen as essentially independent. African cinema is obviously independent of Hollywood studio structures as regards production and distribution, and it has often been seen as consciously alternative in its aesthetics and narrative structure; indeed the cinema has always been low budget with very acute personal viewpoints (Tzioumakis 2006, 6). However, even with that "independence," African cinema has had to fight against its vulnerabilities towards "Western pressures on the content [and style] of the films," implying that filmmakers are forced to look towards "'Western' aesthetics in order to respond to the urgency of raising external funds" (Tcheuyap 2011, 12). This has therefore often besmirched the cinema's label of independence. One might argue that because of the control that European funding bodies have, principally because control is at the level of aesthetic projection, this makes them akin to the majors, especially when these funders are also linked to some of the distribution outlets in their countries as well as to other spheres of influence (this is the case in Iraq as well, discussed in Mary Erickson's chapter in this volume). It is therefore argued that, as discourse, African independent filmmaking "is produced and legitimated by socially authorised groups" (Tzioumakis 2006, 11).

To paraphrase Tzioumakis (2006), these powerful groups are the ones that stand to gain through their association with the cinema because of the exclusion of other parties who might levy some influence. It is therefore not surprising that African cinema has been portrayed as independent, because it also fulfils specific aims and objectives that define the field.

This is not to say that the films do not aim at the entertainment ethic or attain a level of commercial success as per the majors' ethic. There have been a number of films that were, relatively speaking, both commercial and critical successes. Films like *Ezra* (Newton Aduaka, 2006), *Viva Riva!* (Djo Tunda wa Munga, 2010), *Daratt* (Mahamat Saleh Haroun, 2006), *Teza* (Haile Gerima, 2008), *Yellow Card* (John Riber, 2000), *Yaaba* (Idrissa Ouedraogo, 1989), and *Tilai* (Idrissa Ouedraogo, 1991), or even much older ones like *Mapantsula* (Oliver Smitz, 1988) or *Love Brewed in an African Pot* (Kwaw Ansah, 1981), can lay claim to such success. All these films were super low budget and among the few African films to make a commercial return. As film critic Emmanuel Levy (1999, 1) comments, "ideally, an indie is a fresh, low-budget movie with a gritty style and offbeat subject matter that express the filmmaker's personal vision."

The situation in South Africa is somewhat complicated because it is the country with the strongest Hollywood presence in the continent, and since 1994 it has acted as the bellwether of cinema happenings on the continent given its economic power. It has such an incestuous attraction to Hollywood that it does not allow itself to dream the "poor man's dream" like Nollywood and like the rest of sub-Saharan Africa. Only in 2004 was South Africa able to see *Yesterday* (Darrell Roodt, 2003), the first full-length Zulu feature film with English subtitles. With films like *Forgiveness* (Ian Gabriel, 2004), the voice of reconciliation wafted high, but without either critical or commercial success. Even successful and supposedly low-budget films like *Tsotsi* (Gavin Hood, 2005), *Jerusalema* (Ralph Ziman, 2008), and *District 9* (Neill Blomkamp, 2009) – some of which were picked up by major distributors – are way out of league for the rest of the continent. To Africa these films had blockbuster budgets; *Tsotsi* had an estimated US$3 million budget, while *District 9* had an estimated US$30 million budget.

While the voices that come out of these films sound independent, they are muffled by the shrill value system from the co-production necessities with countries like Canada, France, Germany, Italy, Britain, New Zealand, Australia, and Ireland. The National Film and Video Foundation of South Africa (the national funding and film policy body) is torn between supporting the big end of the industry that is supported by co-production treaties, and the low-end disadvantaged youth whose voices we long to hear.

As Tomaselli (2006, 124) warns, "apartheid has left its mark on the South African film industry … At the discursive level, there is need to balance celebratory reconciliation discourses with the more critical engagements with the process of transformation, while at the same time resisting the pressure to always be politically correct. South African films need to draw on a range of narratives and a plurality of meanings."

As creative freedom can now be afforded to everyone in the Rainbow Nation to construct narratives and counter-narratives, from such possibilities we get jewels like *Temba* (Stephanie Scholt, 2006) and *Izulu lami* (Madoda Ncayiyana, 2008), stories with a focus on children, voices that are rarely heard. However, what has dominated the African cinematic discourse is African cinema's attempt and subsequent failure, until the rise of Nollywood, to attract popular audiences and also to be commercially distributed at some significant level. Back in 2009 I wrote: "One of the greatest ironies of film production in Africa is found in the area of distribution. This is because for purposes of commercial earnings that are often meagre or non-existent, African film producers often appeal and attend to the international market for their sustenance. This has translated into total dependence on the festival circuit for the distribution of the African film product.[2] It is important to note, however, that novel methods for distributing the film continue to be tried in many different parts of the continent with diverse results" (Mhando 2009, 19).

As a result of the maintenance of the heavily protected multinational film distribution outlets in the continent, independent African filmmakers have struggled to distribute their product (Nu Metro Times Media Group 2013). The Nu Metro and Ster-Kinekor chains control the mainstream distribution circuit in most of Africa. This has led to the producers adopting novel distribution methods that have evolved with the political economies of the various countries. The phenomenon of the African film festival, for example, existing both inside and outside the continent, has become "a sort of sector for alternative distribution for African cinema."[3] One can certainly conclude that these are the more "appropriate" methods because they derive from the economics of those developing countries.

Historical and Theoretical Contexts

In his book *Post-Nationalist African Cinemas*, Alexie Tcheuyap (2011, 6) makes a bold argument against what he regards as the "prescriptive," "prohibitive," and "exclusionist" cinema of the 1970s in Africa under which the political discourse could not support the aesthetic tenets of film production. He essentially argues that the independent voice of the filmmaker was abdicated in favour of an intellectual cinema as a result of political factors (8). However, one begs to differ over his anointing of the Federation of Pan African Cinema (FEPACI) as the ideological linch-pin of African cinematic expression. While it may be true to a certain extent that FEPACI held sway over some of the francophone filmmak-ing fraternity, it never had the same impact on the anglophone region. The Maghreb region under the leadership of Algeria, Mauritania, and Morocco only peripherally supported its ideology. Indeed, Egypt has always had a strong independent industry. It is obvious, for example, that even before and immediately after South Africa's freedom in 1994 the political regimentation that FEPACI oversaw in the Francophonie failed to take hold among South African filmmakers.

The "brute pan-Africanism" controlled by artists, intellectuals, and social institutions, against which Tcheuyap rallies, cannot really be applied to most anglophone productions, such as *Flame* (2006), *Mapantsula* (1989), or the films produced by Media For Development in Zimbabwe. While nation building was clearly a core-uniting factor among filmmakers in the Anglophonie as it was in the Francophonie, its expression was diversely reflected within the two communities. However the lusophone region maintained a much more revolutionary stance in its cinematic expression, as seen in the films like *Sambizanga* (Sarah Maldoror, 1972, Angola) and *Mueda, memória e massacre* (Louis Guerra, 1979, Mozambique).[4]

Underneath all this, African filmmakers continued to face a very con-strained environment with regard to their production capacities, given that film production was very expensive and control was heavily levied upon any filmmaker who was afforded the opportunity to make a film. As Peter Rovrik (2012) warns, "concerns with co-productions are that foreign countries sometimes require visibility within the film, which can in some cases detract from a good storyline. The same problem exists with overt product placement. Funders, too, often have certain criteria or preferred themes which are imposed on the grant recipients, or self-imposed by filmmakers desperate to secure the funds" (n.p.).

Funding sources always impose control or constrain the independ-ent voice in a film, and this has been the bane of film production in the continent. Apart from the French government funding discussed above and the Centre National de la Cinématographie (CNC), other European countries fund the filmmakers from their ex-colonies. France's World Cinema Fund (formerly Fonds Sud), Arte (Association Relative à la Télévision Européenne, a Franco-German television network channel), Africalia, the Danish Centre for Culture and Development, Hivos, the Hubert Bals Fund, and the Jan Vrijman Fund are some of the funding organizations in Europe that have continued to fund African films. In the Anglophonie the British Film Institute (UK) might be the only consistent funding source.

Some of the obvious constraints are linked to subjects or themes. Notice how often African films appear during periods of themes that have a lot of currency in Europe, such as *Ezra* (2006, focusing on the war in Sierra Leone), *Moolade* (2006, the issue of female genital mutilation worldwide), and *Africa United* (2010, the World Cup held in 2010 in South Africa). The themes might have had currency in Africa for years, but until such time as there was European interest, no film was funded. The late Sembene Ousmane once said that his life's pursuit was to make a film on Sundita Keita (1217 to ca. 1255), founder of the Mali Empire, but no one was ready to fund such a project. However, funding for *Moolade* did not take long to come along, and many wondered if it was the subject of female genital mutilation that had prompted the funding.[5]

The major challenge for an African film practice lies in its need to become a fully fledged industry with the requisite infrastructures of production, distribution, exhibition, promotion, training, and marketing, thus making it sustainable and reducing its dependence on government or donor funding. But, as Peruvian economist Hernando de Soto (2003) argues, although the poor are capable and hardworking, they seem to suffer because they are kept out of the formal economy, unable to expose the capital potential of their entrepreneurship. He says, "The poor inhabitants of these nations – the overwhelming majority – do have things, but they lack the process to represent their property and create capital. They have houses but no titles; crops but no deeds; businesses but no statutes of incorporation" (3).

In the meantime, Louise Kamin (2012) estimated that the Bongo movie industry provided employment for hundreds of thousands of Tanzanians: "There are reportedly over fifty independent producers making films and over twenty-five distributors with strong wholesale networks in Tanzania and East Africa ... Furthermore, there are nearly ten thousand video exhibition halls and about twenty-five thousand video rental libraries across the country. This cultural industry, in

Tanzania, is commercially sustainable and if nurtured will grow and improve over time" (5).

This is the prevailing socio-economic environment in Tanzania with regard to the film industry, where entrepreneurial spirit is high, but those with creativity and talent cannot always avail themselves of the abundant opportunities. The burgeoning Bongo movie industry is straining against the informality of this production system. In the meantime, digital technology and economy beckon with the potential of linking video halls to digital distribution systems, or even the growth of mini multiplexes in the urban centres of the region. At this juncture, however, it appears that we can expect Bongo movies to continue to be "upwardly global and resolutely African" (McCall 2007, 82–97).

I now turn the discussion to the discourses that have come to define what African cinema is or could be in the future. I begin from the premise that the term *African cinema* only exists within two contradictory discourses:

1. The premier discourse concerns cultural production according to the manner in which we have consumed African films in the "cinematic" realm. This is essentially an intellectual discourse, although the nature of African film production and distribution has, until very recently, located it only within the political and cultural spheres. This then is the first contradiction – that the artistic value of the cinema is limited to its historical and political nature or origin.

2. The second contradiction is found in the populist consumption of African visual narratives, where it is defined by its consumerist but equally subversive character. Visit any city in Africa and you will be swamped by the "vulgar" and "cheap" narratives that the masses ravenously consume with total disregard to the politics of their consumption.

These two contradictory discourses inform much of the current "crisis" of global cinematic expression and are enacted by the independent African filmmaker. In recent years we have seen the growth of narratives known by the term *Nollywood*. *Nollywood* describes both the industrial structure and its critical appreciation. Narratives of Nollywood, just like those we find in many African urban cinematic productions (that is, film and video), are very idiomatic in structure and base. These idiomatic constructs appeal to the general population because the characters are composed from a relatively small base of recognizable cultural traits, and their collective meanings follow not just one single interpretation but several modes of interpretations. This is a feature that is recurrent among African audiences because it helps to define the everyday. Like soap operas, the stories that the audiences follow are recurrent, so they do not need to wait to see what will happen. In fact, the audiences "reconnoitre" the narratives and know, as they watch, what is likely to happen next. The growth of Nollywood-like film-production structures all over the continent – as also evidenced in Sheila Petty's discussion herein of digital video in Nollywood, Ghana, Burkina Faso, and elsewhere – has been aided by a number of factors, not least the steady decline in the price of digital cameras that has allowed the making of fast and cheap productions. Second, while television has offered a convenient outlet for the cinematic product, in many countries the African product struggles nevertheless because television is still a middle-class purview.

The middle class's "upward looking" towards Euro-American lifestyles forces television stations to buy cheap American and European products and, at the same time, to look down upon the African product. Poor station management does not help either. The independent voices of African filmmakers therefore work towards not only describing and asserting a view but also mostly fusing the two disparate positions described above by Tcheuyap through an awareness of their need to develop a new cinematic language for the continent.

> The overarching theme of Nollywood films is Africa's troubled journey to modernity. Because Hollywood films tend to show people at the other end of that journey, they fail to resonate. ("Lights, Camera, Africa" 2010)

Independent Filmmakers' Complex Reactions to Hollywood

> "Is there anything in this cinema which is not Africa?
> Fantasy, myth, we got. Walt Disney, we got,
> Lion King, we got. Massacres, we got.
> Comedians, music, we got. Paul Simon, we got.
> Aristotle, catharsis, and kola nut, we got.
> What don't we got?"
>
> Jean-Pierre Bekolo (*Aristotle's Plot*, 1996)

The enunciation of African cinema has always been projected as a vocal criticism of Anglo-American cinema's cultural imperialism, admittedly determined by continental as well as other global concerns (Tcheuyap 2011, 230). As my discussion has thus far shown, there are numerous ways of looking at African cinema through the categories of culture, anthropology, and ideology. As a historically defined and determined social entity, cinema has also come to reveal its complex relations to Hollywood, thus further revealing African cinema as being a complex entity itself. Core to the interrogation of this relationship are the questions, where is contemporary African cinema located and how is it accessed?

This is a fundamental issue for African independent filmmaking as it defines not only the processes of production and conceptualization but also its marketing and valuation. The questions can be divided into two key directions: first, can we predict how African filmmakers will continue to produce films? And second, how is it possible to manage audiences for the African film product?

Central to the question of the accessibility of African films is the issue of piracy. Piracy delineates where the African film is found and the extent of its reach, as well as its conceptual valuation. While we shall discuss piracy as an African cinematic phenomenon, and it probably has a particular "flavour" that is typically African, piracy is not limited to Africa alone. It is a global phenomenon, found even in Malaysia as discussed by Gaik Cheng Khoo in this volume, although it is of particular importance to Africa because media goods are priced considerably higher than the reach of the average low-income earner. More important, the authorized film distribution channels do not work towards serving the majority in society. As Ramon Lobato (2011) puts it, "when pirate discs account for between 80% and 90% of the total DVD marketing in many of the world's most populous nations (...), where illegal file-sharing is estimated to make up around a quarter of total worldwide Internet traffic (...), it is clear that we are no longer talking about a marginal practice at the fringes of cinema culture. Rather we are talking about a fundamental and integral component of the global movie distribution system" (n.p.).

For the African filmmaker, the film business has provided legitimate trade and delivered other important social benefits, while also ensuring that its producers receive enough revenue from the porous piracy (McCall 2007). Therefore, in the context of predicting how African filmmakers will continue to produce their films, it becomes clear that we need to ask ourselves what is actually hidden behind the fear of piracy.

Indeed, Lobato (2011) argues that "piracy is not a coherent and singular practice; rather, there are many and varied piracies, all of which mean different things in different contexts" (n.p.). He continues: "Hence we have in Nollywood an example of piracy working as a structural foundation for new film industries: in other words, piracy as a productive or generative force for new cultural production. This is one very unusual, and quite unique, example of the relations between piracy and emergent national cinemas – in this case, a co-dependent rather than cannibalistic relation" (ibid.).

With regard to the management of African cinema audiences, in the more distant past, African film production was managed through a view of African cinema as a homogeneous entity, predicated by its colonial links and highlighting its difference to other colonial and historical relations. Nationalist and liberationist motivations of African cinema were viewed as necessary projections of a growing vitality during the immediate post-independence period in which the new African countries needed to proclaim their presence in a world that was blind to their geographical and historical locations (Tcheuyap 2011). Furthermore, the "uneven development of African independence assured that revolutionary values would inform African filmmaking as long as colonial domination continued" (Harrow 1999, xiv). But has that domination really stopped? In his article "Thematic Concerns in the Emergent Zimbabwean Short Film Genre," Nhamo Mhiripiri (2010, 94) states: "This article makes the assumption that films made by Zimbabwean filmmakers reflect how Zimbabweans perceive themselves. In implying that the earlier developmental films were influenced by foreign donors, there is again the assumption that it is possible for others to make Zimbabweans view themselves in other ways."

Mhiripiri concludes that identity is also a negotiation influenced by local and global factors. In more recent times a sense of the individuality of expression and the aesthetic joy of experimentation and innovative storytelling has emerged, significantly changing the way African cinema is positioned in world production.

> The export of Nigerian films has been remarkable; ... they are on television in Namibia and on sale in the streets in Kenya. In Congo, they are broadcast with the soundtrack turned down while an interpreter tells the story in Lingala or other languages. In New York, their biggest consumers are now immigrants from the Caribbean and African Americans, not Africans, and Chinese people are buying them too. In Holland, Nollywood stars are recognised on the streets of Suriname, and in London they are hailed by Jamaicans. (Haynes 2007a, 106–7)

Film audiences all over Africa have fallen prey to Nollywood and the many other cinematic "-woods," thus attaching themselves to the allusion of similarities of life and to values that many argue are clearly discernible as being homogeneously African. Audiences of such movies circulate the world as diasporic "Western Union" audiences, attached to their motherland through a diversity of African identities.

All this also needs to be seen in the context of global cinema developments. When in the past Hollywood was structurally linked to American global imperialism, and Europe was seen as the purveyor of avant-gardism, other cinemas positioned themselves as culturally different and oppositional to the Hollywood and European ethics. At present, Hollywood is faced with the fast-changing digital consequences in both production as well as distribution, and the African place in this is eminently consequential. Central to this African challenge is an intrinsic departure from the assumptions, power structures, and ideologies that Hollywood encodes regarding the impact of piracy on the economics of film distribution and in accessing the visual product. Hollywood needs to develop a more complex relationship not only with its American audience but also increasingly with its global audiences, just as these formerly Hollywood markets now view America as Hollywood's "local" market. This is a complex association, as Hollywood will have to renegotiate its relationships with its global audiences and the institutions it protects, while hoping to maintain its power and influence. All these factors are changing, and more so in Africa.

By incorporating new visions, genres, representations, and aesthetic expressions, today's filmmakers are not only interrogating sub-Saharan African identities but also staking out a place for African cultures in global flows where identity oscillates between "global and local, nation and (no) nation" (Petty 2008, 1). Although the films produced and circulating in this new field are African, they conjure up new imaginations of Africa.

So how do we read such cinematic excess? Indeed, as Patricia MacCormack (2005, 34) remarks, cinema has the power to produce pleasure that "is in excess of the meaning of images," and in the case of these films they have currency even over their deferral of political and social contexts. What becomes patently obvious here is that while the definitions of independent cinema are never transparent, as they cannot cover all the criteria for independence, African cinema production is often free from impositions of the dominant or mainstream Hollywood production and distribution system. Thus, whatever other impositions still exist, whether economic, aesthetic, or stylistic, African cinema still has an ostensible independence.

The Independent Vision

In 1961, the Ministère de Coopération was established, developing a Bureau de Cinema for financing films in the Francophone region. By 1975, France would assist more than 125 of 185 films from francophone Africa, totalling close to 70 per cent. Whilst the Bureau was closed by the Mittérrand government in 1980, film financing has continued to exist in different forms in France for the African states, including the Fonds Images Afrique, Fonds Sud Cinema, as well as more international organisations such as the Organisation Internationale de la Francophonie and support from the European Union. 65 of 85 films (or 77 per cent) financed by these organisations between 2001–2003 were produced in francophone Africa. (Armes 2006, 57)

While the productions referenced in the above passage are presented as transnational collaborations, the films have to "satisfy a number of divergent foreign needs and interests," including "a full, dialogued production script in a European language (usually French)" (ibid.), which is necessary for securing foreign investment, and a scenario that "must conform partly to European criteria as to what constitutes an 'African film'" (ibid.). It will come as no surprise that these relations are criticized as being paternalistic and neocolonial, and often participation in such funding processes has labelled filmmakers as French culture mouthpieces. The one way in which a filmmaker could prevail over this view is by manifesting these same contradictions within the African film as text. This is the manner in which two major African filmmakers have indeed come to survive and succeed. I am talking here of Abdremanne Sissako of Mauritania and Jean-Pierre Bekolo of Cameroon. Other influential independent voices with a self-reflexive bent to their production include Jean-Marie Teno (Cameroon), Med Hondo (Mauritania), Cheikh Oumar Sissoko (Mali), and Suleyman Cisse (Mali). For example, in the film *Heremakono* (2002): "Sissako draws on the notion of travel and its connotations – movement, migration, exile – to challenge Eurocentric assumptions regarding Africanness and authenticity in African cinema, assumptions that African Studies scholar David Murphy (...) claims trap Western critics within the Hegelian worldview that imagines Africa as a primitive and incomprehensible 'other'" (Burgin 2011, 27–9).

Through the film, Sissako deals with a self-reflective "African" identity and undermines it, while at the same time revealing the dehumanizing effects of colonialism and indeed of globalization. The village Noua-dhibou in *Heremakono* is set in Mauritania and is the take-off point for Africans attempting to head to the Spanish mainland via the Canary Islands. However, the village is presented as an "authentic" African village, laid back and projecting the same values with which Europe still ascribes Africa. In the meantime we see it as a village of movement, dreams, expectations, intrigue, and death. One could easily see the vil-lage as a postmodern representation of an airline transit lounge – full of mobility, assuring no rootedness. "In this sense, Abdullah, who has lost contact with his familial and cultural ties, becomes representative of the complexities of speaking of 'African identity' and explores the paradox of the African subject caught in the interstices of two or more cultures" (Burgin 2011, n.p.). In one scene the film's Westernized main character, hell-bent to run away from Africa, is shown interned in a room where he hears the pitter-patter of the feet of those making the move to Europe.

In his other very successful film, *Bamako* (2006), Sissako utilizes all possible cinematic skills to narrate a didactic allegory about the World Bank and the International Monetary Fund and their relations with Africa. The story threads the lives of a number of characters attending a court case in an open courtyard. The destinies of the characters are intertwined, and the "characters are not so much as symbols or ciphers as [they] are reminders of the almost incomprehensible gulf between the general and the particular" (Scott 2007).

Sissako compares well with another filmmaker, the Cameroo-nian Jean-Pierre Bekolo, director of three key independent features, *Quartier Mozart* (1992), *Aristotle's Plot* (1996), and *Les Saignantes* / *The Bloodettes* (2005). It is in the personality of Bekolo that we see a major characteristic of independent African filmmaking: the strong personal vision. In all three films Bekolo strives for expressive auton-omy, always with an open-ended structure and a consciously alter-native, non-formulaic, multiple-genre narrative, but filled with the entertainment ethic. In an interview with Akin Adesokan (2008, 3), Bekolo speaks of his use of genre bending: "I would say that, first of all, genre films are part of our culture, as Africans. There's no doubt about that. But the thing is always not just to use them, but to ques-tion them in relation to the choices we have to make in the context of African cultures."

In *Quartier Mozart*, for example, he highlights the need for representing the global through the local, with a specific view. In the film he
describes an African geographical and cultural space that is defined by
economic poverty and stifled by male chauvinism, which to Bekolo is
a form of cultural violence. Using humour and editing techniques to
resemble a music video, he tells a story of two young women whose
struggle for power forces them to realize that it is being a man that con-
fers one power in society. They therefore opt to get themselves penises
through magic and so begin to affect their world. Through this melange
of styles and contradictions Bekolo weaves a narrative about identities
that can only be understood as approximations of otherness.

In 1995 the British Film Institute commissioned Bekolo to make a film
marking the centenary of cinema in Africa. The result was *Aristotle's Plot*,
a satire about the direction and content of filmmaking in Africa through
a narrative of subversion relating to African history, politics, and postcolonial identity. This film questions the relevance of mimesis and conventional storytelling. Bekolo essentially "pokes fun at everyone, pitting
the passive consumers of Hollywood spectacles against the devotees of
French-subsidised *cinéma de calebasse* and social-realist auteur cinema.
Creating a film whereby spectacle, song, diction, thought and character
supersede the plot, Bekolo defies Aristotle, and Western narrative theory
itself, by successfully producing the ultimate tragedy: a reflection on the
pithy state of contemporary African film industry" (Burgin 2011).

Compare this with the humorous treatment of popular memory in
Quartier Mozart, where the young schoolgirl, Queen of the Hood, meets
Maman Thekla, the local sorcerer, who helps her enter the body of a young
stud, My Guy, so that she can understand the real "sexual politics of the
Quartier." To Bekolo the challenge is to create a new semantic through
which one can speak "properly" without having to tread on someone
else's language. Cinema has never been so impregnated! Bekolo explains:
"I was commissioned to make this film for the anniversary of cinema ...
but at the same time, I decided to use this as a tool for self-expression.
Also a discourse about all the aspects of being asked to make a film in
itself, and my criticism of what film's all about" (quoted in Adesokan
2008, 10).

Distribution

Independence in film production lies in the capacity to not only produce
but also distribute the product. Distribution, as the circulation of the

Table 11.1 World Cinema Seat Distribution as of 1964

	Number of Cinemas (35 mm and 16 mm)	Total Seats (Millions)	Seating Capacity per 1,000 Inhabitants
World	170,000	63.0	22
Africa	2,500	1.3	6
North America	22,000	13.5	52
South America	9,000	5.0	37
Asia (excluding USSR)	17,000	10.0	6
Europe	60,000	23.0	55
Oceania	2,600	1.5	93
USSR	59,000	8.8	42

Source: Adapted from Jane Banfield, "Films in East Africa," Transition 3, 13 (March–April 1964), 19.

independent voice, gives visibility to the product and thus gives reason for the production. Writing in 1964, Jane Banfield shows the disproportionate cinema seat distribution in the world (table 11.1). While Africa has never fared better since then in terms of the distribution capacity for films, it remains the bane of the voice of the independent filmmaker throughout the globe, being most evident in Africa. Given the relative isolation of African communities and owing to a weak infrastructure, weak purchasing power, and the intrinsically commercial culture of the value of film distribution, many Africans still do not patronize films in the cineplexes in cities. While in the past the mobile film distribution in the continent was a worthy exercise (linked as it was to the merchandising culture prior to literacy, radio, television, and now digital culture), new forms of distribution have meant its death (mobile cinema has been useful in Iraq recently, however, as discussed in Mary Erickson's chapter in this volume).

Despite the many valiant efforts at diversification, cinema distribution in Africa remains under the control of the major distributors of the world, who supply the products of the major producers of the world. Futile attempts at breaking this cycle were always met with derision until the coming of the Nollywood spectre. "African films are foreigners in their own countries," cried Emmanuel Sama (1996, 148). "They are making a bashful entry in exactly the same way as a stranger entering another country" (ibid.).

In French West Africa, COMACICO (Compagnie africaine cinéma-tographique et commerciale) and SECMA (Société d'exploitation ciné-matographique africaine) control the distribution and exhibition of films. When nationalization took place in countries like Guinea, Burkina Faso, and Mali in the 1970s, COMACICO joined with the Motion Picture Export Association of America (now the Motion Picture Association, a division of the Motion Picture Association of America, the trade association for the major Hollywood film studios) and responded with boycotts until the local authorities capitulated.

The same happened in the anglophone and lusophone countries and, in the 1970s and 1980s, in countries like Tanzania, Mozambique, and Angola. There any effort to give priority to the local or even alternative film exhibition was met with the heavy hand of commercial and political sanctions.

Cultural-historical affinities and some universal appeal of the base aspect of melodrama and humour may explain the popularity of Holly-wood films in Africa. Hollywood has long been an integral part of the cultural memory of African audiences and filmmakers alike. However, it is through the distribution and exhibition structures and their policies that we see the domination of Hollywood.

Despite the fact that there were screening quotas in place, which were designed to allow screen time for other cultural cinematic prod-ucts, local exhibitors often preferred Hollywood films over Indian or European products. During the 1970s and 1980s the more fiscally chal-lenged countries, like Tanzania and Mozambique, could only import cheap B-grade films (like the Italian spaghetti westerns), and of course there was no African cinema production or distribution of any quantity or note. It must, however, be remembered that in the 1960s and 1970s Indian films had also dominated the screen at first-run theatres during the major holiday seasons in many African countries. In addition to the Indian films' proven popularity at these theatres, and despite their language difficulties (they were in Hindi or Gujarat), they still proved to be a viable option for film importers.

Bollywood enjoyed unfettered freedom with an entertainment ethic loosely resembling Hollywood in its impact on the viewer. The effect has then been to acculturate the African viewer into appreciating a specific product, further entrenching the appreciation of colonial culture. It would take a veritable revolution to orient the audiences to another taste.

Television audiences did not fare any better, especially as television remained a medium marketed to and appreciated by the elite whose tastes had already been formed through education, cinema, and class exposure. When the independent filmmakers wanted to speak, they had to engage with these contradictions, which to them were insurmountable. Indeed, they were faced with a greater conundrum when they were asked, as Emmanuel Sama (1996, 148) asks, "But of what value is the finished product if it has no circuit for distribution?" The film festival outlet then became the saviour of the independent African filmmaker.[6] The first films by African filmmakers – produced from the early 1960s onwards – were only exhibited after they had received recognition at festivals outside the continent (Bangré 1996, 157).

Films play an important role in the understanding and appreciation of cultures. However, since African film is never available for consumption beyond the festival circuit, its appreciation remains the subject of the elite audience, otherwise called the alternative audience. Just ten years ago we would often ask ourselves, who sees the African cinema product in Africa? How do films get to be seen? What kinds of distribution circuits exist in the many countries of the continent?

The answer was, they were not being seen! Independent African films and videos were hard to come by not only overseas but also in their places of production. The continued reliance on African film producers on the festival circuit essentially forces filmmakers to accept and depend on the terms of their films' canonization to create other works, thus holding them hostage to that label. As Idrissa Ouedraogo once said, sometimes one finds African films that have won awards in Europe being totally incomprehensible to African audiences, for whom they were initially intended.

The festival, while a valuable tool for African independent filmmakers, also presents a trap. With no possibility of ever getting one's film on the big screen, performance fees at festivals could be one possible source of earnings. However, most festivals no longer pay for unrequested films. Indeed, globalization has meant that often the tendency is to equalize or equate the Westernized view as being universal. This reflects how festivals have become encoded within a "film festival language." Film festivals have become coloured by so many subtle Western pretensions and artistic ornamentations that some festivals now surrender their usefulness as unique cultural documents.

It is in this context that over the last twenty years there has been a mushrooming of African film festivals around the world (especially in Europe), leading to the impassioned appeal for understanding from Lindiwe Dovey (2010), who defends African film festivals outside

Africa in her paper "Directors' Cut: In Defence of African Film Festivals outside Africa." Inside the continent there are now over fifty film festivals, with thirty-one that have been operating for longer than five years (AfriFestNet 2013). Exposure of the independent African product is slowly gathering speed. Recently, with Nollywood also gathering speed and popularity, television stations have begun to buy African film product. M-Net, the South African cable television outlet, has become the owner of the largest archive of African films with its Africa film library, an initiative that showcases the African film industry and makes these African movies easily accessible. Nonetheless, regardless of the importance of M-Net as a market, the price it pays for the African product is abominably low. Indeed it has even reduced the fees it initially paid because of the lack of competition in the television market. It now has two "African Movie Magic" channels and pays as little as US$1,500 per licence for a full-length feature. In the meantime, "digital technology is revolutionizing the landscape and levelling the playing fields. Ghana, Kenya, South Africa and others are embracing the Nigerian model of straight-to-DVD and bypassing cinema. Low budget filmmaking opens up possibilities to filmmakers who previously had little hope of entering the elite domain of high-end cinema" (Rorvik 2012).

Indeed the new independent cinema in the continent has developed ingenious ways to monetize the new cinema product to include a satellite television system, a local DVD hawker distributor system, the stand-alone mini-cinema-hall exhibitor trade, and an overseas DVD market catering to the African diaspora. Lately, even Netflix-inspired websites have been developed. However, and unashamedly, the commercialization of the new cinema is mostly based on the physical sale of cheap DVDs, especially where film distribution has exploded owing to the low production costs, access to the product, and a very large market of the urbanized poor.

Despite these developments, piracy remains a major problem for the independent filmmaker. Short of throwing one's arms up in the air or re-orienting distribution to the production processes (as discussed earlier), the next best alternative is to pursue the legal precepts flanked by lawyers rather than filmmakers, as exemplified by Côte Ouest: "Côte Ouest Audiovisuel is a French, privately owned, independent film and television distribution company, widely recognized as Africa's unrivalled leader in the arena of sales and distribution of audio-visual content for and from Africa. Launched in 1997, it distributes annually to 75 TV channels in over 42 markets an average of 20,000 hours of programs, mostly soap operas and telenovelas, but also feature films, series and TV movies, and serves as a one-stop content destination for African buyers to access high quality programs that have enjoyed broadcast success in the United States, Latin America and Europe" (Côte Ouest Audiovisuel 2013).

While such dynamic and philosophically driven commercial ventures grow, the African independent filmmaker on the continent and in the diaspora now places the African customer at the centre of all business operations and processes. The African diaspora and African cinema now have such a relationship.

There has always been some form of assertive ownership by diasporic Africans towards the African product, be this music, food, fashion, or, as is now happening, film. Beyond the apartheid spectacle or the Mandela dynamic or even the Rwanda genocide, African media producers, including filmmakers, have grown increasingly savvy at promoting Africa to a wider global market that includes the African diaspora. Needless to say, Western domination focuses on the tribal and ritualistic, the ethnographic and the journalistically sensational, where the West sees the diasporic audience as only a small extension of its global market. This is in contrast to the growing, ingenuous methods of embracing the world by Africans as they continue to reinvent ways of addressing their continental and diasporic audiences.

An example of a good "media event" is the Obama factor or the hip-hop scene. African television outlets like M-NET and MTN utilize their capacity to transmit well-orchestrated media spectacles through satellites and other digital platforms as key strategies for reaching out to diasporic, as well as national, audiences.

In all this, it is not the box-office receipts that indicate the popularity or influence of this new film or media culture. While the loud marketing of the short release period helps to attract audiences, it is the subsequent and ancillary markets based on the DVD and the illegal pirate culture that matter. What this continues to reveal is that there are ebbs and flows in the independent film scene that remain unpredictable. Further, this also shows that despite the restrictions and the view of the business as piracy, which inevitably limits growth in the open field, the producers have been successful and influential to the extent that they have been able to attract paying audiences.

Conclusion

The aim of this discussion on the independent filmmakers' voice in Africa has been to reveal how the production and distribution conditions associated with the global film restructuring processes serve to further cement the place and the role of film in clarifying socio-historical transitions. Needless to say, filmmakers in Africa have taken up the challenge, and this has had major implications for the way in which globalization is enacted in the African film. Notice how a film like *Viva Riva!* (Djo Munga, 2011, Democratic Republic of the Congo) ethnicizes the imagery of the dysfunctional African city into a "blaxploitation" drama, allowing the recognition of identities, affinities, and a sense of belonging within specific social contexts. The new voice of the independent filmmaker has shed its national cinema politics and embraced a new global African identity. For this reason, certain pillars of the classical aesthetic, such as cause-and-effect narrative logic, psychological character motivation, and clear-cut generic frameworks, are heavily embraced in the new African narratives.

The stylistic and narrative patterns associated with Hollywood film that include adherence to a narrative structure, narrative as a platform for special effects (as we find in the juju films), increasing emphasis on spectacle with ostentatious living as attraction, and characters as plot functions in adherence to Aristotelian poetics of the supremacy of the plot and genre hybridity have been relearned to embed the entertainment ethic. For many young, untrained African filmmakers, the American film has gradually become a mode of expression and a commemoration of a long and trusted colonial amusement industry, which had succeeded in enticing a very large audience to a specific kind of entertainment but had to date been financially prohibitive.

The extension to this experience that was to be learned was the way in which that effect could be repeated ad infinitum through marginal distribution channels running parallel to the traditional systems that the filmmaker could also control. For the evolving relations between "new" and "traditional" African cinema, the current environment implies that the connection between the broader economic crisis of poverty and the specifics of globalization will serve to further extend the long-run interrogation of the role of media and communication networks, services, and functions across all key spheres of social, political, and economic life. Look for example at the innovative use to which the mobile phone and other social media networks in the African environment have been put; by going way beyond their initial use, they allow for the transformation of both applied technology and society.

That is how the current outlook further amplifies strategic shifts in geopolitical order and in the forms and operations of global power and influence. This is done through acknowledging that the "conceptual shift to independence is best achieved by placing what I call shadow economies of cinema – unmeasured, unregulated and extralegal audiovisual commerce – at the centre of our analytical lens, and by considering the many ways in which they interface with conventional film industries" (Lobato 2011, 1).

The new voice of the independent filmmaker, supported by erstwhile colonial-framed funding, has now come to position both marginal networks and communication as increasingly important features of a contemporary geopolitical order. Notice how the "subterranean" distribution networks across different global cities – from New York to Melbourne to Beijing to Bangkok – now present a viable cinematic culture and commerce (ibid.).

All these will inevitably have repercussions on the global geopolitical order as they highlight tensions between the increasingly global scope of economic and financial relations and national cultural factors and discourses. One can meaningfully talk of Africa being part of a "creative destruction" by contributing to major shifts in the mediation of sociopolitical processes as well as in the structures of power across a number of sectors from commerce and media to technology and culture.

The experience after the International Monetary Fund austerity measures of the 1980s has taught the African filmmaker a lesson – different than that intended by traditional economists – about the devolved economic environment of open markets and economic liberalization. To the discerning African filmmaker or business operator there are clear gaps in the global entertainment market, which, if exploited wisely, can undermine the established order and trigger new, viable socioeconomic configurations.

NOTES

1 The -*wood* attachment is a humorous naming of all the Nollywood-like industries mushrooming across the continent. In Kenya there is Riverwood, in Rwanda it is Hillywood, in Cameroon it is Collywood, and in Tanzania it is Swahiliwood, but the local idiomatic term for the Swahili cinema industry in Tanzania is *Bongo movies*.

2 The southern African region seems to present a different dichotomy here, in that the films do get good distribution in the countries of production and are often later distributed in other countries in the region. Films like *Neria*,

More Time, and *Flame* have been distributed in Zimbabwe, South Africa, Tanzania, Kenya, and Zambia with remarkable ease and success. Indeed experiences of distributing African films remain undocumented in the belief that they are similar. This needs remedying.

3 In my article "Globalisation and African Cinema: Distribution and Reception in the Anglophone Region" I discuss a number of creative distribution structures built to distribute the African film in the continent (Sakbolle, in Dovey 2010, 54).

4 There were also a few "abnormal" films during that period such as *Visages de femmes* (Désiré Écaré, 1985), *Bal Poussière* (Henri Duparc, 1989), *Gito the Ungrateful* (Léonce Ngabo, 1992), *Quartier Mozart* (Jean-Pierre Bekolo, 1992), and *La vie est belle* (Ngangura Mweze, 1987), which straddle the aesthetic and ideological standpoints.

5 Six production companies funded the film including Ciné-Sud Promotion (France), Cinétéléfilms (Tunisia), Direction de la Cinematographie Nationale (Belgium), Filmi Domireew (Senegal), and Les Films Terre Africaine (Cameroon).

6 The 1961 Berlin Festival was the first to select African films, which were by Senegalese filmmakers: Blaise Senghor's *Grand Magal de Touba* (1962), which received a Silver Bear for the Best Short Film; and Paulin Soumanou Vieyra's *Un Nation est née* (1961), which received a Special Mention.

PART THREE

Digital Media and the Independent Voice

Chapter Twelve

Syiok Sendiri? Independent Filmmaking in Malaysia

GAIK CHENG KHOO

This chapter focuses on independent ("indie") filmmaking in Malaysia, which, since 2000, has been spurred by the digital revolution. Although invited to film festivals abroad and winning international accolades, independent films remain relatively unknown or unrecognized within Malaysia.[1] In 2005–6 one local columnist in the Malay newspaper *Utusan Malaysia* even dismissed these film festivals as "mosquito festivals," making Yasmin Ahmad's double awards at the prestigious Berlin International Film Festival even sweeter in 2007 (Hashim 2007).[2] Indie filmmakers are also accused of *"syiok sendiri"* (making films to please themselves). This chapter will first provide a brief outline of the complexities of race in multicultural Malaysia and its influence on the nation's film history, before defining an indie film. A discussion on independent filmmaking in Malaysia necessitates an analysis of its relationship to the mainstream Malay film industry (and to the state), more so than its relationship to Hollywood. Hence I will turn to the specific issues that indie filmmakers face in Malaysia with regard to production, exhibition, and distribution and the differential treatment that independent filmmakers receive in Malaysia, before answering whether they are, indeed, self-indulgent.

Film History and the Race Factor

Malaysia has a long history of cinema, with the earliest record of film screenings being in 1897 and a production industry dominated by Chinese film entrepreneurs in the pre– and post–Second World War era. The first film made in Malaya was *Leila Majnun* (1933–4), a Persian love story directed by Indian director B.S. Rajhans. The Japanese

Occupation (1942–5) disrupted an infant film industry that regained its footing in the post-war years and entered the golden era of Malay film (1950–65). Two competing film studios dominated film production and produced between nine and twenty films per year. Although the casts were ethnic Malays, and the studios were owned by ethnic Chinese producers like the Shaw Brothers and Ho Ah Loke and Loke Wan Tho of Cathay Keris, the crew at the Merdeka Film Productions studio in Ulu Kelang consisted of a multicultural melange of Chinese, Malays, and Indians ("Meet the Film Producers!" 2006). With the rise of Malay nationalism in the 1950s before the country's independence, Malay cultural workers sought to make films with local storylines (for example, with less of an Indian style and cultural influences) and to have Malay rather than Indian or Filipino directors at the helm. P. Ramlee (1929–73) and Hussein Haniff (ca. 1934–66) were two notable Malay directors of the period. Both gave their films an authentic Malay cultural sensibility that had been missing in the films made by Indian directors. The centre of film activity then was Singapore, but, with the split between Malaysia and Singapore in 1965, Malay filmmaking relocated to Kuala Lumpur, where eventually the poorer infrastructure, competition from television, and film imports from Hollywood, Indonesia, Hong Kong, and India heralded the slow demise of the studio era.

Malaysian society is defined and divided according to race, language, and religion. The ethnic breakdown for Malaysia according to the 2011 census was 50.1 per cent Malays, 22.5 per cent Chinese, 6.7 per cent Indians, 12.5 per cent others, and 8.2 per cent non-Malaysian citizens (Yow 2011). Generally, Malays are constitutionally defined as Muslims; the Chinese are Taoist-Buddhists and Christians; and most Tamils are practising Hindus. Language-wise, aside from Malay, the official language, Malaysians speak Mandarin and various Chinese dialects such as Cantonese and Hokkien. Tamil is presumed to be the language spoken by the majority of Indian Malaysians. This linguistic and ethnic diversity is not usually represented in mainstream commercial Malay films because the industry has traditionally conformed to the National Cultural Policy (1971). The policy calls for other Malaysian cultures to assimilate to the indigenous Malay Muslim culture of the archipelago.[3] Such a policy emerged out of the so-called race riots that took place between predominantly the Malays and the Chinese on 13 May 1969, in conjunction with the New Economic Policy (1971–90). The New Economic Policy (which continues under various other names)[4] is perceived as favouring the majority Malays under a racial quota system.

Racialization is reflected first through race-based political parties in the Barisan Nasional (The National Front), which has been in power since independence. The film industry is not immune from the workings of pro-Malay policies. For example, until 2011 an assimilationist agenda was reflected in the state-supported film grants and the tax-rebate policy, which made it a requirement that only Malaysian films with 60 per cent dialogue in the official language, Bahasa Malaysia (Malay), would receive the grant and the 25 per cent entertainment tax rebate from the taxes levied on cinema tickets[5] (more on this point later in the chapter). Ethnic fragmentation is reflected in the market segmentation of targeted audiences in the media landscape, with the majority of media targeting the Malay population, the Chinese language media targeting the Mandarin (and Cantonese) speakers, and, finally, the Tamil and Hindi language media aiming at Indian audiences. English-language media and films appeal to the middle-class, cutting across all ethnic groups, although the audience for local Malaysian films in English is in the minority. Nevertheless, nearly everyone watches Hollywood films and Hong Kong blockbusters, which are subtitled in all three languages. Although Malaysia is multi-ethnic, the commercial film industry since the days of the studio system has targeted a mostly ethnic Malay audience, with plot lines revolving around ethnic Malay characters and Malay society and in the Malay language.

Racial-linguistic segmentation (or segregation) is notable as indie filmmakers often challenge these mainstream boundaries through their cosmopolitan attitude and modus operandi as well as in representations of race relations and hybrid cultures. Featuring Chinese and Indian actors who speak in a variety of languages and dialects instead of only in Malay, this reflection of polyglot Malaysia really began with Yasmin Ahmad's films in the mid-2000s.[6] It is also gradually appearing in the work of more independent-minded Malay filmmakers working in the mainstream industry, especially of a younger generation, notably *Songlap* (Fariza Azlina and Effendee, 2012). Indie filmmakers collaborate with each other across ethnic boundaries, forming film companies together like Kino-i, Dahuang, and Perantauan Pictures. This multi-ethnic cooperation among the indies is "cosmopolitan" in that it transgresses cultural boundaries, deconstructs state racialization, and challenges the ethnocentrism of each group. These cosmopolitan films largely adopt a humanist perspective and transcend issues of race but at the same time highlight ethnic diversity and difference (by reflecting cooperation and everyday interactions among the various ethnic groups).[7]

Factors for the Rise of the Indies

Much like in other parts of the world, the post-2000 wave of independent filmmaking in Malaysia has emerged because of the digital revolution, which has substantially reduced the costs of film production, trimmed down crews, and transformed and simplified the processes of post-production. This digital wave has to be distinguished from earlier independent productions such as *Bejalai* (Stephen Teo, 1989), *Dari Jemapoh ke Manchestee* (Hishamuddin Rais, 1998), and *Spinning Gasing* (Teck Tan, 2000), which were shot in either 16 mm or 35 mm film. Technology has also changed very rapidly as indie filmmakers struggle to keep pace, constantly upgrading digital cameras and learning to use new editing software.[8] In addition, film aficionados gain access to foreign films on the Internet and, through cheap pirated DVDs, to films that would not be screened in the cinemas or taught in film schools. For example, indie filmmakers have access to pirated art-house Asian and European films as well as rare and esoteric Criterion collections, which influence their style and outlook. Thus, indie filmmakers are not averse to piracy, and their films feature DVD pirates as part of the contemporary cultural landscape of Malaysia.[9] This appreciation for bootleg films is a truism for indie filmmakers in neighbouring Philippines, Thailand, and Indonesia, too. With regard to anti-piracy laws, the Malaysian government has faced pressure from other countries (the United States and India) to clamp down on piracy and to observe its Copyright Act of 1987. Periodic raids are carried out, the guilty are charged in court, and hefty fines from RM2,000 to RM20,000 per copy infringement are levied (Ikram 2012). Lately, though, illegal downloading is becoming more popular than pirated DVDs.

Interest in digital filmmaking began in the 1990s when the government established the Multimedia Super Corridor (MSC) and the Multimedia University (MMU) with the goal of transforming Malaysia into an information and communication technology–based society driven by the new economy. Although trained in digital animation, some graduates from the MMU's first and second cohorts, including Tan Chui Mui, Deepak K. Menon, and Liew Seng Tat, made digital feature films that won critical acclaim and awards (at festivals in Pusan[10] and Rotterdam) (Cremin 2011). The MSC under the Multimedia Development Corporation also funded short films by indie filmmakers through a system of internship training. These indie filmmakers, most born in the 1970s and 1980s, are media savvy and cosmopolitan, having grown up in a globalized era and been exposed to other cultures, whether through travel, living, or studying overseas, or to global pop culture and the Internet. As is the case with many filmmakers in other countries discussed in this volume (such as Iraq), some are trained overseas (though not necessarily in film), while others are locally trained or self-taught. Technologically astute and accustomed to a do-it-yourself style of working quickly on their own with slim budgets (no government largesse means no red tape), they have impressed foreign film programmers by producing interesting, high-quality work on digital.[11]

Definition of "Indie" Film

Initially I defined the independent filmmaking movement as "being underground, low-budget, non-profit oriented, guerrilla filmmaking, and made without consideration of being screened in the censor-ridden mainstream cinemas" (Khoo 2007, 228). This definition was largely influenced by the manifesto issued around 2001 by one of the two progenitors of the Just-Do-It-Yourself digital indie film movement, James Lee, on his former website. While true for Lee's Doghouse73 Productions and the movement in its infancy to the mid-2000s, the landscape has also broadened substantially today to include less avant-garde-style, independently funded films that have commercial potential or may no longer be low budget. The indie filmmaking scene in the early to mid-2000s was fuelled by a handful of filmmakers of various ethnic backgrounds, many of whom had worked on Amir Muhammad's groundbreaking documentary, *The Big Durian* (2003). This group (some of whom went on to establish Dahuang Pictures)[12] worked collaboratively, taking turns to produce, edit, perform the duties of director of photography, and act in each other's films. In the smallish indie filmmaking scene centred in Kuala Lumpur the "six degrees of separation" rule applies because the same editors (for example, Azharrudin), directors of photography (such as Malek aka Albert Hue, and Khoo Eng Yow), and music composers (such as Hardesh Singh) work with filmmakers from different but overlapping circles.

The incipient scene in the early to mid-2000s was characterized by short films and documentaries made by amateurs, students, and professionals, with a sprinkle of feature films that began to travel outside of Malaysia to film festivals. Dahuang Pictures' founding members Tan Chui Mui and Liew Seng Tat, both graduates from the Multimedia University, attracted attention with their short films before venturing into feature films. In interviews with the author,[13] filmmakers like Liew and Khairil M. Bahar admitted that considerations of distribution were not their priority in making their first feature film, but these issues have now become more urgent with experience.

With the gradual professionalization of some of these independent filmmakers and new emerging players, the above description of "underground, low-budget, non-profit oriented, guerrilla filmmaking" no longer applies across the board. The successful first feature film of singer-turned-filmmaker Ah Niu, *Ice Kacang Puppy Love* (2010), was made for US$1.24 million – above the average cost of a commercial Malay film (US$ 463,000),[14] and way above the RM70,000 (US$23,000) budget of the first Malaysian indie digital film, *Lips to Lips* (Amir Muhammad, 2000) (National Film Development Corporation Malaysia 2013). Liew Seng Tat, whose first feature film, *Flower in the Pocket* (2007), cost below RM100,000 (US$32,653), had a larger budget for his second feature, *In What City Does It Live?*, costing RM2.4 million (Torino Film Lab). At the same time, the indie spirit of do-it-yourself persists with the cooperation of friends of various ethnic backgrounds.[15]

Since the demise of the studio system in the 1970s all Malaysian films have been economically independent of studio interests and mandates (Lim 2004, 8–9). However, there are several media corporations that produce films and act as distributors and can be regarded as being similar to studios. These include, for example, satellite television company Astro, through its film production company Tayangan Unggul; and Media Prima, through its film production arm Primeworks (formerly Grand Brilliance). Together with Metrowealth, Skop Productions, and KRU they dominate the commercial film landscape and constitute the major players in the local film industry, according to interviews with producer Nandita Solomon and Yeo Joon Han.[16] Technically, surmises filmmaker Yeo Joon Han, releasing an indie film at the same time as a film produced by Astro or Media Prima – which together own all the "private" television stations, most of the radio stations, and several print publications[17] – "would be a nightmare" since these two corporations wield such marketing power (email with author, 2011). When the industry was ailing from a surplus of formulaic poor-quality plots, these "studios" also hired indie filmmakers like Amir Muhammad, James Lee, and Woo Ming Jin to inject new ideas into popular genre films. This means that the label *indie* applies more accurately to specific films than to the filmmaker, whose whole body of work needs to be taken into consideration with regard to the label *indie* or *mainstream*.

To complicate matters further, *Sell Out!* (Yeo Joon Han, 2008) was funded by a studio, but the filmmaker had full creative control of the film and also the support of the company's chief executive officer (email to author, 2 December 2011).

In 2004 one of the fathers of the Just-Do-It-Yourself indie film movement, Amir Muhammad, jokingly defined an indie Malaysian film as one that does not qualify to be in the annual Malaysian Film Festival (Khoo 2004), an industry-run event with officially appointed jurors made up of various members of the industry who are politically conservative. Moreover, according to film historian Hassan Abdul Muthalib, these jurors are generally not knowledgeable enough in film to be on the jury (Hassan 2011). There is also a Malay ethno-nationalist agenda at the heart of state institutions such as FINAS (National Film Development Corporation), and a similar mentality among certain people in the mainstream film industry. For example, actor-comedian-director Afdlin Shauki and director Mamat Khalid air their views about Malay pride and preserving the Malay film industry through the *wajib tayang* (mandatory screening scheme) on their blogs.[18] Political ambitions and economic survival on the basis of crony politics cannot be discounted in any business in Malaysia, and the film industry is no different. Afdlin Shauki publicly joined the ruling party, United Malays National Organisation (UMNO), in January 2012, stating his reason as wanting to influence young Malaysians to vote for the party in the upcoming general elections (Zieman 2012). In the past, big budget films, which are made with state funding in the mainstream industry, like *Embun* (2002), *1957: Hati Malaya* (2007, RM3 million), and *Tanda Putera* (2013, RM5 million), have been brought about thanks to political connections (Khoo 2006).[19]

In the annual Malaysian Film Festival, local films made in languages other than Malay do not compete in the same category as Malay films: instead they are classified and compete for awards under the categories of "digital films"[20] or "non-Malay language films,"[21] because most of these films are shot on digital. For instance, a Tamil-language film, *Chalanggai / Dancing Bells* (Deepak Kumaran Menon, 2007), won the digital film award, and a Mandarin horror film, *Possessed*, won in the "non-Malay film" section in the 2007 Malaysian Film Festival. This segregation acts to protect Malay mainstream films from competing with other Malaysian films that have won critical acclaim overseas, and perpetuates a double standard whereby Malay industry films remain parochial and insular despite the industry's claims to make Malaysian films internationally competitive (Lee 2010).[22]

A general keyword to describe independent Malaysian films would be *diverse*. Independent films as a whole reflect Malaysia as a multicultural society, unlike the commercial, locally made films playing in the cinemas, which are made in Malay language and feature ethnic Malay actors and stories that revolve around Malay society for a majority Malay audience. Diversity reflects not only the various ethnic groups in Malaysia and the stories that filmmakers tell about their communities (in multiple languages); it is also reflected in the rural and urban landscapes, the film styles, and the target audiences, which range from very niche local audiences to international art-house and commercial audiences. Indie filmmakers using spare dialogue, striking visuals, non-professional actors, long takes, and medium-to-long shots depicting stories of everyday marginalized characters are more likely to be influenced by world cinema directors like the Dardenne brothers, Wong Kar Wai, Hou Hsiao Hsien, Aki Kaurismaki, a number of Iranian filmmakers, Yasujirō Ozu, and American independents like John Cassavettes and Kevin Smith than by local Malay filmmakers (Macauley 2011).[23]

As independent productions, Malaysian films are also liberated from the commercial need to conform to conventional narrative styles, pacing, and genre (and, in some cases, censorship) if they are not being screened in the Malaysian cinemas. After all, as Yeo Joon Han explains, "independence means not having to answer to anyone for [one's] creative decisions" (email to author, 2 December 2011). With low budgets, they do not try to compete against foreign blockbuster films with special effects and instead try to offer something Malaysian yet different from the mainstream industry. Yeo's *Sell Out!* provides something completely unique by being an entertaining Malaysian English-language comedy with songs that are at times laugh-out-loud silly but also intelligent in critiquing attitudes such as the elevation of a culture of mediocrity and the validation of commercial values over artistic integrity. *Pungguk Rindukan Bulan / This Longing* (Azharrudin, 2008), produced by Dahuang Pictures, however, is a slow-paced introspective Malay film that captures the lives of those living in a run-down, low-cost apartment building that is slated for demolition in the city of Johor Bahru. Some indie filmmakers are equally aware of and are fans of the Hong Kong nonsensical (*mo lei tau*) kung fu comedies by Stephen Chow, and also understand the power that Bollywood musicals hold over local audiences, as these films are also screened in the cinemas.[24] Simultaneously, non-profit, independent documentaries, which may not clear the

National Censorship Board to screen in the mainstream cinemas, can take a bolder political and critical stance.

Independent filmmakers are increasingly conscious of producing films for particular niche markets; for example, making art-cinema-style films that are mostly screened at international film festivals rather than at the local cinemas. Alternative means of funding, distribution, and exhibition from film festivals in Rotterdam and Busan give independent filmmakers room to experiment with less commercial forms of visual storytelling. Their films differ from most Malaysian mainstream films, many of which are horror stories and romantic comedies.

Production

Most indie filmmakers make a living and fund their indie film projects through creating corporate videos; working in post-production houses; directing commercials, music videos, and television shows; lecturing; and producing photography and video installations (fewer from selling their movie rights). A few rely on winning awards, grants, and commissions from film festivals overseas; for example, Tan Chui Mui's New Currents Award money for *Love Conquers All* (2006) from the Pusan International Film Festival funded the first feature film of fellow Dahuang filmmaker Liew Seng Tat, *Flower in the Pocket* (2007). When *Flower in the Pocket* won several awards, they went back to fund Tan's second film. Some may also participate in the film labs, talent camps (Berlinale), and film markets attached to international film festivals, which act as social networking sites that further lead to greater international visibility and possibility of future funding and sales. Both Tan Chui Mui and Liew Seng Tat were selected at different times for the Cinefondation Cannes Residency in Paris, which helps young directors to prepare their first or second feature film. Malaysian filmmakers, much like filmmakers in parts of Africa and Iraq, have received funding from the Hubert Bals Foundation (Rotterdam), the Asian Cinema Fund (Pusan), the World Cinema Fund (Berlin), and the Jan Vrijman Fund for documentaries from the developing world at the Documentary Festival of Amsterdam (recipients include *The Last Communist*, Amir Muhammad, 2006, and *World without Shadows*, Khoo Eng Yow, 2011). For his more ambitious second feature film, *In What City Does It Live?*, Liew was awarded several grants (Torino Film Lab)[25] but at the time of the interview still needed much more to shoot the film and have enough for marketing and distribution, two of the biggest problems facing indie filmmakers.[26] Nonetheless, grants and self-funding allow indie filmmakers to maintain creative control of their works.

With regard to local funding and support for indie filmmakers, conflicting accounts exist about whether the system is unfair to Malaysian films in languages other than Malay, with regard to not qualifying for the 20 per cent tax rebate or the mandatory screening status and also in terms of obtaining grants and loans through FINAS (Sia 2004; Lim 2007; Bertolin 2011), according to Anwardi Jamil (email to author, 20 January 2012). In addition, exceptions made for certain films generate difficulties in understanding the way in which the rules actually work and the rationale that necessitated their exclusions in the first place, a convoluted system matched in other parts of the world like Canada, where Inuit filmmakers vie for funding with English-language and French-language productions. In Malaysia, for example, the English-language film *The Red Kebaya* (Oliver Knott, 2006) was allowed to be on the *wajib tayang* scheme, but the film was not eligible for the 20 per cent tax rebate because it was in English (Meor 2010).

The Tax Rebate and Producer's Incentive Scheme

From 2005 to early 2011, a ruling disqualified the Malaysian films with less than 60 per cent dialogue in Malay from obtaining a 20 per cent tax rebate from FINAS. In 2011, numerous complaints from indie filmmakers whose films were in Mandarin and Tamil, backed surprisingly by the Malaysian Film Producers Association president, Ahmad Puad Onah, compelled the Ministry of Information, Communication, and Culture to change its policy (Meor 2010; "Top M'sian Filmmakers Welcome Tax Rebate" 2011). The policy change was also made in line with Prime Minister Najib Razak's national unity program, 1Malaysia, a slogan featured as part of FINAS's vision that was ostensibly meant to reflect Malaysian unity through diversity. The new ruling allows Malaysian films in Chinese, Tamil, and English made from 2010 onwards to qualify for the tax rebate as long as they have Bahasa Malaysia subtitles. Two of Dahuang Pictures' productions, according to Amir Muhammad, *Flower in the Pocket* (mostly in Mandarin) and *Punggok Rindukan Bulan* received the tax rebate, even though both films did not go through the *wajib tayang* scheme.[27]

Despite this policy change, *Nasi Lemak 2.0* (Wee Meng Chee), released late in 2011, did not receive the tax rebate because the new ruling ties the tax rebate to the mandatory screening scheme[28] for which *Nasi Lemak 2.0* did not qualify (Noorsila 2010). Apparently, a film by controversial rapper-turned-filmmaker Namewee did not qualify for the *wajib tayang* scheme either, not because it was 60 per cent in Mandarin (according to previous FINAS Director-General Mahyudin in 2010), but because the scheme is no longer limited to Malay films (Koay 2010). The present FINAS director-general, Mohd Naguib Razak, explained: "The film *Nasi Lemak 2.0* has been viewed with prejudice [by the National Censorship Board] because the producer (Namewee) had sparked a controversy before," which made FINAS's ruling on the matter seem political (Noorsila 2010).[29] As if to placate his critics, Namewee's film, which features a truly multicultural Malaysia, is about the humbling experience of a chauvinist ethnic Chinese Malaysian chef as he gradually learns to appreciate the rich cultural and hybrid diversity that Malaysian society has to offer. Owing to Namewee's controversial rap music, ethno-nationalist Malay critics advocated a boycott of the film in the town of Ipoh and published an article in the Malay newspaper *Utusan Malaysia* voicing opposition to the film because of its filmmaker (Lee 2011). Despite this negative publicity and not getting the largest screens under *wajib tayang*, *Nasi Lemak 2.0* still managed to generate RM7 million at the box office.

The independent filmmakers and critics of the tax rebate system that I interviewed believe that all Malaysian films, regardless of language, should be granted the tax rebate (which has been replaced by the producer's incentive plan, as of July 2011). Although the producer's incentive does not discriminate against non-Malay language films as long as they have Malay subtitles, it is only given to films that go under the mandatory screening scheme (National Film Development Corporation Malaysia 2012b). Under the incentive, films that make RM2 million and below either receive 10 per cent of box-office takings or are reimbursed for the costs of bulk print (RM3,500 per copy, up to a maximum of forty copies), whichever is higher. Films that earn up to RM6 million receive a 10 per cent tax rebate to a maximum of RM500,000. Some people feel that the minimum that is set for a film's earnings of RM2 million or below may encourage producers to take advantage of the cost for bulk printing and consequently print up to forty prints for circulation even though the film might be of poor quality. While this new incentive might seem fair on the surface, the fact that it is limited to films that undergo mandatory screening proves problematic.

Wajib Tayang (Mandatory Screening) Scheme

To protect the local film industry against Hollywood and other foreign imports, the government introduced a mandatory screening scheme in July 2005. It stipulates that a Malaysian film should have a mandatory, consecutive fourteen-day exhibition in the biggest screening hall, once it has fulfilled certain conditions, regardless of the language used in the film (Koay 2010, 9).[30] However, because only two local films can open in a month and there has to be a two-week gap between the release of the two films (Nur 2006), compounded by the fact that annual local film production has increased substantially (from thirty-nine films in 2010 to over seventy productions in 2012), there is a long queue for Malaysian films to be screened (National Film Development Corporation Malaysia 2013). Hence, the fourteen-day mandatory scheme was shortened unofficially to one week in the main hall, with the first day in the largest cinema hall. However, after only three days, the film would be moved to smaller halls if ticket sales fell below 15 per cent of the seating capacity (Shauki 2008).[31] The problem with this stipulation is that it relies heavily on publicity to attract viewers to the first three days of screening, and it works against local niche art films, which may not attract large numbers of viewers. Indeed, many independent films rely on word of mouth to draw audiences to the cinemas and, as Yeo Joon Han suggests, would benefit from a gradual roll-out, "starting with one or two screens in the city, and then, if and when word of mouth grows (trackable nowadays by monitoring blogs and Facebook feedback), more cinemas around the country could start screening them" (email to author, 2 December 2011).

Under *wajib tayang*, if a film does well at the box office, exhibitors can extend the screening for another week or longer. However, this may not work if the film is competing simultaneously with Hollywood blockbusters during the school holidays. In addition, film producers have no say over the date of release under *wajib tayang* because they are slotted in the queue by FINAS. *Relationship Status* (Khairil Bahar, 2011), a mainly English-language independent local film, was classified and screened under the International Screen category, partly because Khairil preferred to have control over the screening dates. Azharr Rudin's Malay-language digital feature film, *This Longing* (2008), though not well attended, had a month-long screening at the Golden Screen Cinemas because it came under the International Screen category rather than the *wajib tayang* (for local films). There are fewer foreign films shown under the former category. The long queue under *wajib tayang* disadvantages smaller independent companies that need to repay loans and recoup their capital as soon as possible: "Companies with more holding power may be able to wait, but a smaller independent one like ours cannot do so and will have to turn immediately to VCDs and TV to recoup our capital," says the indie filmmaker of cult action films Julian Cheah (Rizal 2005).

Other conditions under the scheme also enable exhibitors to undermine the protectionist intentions of the scheme;[32] the stipulation that the exhibitor can exercise its right to pull out the film if audience figures fall below 15 per cent of the hall capacity, with permission from FINAS, means that local art films, which already command a small audience, do not even get the full fourteen-days' screening time. Finally, FINAS schemes and policies are not enforced, and exhibitors who unfairly pull a local film before its mandatory screening time has been completed, or replace it with a blockbuster, are not fined or given a warning. Filmmakers like Yasmin Ahmad and Yeo Joon Han have had problems before with exhibitors who informed interested viewers that their films had limited seats left, only to find that the cinema halls were mostly empty (Chan 2009).

As for local exhibition, digitally shot independent films faced additional hurdles in these early years as there were only four digital screens nationwide. What filmmakers saved by shooting on digital cameras went towards transferring digital to film for cinema projection, which was a costly endeavour. Indie filmmakers could not afford the transfer fees, and therefore their films, unlike 35 mm films, were not exhibited widely. Luckily, the popularity of 3-D projection after *Avatar* (2009) has encouraged a few cinema chains to convert film halls into digital halls in the hopes of screening more 3-D films. In addition, commercial filmmakers are also shooting on digital cameras, which accounts for the increased number of locally produced films screening in the cinemas.

Local Grants and Loans

The perception that loans and grant support are based on the criterion that films have to be at least 60 per cent in Malay also deters applications by many indie filmmakers who make films in Chinese, English, or other languages. For example, the highest grant of RM15 million shown on the FINAS website comes from the Nationhood and Heritage film production fund, but the film has to be 100 per cent in Bahasa Malaysia, and the fund prioritizes patriotic historical films that might have less commercial potential. This usually means making films that support the ideology of the ruling government. Notably, Namewee's *Nasi Lemak 2.0*, written with Prime Minister Najib Tun Razak's 1Malaysia in mind, was "rejected as a recipient of government funding on the basis that not enough of his script was in Malay" (Naidu 2011).

Independent filmmakers have been able to secure small FINAS grants for up to RM40,000 (usually they receive RM20,000) for short films through the Film Art and Multimedia Development Fund, though this also has the national language requirement.[33] However, while submitted scripts may contain the required 60 per cent Malay dialogue, sometimes, after shooting and editing, the film may end up having less than the required amount (say, 50 per cent). But even then, FINAS may still release the balance of the payments. This happened to Foo Mee Teng and Tham Wai Fook's short films *What Happened between Agusta and I* (2011) and *Rompin* (2010). Under the same category, FINAS additionally provides not more than RM10,000 to support travel, expenses, and accommodations for indie filmmakers whose films have been selected to compete in film festivals, or to support promotion and film marketing. Reported beneficiaries have included "award-winning editor Akashdeep Singh, Margaret Bong and Aaron Chung" (Koay 2010).

In 2010 the government, through FINAS, set aside funding for two types of bank loans (with low 2–4 per cent interest rates), which were not tied to language restrictions. Unfortunately independent filmmakers like Tan Chui Mui whose art-house films are not commercially viable would have difficulty applying for the loan because the bank would want to see a return on investment (Koay 2010). The pitching criteria stated on the FINAS website, which require the films to have strong commercial values and positive elements and to attempt to showcase and promote local attractions as part of the tourism industry, may act as further deterrents to indie filmmakers who may not share such commercial inclinations (National Film Development Corporation Malaysia 2012a).

Moreover, the loan application process can cause substantial delays in production and involve unnecessarily complicated bureaucratic procedures with additional expenses and time wasted (applying for permits and making sure that all the crew working on the film are members of various unions, which some indie filmmakers claim do not do anything to assist their members). Motivated by an independent spirit of self-reliance, indie filmmaker Khairil M. Bahar, who is influenced by American filmmakers like Robert Rodriguez and Kevin Smith, prefers to avoid cumbersome rules (like obtaining permits to film at the airport) and "just do it." The filmmakers I interviewed were aware of the limits of shooting a film with few commercial prospects. They explained that, were their films marketable, they would have tried harder to find investors and market them through the appropriate channels. Despite the lack of economic support for such films, they persist out of passion.

When it comes to local exhibition, one final source of revenue is Astro First, a subscription satellite television channel, where viewers pay RM15 to watch the latest local movie release within forty-eight hours. Launched in January 2011, Astro First showcases newly released Malaysian films almost immediately after their initial two-week theatre screening. Although more expensive than buying a pirated DVD copy (between RM5 and RM10), it provides a cheaper alternative for families who cannot afford to attend the cinema. Nevertheless, it is unclear yet how useful an avenue it is for independent art films.

International Connections for Independent Film Production, Exhibition, and Distribution

Asian regional connections are important for Malaysian filmmakers with regard to production and distribution, particularly those making films in Cantonese or Mandarin. Ho Yuhang's third feature, *Raindogs* (2006), was funded by the film production and distribution company of Hong Kong actor Andy Lau under a project called Focus First Cuts, a high-definition-film project involving new and upcoming directors from across China, Hong Kong, Malaysia, Singapore, and Taiwan. His following film, *At the End of Daybreak* (2009), received Korean, Taiwanese, and Hong Kong production and post-production support. Both *Raindogs* and *At the End of Daybreak*, though shot in Malaysia, included veteran Hong Kong actors. *At the End of Daybreak* revived the career of actress Kara Hui, whom Ho cast again in his short film *Open Verdict* (2011); this short was part of *Quattro Hong Kong 2*, the omnibus feature about Hong Kong that was commissioned by the Hong Kong International Film Festival (Kerr 2011).[34] Ho is considering casting the same two Hong Kong actresses from *Open Verdict* in a new feature.

For Mandarin-language Malaysian films, Taiwan and Singapore are potential places for distribution. *Ais Kacang Puppy Love*, directed by and featuring Malaysian singer Ah Niu, who is popular in Taiwan, China, and Hong Kong, was the first Malaysian film to be theatrically released in these three countries. The commercial success of local

Chinese-language films like *Tiger Woohoo!* (2010) and *Ais Kacang Puppy Love* proves that a local market for Mandarin-language Malaysian films exists. It has also encouraged co-productions between Chinese-language Malaysian and Singaporean film production companies, like *The Wedding Diary* (2012), which has ready-made distributors in Malaysia (Golden Screen) and Singapore (Golden Village). Arguably, films like *Tiger Woohoo* and *A Great Day*, which are produced by satellite television station Astro Wah Lai Toi, are not "independent" of the studios, but, when defined against the Malay-language national film industry, they are still considered independent.

In Malaysia, ironically, winning awards at foreign film festivals is detrimental to the reputation of an indie film because it is then labelled as boring and slow paced and therefore unlikely to attract audiences at the local cinemas. This is partly owing to the shortcomings of local distributors who are not marketing professionals but, rather, are theatre bookers and media buyers. Indie filmmakers complain that distributors are not experienced, diligent, or creative enough to market a film. They tend to pigeonhole films into existing categories such as horror, action, or "festival movie and therefore unmarketable" and may not even have watched a film before deciding on a distribution strategy. For that reason, indie filmmakers like Khairil and his producer Bahir Yeusuff self-distributed and self-marketed Khairil's third feature, *Relationship Status*, by liaising directly with the cinemas. Indie filmmakers do not usually have large budgets for marketing their films, and oftentimes debut feature films do not circulate very widely because resource-short filmmakers concentrate solely on production rather than on marketing. Even when cinema chains agree to screen Malaysian indie films,[35] filmmakers are still expected to handle most of the marketing and publicity themselves; this includes sending out media releases, doing interviews, building hype by making trailers and releasing them online, blogging information about production, and screening to the press. *Flower in the Pocket*, for example, made money from the local box office, even though half of the money earned was not recorded through the box-office receipts. This is because Dahuang Pictures pre-bought two thousand to three thousand tickets and sold most of them online, to friends and family, and at bazaar events like Arts for Grabs.

As for overseas sales, Dahuang sold the DVD rights for *Flower in the Pocket* to the Rialto, an art-house cinema in Amsterdam, together as a double bill with *Mukhsin* and with Dutch subtitles under different packaging and bonus materials (quite a different selection than that of a DVD purchased directly from the Dahuang website). When asked for his retrospective thoughts on distributing *Flower in the Pocket*, Liew says: "I was glad for *Flower* to go so far because when we started, we didn't think that far. We had a script and just shot it. We never thought of distributing it. We never planned to release it elsewhere or we would have done a better job – quality, proper shoot, have money to transfer it to 35 mm. [Regardless of what we digital indies think], people still look for that. Most of the feedback from overseas [on *Flower* is that] they think it's a very small film, digital, TV; they feel it's so small that it's not worth distributing. They would need to spend additional money to transfer from digital to film" (interview, 12 January 2012).

Some other indie films are distributed overseas by European distributors and sales agents, but since the distributor covers marketing and promotion costs, the profit is insubstantial.[36] For example, having a French distributor means paying a 33.33 per cent government tax on the sale of a film, on top of the paid commission to the distributor. After deducting bank commissions and exchange rate losses when money is transferred from the buyer to the distributor and from the distributor to the Malaysian filmmaker, there are hardly any earnings.[37] High rental fees charged by European distributors and sales agents for an Asian film (typically between €500 and €1,000) may also counteract wide circulation of independent films.[38]

Are Indie Filmmakers *Syiok Sendiri*?

Whether making art cinema or more audience-friendly films, most indie filmmakers still assert that Malaysian audiences are their main target. After all, the films are about characters living in Malaysian society. So the question of whether indie filmmakers make films to please themselves can be answered in two ways. If *syiok sendiri* means merely indulging their own egos by making films that do not please local audiences because their films are too esoteric, slow paced, and boring, indie filmmakers are equally frustrated with audiences who expect an easily consumable product that caters to the lowest common denominator. In this regard, several filmmakers to whom I spoke advocated film education in school: "I learned about 3-act structure, themes and character in secondary one in Singapore. I strongly believe that unless Malaysian audiences' tastes and insights improve, our films will be hard-pressed to do so. Everything begins with education," says one filmmaker.

Indie filmmakers are also very much aware of their responsibility to the producer and how costly production can be. Yet often, even films that have some commercial or entertainment value do not become box-office successes, owing to poor marketing. Thus indie filmmakers have to turn to markets outside of Malaysia. B-movie indie filmmaker Julian Cheah (often known as Malaysia's Ed Wood) reportedly sold his film *The Fighter* to the video and television market in the United States, Canada, and Australia (Rizal 2010). More important, Dahuang Pictures became inactive when Tan Chui Mui relocated to Beijing to work for Chinese filmmaker Jia Zhangke in the hopes of sourcing production funds from China from 2011 to mid-2013.

Meanwhile, back home, the hard-core indie filmmaker still relies on the alternative route of screening in schools, colleges, and film clubs, for "all one really needs is a projector and some seats," according to Khairil Bahar. To finance such endeavours, the Hubert Bals Fund offers a small grant that supports alternative distribution in the country of origin. *Year without a Summer* (Tan Chui Mui, 2010) received this grant, enabling the non-commercial art film to tour various institutions and universities in Malaysia, as well as in rural places or small towns that had no cinemas. The grant covers screening costs such as venue and equipment rental so that the screenings can be free.[39]

James Lee prophesies that in the future his films will be seen not only at festivals but eventually via streaming or downloading over the Internet. If there are any lessons to be learned as the indie film-makers become more professional, it is that budgets need to account substantially for promotion and distribution in order for films to reach broader audiences. As a slightly jaded Liew states, "there's no point making a film just for festivals" (interview, 19 January 2012). While the independent filmmakers do not wait for handouts from the state and they differentiate themselves from the mainstream because of their not-for-profit status, their dialectical relationship to the ethno-nationalist Malay mainstream film industry remains.

In some ways, the idea of *syiok sendiri* cinema can be turned against the mainstream industry that rewards or supports weak films. One film-maker who prefers to remain anonymous explains his feelings about the local film industry: "I would like to see people who understand film and filmmaking, people who appreciate originality and good sto-rytelling, and people with no conflict of interests sit on the panels who decide to which projects these funds should go" (email to author, 10 January 2012). Another, Liew Seng Tat, feels that local grants should be made available to non-commercial, high-quality projects. Frustrated, he expressed that there should be better communication between indie filmmakers and FINAS so that FINAS is aware of indie film projects such as *In Which City*, which has already received international assistance but requires extra support from within Malaysia in order to be brought to fruition.[40] Clearly, independent filmmakers in Malaysia generally feel marginalized with regard to state support for the production and distribution of their works because of ethno-nationalist linguistic barriers, inefficiency, bureaucratic red tape, and film policies that are motivated by commercial values.

ACKNOWLEDGMENTS

I would like to thank the filmmakers who generously made time to fill out my email questionnaire, chat online, and meet for interviews in Petaling Jaya and Kuala Lumpur (Malaysia) between December 2011 and mid-January 2012: Azharrudin, Liew Seng Tat, Yeo Joon Han, James Lee, Ho Yuhang, Khairil M. Bahar, Khoo Eng Yow, Foo Mee Teng, Edmund Yeo, Bryant Low, Stephen Teo, Linus Chung, Amir Muhammad, Anwardi Jamil, Dain Said, and producer Nandita Solomon. Additional thanks go to film historian Hassan Muthalib for proofreading. Any errors are mine alone.

NOTES

1 *Beautiful Washing Machine* (James Lee, Bangkok International Film Festival 2005), *The Gravel Road* (Deepak Kumaran Menon, 2005 Special Jury Award, Nantes Festival 3 Continents), *Raindogs* (Ho Yuhang, in competition in Venice 2006), *At the End of Daybreak* (Ho Yuhang , 2009), *Love Conquers All* (Tan Chui Mui, New Currents and Fipresci Awards, Pusan International Film Festival 2006), *Flower in the Pocket* (Liew Seng Tat, New Currents Pusan International Film Festival 2007; VPRO Tiger Award at International Film Festival Rotterdam 2008), *Sell Out!* (Yeo Joon Han, 2008, world-premiered at the Venice Film Festival in 2008 and won the Young Cinema Award for Altre Visioni), *Karaoke* (Chris Chong Chan Fui, Director's Fortnight Cannes 2009), *The Tiger Factory* (Woo Ming Jin, Asian Film Award, International Film Festival Rotterdam 2010; Special Mention, Tokyo International Film Festival 2010), and *Woman on Fire Looks for Water* (Woo Ming Jin, SEA Competition; Special Mention, Cinemanila Film Festival 2009).

2 Yasmin Ahmad's *Mukhsin* (2006) won two awards at the Berlin International Film Festival in 2007 (the Crystal Bear Special Mention, and the Deutsches Kinderhilfswerk Grand Prix) and, unlike her earlier two films, was acknowledged by the mainstream Malaysian film industry with a few prizes at the annual Malaysian film festival that year.

3 The archipelago refers to Malaysia, Indonesia, Brunei, and the Philippines.

4 The National Development Policy (1991–2000), the National Vision Policy (2001–10), and the New Economic Model (2011–).

5 The 25 per cent is off the net price of the ticket. Other reports claim that it is 20 per cent, but that is off the gross price of the ticket.

6 The late auteur Yasmin Ahmad (1958–2009), who was more famous for her emotional Petronas advertisements than for her films, is an example of a filmmaker who straddles the divide between the independent and the mainstream because her films, unlike those of her peers, had the most potential to be commercial.

7 For example, Deepak K. Menon's Tamil-language films *Chemman Chaalai / The Gravel Road* (2005) and *Chalanggai / Dancing Bells* (2007), films by James Lee, Tan Chui Mui, Amir Muhammad, Liew Seng Tat, Woo Ming Jin, and the late Yasmin Ahmad, and *Min* (2003) by Ho Yuhang .

8 This is not to say that post-2000 independent filmmakers are not shooting on 35 mm or 16 mm film. As an example of how fast technology has moved, Khairil M. Bahar explains in an interview with the author that he shot his second feature film, *London Calling* (2007), on the same camera as the one he used for his first feature film, *Ciplak*. However, he has not really released *London Calling*, because he feels that the quality and standard of the technology used is no longer acceptable when better cameras are now available on the market.

9 *Sepet* (2004) tells the story of a Malay girl who falls in love with Jason, a DVD pirate, and *Ciplak* (2006) is about Joe who is a student DVD pirate. DVD pirates make appearances in James Lee's *Beautiful Washing Machine* and Woo Ming Jin's short film *Slovak Sling* (2009). James Lee's commercial, costumed, martial arts comedy, *Petaling Street Warriors*, set at the turn of the twentieth century, makes anachronistic jokes about not buying pirated goods. Petaling Street is in Kuala Lumpur's Chinatown and is *the* place to find pirated goods.

10 Re-spelled as *Busan* in 2011.

11 See the Rotterdam Film Festival programmer's notes about Sherman Ong (Ong 2010); also see the interview with Ong by Jeremy Sing (2010).

12 Dahuang Pictures was established in 2005 by Amir Muhammad, James Lee, Tan Chui Mui, and Liew Seng Tat.

13 All interviews with the author took place over a period of time in late 2011 and early 2012 on different media and on different occasions.

14 This figure from FINAS is from January 1 to October 31, 2011; US$1 = RM3–RM3.5.

15 This is true for *Relationship Status* (2012) and *Survival Guide Untuk Kampong Radioaktif / Survival Guide for Radioactive Village* (2011), which features a series of four short films mostly using parody to broach the subject of radioactive issues in Malaysia in light of the struggle against Lynas, an Australian mining company that is building the world's largest rare-earth processing plant in Gebeng, Malaysia. The cast and crew of *Kampung Radioaktif* volunteered their services and were only remunerated for transportation costs and food.

16 The author conducted interviews with producer Nandita Solomon in 2012 and Yeo Joon Han in 2011 (via email).

17 All mainstream media (television, radio stations, and print media) are controlled by the government or individuals close to the government.

18 See blogs by Mamat Khalid (2011) and Afdlin Shauki (2008).

19 According to Hassan Muthalib, the brother-in-law of the director of the last two films was the FINAS director-general at the time.

20 The Best Digital Film award was subsequently made redundant as mainstream film companies also began to shoot using digital cameras.

21 The exception is the English-language film *The Red Kebaya* (2006), which participated in the main category and won four awards at the 20th Annual Malaysian Film Festival in 2007.

22 The criticism of the twenty-third Malaysian Film Festival in 2010 was no different.

23 Khairil M. Bahar names the late P. Ramlee among his favourites, but his films are more immediately influenced by American independents like Robert Rodriguez and Kevin Smith for being witty, dialogue-driven, and in English. Dain Said, director of *Bunohan* (2011, premiered at the Toronto International Film Festival 2011), claims admiration for Malaysian filmmaker U-Wei Haji Saari whose telemovie, *The Arsonist* (1995), was invited to Un Certain Regard at Cannes in 1995, and fellow indie filmmaker, Ho Yuhang.

24 Again the influence of Bollywood is evident in *Nasi Lemak 2.0* (Namewee, 2011) and *Rabun* (Yasmin Ahmad, 2003).

25 So far the film has received €100,000 from the 2010 Torino Film Lab's Production Award; €50.000 production grant from the Berlinale World Cinema Fund (Germany) in July 2011; and CHF50,000from Visions Sud Est (Switzerland), plus €50,000 from 2011 Hubert Bals Fund; €10,000

from the Hubert Bals Development Funds; €15,000 from the Prince Claus
Fund; and US$2,500 from the Sundance Feature Film Program.

26 Shooting completed in January 2013. Retitled *Lelaki Harapan Dunia / Men
Who Save the World*, the film opened in Malaysia in November 2014.

27 See also "FINAS Gives Out RM2.4 Mil" (2009).

28 The qualification of Malaysian films for the fiction film incentive, as stated on
the FINAS website under 2.1, is: "local fiction films which have been screened
in the cinemas and registered through the mandatory screening scheme
on or after 1 July 2011" (translation by author; National Film Development
Corporation Malaysia 2012b). See FINAS's website for more information.

29 Rapper Namewee (real name Wee Meng Chee) had stirred up controversy
in 2007 as a Malaysian university student in Taiwan with his controversial
rap version of the Malaysian national anthem on YouTube. The song raised
issues about endemic police corruption and uneasy race relations and was
deemed disrespectful towards Malay Muslims, sparking calls for the revoca-
tion of Wee's citizenship, and death threats towards his family in Malaysia.

30 According to the then FINAS director-general, Mahyiddin Mustakim.
However, many independent filmmakers whom I interviewed thought
that the mandatory screening scheme was limited only to Malay-language
films. A November 2008 report by the Australian Media, Entertainment,
and Arts Alliance to the Australian Department of Environment, Water,
Heritage, and the Arts regarding a proposed bilateral film co-production
agreement between Australia and Malaysia also supports the latter point.

31 This one-week figure for *wajib tayang* was given to me by several filmmakers.

32 A quick scan of the Golden Screen Cinemas' offerings on 15 November
2012 suggests that 60 per cent of the films are from Hollywood. Out of a
total of twenty-five, there were four Chinese language films, three Indian
films (Hindi and Tamil), one Korean film, fifteen Hollywood films, and
two Malaysian films.

33 See http://www.finas.gov.my/index.php?mod=dana&sub=
pembangunan_seni

34 Four award-winning directors, Apichatpong Weerasethakul, Brillante
Mendoza, Ho Yuhang, and Stanley Kwan were commissioned by Brand
Hong Kong to make short films about Hong Kong. A "festival film created
for festivals by a festival," the *Quattro Hong Kong 2* was produced by the
Hong Kong International Film Festival Society to premiere at the thirty-
fifth Hong Kong International Film Festival (Kerr 2011).

35 Independent American films rarely play in the cineplexes, if at all. Most
cineplexes screen the same commercial mainstream Hollywood films that
are released worldwide, together with a sprinkling of mainstream Asian

offerings. Five cinema chains compete for the local market; locally owned chains include Golden Screen Cinemas, Tanjung Golden Village, MBO, Lotus Five Star, and an Indian international chain, Big Cinemas.

36 Usually the producer gets 40 per cent while the distributor gets 60 per cent from sales.

37 Yeo Joon Han discussed his short film *Adults Only* (2006) in an interview with the author.

38 I would like to thank Quentin Turnour, film programmer for the Australian National Film and Sound Archive, for this information.

39 For the funding rules, see International Film Festival Rotterdam (2013a). For results showing award winners of the 2010–11 Hubert Bals Fund, see International Film Festival Rotterdam (2013b).

40 As FINAS's objective is merely to "promote, maintain, and facilitate film production development in Malaysia," it does not have much power to reformulate media policy, which is the role of the Ministry of Information, Communications, and Culture under which FINAS falls.

Chapter Thirteen

Independent Filmmaking in the Canadian Arctic

DORIS BALTRUSCHAT

Canada's independent film movements have their roots in the experimental arts and broadcasting initiatives dating back to the 1960s. With the emergence of portable video equipment in the 1980s, independent film and video proliferated and found their outlets and exhibition venues at cultural centres, arts venues, and small film festivals. Initiatives such as Videoazimut in Montreal, and Women in Film in Video, as well as the Western Front Society, in Vancouver, set examples for enhanced media accessibility, as their outreach campaigns invited anyone interested in film and video production to join workshops, educational forums, and exhibition venues. On the broadcasting side, community television stations recruited volunteers for local program production, thus creating a training base for new media producers and filmmakers. In addition, independent filmmakers produced a plethora of alternative works, from experimental films to provocative documentaries (Thede and Ambrosi 1991). Many of these works remain in the vaults of non-profit distribution houses, most of them never properly archived or cross-referenced with a countrywide database. As a result, most of Canada's independent film production appears to be linked to the National Film Board of Canada (NFB), even though funds from the Canadian Film Development Corporation (now Telefilm Canada),[1] the Canadian Independent Film and Video Fund, and the Canada Council for the Arts have supported the development of many creative works outside the NFB for decades.

In spite of a history of independent film and alternative video, Canada has one of the highest media concentrations in the world as only a few media oligopolies dominate the film and television sector today (Baltruschat 2010). This trend in media concentration intensified from the mid-1990s onwards, causing some sectors in society to push back and create new initiatives such as the Media and Democracy movement with a focal point for debate and community action around greater diversity of media ownership and rights for media professionals. This movement, with links to media activist groups around the world, continues to work towards greater transparency and accountability of today's media organizations in Canada.[2]

Much has been written about the new indie media movements that use digital technologies to seize their right to communicate, within the context of calling for greater "media democracy."[3] Yet, caution needs to be expressed in response to an overly optimistic uptake on the new media landscape because digital media facilitate not only widespread access to the means of communication and media production but also wide-scale surveillance of all digital activities and "footprints" across the political-economic and socio-cultural fields. Previous initiatives such as alternative radio, film, and video are now perceived to be outdated, but one needs to be reminded that these earlier initiatives often provided greater freedoms in formulating and expressing dissident voices than they do today in heavily circumscribed and traffic-shaped Internet[4] and mobile media environments (Mosco, 2004).

In contrast to "alternative" and independent initiatives, Canada's film and broadcasting traditions are also rooted in documentary production, spearheaded by the NFB and Canada's public service broadcaster, the Canadian Broadcasting Corporation (CBC). A key figure here is the British documentary filmmaker John Grierson, who was invited by the Canadian government in the late 1930s to develop the country's documentary production. Grierson proposed the establishment of the National Film Commission in 1939, which was renamed the National Film Board soon afterwards. The NFB remains the leading documentary-producing agency across the country. It commissions, produces, and co-produces many award-winning productions for the national and international markets, including the widely acclaimed Inuit film *Atanarjuat: The Fast Runner* (2001), which will receive more detailed attention in the following pages.

Considering the varied approaches to Canadian film and video production, independent filmmaking in Canada has to be defined from a variety of angles because a filmmaker's "independence" is greatly affected by available budgets for production. Any large project (over C$250,000) necessitates the input of some public funding, which ultimately is attached to official mandates and guidelines. While some

Canadian film producers would prefer to have a more commercial approach to filmmaking – using a U.S. private investment model, for example – others realize that the proximity of a market as large as the United States inevitably requires some sort of protection for Canada's cultural industries (Baltruschat 2003). This is also poignantly expressed by Acheson and Maule (2003, 2) with regard to Canada's audio-visual policies, which tend to "restrict the inflow of content from the United States, either directly or indirectly, control foreign ownership of firms engaged in production and distribution, encourage the production of Canadian content and assure that it is given 'shelf-space' by distributors."

The meaning of independence within a Canadian context therefore has to be understood as a cinema that not only strives to be different from Hollywood-type storylines and aesthetics (and often achieves just that, such as in films by Sarah Polley) but also depends to a certain degree on government funding to supplement as well as augment budgets. The unique aesthetic of Canadian independent films cannot necessarily be summarized within one neat formula, given the vast differences in filmmakers' approaches as well as the English, Québécois, and Aboriginal artistic traditions, the genres, and the newly emerging film formats (for example, interactive film). Yet certain distinct features differentiate many Canadian independent films from popular Hollywood fare, be it through the extensive use of metaphors, a slower pace in narration, or story arches that are often left unresolved (that is, no neat and simple happy endings). In the case of some filmmakers, such as Atom Egoyan and Sarah Polley, the use of flashbacks and a non-linear narrative style characterizes their approach, as exemplified in *The Sweet Hereafter* and *Away from Her* (Baltruschat 2014). At the same time, these examples of Anglo-Canadian filmmaking are not – or cannot be – representative of the entire Canadian independent film oeuvre given the distinct film traditions in Quebec and among Aboriginal and Inuit filmmakers, the latter being the focus of this chapter.

Even though many Canadian filmmakers rely on public funding mechanisms, some filmmakers finance their production with the help of family and friends, which consequently situates them outside government guidelines and restrictions (for example, the need to follow the Canadian-content rules associated with hiring a certain percentage of Canadian talent). However, this type of independent film production does not necessarily translate into elevating art over commerce. On the contrary, the need to recoup private financing is often accompanied by forcefully and skilfully executed promotional campaigns using social media platforms like Twitter, Facebook, and Tumblr to engage potential viewers (and fans) in a dialogue about the film with the aim to sell theatre seats, DVD copies, and Internet downloads.[5]

The influence of official policies for audio-visual content in Canada cannot be under-estimated, however, as government agencies provide an essential framework for Canada's media industries. In particular, the Department of Canadian Heritage and the Canadian Radio-Television Telecommunications Commission (CRTC) regulate Canada's cultural industries with the help of other ministries – Industry Canada (ownership) and Revenue Canada (tariffs and taxes) – and several agencies that include Telefilm Canada, the CBC, and the NFB (Gurd 1998). The Department of Canadian Heritage is responsible for national policies and programs designed to maintain Canada's identity and cultural sovereignty (Canadian Heritage 2000, 26), while the CRTC administers the Broadcasting Act and stipulates, through content regulations, that Canada's public and private broadcasters must reflect diversity in their programming.

As outlined above, small productions not supported by government funding also exist, especially with regard to producing digital media for multi-platform distribution. These tend to be self-funded through private investments (including donations from family and friends) as well as through online fund-raising campaigns, comparable to the crowd-funding website Kickstarter in the United States (Canada Media Fund 2012). Examples of Canadian crowdfunding platforms include Ideacious, Boumchicaboum (French Canadian media), and Fundweaver (for Aboriginal productions), which are based predominantly on a lending model. Yet, given the high-risk nature of film and video production, most Canadian projects still fall within the publicly funded media category, which as noted above does come with prescribed guidelines for Canadian content and the necessity to involve Canadian talent in production. In other words, the "independence" of a filmmaker may be curtailed, in some instances, in his or her approach to narrative development and production, especially if a film necessitates international location shooting and talent. In this case, a producer may have to find a co-producing partner in another country to collaborate on a film, which further ties the filmmakers to a complex set of official rules mandated by two or even three different governments. Nonetheless, as many Canadian filmmakers tend to focus on Canadian stories set in Canada, in the final analysis these seemingly restrictive guidelines may not undermine a filmmaker's unique vision at all. In other words, the meaning of independence within the context of Canadian filmmaking relates to efforts to differ from Hollywood, building a local industry, and finding international acclaim, and profits, for unique cinematic works. At the same time, one has to consider film production on a case-by-case basis; whereas some filmmakers may be curtailed in their approach to production and narrative development (or even face discriminatory practices with regard to funding allocations), others may experience a great amount of creative freedom because of their focus on Canadian stories, involving Canadian talent and locations.

Trade, Cultural Protectionism, and the Global Market

Canada's geographical proximity to the United States has shaped the country's domestic media landscape. The dominance of American movie products is reflected in feature-film distribution where the six major, foreign-controlled distributors (Walt Disney, Paramount Pictures, Sony Pictures Entertainment, Twentieth Century Fox, Universal City Studios, and Warner Bros.) achieved a 77 per cent share of all box-office receipts from Canadian theatres in 2012 (De Rosa 2012).[6] Since Canada is a much smaller market than the United States, producing domestic film and television is about ten times more expensive than importing foreign programs (Canadian Heritage 2000, 1). This imbalance in cultural production and distribution provides the basis for Canada's cultural protectionism, which has underscored every trade negotiation between the two nations for the past decades. Canada's economic alliance with the United States is anchored in the North American Free Trade Agreement of 1993. Canada succeeded in exempting cultural industries from the agreement but also faced the inclusion of a notwithstanding clause that allows the United States to take countermeasures if Canada does not adhere to its guidelines (Hoskins, Finn, and McFadyen 1996, 65). The exemption was an important provision to "prevent the cultural standardization of content and the complete foreign control of distribution" (Government of Canada 1993).

Within a global economic context, cultural protectionism tends to be often underscored by economic motivations and regional competition even though it is expressed as cultural policy emphasizing culture as a national right within a liberal democratic paradigm. However, cultural development is more than economic progress; it constitutes an essential public good, especially in places where a large number of cultural groups coexist. Canadian society, like many societies in the world – as described by Gaik Cheng Khoo in this volume's chapter on Malaysian independent film – is culturally and ethnically highly diverse.

Given the neoliberal context of the 1990s, the international market became a strategic priority for Canada during that decade. This was especially evident in the growth of co-productions between Canada and Europe and other countries around the world, which were perceived as a gateway to "finance high-quality products for distribution in the global marketplace" (Telefilm Canada 1999). Yet, the increase in co-productions occurred at the same time as the levelling-off of public financing for Canadian productions, especially in the local drama category. Local film production has actually declined over the past two decades, and independent producers find it increasingly difficult to access funding; larger production companies such as Ciné-Groupe rely on co-productions and distribution deals with foreign investors (CFTPA and APFTQ 2000, 3, 9).

In spite of the increasing public-funding challenges, Canada's independent filmmakers continue to carve out an important niche for themselves through using many of the country's smaller public and private investment funds. The guarantee of one fund often triggers another funding stream, allowing filmmakers to gradually build a sufficient production budget. For example, the Canada Council for the Arts offers grants to film and video artists, Telefilm accepts application for its Feature Film Fund (as well as co-productions), and the Canada Media Fund provides financing for film and new experimental digital production. In addition, a great variety of smaller private funds help independent filmmakers to get their projects started. These range from the Astral Media Fund to the Bell Broadcast and New Media Fund (especially for new media projects). However, as the following case studies reveal, access to various funding streams is not without its challenges or built-in biases towards applicants from Canada's diverse and multiethnic population.

Independent Film Production in the Canadian Arctic

The complexity of Canadian society, comprising multinational elements – French Canadians, English Canadians, and Aboriginal peoples (called First Nations, Inuit, and Metis in Canada)[7] – and the official recognition of multiculturalism, necessitates a broad definition of culture. Poignantly, Starowicz suggests the following paradigm for Canada's diverse cultural landscape: "a country's or ethnic group's aggregate values (social, political, economic, ethnical and artistic), not necessarily harmonious, at any given time; a constant process. This definition does not require homogeneity; it recognizes culture as dynamic; it allows art and entertainment to be defined as a form of communication, rather than as a product" (Starowicz 1993, 93).

First Nations and Inuit filmmakers create and showcase a great variety of film and media throughout Canada and the rest of the world. Some filmmakers began their work in the early 1980s, such as Zacharias Kunuk from Kingulliit Productions (formerly known as Isuma Productions). Others like Dana Claxton used community television in 1984 as an outlet for news stories about Aboriginal events. Since the 1990s, Aboriginal filmmakers like Barb Cranmer, Loretta Todd, and Catherine Martin have developed documentary films to tell stories about their respective communities and Nations' histories: the 'Namgis people of the west coast of Canada, the Cree, and the Mi'kmaq First Nation of the Maritimes, respectively. As noted by Catherine Martin (2002), "the media is a powerful tool to help our nations heal and bring understanding through the telling of our own stories."

In the Canadian north, independent filmmakers such as Elisapie Isaac are creating works from an Aboriginal and Inuit point of view. Isaac collaborated with the NFB for her first documentary, *If the Weather Permits* (2003), about the changing lifestyles of the Inuit of Nunavik. The NFB was also instrumental in producing the documentary *Inuuvunga: I Am Inuk, I Am Alive* (2004), which involved training Inuit youth to film and document their experiences of growing up in the town of Inukjuak, Nunavik – amidst a changing culture and coping with issues such as substance abuse and suicide.[8] Where broadband technology is available, young Inuit are able to develop and maintain news- and information-based websites such as the *Nunavut Echo*, run by students and youth of the Arviat Film Society. The website features Inuit-produced videos and uses Twitter and Facebook to establish social networks throughout Canada (http://arviat.tv/).[9]

In 2011 the NFB developed a historical collection of two hundred Inuit films (about Inuit peoples and by Inuit filmmakers) titled *Unikkausivut: Sharing Our Stories* (2011), which covers four decades of films about (mostly) Inuit peoples. Interestingly, the collection provides a glimpse into the changing perception of Inuit peoples and their lifestyle as recorded by anthropologists and documentary filmmakers. In particular, a 1944 short film reveals many of the misperceptions of Inuit peoples that were particular pronounced in earlier documentaries.

In *Eskimo Summer* the official British narrator from the NFB describes an Aboriginal settlement in northern Canada as resembling "a small English town" (Dixon 2012), highlighting how little Inuit culture was understood at that time. A similar sentiment was expressed in Robert Flaherty's documentary *Nanook of the North* from 1922, in which he created a romanticized image of an Inuit family living in a pre-industrial setting amidst a hostile natural world. Flaherty constructed an image of the "happy Inuit," an image that was far removed from the social and political conditions of the time (Raheja 2007). On the contrary, Alakariallak, who played Nanook, and his family were from the Inukjuamiut community that would be relocated thirty years later to the barren High Arctic by the Canadian government.

In sharp contrast to these early depictions of social life and culture in the Canadian Arctic, filmmakers like Zacharias Kunuk present a distinctive Inuit point of view, clarifying, documenting, and challenging misconceptions and misrepresentations. These Inuit filmmaking practices have to be contextualized by early broadcasting initiatives and projects such as "Inukshuk" from 1978 (Inuit Broadcasting Corporation 2006). According to Debbie Brisebois, executive director of the Inuit Broadcasting Corporation, Canadian Inuit have been active in media production since the 1960s and 1970s, volunteering in local community radio stations and working as crew members in broadcasting and filmmaking in Canada's south. A key development was the launch of the Native Communications Program by the Canadian government in 1973, which resulted in the establishment of numerous Inuit communications societies. These ranged from community newspapers and community radio to a film society in Iqaluit, Nunavut, on Baffin Island. Another milestone was the installation of the Anik B satellite in 1978, which facilitated connections between regions, as well as nationwide broadcasting of programming between northern and southern communities. Inuit Tapirisat, the national Inuit organization of the time, seized the opportunity to broaden communications networks and initiated the Inukshuk Project, which established the basis for the Inuit Broadcasting Corporation in 1981 (Roth 2002).

During the same year the CRTC licensed Cancom (Canadian Satellite Communications) to broadcast programs from the Canadian south to remote northern communities and to carry locally produced programs developed by First Nations broadcasters.[10] The CBC was also mandated to provide public-service channels for Native-language programming (Baltruschat 2004, 47–59). All of these developments laid the groundwork for a northern satellite distribution system and resulted in the launch of Television Northern Canada (TVNC) in 1991, and eventually the founding of the Aboriginal Peoples Television Network (APTN) in 1998.[11] Another important development in the history of Inuit film and media production includes the establishment of the non-governmental Nunavut Film Development Corporation (NFDC) in 2002–3. With a budget of C$1.3 million, of which C$600,000 goes directly to filmmakers, the corporation seeks to connect producers between Canada's north and south as well as overseas and to create training programs for filmmakers in the region.[12]

Today, an estimated C$6 million to C$8 million is spent on Indigenous film production each year (Dixon 2012). With about six active production companies in the region, including the Inuit Broadcasting Corporation (now mainly a production company) and APTN as the two biggest producers, it is obvious that large-scale production requires additional funding sources – facilitated through co-production arrangements for example. In the case of *The Journals of Knud Rasmussen* (2006), the second major feature film of Igloolik Isuma Productions in collaboration with Barok Film in Denmark, the budget received a huge boost by having a co-producer on board and as a result reached nearly C$6.3 million. Igloolik Isuma Productions, today known as Kingulliit, continues to be the most widely known Inuit production company in Canada and internationally. Founded by Zacharias Kunuk and Norman Cohn in Igloolik, Nunavut, over twenty-five years ago,[13] the company achieved international success with its first feature-length movie, *Atanarjuat: The Fast Runner*, which won a Camera d'Or award for best first feature film at the 2001 Cannes Film Festival. Isuma Productions was founded in 1990, but the founding members' experience with independent film dates back to the early 1980s, coinciding with the development of media infrastructures in the region during that decade.

Kunuk created his first independent video, *From Inuk Point of View*, in 1985. Besides experimenting with media production, he also managed the production centre of the Inuit Broadcasting Corporation in Igloolik, the only Aboriginal-controlled television network in North America. Norman Cohn, the only non-Inuit member of the team, which also includes Paul Apak Angilirq[14] and the late Paul Qulitalik, became involved in alternative media while living in New York City. He became interested in Kunuk's and Angilirq's media art after seeing their work exhibited in Montreal. Looking for a "context in which to work that was more serious than the exclusively self-referential world of contemporary video art" (Isuma Productions 2013c), he decided to move to Igloolik and co-founded Isuma Productions. As noted, video and light-weight camera equipment sparked a revolution in independent video productions during the 1980s. Consequentially Inuit storytelling values, which are based on collective and community-based activities,[15] could be combined with alternative video to create films that allowed for insights into an "authentic world." The third vector in this equation, as Cohn suggests, is digital media and its development into user-friendly applications, which provide access to portable recording and editing equipment. He further states:

> As a marriage of art and politics, Isuma's video-making synthesizes several related themes in a new way. First, Inuit oral storytelling is a sophisticated mix of fact, fiction, performance, improvisation, past and future, which has maintained Inuit culture successfully through art from Stone Age to Information Age. Second, being colonized offers artists a fertile reality for original progressive self-expression. Third, the invention of low-cost video at the end of the 1960s enabled people from Harlem to the Arctic to use TV as a tool for political and social change in local communities. And finally, after thirty years on the margins, video, reincarnated as "digital filmmaking," finally moved to the mainstream. (Isuma Productions 2013c)

Isuma's feature films were shot on wide-screen digital Betacam and, in the case of *Atanarjuat: The Fast Runner* and *The Journals of Knud Rassmussen*, were later transferred to 35 mm film stock.[16] This approach allowed for preliminary digital post-production on site. Digital technologies greatly enhance independent filmmaking, especially in regions that are hundreds of kilometres away from post-production facilities. Rushes from the daily shoot in Igloolik could be screened on location and did not have to be sent to Montreal, which would have resulted in lengthy delays and increased production costs. Digital technologies therefore allowed Isuma filmmakers to complete most of their film production in Igloolik (Chun 2002, 21–3).

The key to Isuma's philosophy was the creation of films that accurately reflected Inuit history and daily life. This vision continues in the company that has superseded Isuma Productions – Kingulliit, which means "Those who came after." For Zacharias Kunuk, the Inuit point of view in filmmaking is based on the authentic representation of Arctic settings, peoples, and their environment. In *Atanarjuat*, which is based on an ancient Inuit legend, this is reflected in the portrayal of traditional skills, from using the right tools for building an igloo to attending oil lamps to hunting. The film also introduces audiences to traditional child care, food preparation, music, dance, the art of facial tattoos, and the sewing of clothes. These depictions show audiences that an ancient culture continues to thrive. In turn, community involvement in the filmmaking processes allows participants to learn about ancient customs and communicate their insights to local and international audiences. To exemplify, for the film *Atanarjuat*, Kunuk and Cohn involved the entire community of Igloolik in every aspect of the production process; from costume making, set construction, and make-up to acting, scriptwriting, and technology, over one hundred Igloolik residents took part in the film.

Similarly, in *The Journals of Knud Rasmussen*, a film about the encounter between a group of Danish explorers and the Inuit of the Igloolik region, the filmmakers used historical records to retrace events from the early twentieth century. Photographs served to map locations and to find people who had been in contact with Knud Rasmussen, Therkel Mathiassen, and Peter Freuchen. The journals of explorers, missionaries, and whalers, as well as government documents and museum artefacts, were researched to learn about previous customs, beliefs, facial adornment, and clothing. In the reclamation of these artefacts and memorabilia for the creative interpretation of history, colonial traces were redrawn and used as a form of empowerment for the present. The result is a deeper understanding of the impact of colonial forces on the community and the reconnection of collective memory to its social world (see figure 13.1).

Atanarjuat, the first feature film to showcase Isuma's "unique style of 're-lived' drama" (Isuma Productions 2013a), highlights key aesthetic elements, which can be found in most of Kunuk's and Cohn's films: a focus on oral history and mythologies, authenticity in depicting Inuit traditions, and a slow-paced editing style that allows for scenes and scenery to gradually unfold and linger. *Atanarjuat* received most of its C$1.96 million funding from Telefilm Canada and the National Film Board. The well-documented struggle to obtain funding for *Atanarjuat* revealed in-built discriminatory perceptions of Aboriginal filmmaking practices and expectations of financial returns (Ginsburg 2003, 828–9). Production for *Atanarjuat* began in 1996 but had to be halted owing to the lack of funding in 1998. After applying to Telefilm Canada, Isuma producers were confronted with a choice between the different funding

13.1 On the set of *The Journals of Knud Rasmussen* (Norman Cohn and Zacharias Kunuk, 2006). Image courtesy of Norman Cohn, Isuma Distribution International, www.isuma.tv/fastrunnertrilogy.

streams for English, French, and Aboriginal programming; the latter was capped at C$200,000 for all types of Aboriginal productions.[17] However, Isuma producers did not want to be confined to the Aboriginal Production Fund and its limited funding stream, and applied to the other funding envelopes instead. Their subsequent rejection highlighted what Ginsburg has termed "under-resourced 'media reservations'" and a "cultural glass ceiling" (ibid.), as the perception of Aboriginal productions clearly indicated that they were delimited to low-budget filmmaking and limited distribution. According to Kunuk, "classifying our application by ethnicity rather than eligibility, measuring us by race rather than merit, Telefilm excluded *Atanarjuat* from the competitive evaluation process that decides what Canadian films got made this year" ("Inuit Film Unfairly Excluded" 1998). In response, Isuma staged a protest campaign through letters to the government and the press and found an ally in Matt Radz of the *Montreal Gazette* newspaper, who brought the situation to the attention of the Canadian public. Ultimately, Isuma's producers were successful in convincing the government that the company should be able to access the funding stream marked for Canadian productions rather than the smaller envelope designated for Aboriginal films. The production budget for *Atanarjuat* increased significantly after Telefilm Canada invested C$537,000 in the feature. In addition, after the NFB had signed on as co-producer and committed to 23 per cent of the financing, the Canadian Television Fund also contributed C$390,000.[18] The whole situation shed an important light on in-built discriminatory perceptions of Aboriginal filmmaking and increased the awareness of unfair practices. It also highlighted that Inuit films can make an important cultural contribution nationally and internationally, especially with regard to the recognition of *Atanarjuat* at the Cannes Film Festival.

In addition to raising awareness about Inuit-specific issues, Isuma provided economic opportunities in the region: during production, local talent was employed, including actors, set builders, and costume designers. In the end, *Atanarjuat: The Fast Runner* contributed C$1 million to the local economy and created over sixty part-time and twenty full-time jobs in a region marked by high unemployment. Isuma's approach was therefore fundamentally different from that of other film production units, starting with community involvement in all of the production processes. Another unique feature relates to Isuma's film narratives, which are rooted in Inuit spirituality and symbolism. These are not translated for non-Inuit viewers to attain easier access to their meaning.[19] The films are therefore as much a celebration of cultural continuity as they are mnemonic devices to reconnect to memories of the past. Their purpose goes beyond educational aims as they allow Inuit participants and audiences to engage and reflect upon issues that are important to the community. Within the context of colonial legacies and unresolved land claims, the films represent a political voice for Indigenous rights that extend beyond national borders.

In its twenty-five-year history Isuma Productions has been instrumental in establishing and supporting many Inuit initiatives such as the Tarriaksuk Video Centre, one of the first independent non-profit video training and access centres in the Arctic. In turn, throughout the 1990s Tarriaksuk sponsored programs such as Arnait Video Productions, a Women's Video Workshop, and the Inuusiq (Life) Youth Drama Workshop. In 1999 Arnait Video Productions incorporated as the first women's collective independent production company in the Arctic. Arnait produced programs mainly from a female perspective. These have been exhibited in festivals and museums in many countries, and include

Ninguira / My Grandmother (1999), a half-hour drama about women and health, and *Anaana / Mother* (2002) and *Unakuluk / Dear Little One* (2006) about Inuit adoptions. Key members of the Arnait women's group were also instrumental in writing and directing Isuma's third feature film, *Before Tomorrow* (2009), which today forms part of the remarkable Inuit movie trilogy by Isuma, together with *Atanarjuat: The Fast Runner* and *The Journals of Knud Rasmussen*.

In many ways *Atanarjuat* and *The Journals of Knud Rasmussen* exemplify the confluence of traditional storytelling, community-based independent filmmaking practices, and new media technologies, which resulted in films that are fundamentally different from mainstream productions. They represent an approach that transforms "media that dissolve and homogenize cultures into tools of cultural preservation" (Scott 2002, 11–12). The success of films like *Atanarjuat* led Isuma to pioneer several other digitally based media projects such Isuma TV, which uses the Internet as a digital distribution platform for a wide variety of Indigenous programming (Isuma TV 2013). Isuma also launched the SILA project, which consists of an interactive website that functions as a narrative map for entry points into traditional Inuit songs, stories, and historical events. In addition, Kunuk and Cohn use their public platform to raise issues of concern for Inuit communities and the world in general. For one, they have highlighted the high suicide rates among Inuit youth and the desperate living conditions that many Inuit communities face because of unemployment and health risks, especially diabetes. On an international scale, Isuma is working with environmental groups to relate observations and insights from Inuit elders to the researchers who are investigating climate change connected to global warming. The results of these collaborations were presented at the UN Climate Change Conference in 2009 and culminated in Isuma's documentary *Qapirangajuq: Inuit Knowledge and Climate Change* (2010).

However, in spite of the increasing use of digital technologies for Inuit films and Internet platforms, the overall infrastructure of social media applications like Twitter and Facebook remains limited owing to the lack of high-speed Internet access in the Arctic. As outlined in a report by the Centre for the North of the Conference Board of Canada (2013), Arctic Internet services are often slower, less reliable, and more expensive than in other parts of the country. Along the same line, Rachael Petersen's (2013) research on Indigenous use of digital media points out that most Inuit youth do not use Twitter because the required 3G technology has yet to be implemented. In addition, limited access to high-speed Internet, in most regions, effectively prevents Inuit communities from downloading or uploading video from or to sites like YouTube and Vimeo. Yet since the spoken word is one of the predominant communication methods among Inuit, increased accessibility to a technology that permits the transmission of audio-visual content would be logical and desirable.

Where the Internet can be accessed for uploading and downloading video, Inuit communities embrace the opportunity to document day-to-day life and special occasions, such as hunting excursions. Social media sites like Facebook are used to post events, warn others about potential predators in the region (for example, polar bears), and send out invitations to join in local gatherings. In the case of a Facebook page on "Nunavut hunting stories," nearly twenty-three thousand Inuit share their experiences, reach out to the next generation, and raise awareness about Native hunting rights.

Another development in digital media use is the appropriation of popular Internet memes and giving them an Inuit connotation. These memes feature Inuktitut written in roman script, which is rare in social media but important with regard to preserving a language (see figure 13.2). Given this high interest in connectivity on the one hand, and the lack of a region-wide broadband infrastructure on the other, more has to be done to guarantee access to digitally based social media, especially in view of Nunavut's Internet subsidies that are set to expire in 2016.[20]

Currently most broadband initiatives are based on military needs and emergency response set-ups. Commercial interests in the north (for example, mining) are also linked to the expansion of digital communication networks to serve local industry. More promising are discussions around the development of a fibre optic telecommunications network in the Canadian Arctic. Arctic Fibre proposes to install a 15,600 kilometre network between Tokyo and London through the southern portion of the Northwest Passage, which would connect Nunavut communities (Arctic Fibre 2013). Yet, as Petersen (2013) rightly points out, the necessary discourse about how these networks will ultimately interact with traditional culture is currently missing. A key question that has yet to be explored is, how can the Internet and social media be shaped according to Inuit values and culture?

With respect to independent filmmaking, digital production provides a great advantage over analogue production, as described in detail with the works of Isuma. Digital media production promotes

13.2 An Inuit meme.

participatory forms of communication because it allows smaller communities to access film production technologies. It enables Inuit and other Aboriginal communities to explore issues of concern and to tell their stories in dramatic ways. Independent film practices and alternative media therefore provide the basis for Indigenous peoples to pursue social change through politics of identity and representation. Within this paradigm, cultural production is transformed into political mobilization, and, according to Ginsburg (2003, 828–9), this "cultural activism" defines Indigenous media as promoting differences rather than assimilation.

Furthermore, the decentralization of media practices is an exercise in empowerment, which at various points intersects with mainstream media to redirect nationwide focuses and international debates. Global interest in the Arctic is intensifying, especially with regard to the environment and global warming, and in international politics (for example, sovereignty claims on the North), as well as in the popular imagination of the public, which ranges from animal preservation to tourism and northern iconography (for example, the image of the polar bear) in advertising campaigns. Inuit films, web initiatives, and social media outreach campaigns therefore provide an opportunity to contribute to a vital international cross-cultural dialogue about climate change, cultural identity, and globalization.

As shown by chapters throughout this volume, in particular Sheila Petty's discussion on "independent" African cinema and Gabriela Martinez's chapter, "Independent Filmmaking in the Peruvian Context," digital technologies greatly enhance independent film production and distribution where access to traditional means of production is limited owing to great expense or unavailability. In the case of independent film production in the Canadian Arctic, additional questions around broadband and high-speed Internet access are being raised, especially with respect to cultural sustainability and the need for Inuit communities to control their own means of production and distribution across newly emerging digital platforms.

NOTES

1 Established in 1968, the Canadian Film Development Corporation (CFDC) was renamed Telefilm Canada in 1984.
2 The Media Democracy movement developed out of the Campaign for Press and Broadcast Freedom (CPBF), a non-profit organization committed to raise awareness of media-related issues. It is dedicated to public education and action to promote greater diversity of media ownership and to enhance the rights of media professionals. It also monitors and comments on key developments in the news and information industries (see Baltruschat 2006).
3 For example see Jenkins (2006); Rheingold (2002).
4 The ability to limit, slow down, or restrict data streams by Internet service providers is known as traffic shaping.
5 An example of this kind of campaign can be found in the promotional campaigns for the indie horror film American Mary (2013). Jen and Sylv Soska (also known as The Twisted Twins), who wrote, produced, and directed the film have proven to be masters at promoting their film through a wide range of social media.
6 In 2009 the six major U.S. distributors generated nearly three-quarters of the total distribution revenues in Canada, or C$1.38 billion (De Rosa 2012, 24).
7 The Aboriginal peoples of Canada refer to presettler societies across Canada, of which the majority are recognized as bands and self-governing

communities. The Inuit, in particular, is a group of indigenous peoples and communities inhabiting the Canadian Arctic, as well as regions in the United States, Greenland, and Russia.

8　According to Health Canada (2013), suicide rates for Inuit youth are among the highest in the world, at eleven times the national average.

9　http://www.nunatsiaqonline.ca/stories/article/65674arviat_film_society_to_launch_local_television_channel/

10　The licence required CANCOM to provide one video and two audio uplinks in Canada's north for northern programming and to substitute up to ten hours each week of programming originating in the south with Native television programming (Indigenous Communications in Canada 2013).

11　For a more detailed history of APTN see Baltruschat (2004).

12　The NFDC's funding is derived from a variety of private and public sources, such as the Canadian Northern Economic Development Agency (CanNor), which invested C\$140,000 in the NFDC in 2010.

13　Igloolik Isuma Productions went into receivership in 2011 after the company was unable to repay loans to Atuqtuarvik Corporation and several other lenders. Isuma's online television service, Isuma.tv, was not affected and continues to operate as an online platform for Indigenous films and video programs. Zacharias Kunuk introduced Kingulliit (Those who came after) soon afterwards, which follows a similar mandate to that of Isuma but on a smaller scale ("Igloolik Isuma Productions Going Out of Business" 2011).

14　Paul Apak Angilirq (1954–98) was vice-president and co-founder of Isuma. Apak began his career in 1978 as a trainee in Canada's Inukshuk Project, the first project to train Indigenous television producers in remote communities.

15　Inuit communities have a long tradition of oral literature and storytelling. Before the introduction of a writing system, the local histories, myths, and stories were passed along from generation to generation by word of mouth.

16　With the introduction of digital projection systems in theatres across North America, this type of transfer, from digital to 35 mm film, will likely no longer occur in the near future.

17　Since 2010 the newly formed Canadian Media Fund (2012) has fostered innovation through supporting experimental and digital media projects. Concurrently, Telefilm Canada maintains different funding streams for English and French films, as well as films featuring Aboriginal stories. Funding for the latter, through the Featuring Aboriginal Stories Program, has increased significantly since the production of *Atanarjuat* and now ranges between C\$1.5 million and C\$2 million.

18 The case of *Atanarjuat* provides a good example of how additional film
    funding is being "triggered" by the involvement of major public funding
    bodies in financing.
19 Isuma's films are in Inuktitut with English or French subtitles.
20 Nunavut Internet access is serviced by the QINIQ network, which is subsi-
    dized by federal funding from the Nunavut Broadband Development
    Corporation to ensure lower monthly costs for individual and business
    broadband accounts.

Chapter Fourteen

Digital Video Films as "Independent" African Cinema

SHEILA PETTY

As a transnational space, Africa is still mired in what may be described as the "digital divide" where access to information and communication technology (ICT) lags behind that of many developing and developed countries (Fuchs and Horvak 2008, 100). Still, it would be incorrect to assume that all African cinema is digitally or otherwise inaccessible. For example, the Nollywood industry, centred in Lagos, Nigeria, has become "the third largest film industry in the world" (Haynes 2007b, 131). Based on a low-budget production model, Nollywood cinema is populist in content, innovative in technology, and driven by profit. In an era of deteriorating movie houses, where violence has made home viewing more palatable, Nollywood films fill a niche comprising small screens that require an endless stream of entertainment (Barlet 2010, 84).

If that were all there was to it, Nollywood cinema would simply be a successful local phenomenon. Yet it is an international success story, where Internet streaming, whether of trailers or films, has brought Nollywood to a world audience that is seemingly eager to buy, and "since the early 1990s" video filmmaking "partake[s] of a mix of local, national and global discourses and aesthetics" (McCall 2002, 79–80). Now "a significant cultural and commercial presence within contemporary Nigeria and in the Nigerian diaspora abroad," such video films represent a transactional exchange between Africa and the rest of the world (Adejunmobi 2002, 77). More to the point, the success of its production methodology has led to the development of video film industries in other African countries, including Burkina Faso, Ghana (Ghallywood), Cameroon (Collywood), Kenya (Riverwood), Tanzania (Bongowood), and Uganda (Ugawood).

Cinema in most areas of the African continent developed as a post-colonial industry, born alongside nations' independence. In British-colonized areas the film units were not maintained, owing to other pressing needs, and in French-colonized areas a form of dependency was maintained through the French Ministry of Cooperation, especially during the 1960s and 1970s, which stipulated the way in which Africans could create their cinema projects. The major production imperative during those two decades was the reversal of the colonist's gaze and the re-appropriation of African cultural space, ideology, and images. By the 1980s and 1990s, nations' debt to the International Monetary Fund and the devaluation of African currencies made it increasingly difficult for Africans to shoot films in Africa, and many filmmakers began to pursue north-south co-production partnerships with European nations (NeuCollins 2007). Furthermore, as the "cinematic infrastructure" (read one that is celluloid driven and state controlled) of most African nations has all but disappeared, many, including Nigerian Tunde Kelani, believe that Africa can overcome the digital divide by embracing the digital video revolution. Kelani (2008, 90–1) maintains that high-quality production does not necessarily require shooting on celluloid (which relies mainly on foreign post-production facilities and is payable in non-African currencies) and that low-cost digital technologies can provide a suitable alternative.

Beginning with a brief analysis of the Nollywood video film phenomenon, this chapter will examine how some filmmakers from other African nations have turned to the digital video model when state-owned film industries have ceased production (Ghana); as a means of exploring new aesthetics or production models (Yousry Nasrallah, Egypt); as a means of exploring genre video style (Boubacar Diallo, Burkina Faso); or as a way of producing socially committed videos that challenge the official cinema controlled by the state (Amazigh films produced by Chleuh Berbers in southern Morocco). In many ways these initiatives have brought to the fore new "independent" cinemas that challenge and reconfigure identity constructions in a globalizing Africa.

A large part of identity building in these new nations focused on language as a unifying force of culture and heritage. New forms of visual expression were necessary to raise Africans' consciousness of themselves and portray the urgent realities of newly formed nations. In terms of film and video style, realism and didacticism dominated the emerging industries, almost to the exclusion of other narrative forms or aesthetics. Independent digital video filmmaking has afforded directors a great deal of freedom to challenge established conventions and create their own aesthetic and narrative models, which, in the case of Nigerian and Ghanaian video films, has often meant the use of Brechtian techniques such as direct camera address, and the use of flashbacks as a narrative device. In Egypt, Yousry Nasrallah has concentrated on character development in his work while, in Burkina Faso, Boubacar Diallo has explored almost every type of genre narrative structure possible. Finally, the ideology-driven Amazigh videos from Morocco employ an abundance of static medium two-shots to link two characters in conversation and social space, but punctuate scenes with long shots to foreground-sweeping landscape vistas of the Atlas mountains.

The Nollywood Phenomenon

Nigerian-based video film, often referred to by the sobriquet "Nollywood" film, denotes a strand of low-budget film within African cinema that is based on popular culture, and promotes a production model involving market-driven entrepreneurial financing, independent of state funding, and product placement as a means of financing. Nollywood has long been controversial among African cinema film scholars, who seem divided on the authenticity and cultural worth of an industry noted for its ability to churn out low-budget, straight-to-video or DVD film product at what seems to be an astounding rate. Ikechukwu Obiaya, for example, lauds Nollywood for its populist approach, describing it as "created by the people for the people" (Obiaya 2010, 321). Others, such as Olivier Barlet, lament that the popularity of such works might spell "the end of African auteur cinema" (Barlet 2010, 81). Regardless of the boom and gloom surrounding Nollywood cinema, it has nevertheless demonstrated a profound resilience grounded in an extraordinary relationship with technological advancement and has made significant inroads across the African continent as a production and distribution model.

Nollywood has its roots in the traditions of Yoruba travelling theatre, which in turn derives from church year-end and harvest performances as well as "Yoruba *alarainjo* (or *apidan*) masquerade performance practices that predate colonialism by centuries" (Ogundele 2000, 92). At its height in the early 1980s, at least a hundred theatre companies travelled Nigeria, bringing to audiences a mixture of Christianity and folk-based productions (91). The first link to Nigerian video film is found in the 1970s, when leading Nigerian dramatist Hubert Ogunde pioneered the use of film inserts during the plays. These were intended to connote "fantasy actions or elements (transformation of human being into animals, for instance), that were meant to convey the supernatural dimensions of Yoruba cosmology" (95), which could not realistically be portrayed during live performances. Later, recognizing the potential of television for spectacle and sensationalism, Ogunde began producing full-length, low-budget feature films on video, taking the first tentative steps in the development of Nollywood (96).

The second influence on the development of the Nigerian video film industry comes from Ghana, which pioneered the development of a market-driven, low-budget video film industry based on popular local cultural interests (Ghana will be discussed later in this chapter). Often created by "private producers" without formal film training, these films are distributed through a network of "small video theatres" and home sales, making them very popular and potentially lucrative (Meyer 1999, 93). Olivier Barlet (2008, 121) credits producer Holy Rock as the first to see the potential of adopting the Ghanaian production model when he received a large shipment of blank videotapes and commissioned a Yoruba language film on VHS. The Igbo language video film *Living in Bondage* (Chris Obi Rapu, 1992) followed and focused on a man who makes a deal with the devil to advance his social and economic position. This is arguably Nollywood's first financial and popular success (Barlet 2008, 121–2). This film, and the others that followed, are supported by "15,000 video clubs" and "individual cassette sales, which can reach up to 200,000 copies of the same film" (ibid., 122). In addition to private financing, additional production financing comes from product placements, including virtually any marketable item that can be placed in front of the spectator (Barlet 2010, 87–8).

The third element delineating the rise of Nollywood includes a series of cultural factors. As Olivier Barlet (2008) explains, the collapse of Nigerian currency made celluloid film production prohibitively expensive versus the much less expensive alternative offered by video production. In addition to the collapse of the currency, social conditions deteriorated, resulting in many Nigerians choosing to stay in at night, no doubt contributing to "the sharp rise in the number of VCRs and V-CD players in homes" (125–6).

Finally, the presence of multiple ethnic groups and languages, including Hausa, Yoruba, and Igbo, provided ready-made audiences predisposed to video films that focused on local folklore and imperatives (125). Manthia Diawara (2010, 169) cautions that "even in Nigeria,

Nollywood videos are not to be confused with the Yoruba videos,"
which are mostly historical and employ acting and narrative techniques
firmly ensconced in Yoruba theatre traditions. The Nollywood product,
according to Diawara, represents "stories of mobility" (179) and "is full
of the elements that facilitate the projection of the spectator's fantasies
or fears onto the screen, and thus constitute narrative desire and identi-
fication" (170). These films are star driven, rely heavily on spectacle and
melodrama, and use Nigerian English (170).

Not only has the Nollywood-style storytelling contributed to the
industry's boom, but also there are technological, distribution, marketing, and cultural factors that have helped fuel Nollywood's rise.
Technological elements include affordable production and home
equipment, now including DVD and V-CD players and recorders. Perhaps more to the point, Nollywood became an aggressive marketing
machine that saw the potential of making its product available to more
than a Nigerian-based audience. Innovative marketing and distribution methods include selling DVDs in hair salons and street stalls, by
hawkers; through video clubs or by promotional events and posters;
press coverage including magazines; sponsorships by automobile ·
and beverage companies; and in hotels. With "a declared production
of nearly 700 films" in approximately ten years, Nollywood has been
promoted along cultural lines, with Hausa films finding an audience
in Niger, and Yoruba films finding secondary markets in Benin and
Togo (Barlet 2008, 125). Dubbing in French has opened up opportunities in sub-Saharan francophone countries, and dubbing in English
has opened up the market to the Nigerian diaspora who access films
via distribution websites (ibid.). Onookome Okome has argued that
the Nigerian video film is instrumental in forging the local-global connection between transnational communities and home (Okome 2004, 5).
Finally, the low production budgets, typically US$8,000 to produce a
ninety-minute video film, necessitate volume sales, and, as a result,
Nollywood films are among the most competitively priced, certainly
undercutting the rental or purchase cost of African auteur, American,
Asian, and Indian films (Oladunjoye 2008, 64).

Increasingly Nollywood is successfully exploiting streaming as a
means to reach an African and Nigerian diasporic audience. A recent
study of Nollywood's presence online conducted by Ikechukwu Obiaya finds that Nollywood "commands a fairly high online presence,"
including "twelve websites, fifteen blogs and 107 Facebook groups all
fully dedicated to" topics centring on all aspects of Nollywood film,

including reviews, performers, and "industry news" (Obiaya 2010, 325). What this indicates is a computer-literate international audience prepared to consume Nollywood films through an Internet medium. Interestingly, this wide audience base includes Nigeria-based members who, statistically, have a higher percentage of Internet users than the African average. For example, Africans constitute only 3.4 per cent of worldwide users (ibid.). With ten million potential users in Nigeria, Nigeria's national average includes 6.8 per cent Internet coverage in its own population and represents 18.5 per cent of all African Internet users (ibid.). This suggests that, as a nation building infrastructure, Nigeria remains committed to the development of technological advancement.

A quick search of YouTube for "African films" retrieves a vast number of items bearing the Nollywood brand. For example, out of twenty-five possibilities drawn up by one search, at least two-thirds either promoted Nollywood films or offered sites that allowed the streaming of select films. Ironically, a search for "African cinema" unearthed more traditional offerings pertaining to African auteur cinema. The contrast between these two phrases bears out the struggle perceived by Olivier Barlet and other African film studies scholars that Nollywood has become a sort of low-budget predatory colonizer that has "invaded markets in neighboring countries (Ghana, Cameroon, Niger, Benin, and the African market in general) thanks to dumping and aggressive sales practices" (Barlet 2008, 126). Certainly, some of these complaints are accurate, and a look at Nollywood's presence on YouTube demonstrates why this is so.

Streamed Nollywood product on YouTube includes clips, trailers, and full-length feature films. Some of these trailers are clearly professionally produced, including slick production values and centring on highlights from the film promoted. Others take the form of simple clips, often promoting the film from which they have been taken by simply presenting a dramatic or climatic scene without further context. Full-length feature films are presented in a series of clips as per the limitations of YouTube's technology. Streaming quality can be quite uneven and, given the weaker production values of some films, quite problematic. However, as a marketing and fan resource, the streaming of Nollywood film on YouTube offers an effective way of building an international audience.

Another way for Nollywood producers and distributors to access African diaspora and international audiences is through so-called fansites, forums, and e-zines. Often promoting free access to streamed

Nollywood films, such fansites and forums are geographically mobile, allowing fans and other interested parties to connect worldwide (Obiaya 2010, 326). Another function of such sites is the ability to provide audience feedback, and, as Obiaya notes, "the technology has permitted a shift in the balance of power between media producers and consumers, in that the audience can now compete online with the producers" (327). Thus, the forum format coupled with the streaming of Nollywood film provides a hub around which audiences can coalesce.

An example of such a community may be found on Naijapals.com and Naijarules.com. *Naija* is a colloquial term for "Nigeria" and signals the site's interest in Nigerian culture (ibid., 326). As is the case with many of these sites, Naijapals.com offers a wide range of focuses, including Nigerian entertainment, politics, celebrity gossip, music, and Nigerian and African films. Under the category of videos, Naijarules.com provides a free video streaming and/or download service for members of the site. A quick perusal of films such as *Freefall* and *Freefall 2* demonstrates the tendency of Nigerian video filmmakers to make sequels of successful films, following the U.S. system and thus capitalizing on ready-made audiences. Other notable examples include *Living in Bondage 1, 2,* and *3; Glamour Girls 1* and *2;* and *Issakaba 1, 2, 3,* and *4.*

Sites like Naijapals and Naijarules, while clearly assisting Nollywood film in the promotion of their products, raise some concerns about one of the most debilitating activities in the film industry, namely pirating. On free streaming sites like Naijapals, Naijarules, and YouTube, it is often difficult to find attribution for the films housed on site. Barlet (2008, 129) notes that "video pirating is rampant" in Africa and relates the allegation that "Nigerians even go as far as changing the credits and adding scenes with their own actors in order to give the films greater commercial appeal when they pirate Ghanaian films." Streaming pirated films purportedly adds to the loss of revenues in Nollywood film and seems virtually unstoppable although Nollywood producers have had occasion to require their films be removed from such sites. Opinion is mixed on the issue of piracy. As an industry unto itself, it keeps many people employed (upwards of twenty thousand in Kano alone). Some producers, however, such as the Ghanaian director and producer Socrate Safo, believe that although it is impossible to fight pirates, it is possible to undermine them by flooding the markets with CDs or DVDs when a film is first released (Oladunjoye 2008, 66–7).

Another venue for African film is AfricanMovieChannel.com (AMC), which came into existence in the United Kingdom in 2006 as a pioneering effort to provide the first television channel "dedicated to African movies from Nollywood (the very popular Nigerian film industry)" outside Africa (African Movie Channel 2013). Although other African films may be represented here, the focus of the channel remains primarily on Nollywood film. The fact that the United Kingdom was the site for such an endeavour is not surprising, given that it possesses one of the largest Nigerian diasporic communities in the world, estimated in 2009 at 154,000 (ibid.). The obvious attraction here is an international market with a ready-built audience and opportunities for expansion. As well, unlike Naijapals, Naijarules, and YouTube, AMC is a fee-for-service site that sells its offerings via online downloads, worldwide streaming, and television syndication (ibid.). Films are purchased in "credit packages," the least expensive of which amounts to fifty credits for £5. Given that an individual streaming of a film costs approximately ten credits, the cost of procuring a film is relatively inexpensive. In addition to films, AMC also offers streaming and download services for other types of programming, including television series, documentaries, and talk shows originating in Africa.

Given the strong presence of Nollywood films on the Internet and the variety of streaming options available, it seems possible that Nollywood video films, despite uneven aesthetics and genre-based story structures, is emerging as the "first" face of African cinema. Regardless of its detractors who question whether such manifestly commercial and popular cinema could ever authentically represent African needs and imperatives on the world's screens, Nollywood cinema has clearly exploited technology in a calculated way in order to bring its products to a local and international audience. Although somewhat grudgingly, Barlet (2008, 127–8) admits that Nollywood video film's "democratization of image production" signals that digital film has given "Africa the potential to produce its own images without foreign backing." Indeed, what began as a popular art has transformed into a formidable industry within the field of African screen media, commanding considerable academic attention on par with that of the celluloid art films produced in francophone West Africa. In the future, legitimate licensed streaming at a modest cost will continue to give Nollywood video film an edge on its competitors, a fact that other image industries on the continent will need to take into consideration in order to survive.

The Ghanaian Independent Video Scene

One of the most striking examples of the development of a video film industry occurred in Ghana in the late 1980s with the creation of low-budget video films (Meyer 1999, 93). Spurred on by the inexpensiveness, accessibility, portability, and ease of post-production made possible by video technology, the Ghanaian film industry was revitalized, and a new set of narrative and aesthetic imperatives, albeit controversial ones, entered the lexicon of African cinema (ibid., 94–5). Manthia Diawara (2010, 169) describes Ghanaian videos as "remakes of [Kwah] Ansah's films, but without the same dramatic tension, with less characterization, fewer special effects, more slowly paced narratives, and predictable, didactic endings." Diawara is inferring here, via a reference to one of Ghana's most well-known (celluloid) cinema directors, that Ghanaian video films tend to take up Ansah's project in his two groundbreaking films, *Love Brewed in the African Pot* (1981) and *Heritage Africa* (1988); this project is aimed at rehabilitating African history and identity via the African male protagonist's "correct" choices vis-à-vis tradition and heritage (ibid.). Birgit Meyer (2010b) has argued that the comparison of "tradition" and "heritage" in *Heritage Africa* to the plots in video films merits a much more complex analysis than simple rehabilitation or retrieval from "colonial brainwashing." She demonstrates how, in video films, tradition and heritage were "framed differently" and were a "major source of trouble and anxiety – indeed, a burdensome 'legacy' more than simply 'heritage' – that had to be gotten rid of" (13). Ultimately, Meyer advocates for more flexible understandings and applications of these notions so that they are not fixed definitively to the colonial past, as demonstrated in Ansah's work (19).

Interestingly, Ansah's films are the prototypes of "appropriate representations" sanctioned by the "once state-owned Ghana Film Industry Corporation (GFIC)" (Meyer 2010b, 8). However, from its inception in 1957 to its closure in 1996, the GFIC only produced thirteen feature films on celluloid (among the numerous documentaries and newsreels produced). With the introduction of television and subsequently video technology, local entrepreneurs considered video as a way to revitalize the local cinema industry. Kwah Ansah himself declared in 2002, "Film or celluloid is expensive, and ideally that's the format by which I would prefer telling my story, but realistically no African filmmaker on his own can afford celluloid as things stand now. And neither can we wait for our mismanaged economies to be revamped before telling our stories" (quoted in Ukadike 2002, 17).

Although the Ghanaian video industry began well before Nollywood, it was slow to develop compared to the Nigerian industry, which finally overtook that of Ghana by the late 1990s. This was mainly owing to the fact that many viewers preferred Nigerian videos. Meyer (2010a) argues, for example, that style, fashion, and the latest fads are highly prized values in Ghana and that, for a long period, Ghanaian video films appeared modest and "old-fashioned" compared to the flashy Nigerian product. Even more important, however, Ghanaian viewers tended to prefer the stories and content of Nigerian movies because the "films resonated more than Ghanaian ones with the concerns of people in the street" (53–5). The depiction of melodramatic excess, opulent displays of wealth, and stories centred around issues of witchcraft and juju (sorcery) versus Christianity were especially attractive to viewers who considered juju to be a part of everyday life. Thus, Nigerian product continued to be dumped on the Ghanaian market (to a large extent by Ghanaian business people because it was more profitable than Ghanaian movies). Pierre Barrot (2008, 44) cites the Ghanaian director and producer Socrate Safo who claims that at the end of the 1990s there were forty-seven registered Ghanaian producers, and by 2004 there were only seven. As well, by the same year, eighteen out of twenty-six officially registered active distributors were Nigerian. In another context, Safo has described how Nigerian directors pirate Ghanaian videos, change the credits, and embellish the stories with scenes using Nigerian actors in an attempt to heighten commercial and audience appeal (Barlet 2008, 129).

Aboubakar Sanogo (2009) writes of African cinephilic traditions and attitudes "such as renaming oneself, adopting the demeanors of actors, knowing songs by heart, changing accents, frantically watching films over and over again, reciting lines by heart, reenacting scenes and sequences with gestures, words, and swear words," and wonders if these are possible mechanisms for forging "a continental and global cinephilia for African-produced cinema" (228). Although these traditions were created as viewer responses to Hollywood, Bollywood, and Hong Kong films, they increasingly pertain to Nollywood, according to Sanogo, and, thus I would argue, Ghanaian video films (ibid.). These attitudes have evolved in concert with the revival of the Ghanaian industry. Since 2005, according to Meyer (2010a, 55–6), there has been an improved aesthetic quality to the videos, which deal with juju and witchcraft in local languages and in VCD format. Video producers now speak with pride of a "Ghallygold" industry where Ghanaian audiences are prepared to pay more for Ghanaian video films than Nollywood films.

African Independent Video "Auteurs"

A number of filmmakers across the continent have turned to independent digital video production in an effort to reach audiences through popular genres and experimental or alternative production models. For example, the Burkinabé filmmaker Boubacar Diallo began his career as a journalist, creating the weekly satire newspaper *Le Journal du Jeudi*; after publishing two detective novels and numerous screenplays, he turned to filmmaking in 2004 with the thriller *Traque à Ouaga? / Pursuit in Ouaga* and the romantic comedy *Sofia*. These were immediate hits with huge audiences, and Diallo has claimed that genre movies are the way to attract audiences: "if people aren't going to see movies, it's because we're not showing what they want to see" (quoted in Barlet 2010, 88). He has attempted almost all cinematic genres from the political thriller *Code Phoenix / Phoenix Code* (2005) to the western *L'Or des Youngas / The Youngas Gold* to the fantasy film *Julie et Roméo / Julie and Romeo* (2011), a "re-make" of the Shakespearean production. Produced quickly and on very low budgets of €0,000–50,000 per feature, the video films are financed through promotion of bottled water, cellular telephones, mopeds, et cetera (Barlet 2010, 87). Interestingly, other independent filmmakers such as Franco-Tunisian Nadia El Fani have tested alternative funding models that involve multiple co-production via the Internet in order to cover post-production costs. She sent a mass email to all her friends and acquaintances, inviting them to become co-producers for €35 each. All who donated were listed in the credits of her 2012 documentary, *Même pas mal / No Harm Done* (Florence Martin, personal communication).[1] The Burkinabé filmmaker and television director and producer Apolline Traoré was able to complete her digital feature film *Moi, Zaphira / I, Zaphira* in 2012 by using all the money she made through directing or producing television serials for the state-run television station.

Diallo has been described as an auteur video filmmaker who speaks and thinks like an entrepreneur. He has been heard to say, "All activity should possess an economic logic. The day the subsidy tap runs dry, African cinema will no longer exist. However, as far as I'm concerned, from Dakar to Libreville, there is only one audience. It's a shame to not capitalize on that" (Lequeret 2005).[2] Lequeret goes on to claim that, for Diallo, video is much more than just an aesthetic choice; it allows him artistic licence and independence while he is able to produce films quickly and regularly, often completing two features per year (ibid.). This is in stark contrast to filmmakers working in 35 mm film, many of whom would struggle to complete one feature every ten years![3]

On the other side of the African continent, in Egypt, Yousry Nasrallah, a former assistant to filmmaking giant Youssef Chahine, began making socially committed films infused with autobiographical tendencies, such as his 1988 *Summer Thefts* in which personal memories are superimposed on political images and narrative. The observance of social commitment (*iltizam*), while referencing the personal, is typical of other North African filmmakers such as the Tunisian Nouri Bouzid, the Franco-Tunisian Nadia El Fani, and the Franco-Algerian Fatima Sissani. Like his counterparts, Nasrallah depicts all points of view, creating a space for the audience members to consider and form their own opinions on the subject. With *The City* in 1999, Nasrallah turned to digital video to afford his actors "more space for improvisation" (Shafik 2007, 192–3, 226). In 2011 Nasrallah participated in the collective-driven film *Tamantashar Yom / Eighteen Days*. Ten directors each agreed to direct, without a budget and on a volunteer basis, a short film from his or her own point of view, centred on the events of 25 January to 11 February 2011 during the Egyptian revolution. Nasrallah's short is titled *Interior/Exterior*, and he used his small Sony high-definition camera to film images of his actors mixing with demonstrators in Tahrir Square. The goal of the film project was to support the democracy movement and depict the courage of ordinary citizens and their multiplicity of viewpoints on the revolution via fiction films that could be posted to YouTube, as opposed to recording live events like the media did (Barlet 2011). Nasrallah continues his practice of exploring different character viewpoints in *After the Battle* (2012), which depicts complex characters over a wide social spectrum but, in particular, focuses on a horseman who was pulled off his horse while he was charging demonstrators during "The Battle of the Camels."

Although YouTube exists as a form of distribution, it is still fraught with contradictions: on the one hand, it provides access to films; on the other hand, the works are often pirated, and many filmmakers are unaware that their films have been uploaded or posted to the Internet. At the recent edition of the Festival International de Cinéma Vues d'Afrique in Montreal, 26 April to 5 May 2013, an African participant declared that there is currently no platform for distribution in Africa; the focus is solely on production.

The Amazigh Experience

In the late 1990s in southern Morocco, Amazigh (Berber)-produced video films began challenging the national cinematic construct. Independent, socially committed, low-budget music videos and narrative features in the Tamazight language, with local actors and locations, provided political edutainment for local audiences. Imazighen (the plural of *Amazigh*) are the original peoples of Morocco, who occupied the land long before the Arab-Islamic conquest of the Maghreb in the AD 600s. In Moroccan history, Imazighen have long been linked with the notion of *bilad-al-siba*, the "lands of dissidence" often beyond the reach of the central authorities (Maddy-Weitzman 2001, 28). In fact, Arabization, Islamization, and homogenization of the nation have led to much unrest in Morocco ever since the days of independence (as it did among the Kabyle in Algeria), despite the recognition of Amazigh as an official language during the last constitutional reforms, in 2011. For many years, and especially under the rule of Hassan II, "explicit articulation of Berber identity was considered threatening and was thus forbidden" (ibid., 30). Moroccan society experienced extreme strife and tension, and by the 1990s Amazigh activists had begun to challenge the nature of Moroccan identity by declaring that "abandoning or neglecting the Amazigh aspects" of their identity "would be a veritable outrage ... an intolerable mutilation of our personality, an amputation of our patrimony, and a denial of history" (ibid., 33).

Sandra Carter (2009, 21) points out that "Berber videos do not fill a void created by *neglect*, but by *repression* of cultural identity, which is quite different." Although Carter argues that Berbers are no longer repressed by the State, they are still culturally marginalized, leading to their use of "marginalized media rather than cinema and filmmaking"; Carter claims that this is beginning to change with Mohamed Asli's *In Casablanca Angels Don't Fly / Al Malaika la tuhaliq fi al-dar albayda* (2004), a popular comedy about three men from a Berber village in the Atlas mountains who journey to Casablanca to work in a restaurant (ibid.).

Although it was widely believed that Amazigh videos would not appeal to large audiences, producers strongly believed that their films would have the opposite effect, and Amazigh films gained popularity beginning with the production of *Tamghart wurgh / Femme d'or / Golden*

Woman in 1993. The video's director, Lahoucine Bizguaren, struggled for three years to complete his project, which many predicted was doomed for failure because of insufficient production funds and the fact that Tamazight was considered to be an oral language used only for everyday conversations. The video proved to be a hit, however, and audiences adored the story of a strong female character, capable of confronting and overcoming difficult obstacles while her husband was working abroad (Idtnaine 2008b). One hundred and fifty-eight films were subsequently produced in the aftermath of the film's success (1992–2008). These films rehabilitated ancient heroes from Amazigh mythology in tales such as *Dda Hmad Boutfounast and the Forty Thieves* and capitalized on the star appeal of the popular actor Lahoucine Ouberka (Idtnaine 2008a). Shot and produced in often difficult conditions, with a lack of electricity and infrastructure, the video films are immensely popular and a source of distraction in cafes, or for villagers in rural areas who gather in *tikbilines* (a large family gathered in a small area) to watch the videos together. Video is easier and cheaper to produce and circulate, and, as Carter (2001, 21) affirms, "local individuals and groups found they could use video technology to preserve, promote, and manipulate their own histories." Furthermore, she goes on to add that "these videos indicate that Berber culture groups are not yet willing to have their identity subsumed into the wider homogenous Moroccan, Arabic, and Muslim identity fostered by the State" (ibid.).

Conclusion

Digital video film production on the African continent has clearly seen many avenues of expression for a multiplicity of purposes. From the entrepreneurist Nollywood industry to its neighbouring competitor, Ghallywood, to independentist incarnations by auteur producers in Egypt and Burkina Faso, to socially committed videos by Moroccan Imazighen, the low cost and flexibility of video production allows localization of cultural forms (Carter 2001, 21–2). These forms of cultural media and expression derive their very essence of being from their "independence from colonial, postcolonial, and neo-colonial power structures in terms of production and distribution" (Hoffmann 2012, 228). While making invaluable contributions to African screen media cultures, digital video film production contributes to global media flows and validates cultures and identities in increasingly networked societies. A question recently was posed at the 2013 Vues d'Afrique: is it not better for Africa to create images first and foremost and then afterwards worry about quality and technical perfection? This foresees a blending of artistic creativity and entrepreneurship – a digital screen media product that "will be finished on a laptop ... be delivered by broadband, and viewed on a mobile TV" (Saul 2010, 153).

ACKNOWLEDGMENTS

Special thanks go to Brahim Benbouazza for his assistance with this paper and to the late Donna-Lynne McGregor who always inspired me. An early version of the Nollywood section was presented at "World Cinema on Demand," Queen's University Belfast, 2012.

NOTES

1 Florence Martin, email to author, 17 March 2013.
2 Translated from the French article by Elisabeth Lequeret: "Toute activité doit avoir une logique économique. Le jour où le robinet des subventions est coupé, il n'y a plus de cinéma africain. Or, pour moi, de Dakar à Libreville, il y a a un seul et même public. C'est dommage de ne pas s'appuyer dessus."
3 According to Tunde Oladunjoye (2008, 68), no feature-length 35 mm films were released in Nigeria between 1994 and 2006.

Glossary

Co-productions; Co-productions are governed by official (bilateral) treaties or consist of co-venture-type arrangements between producers for the duration of film or television production and distribution. Co-productions allow producers to pool resources such as government funding, talent, and labour into a production package that exceeds most budgets for domestic feature films and television programs. Treaty co-productions guide administrative and regulatory processes involved in the international movement of goods and services as well as equipment.

Copyright; Copyright is one aspect of intellectual property law that protects the intellectual and intangible nature of an object in contrast to the physical and tangible aspects of an object. It gives owners of creative works (that is, literary, dramatic, musical, or artistic) the sole and exclusive right to publish or reproduce a work. A work is copyrightable if it meets three criteria for protection: (a) originality, which is measured as the expression of ideas (neither ideas nor facts are copyrightable); (b) fixation, which means that this expression has been given material form; and (c) nationality.

Crowdfunding; Crowdfunding is a fund-raising platform that enables individuals to pledge and donate money to finance projects, research, development, campaigns, and other projects. They are most often art projects (such as dance, music, film, and visual arts) or science (such as patents and inventions). In the context of film, crowdfunding has become an oft-used method of raising funds for production, distribution and marketing. Kickstarter (kickstarter. com) and Indie GoGo (indiegogo.com) are two of the most well-known crowdfunding platforms both in the United States and in other parts of the world. Ideacious (ideacious.com) is a well-known Canadian platform.

Eurimages; Eurimages is the Council of Europe fund for the co-production, distribution, and exhibition of European cinematographic works. Set up in 1988 as a partial agreement, it currently has thirty-six member states. Eurimages aims to promote the European film industry by encouraging the production and distribution of films and fostering cooperation between professionals. Eurimages's first objective is cultural, in that it endeavours to support works that reflect the multiple facets of a European society whose common roots are evidence of a single culture. The second one is economic, in that the fund invests in an industry that, while concerned with commercial success, is interested in demonstrating that cinema is one of the arts and should be treated as such. (Source: http://www. coe.int/t/dg4/eurimages/About/default_en.asp)

Euromed Audiovisual Program; Funded by the European Union, Euromed Audiovisual Program focuses on the development of films and the audio-visual sector in southern Mediterranean countries, including Algeria, Egypt, Jordan, Israel, Lebanon, Libya, Morocco, Palestine, Syria, and Tunisia. The program is intended to facilitate the training of professionals and to benefit the overall socio-economic development of the region.

European Convention on Cinematographic Co-production; The aims of the European Convention on Cinematographic Co-production are to promote the development of European multilateral cinematographic co-production, to safeguard creation and freedom of expression, and to defend the cultural diversity of the various European countries. In order to obtain co-production status, the work must involve at least three co-producers, established in three different parties to the convention. The participation of one or more co-producers who are not established in such parties is possible, provided that their total contribution does not exceed 30 per cent of the total cost of the production. The co-produced work must also meet the definition of a European cinematographic work as set forth in appendix II to the convention. This convention entered into force on 1 April 1994.

MEDIA; MEDIA is the European Union's support program for the European audio-visual industry, established in 1991. It co-finances training initiatives for audio-visual industry professionals and the development of production projects (feature films, television drama, documentaries, animation, and new media), as well as the promotion of European audio-visual works. The MEDIA 2007 program (2007–13) was the fourth multi-annual program established since 1991 and had a budget of €755 million. Its objectives were (a) to strive for a stronger European audio-visual sector, reflecting and respecting Europe's cultural identity and heritage; (b) to increase the circulation of European audio-visual works inside and outside the European Union; and (c) to strengthen the competitiveness of the European audio-visual sector by facilitating access to financing and promoting use of digital technologies. (Source: http://ec.europa.eu/culture/media/index_en.htm)

Media, Entertainment, and Arts Alliance (MEAA); MEAA, also known as the Alliance, is Australia's largest union and professional organization, which covers personnel in the media, entertainment, art, and sports industries. In 1992 the Alliance was created through a merger of unions covering actors, journalists, and entertainment industry employees, including Actors Equity (AE), the Australian Theatrical & Amusement Employees Association (ATAEA), and the Australian Journalists Association (AJA). Today it also covers the Symphony Orchestra Musicians Association (SOMA), the NSW Artworkers Union, and the Screen Technicians Association of Australia (STAA).

Media Mundus; Funded by the European Union, the Media Mundus program aims to enhance collaboration in the audio-visual sector between European professionals and non–European Union partners from around the world for the following purposes: co-production and distribution, international sales and promotion, and the circulation and exposure of audio-visual materials across distribution platforms.

Mercosur Audiovisual; Funded by the European Union, the Mercosur Audiovisual program aims to promote and create audio-visual collaboration, as well as the circulation of audio-visual content, between the European Union and the Mercosur region, which includes countries like Brazil, Argentina, Paraguay, Uruguay, Venezuela, and Bolivia.

Motion Picture Association of America (MPAA); Since 1922 the trade organization MPAA has represented Hollywood's studios. Today this includes Walt Disney Studios, Sony Pictures Entertainment, Paramount Pictures, Twentieth Century Fox, Universal Studios, and Warner Bros. The organization lobbies for the interests of its members, especially with regard to copyright protection and removal of trade barriers. Currently the MPAA also administers the film-rating system.

National Film Development Corporation Malaysia (FINAS); FINAS is Malaysia's film agency responsible for developing the audio-visual industry. It was established in 1981 under the Ministry of Information, Communication, and Culture. Today FINAS promotes the local film industry and assists and supports all foreign film production in Malaysia.

Negative pick-up; The term *negative pick-up* refers to a film financing and distribution method whereby a film studio or other company agrees to pay an independent filmmaker a fixed amount of money at a certain date for a finished motion picture. The studio then markets and distributes the film. Also typically involved in this agreement is a lender (bank or other investor) who provides "gap" financing – money to cover the film's budget until the film has been completed – based on the strength of the negative pick-up deal.

Nollywood; *Nollywood* is a term used to describe the film industry centred in Lagos, Nigeria, which has become the third-largest film industry in the world (after Bollywood and Hollywood). According to Sheila Petty, Nollywood cinema, based on a low-budget production model, is populist in content, innovative in technology, and driven by profit. There are a number of other "-wood" cinemas that have emerged in Africa, including Ghallywood (Ghana), Collywood (Cameroon), Riverwood (Kenya), Bongowood (Tanzania), and Ugawood (Uganda).

Non-linear Editing; Non-linear editing is a technique of digitally editing video footage on a computer. Some of the most-used edit suites in the film industry include Final Cut Pro and Avid. Final Cut Pro, for example, is a video-editing software program developed by Macromedia Inc., and later Apple Inc., that allows users to transfer their video to a hard drive for editing. The video can then be prepared for a number of formats. Final Cut Pro is popular with independent filmmakers and with people who create videos for personal use.

Ocker; The term *ocker* refers to a genre of Australian film extremely popular in the 1970s that celebrated vulgar, unsophisticated characters and made fun of Australian culture. These low-budget feature films were, in many ways, the antithesis of the types of films supported by the state. Some of the most well-known ocker films were *The Naked Bunyip* (1970), *Stork* (1971), *The Adventures of Barry McKenzie* (1972), and *Libido* (1973).

Prosumer; The term *prosumer* is a combination of the words *professional* and *consumer*. In the context of filmmaking, it usually refers to software and equipment that offers decent quality and usability but does not cost as much as high-end professional gear. It is, however, usually more sophisticated than the average consumer-grade gear. Prosumer equipment has enabled independent filmmakers to make high-quality films with low budgets.

Screen Australia; Formerly known as the Australian Film Commission, Screen Australia is a government agency that provides funding for Australia's film and television production sectors. Screen Australia also administers international co-production treaties.

Telefilm Canada; Telefilm Canada is a federal cultural agency dedicated to the development and promotion of Canada's audio-visual industry. It administers international co-production treaties for the Department of Canadian Heritage.

Video Compact Disc (VCD); The home exhibition format VCD similar to that of a digital versatile disc (DVD); it is a lower-capacity digital disc on which video is stored, and it is generally played on a dedicated VCD player. As a result, VCDs generally have lower quality in terms of picture and audio than do DVDs and are often compared in quality to that offered by video home system (VHS) cassettes. VCDs are used for distributing movies, often in regions of the world that have less access to high-end digital technology. Regions in Africa and Asia, for example, sell movies on VCDs as well as on DVDs.

World Cinema Support; The World Cinema Support fund is administered by France's Centre national du cinéma et de l'image animée (CNC) and the Institut français. This fund, created in 2012, is intended to support foreign feature-length films that are also French co-productions. Its budget in its inaugural year was €6 million, and the fund is open to film productions from anywhere around the world. Funding for a single project is capped at €250,000 for pre-production work and at €50,000 for post-production work. The World Cinema Support fund replaces the CNC's Fonds sud cinéma, which was phased out in 2012 and which was intended for filmmakers in the developing world. It also replaces Aid to Foreign Language Films (AFLE), which was aimed at film directors with at least two directing credits.

Filmography

The filmography compiles titles of some of the most representative films of each country's or region's independent film scene. It is not an exhaustive list, nor does it compile titles of every film mentioned in this volume.

Africa (Central)
Daratt (Mahamat Saleh Haroun, 2006, Chad)
La vie est belle (Ngangura Mweze, 1987, Democratic Republic of the Congo)
Viva Riva! (Djo Tunda wa Munga, 2010, Democratic Republic of the Congo)

Africa (East)
Gito the Ungrateful (Léonce Ngabo, 1992, Burundi)
Mueda (Louis Guerra, 1979, Brazil/Mozambique)
Teza (Haile Gerima, 2008, Ethiopia)

Africa (North)
Al Malaika la tuhaliq fi al-dar albayda / *In Casablanca Angels Don't Fly* (Mohamed Asli, 2004, Morocco)
Après la bataille / *After the Battle* (Yousry Nasrallah, 2012, France, Egypt)
Bamako (Abderramane Sissako, 2006, Mauritania)
Ehki ya shahrazade / *Scheherazade Tell Me a Story* (Yousry Nasrallah, 2009, Egypt)
Heremakono (Abderramane Sissako, 2002, Mauritania)
Itto Titrit / *Morning Star* (Mohamed Oumouloud Abbazi, 2010, Morocco)
Tamghart wurgh / *Femme d'or* / *Golden Woman* (Lahoucine Bizguaren, 1993, Morocco)

Africa (South)
Africa United (Debs Gardner-Paterson, 2010, Rwanda / South Africa / United Kingdom)
District 9 (Neill Blomkamp, 2009, South Africa)
Izulu Lami (Madoda Icayiyana, 2008, South Africa)
Jerusalema (Ralph Ziman, 2008, South Africa)
Love Brewed in an African Pot (Kwaw Ansah, 1981, Ghana / South Africa)
Mapantsula (Oliver Schmitz, 1988, South Africa)
Temba (Stephanie Scholt, 2006, South Africa / Germany)
Tsotsi (Gavin Hood, 2005, South Africa)
Yellow Card (John Riber, 2000, Zimbawe / United States)

Africa (West)
Aristotle's Plot (Jean Pierre Bekolo, 1996, Cameroon/France)
Bal Poussière / Dancing in the Dust (Henri Duparc, 1989, Côte d'Ivoire)
The Beast Within (Nana King, 1993, Ghana)
Code Phoenix / Phoenix Code (Boubacar Diallo, 2005, Burkina Faso)
Diabolo (William Akuffo, 1991, Ghana)
Ezra (Newton Aduaka, 2006, Nigeria/France)
Le Grand Magal de Touba (Blaise Senghor, 1962, Senegal)
Living in Bondage, I (Chris Obi Rapu, 1992, Nigeria)
Living in Bondage, II (Christian Onu, 1993, Nigeria)
Moolade (Ousmane Sembene, 2006, Senegal)
The Narrow Path (Tunde Kelani, 2006, Nigeria)
Un Nation est née (Paulin Soumanou Vieyra, 1961, Senegal)
Not Without (A. Hackman, 1996, Ghana)
Osuofia in London (I and II) (Kingsley Ogoro, 2003 and 2004, Nigeria)
Quartier Mozart (Jean Pierre Bekolo, 1992, Cameroon/France)
Les Saignantes (Jean Pierre Bekolo, 2005, Cameroon/France)
Sambizanga (Sarah Maldoror, 1972, Angola)
Thunderbolt (Tunde Kelani, 2000, Nigeria)
Tilai (Idrissa Ouedraogo, 1991, Burkina Faso)
Traque à Ouaga / Pursuit in Ouaga (Boubacar Diallo, 2004, Burkina Faso)
Visages de Femme (Désiré Écaré, 1985, Senegal)
Yaaba (Idrissa Ouedraogo, 1989, Burkina Faso)
Zinabu (William Akuffo and Richard Quartey, 1987, Ghana)

Australia
The Adventures of Priscilla, Queen of the Desert (Stephan Elliott, 1994)
Animal Kingdom (David Michôd, 2010)

Kenny (Clayton Jacobson, 2006)
Muriel's Wedding (P.J. Hogan, 1994)
The Piano (Jane Campion, 1993)
Red Dog (Kriv Stenders, 2011)
The Sapphires (Wayne Blair, 2012)
Shine (Scott Hicks, 1996)
Strictly Ballroom (Baz Luhrmann, 1992)
Tomorrow, When the War Began (Stuart Beattie, 2010)
The Tunnel (Carlo Ledesma, 2011)
Wolf Creek (Greg Mclean, 2005)

Canada (Indigenous)
Atanarjuat: The Fast Runner (Zacharias Kunuk and Norman Cohn, 2001)
Barefoot (Danis Goulet [Cree Metis], 2012)
Bearwalker (Shirley Cheechoo, 2000)
Before Tomorrow (Marie-Hélène Cousineau, Madeline Ivalu, Madeline Piujuq Ivalu 2009)
The Cave (Helen Haig-Brown [Tsilhqot'in], 2009)
File Under Miscellaneous (Jeff Barnaby [Mi'kmaq] 2010)
Gwishalaayt "The Spirit Wraps Around" (Barb Cranmer [Kwakwaka'wakw], 2001)
If the Weather Permits (Elisapie Isaac, 2003)
Inuit Cree Reconciliation (Zacharias Kunuk and Neil Diamond, 2013)
Inuuvunga: I Am Inuk, I Am Alive (National Film Board of Canada, 2004)
The Journals of Knud Rasmussen (Zacharias Kunuk and Norman Cohn, 2006, Canada, Denmark)
Kanehsatake: 270 Years of Resistance (Alanis Obomsawin, 1993)
The Legend of Sarila / La Légende de Sarila (Nancy Florence Savard, 2012)
Maïna (Michel Poulette, 2012)
Nanook of the North (Robert Flaherty, 1922, United States, Canada-France)
Path of Souls (Jeremy Torrie, 2012)
Qapirangajuq: Inuit Knowledge and Climate Change (Zacharias Kunuk and Ian Mauro, 2010)
Storytellers in Motion (Catherine Martin [Mi'kmaq], 2006–13)
Today Is a Good Day: Remembering Chief Dan George (Loretta Todd, 1998)
Tungijuq (Félix Lajeunesse and Paul Raphaël, 2009)
Unikkausivut: Sharing Our Stories (National Film Board of Canada, 2011)

China
Beijing Bastard /*Beijing zhazhong* (Zhang Yuan, 1993)
Beijing Bicycle / *Shiqisui de dance* (Wang Xiaoshuai, 2000, China/Taiwan/ France)
Blind Shaft / *Mangjing* (Li Yang, 2003)
East Palace West Palace / *Donggong xigong* (Zhang Yuan, 1996, France)
Lunar Eclipse (Wang Quanan, 1999)
The Orphan of Anyang / Anyang yinger (Wang Chao, 2001, China/ Netherlands)
Postman (He Jianjun, 1995)
Platform (Jia Zhangke, 2000, Hong Kong/Japan)
Rainclouds over Wushan / Wushan yunyu (Zhang Ming, 1996)
So Close to Paradise / Biandan guniang (Wang Xiaoshuai, 1998)
Suzhou River / Suzhou He (Lou Ye, 2000, China/Germany)
Xiao Wu (Jia Zhangke, 1997, Hong Kong)
Unknown Pleasures / Ren xiaoyao (Jia Zhangke, 2002, Hong Kong / Japan / United States)

European Film Academy - Nominations for Best Film (2012–13)
Amour (Michael Haneke, 2012, Austria, Germany, France)
Barbara (Christian Petzold, 2012, Germany)
The Best Offer (Giuseppe Tornatore, 2013, Italy)
Blancanieves (Pable Berger, 2013, Spain, France)
The Broken Circle Breakdown (Felix van Groeningen, 2013, Belgium)
Caesar Must Die (Paolo and Vittorio Taviani, 2012, Italy)
La Grande Bellezza / *The Great Beauty* (Paolo Sorrentino, 2013, Italy/France)
The Hunt (Thomas Vinterberg, 2012, Denmark)
Intouchables (Olivier Nakache and Eric Toledano, 2012, France)
Oh Boy! (Jan Ole Gerster, 2013, Germany)
Shame (Steve McQueen, 2012, United Kingdom)
La vie d'Adèle: Chapitres 1 et 2 / *Adele: Chapters 1 and 2* (Adellatif Kechiche, 2013, France)

Greece
Akadimia Platonos / *Plato's Academy* (Fillipos Tsitos, 2010, Germany/ Greece)
Anaparastas/*Reconstruction* (Theodoros Angelopoulos, 1970, Greece)
Attenberg (Athina Rachel Tsangari, 2010, Greece)
I Aionia Epistrofi tou Antoni Paraskeva / *The Eternal Return of Antonis Paraskevas*] (Elina Psikou, 2013, Greece / Czech Republic)

Kynodondas / Dogtooth (Yorgos Lanthimos, 2009, Greece)
Luton (Michalis Konstandatos, 2013, Greece/Germany)
Macherovgaltis/Knifer (Yannis Economides, 2010, Greece)
Magiki Polis / Magic City (Nikos Koundouros, 1952, Greece)
Miss Violence (Alexandros Avranas, 2013, Greece)
O Drakos / The Ogre of Athens (Nikos Koundouros, 1956, Greece)
Ouranos/Sky (Takis Kanellopoulos, 1962, Greece)
Thiasos / The Travelling Players (Theodoros Angelopoulos, 1974, Greece)
To Agori Troei to Fagito tou Poulio / Boy Eating Bird's Food (Ektoras Lygizos, 2012, Greece)
To Bloko / The Roundup (Adonis Kyrou, 1965, Greece)
Wasted Youth (Argyris Papadimitropoulos and Jan Vogel, 2011, Greece)

Iraq
Ahlaam/Dreams (Mohamed al-Daradji, 2006)
The Dreams of Sparrows (Haydar Daffar, 2007, Iraq/USA)
In My Mother's Arms (Mohamed al-Daradji, 2011, United Kingdom / Netherlands / Iraq)
In the Sands of Babylon (Mohamed al-Daradji, 2013, United Kingdom / United Arab Emirates / Iraq / Netherlands)
Jani Gal (Jamil Rostani, 2007, Iraq/Iran)
Jiyan/Life (Jano Rosebiani, 2002, Iraq/USA)
Kilometre Zero (Hineer Saleem, 2005, France/Iraq/Finland)
Leaving Baghdad (Koutaiba al-Janabi, 2010, Iraq / United Arab Emirates / Hungary / United Kingdom)
My Sweet Pepper Land (Hineer Saleem, 2013, France/Germany/Iraq)
Qarantina (Oday Rasheed, 2010, Germany/Iraq)
Son of Babylon (Mohamed al-Daradji, 2009, Iraq / United Kingdom / France / Netherlands / United Arab Emirates / Egypt / Palestine)
Turtles Can Fly (Bahman Ghobadi, 2004, Iran/France/Iraq)
Underexposure (Oday Rasheed, 2005, Germany/Iraq)

Malaysia
Beautiful Washing Machine (James Lee, 2004)
The Big Durian (Amir Muhammad, 2003)
Bunoha / Return to Murder (Dain Said, 2011)
Chalanggai / Dancing Bells (Deepak Kumaran Menon, 2007)
Flower in the Pocket (Liew Seng Tat, 2007)
Ice Kacang Puppy Love (Ah Niu, 2010)
Karaoke (Chris Chong Chan Fui, 2009)

The Last Communist (Amir Muhammad, 2006)
Love Conquers All (Tan Chui Mui, 2006)
Nasi Lemak 2.0 (Wee Meng Chee, 2011)
Raindogs / Tai Yang Yue (Ho Yuhang, 2006)
Sell Out! (Yeo Joonhan, 2008)
Sepet (Yasmin Ahmad, 2004)
Spinning Gasing (Teck Tan, 2000)
The Tiger Factory (Woo Ming Jin, 2010)
This Longing / Punggok Rindukan Bulan (Azharr Rudin, 2008)

Peru
Alias "la gringa" (Alberto "Chicho" Durant, 1991)
Allpa kallpa (Bernardo Arias, 1975)
La boca del lobo / The Lion's Den (Francisco Lombardi, 1988)
Chicama (Omar Ferrero, 2013)
Entonces Ruth (Fernando Montenegro, 2013)
Gregorio (Grupo Chaski, 1984)
Kuntur wachana (Federico García Hurtad, 1977)
Malabrigo (Alberto "Chicho" Durant, 1986)
Las malas intenciones (Rosario Garcia Montero, 2011)
Marcados por el destino (Oscar Gonzales, 2009)
Muerte al amanecer / Death at Dawn (Francisco Lombardi, 1977)
Los perros hambrientos (Luis Figueroa Yabar, 1976)
Profesión: Detective (José Carlos Huayhuaca, 1986)
Reportaje a la muerte (Danny Gavidia Velezmoro, 1993)
Talk Show (Sandro Ventura, 2006)

Turkey
Anayurt Oteli / Motherland Hotel (Ömer Kavur, 1986)
Bal/Honey (Semih Kaplanoğlu, 2010).
Bereketli Topraklar Üzerinde / On Fertile Soil (Erden Kıral, 1979)
Beş Vakit / Times and Winds (Reha Erdem, 2006)
Çoğunluk / Majority (Seren Yüce, 2010)
Gemide / On Board (Serdar Akar, 1998)
Gitmek / My Marlon and Brando (Hüseyin Karabey, 2008)
Güneşe Yolculuk / Journey to the Sun (Yeşim Ustaoğlu, 1999)
Gurbet Kuşları / Birds of Exile (Halit Refiğ, 1965)
Karpuz Kabuğundan Gemiler Yapmak / Boats out of Watermelon Rinds
    (Ahmet Uluçay, 2004)
Masumiyet/Innocence (Zeki Demirkubuz, 1997)

Soluk Gecenin Aşk Hikayeleri / *Love Stories of the Pale Night* (Ali Zeki Heper, 1966)
Sonbahar/Autumn (Özcan Alper, 2008)
Susuz Yaz / *Dry Summer* (Metin Erksan, 1963)
Tabutta Rövaşata / *Somersault in a Coffin* (Derviş Zaim, 1996)
Tatil Kitabı / *Summer Book* (Seyfi Teoman, 2008)
Tepenin Ardı / *Beyond the Hill* (Emin Alper, 2012)
Uzak/Distant (Nuri Bilge Ceylan, 2002)
Yol / *The Way* (Yılmaz Güney, 1982)

United Kingdom
Behold the Lamb (John McIlduff, 2011)
Edge (Carol Morley, 2012)
I am Nasrine (Tina Gharavi, 2012)
Kandahar Break (David Whitney, 2010)
My Brother the Devil (Sally El Hosaini, 2012)
N.F.A. (No Fixed Abode) (Steve Rainbow, 2012)
The Raven on the Jetty (Erik Knudsen, 2014)
Trishna (Michael Winterbottom, 2011)
Tyrannosaur (Paddy Considine, 2011)
Verity's Summer (Ben Crowe, 2013)

United States
Brokeback Mountain (Ang Lee, 2005, United States / Canada)
Eternal Sunshine of the Spotless Mind (Michel Gondry, 2004)
The Grifters (Stephen Frears, 1990)
Heartland (Richard Pearce, 1980)
Juno (Jason Reitman, 2007)
Lost in Translation (Sofia Coppola, 2003, United States / Japan)
Magnolia (Paul Thomas Anderson, 1999)
My Own Private Idaho (Gus Van Sant, 1992)
Northern Lights (John Hanson and Rob Nilsson, 1978)
Poison (Todd Haynes, 1991)
Pulp Fiction (Quentin Tarantino, 1994)
Reservoir Dogs (Quentin Tarantino, 1992)
sex, lies, and videotape (Steven Soderbergh, 1989)
She's Gotta Have It (Spike Lee, 1986)
Stranger than Paradise (Jim Jarmusch, 1984, United States / West Germany)
Traffic (Steven Soderbergh, 2000, United States / Germany)

Bibliography

24-Hour Party People. 2002. Film. Directed by Michael Winterbottom. UK: Revolution Films, Baby Cow Productions, Film Consortium.

28 Days Later. 2002. Film. Directed by Danny Boyle. UK: DNA Films, British Film Council.

Aburish, Saïd K. 2000. *Saddam Hussein: The Politics of Revenge.* London: Bloomsbury Publishing.

Acheson, K., and C.J. Maule. 2003. *Canada—Audiovisual Policies: Impact on Trade.* Hamburgisches Welt-Wirtschafts-Archiv (HWWA) Report 288. http://ageconsearch.umn.edu/bitstream/26070/1/re030228.pdf

Adams, J. 2011. "UK Film: New Directions in the Glocal Era." *Journal of Media Practice* 12 (2): 111–24. http://dx.doi.org/10.1386/jmpr.12.2.111_3.

Adejunmobi, Moradewun. 2002. "English and the Audience of an African Popular Culture: The Case of Nigerian Video Film." *Cultural Critique* 50 (Winter): 74–103. http://dx.doi.org/10.1353/cul.2002.0001.

Adesokan, Akin. 2008. "The Challenges of Aesthetic Populism: An Interview with Jean-Pierre Bekolo." *Postcolonial Text* 4 (1): 1–11.

African Movie Channel. 2013. Accessed 18 June. http://www.african-moviechannel.tv/

AfriFestNet: African Festival Network. 2013. "African Festivals Directory." Accessed 12 January. http://africanartsfestivals.com/en/liste-festival.

Akser, Murat. 2010. *Green Pine Resurrected: Film Genre, Parody, and Intertextuality in Turkish Cinema.* Saarbrücken, Germany: Lambert Academic Publishing.

Akser, Murat. 2013. "Blockbusters." In *Directory of World Cinema: Turkey,* ed. Eylem Atakav, 124–45. London: Intellect.

Allawi, Jabar Audah. 1983. "Television and Film in Iraq: Socio-political and Cultural Study, 1946–1980." PhD diss., University of Michigan.

Anderson, C. 2006. *The Long Tail*. London: Random House.

Ansary, Khalid al-. 2011. "Iraq Aims to Revive Movie-Going Stifled by Saddam, War." *Reuters*, April 28. http://www.reuters.com/article/2011/04/28/us-iraq-cinema-idUSTRE73R2E420110428.

Arctic Fibre. "Welcome to Arctic Fibre." 2013. Accessed 9 April. http://arcticfibre.com/.

Arendt, Paul. 2006. "Happy Feet." *BBC Film Reviews*, 7 December. http://www.bbc.co.uk/films/2006/12/04/happy_feet_2006_review.shtml.

Armes, Roy. 2006. *African Filmmaking North and South of the Sahara*. Bloomington: Indiana University Press. http://dx.doi.org/10.3366/edinburgh/9780748621231.001.0001.

Armes, Roy. 2010. *Arab Filmmakers of the Middle East: A Dictionary*. Bloomington: Indiana University Press.

Arslan, Savaş. 2009. "The New Cinema of Turkey." *New Cinemas: Journal of Contemporary Film* 7 (1): 83–97. http://dx.doi.org/10.1386/ncin.7.1.83_1.

Arslan, Savaş. 2011. *Cinema in Turkey: A New Critical History*. New York: Oxford University Press.

Atam, Zahit. 2011. *New Turkish Cinema in Close-Up* [in Turkish, *Yakın Plan Yeni Türkiye Sineması*]. Istanbul: Cadde Yayınları.

AusFilm. 2012. "Significant Australian Content (SAC) Test." *Co-Productions and Co-Ventures*. http://www.ausfilm.com.au/incentives/co-productions-co-ventures/.

Baltruschat, Doris. 2003. "International Film and TV Co-productions: A Canadian Case Study." In *Media Organization and Production*, ed. Simon Cottle, 149–69. London: Sage Publications. http://dx.doi.org/10.4135/9781446221587.n9.

Baltruschat, Doris. 2004. "Television and Canada's Aboriginal Communities: Seeking Opportunities through Digital Technologies." *Canadian Journal of Communication* 29 (1): 47–59.

Baltruschat, Doris. 2006. "Global Civil Society and Media/Democracy Action." *International Journal of the Humanities / The Humanities Collection* 3 (3): 53–64.

Baltruschat, Doris. 2010. *Global Media Ecologies: Networked Production in Film and Television*. New York and London: Routledge.

Baltruschat, D. 2014. "Sarah Polley Directs *Away from Her*." In *Encyclopaedia of Films*, ed. S. Barrow, S. Haenni, and J. White. London: Routledge.

Banfield, Jane. 1964. "Films in East Africa." *Transition* 3, 13 (Mar–Apr): 18–21.

Bangré, Sambolgo. 1996. "African Cinema in the Tempest of Minor Festivals." In *African Experiences of Cinema*, ed. Imruh Bakari and Mbye Cham, 157–61. London: British Film Institute.

Barlet, Olivier. 2008. "Is the Nigerian Model Fit for Export?" In *Nollywood, the Video Phenomenon in Nigeria*, ed. Pierre Barrot, 121–9. Bloomington: Indiana University Press.

Barlet, Olivier. 2010. "Africultures Dossier." *Black Camera, an International Film Journal* 1 (3): 63–102.

Barlet, Olivier. 2011. "18 Jours: La revolution égyptienne en dix chapitres." *Africultures*, 20 August. http://www.africultures.com/php/?nav=article&no=10361.

Barrot, Pierre. 2008. "Audacity, Scandal, and Censorship." In *Nollywood, the Video Phenomenon in Nigeria*, ed. Pierre Barrot, 43–50. Bloomington: Indiana University Press.

Barrow, Sarah. 2005. "Images of Peru: A National Cinema in Crisis." In *Latin American Cinema: Essays on Modernity, Gender, and National Identity*, ed. Lisa Shaw and Stephanie Dennison, 39–58. Jefferson, NC: McFarland Publishers.

BBC Radio Four. 2011. *The Film Programme*. Online broadcast, 30:00. 5August. http://www.bbc.co.uk/programmes/b012x12w.

Bedoya, Ricardo. 1997. *Dictionary of Peruvian Films* [in Spanish, *Un Cine Reencontrado: Diccionario Ilustrado de Películas Peruanas*]. Lima: Universidad de Lima.

Bedoya, Ricardo. 2009. *Sound Film in Peru* [in Spanish, *El Cine Sonoro en el Perú*]. Lima: Universidad de Lima.

Beijing Scene. 1999. "Jia Zhangke: Pickpocket Director." *Beijing Scene* video, 5:23. 27 August–2 September. http://www.beijingscene.com/V051023/feature/feature.htm.

The Bellboy and the Playgirls. 1962. Film. Directed by Francis Ford Coppola. United States: Defin Film, Rapid Film, Screen Rite Picture Company.

Bengio, Ofra. 1998. *Saddam's Word: Political Discourse in Iraq*. New York: Oxford University Press. http://dx.doi.org/10.1093/acprof:oso/9780195114393.001.0001.

Berry, Chris. 1988. "The Sublimative Text: Sex and Revolution in Big Road." *East-West Film Journal* 2 (2): 66–86.

Bertolin, Paolo. 2011. "The Turning Point? Malaysian Films in 2010–2011." *FarEastFilm.com*. http://www.fareastfilm.com/easyne2/LYT.aspx?IDLYT=7803&CODE=FEFJ&ST=SQL&SQL=ID_Documento=3057

Biskind, Peter. 2005. *"Down and Dirty" Pictures: Miramax, Sundance, and the Rise of Independent Film*. London: Simon & Schuster.

Blaney, Martin. 2011a. "European Film Industry Faces MEDIA Showdown with EU." *ScreenDaily*, 18 March. http://www.screendaily.com/news/finance-news/european-film-industry-faces-media-showdown-with-eu/5025057.article

Blaney, Martin. 2011b. "Mobilising for MEDIA" *ScreenDaily*, 6 May. http://www.screendaily.com/features/features/mobilising-for-media/5026891. article

Bodey, M. 2009. "Films in Search of an Audience". *The Australian*, 11 December. http://www.theaustralian.com.au/arts/films-in-search-of-an-audience/story-e6frg8n6-1225809216615?nk=ec99d52dabaaef2a345882264d96fa86

Bodey, Michael. 2010. "Lack of Clarity Offsets Benefits." *The Australian*, 27 January 27. http://www.theaustralian.com.au/arts/lack-of-clarity-offsets-benefits/story-e6frg8n6-1225823745715

Box Office Guru. 2012. "Worldwide Box Office Grosses." Accessed 1 March. http://www.boxofficeguru.com/intlarch4.htm.

Brandis, G. 2007. *Film Laws Introduce New Era for Australian Film*.Media Release, 20 September. Canberra: Commonwealth Government of Australia.

Bresson, R. 1975. *Notes on Cinematography*. New York: Urizen.

British Film Institute (BFI). 2012. *Statistical Yearbook 2011*. London: British Film Institute.

Bruno, Chatelin. 2009. "Rotterdam Hubert Bals Fund Selects 27 Projects." *Film Festivals.com: Editor's Blog*, 5 November. http://pourwww.filmfestivals.com/blog/editor/rotterdam_hubert_bals_fund_selects_27_projects.

Burgin, Alice G. 2011. "Waiting for Happiness in the Global South: Challenging Unequal Flows in West African Cinema." Paper presented at the World Cinema Now Conference, Monash University, Victoria, Australia, 27–9 September.

Burnshaw, S. 1991. *The Seamless Web*. New York: George Braziller.

Canada. Ministry of Foreign Affairs, Trade, and Development. 1993. *International Trade Business Plan, 1993–94*. Ottawa: Ministry of Supply and Services.

Canadian Heritage. 2000. *A Guide to Federal Programs for the Film and Video Sector*. Hull, QC: Minister of Public Works and Government Services.

Canada Media Fund. 2012. "Crowdfunding in a Canadian Context." http://www.cmf-fmc.ca

Canadian Media Fund (CMF). 2012. "Profile 2011." http://www.thecanadianencyclopedia.com/articles/film-distribution.

"Cannes Film Festival Archives." 2012. Cannes Film Festival. Accessed 5 March. http://www.festival-cannes.fr/en/archivesPage.html.

Carbone, Giancarlo. 2007. *Cinema in Peru: The Short Movie, 1972–1992* [in Spanish, *El Cine en el Perú: El Cortometraje, 1972–1992*]. Lima: Universidad de Lima.

Caravaggio. 1986. Film. Directed by Derek Jarman. UK: British Film Institute (BFI).

Carter, Sandra Gayle. 2009. *What Moroccan Cinema? A Historical and Critical Study, 1956–2006*. Lanham, MD: Lexington Books.

Carver, Benedict. 1998. "Fine Line Grows Int'l Sales Arm." *Weekly Variety*, 30 March.

Celik, Ipek A. 2013. "Family as Internal Border in Dogtooth." In *Frontiers of Screen History: Imagining European Borders in Cinema, 1945–2010*, ed. Raita Merivita, Kimmo Ahonen, Heta Mulari, and Rami Mähkä. Bristol, UK: Intellect/University of Chicago Press.

CFTPA and APFTQ (The Canadian Film and Television Production Association and l'Association des producteurs de films et de télévision du Québec). 2000. *The Canadian Film and Television Industry: Profile 2000*. Toronto: CFTPA.

Chalkou, Maria. 2009. "Towards the Creation of 'Quality' Greek National Cinema in the 1960s." PhD diss., University of Glasgow.

Chan, Clement. 2009. "Local Cinemas and SellOut! Sabotage, or Plain Coincidence?" *Cinematic Concerns*, 11 May. http://filmgarmott.blogspot.com/2009/05/best-malaysian-film-ever-and-gsc-is.html.

Chebli, Hakki. 1966. "History of the Iraqi Cinema." In *The Cinema in the Arab Countries*, ed. George Sadoul, 117–24. Beirut: Interarab Centre of Cinema and Television.

Chun, Kimberly. 2002. "Storytelling in the Arctic Circle: An Interview with Zacharias Kunuk." *CINEASTE*, 21–3.

Clarke, Cath. 2009. "Heroes and Handycams." *The Guardian*, 30 April. http://www.guardian.co.uk/film/2009/may/01/maysoon-pachachi-iraq-baghdad-film.

Cohen, David S. 2013. "Filmmakers Lament Extinction of Film Prints." *Variety*, 17 April. http://variety.com/2013/film/news/film-jobs-decline-as-digital-distribution-gains-foothold-1200375732/

The Conference Board of Canada. 2013. *Mapping the Long-Term Options for Canada's North: Telecommunications and Broadband Connectivity*. Ottawa, ON: Conference Board of Canada.

Connolly, Kate. 2011. "Son of Babylon: 'I Made It for My Family, For Iraq.'" *The Guardian*, 3 February. http://www.guardian.co.uk/film/2011/feb/03/son-of-babylon-iraq-film.

The Cook, the Thief, His Wife, and Her Lover. 1989. Film. Directed by Peter Greenaway. UK: Allarts Cook, Erato Films, Films Inc.

Corliss, Richard. 2001. "Crouching China, Hidden Agenda." *Time* (3 March): 1–3. http://www.time.com/time/arts/article/0,8599,101297,00.html.

Cornwell, Regina. 1981. "Cents and Sensibility or Funding without Tears." *American Film* 6 (10): 62–4, 80.

Côte Ouest Audiovisuel. 2013. Accessed 12 January. http://coteouest.tv/societe_test.php.

Council of Europe. 2003. *Resolution 1313. Cultural Co-operation between Europe and the South Mediterranean Countries.* http://assembly.coe.int/ASP/XRef/X2H-DW-XSL.asp?fileid=17070&lang=EN

Council of Europe. 2009. *Regulations for the Support of Co-productions of Full-Length Feature Films, Animations, and Documentaries.* www.coe.int/t/dg4/eurimages/.../Co-productionRegulations2009_EN.doc

Council of Europe. 2012. *EURIMAGES – European Cinema Support Fund.* http://www.coe.int/T/DG4/Eurimages/About/default_en.asp.

Craven, Ian, ed. 2001. *Australian Cinema in the 1990s.* London: Frank Cass Publishers.

Cremin, Stephen. 2011. "Pusan Becomes Busan." *Film Business Asia,* 24 February. http://www.filmbiz.asia/news/pusan-becomes-busan.

Dai, Jinhua. 2002. *Cinema and Desire: Feminist Marxism and Cultural Politics in the Work of Dai Jinhua.* New York: Verso.

Dallas, Sam. 2011. "Daybreakers: In Top 50 Worldwide Highest-Grossing Independent Films of 2010." *Inside Film* 140 (April–May): 6.

Dargis, Manohla. 2006. "*Bring in da Hoofers on Ice.*" *New York Times,* 17 November. http://query.nytimes.com/gst/fullpage.html?res=9F03E4DC143EF934A25752C1A9609C8B63.

Davis, Darrell William. 2003. "Compact Generation: VCD Markets in Asia." *Historical Journal of Film, Radio, and Television* 23 (2): 165–76. http://dx.doi.org/10.1080/0143968032000091095.

Deasy, Kristin. 2010. "Backers of Baghdad Film Production Center Seek Iraqi Cinema Revival." *Radio Free Europe /Radio Liberty,* 29 September. http://www.rferl.org/content/Iraq_Cinema_Revival_New_Film_Production_Center_Baghdad/2169628.html.

The Deep Blue Sea. 2011. Film. Directed by Terence Davies. UK: Camberwell/Fly Films, Film4, UK Film Council.

Delveroudi, Eliza Anna. 2011. "Silent Greek Cinema: In Search of Academic Recognition." In *Greek Cinema: Texts, Histories, Identities,* ed. Lydia Papadimitriou and Yannis Tzioumakis, 115–28. Bristol, UK: Intellect/University of Chicago Press.

Demopoulos, M. 2011. "Neo aima kyla stis fleves tou Ellenikou cinema / New Blood Is Flowing in the Veins of Greek Cinema." *Cinema* 219 (Winter): 52.

De Propris, Lisa, and Laura Hypponen. 2008. "Creative Clusters and Governance: The Dominance of the Hollywood Film Cluster." In *Creative Cities, Cultural Clusters, and Local Economic Development,* ed. P. Cooke and L. Lazzeretti, 258–86. Cheltenham, Northampton, UK: Edward Elgar.

Dermody, Susan, and Elizabeth Jacka. 1988. *The Screening of Australia: Anatomy of a National Cinema.* Vol. 2. Sydney: Currency Press.

De Rosa, Maria. 2012. *The Canadian Feature Film Distribution Sector in Review: Trends, Policies, and Market Developments.* http://www.communicationsmdr. com

Diawara, Manthia. 2010. *African Film: New Forms of Aesthetics and Politics.* Munich: Haus der Kulturen der Welt. Berlin: Prestel Verlag.

Distant Voices, Still Lives. 1988. Film. Directed by Terence Davies. UK: British Film Institute (BFI), Channel Four Films.

Dixon, Guy. 2012. "Out in the Cold: the Struggle of Inuit Film." *Globe and Mail,* 6 September. http://m.theglobeandmail.com/arts/film/ out-in-the-cold-the-struggle-of-inuit-film/article4197448/?service=mobile.

Dönmez-Colin, Gönül. 2008. *Turkish Cinema: Identity, Distance, and Belonging.* London: Reaktion Books.

Douhaire, Samuel. 2002. "Far from the Mandarins of Beijing." *Liberation* (New York, NY) (25 May), online. http://www.liberation.com/.

Dovey, Lindiwe. 2010. "Directors' Cut: In Defence of African Film Festivals outside Africa." In *Film Festival Yearbook 2: Film Festivals and Imagined Communities,* ed. Dina Iordanova and Ruby Cheung, 45–7. St Andrews, UK: St Andrews Film Studies.

Durant, Alberto. 2010a. *El cine peruano en debate: "Peruvian Indie,"* Parte 1. *FAQ.TV* video, 5:23. 25 February. http://www.youtube.com/ watch?v=57pdCPKg_9k.

Durant, Alberto. 2010b. *¿Existe un cine independiente en el Perú?* Parte 2. *Intervencion Chicho Durant.* University of Lima video, 10:30. 8 March. http:// www.youtube.com/watch?v=LLvEc1iOifI.

Elberse, Anita, and Felix Oberholzer-Gee. 2008. *Superstars and Underdogs: An Examination of the Long-Tail Phenomenon in Video Sales.* Working paper. Boston: Harvard Business School.

Eleftheriotis, Dimitris. 1995. "Questioning Totalities: Constructions of Masculinity in the Popular Greek Cinema of the 1960s." *Screen* 36 (3): 233–42. http://dx.doi.org/10.1093/screen/36.3.233.

Eraserhead. 1980. Film. Directed by David Lynch. United States: American Film Institute (AFI), Libra Films.

Erdogan, Nezih. 1998. "Narratives of Resistance: National Identity and Ambivalence in the Turkish Melodrama between 1965 and 1975." *Screen* 39 (3): 259–71. http://dx.doi.org/10.1093/screen/39.3.259.

Erdogan, Nezih. 2002. "Mute Bodies, Disembodied Voices: Notes on Sound in Turkish Popular Cinema." *Screen* 43 (3): 233–49. http://dx.doi.org/10.1093/ screen/43.3.233.

Euréval and Media Consulting Group (MCG). 2010. *Interim Evaluation of MEDIA 2007: Final Report, 4 June 2010.* http://ec.europa.eu

European Audiovisual Observatory. 2008a. *The Circulation of European Co-productions and Entirely National Films in Europe, 2001 to 2007.* Report by Martin Kranzler in collaboration with Susan Newman-Baudais and André Lange. Strasbourg: European Audiovisual Observatory.

European Commission. 2001. *Communication from the Commission to the Council, the European Parliament, the Economic and Social Committee, and the Committee of the Regions on Certain Legal Aspects Relating to Cinematographic and Other Audiovisual Works.* COM/2001/0534 final/. http://eur-lex.europa.eu/LexUriServ/LexUriServ.do?uri=CELEX:52004DC0171:EN:NOT

European Commission. 2007. *MEDIA, a Programme of the European Union: Guidelines for the Submission of Proposals to Obtain Financial Support.* Council Decision no. 1718/2006/EC of the European Parliament and the Council. http://ec.europa.eu/culture/media/media.../eacea_14_07_guidelines_en.doc

European Commission. 2008. *State Aid: Future Regime for Cinema Support.* Memo/08/329. http://europa.eu/rapid/press-release_MEMO-08-329_en.htm?locale=FR

European Commission. 2009. *Communication from the Commission Concerning the State Aid Assessment Criteria of the Commission Communication on Certain Legal Aspects Relating to Cinematographic and Other Audiovisual Works (Cinema Communication) of 26 September 2001.* 2009/C 31/01. http://eur-lex.europa.eu/

European Commission. 2011. *Commission Staff Working Paper: Impact Assessment; Accompanying the Document Regulation of the European Parliament and of the Council Establishing a Creative Europe Framework Programme SEC(2011) 1399 final.* Brussels, 23 November, 170.

European Commission. 2013a. *The Cotonou Agreement.* Accessed 20 November. http://ec.europa.eu/europeaid/where/acp/overview/cotonou-agreement/

European Commission. 2013b. *Treaty Provisions on State Aid.* Accessed 2 April. http://ec.europa.eu/competition/state_aid/legislation/compilation/a_01_12_09_en.pdf

Evren, Burçak. 2004. "A New Era in Turkish Cinema: Independent Filmmakers" [in Turkish, "Türk Sinemasında Yeni Bir Dönem: Bağımsız Sinemacılar"]. *Antrakt* 75–6:14–39.

Feng, Rui. 2004. "Jia Zhangke Answers Five Questions Regarding the World" [in Chinese, 贾樟柯细解<<世界>>五问"]. http://yule.sohu.com/20050416/n225212381.shtml.

"FINAS Gives Out RM2.4 Mil as Entertainment Duty Refund to 26 Films." 2009. *Bernama.com.* 21 December. http://www.bernama.com/bernama/v3/news_lite.php?id=463650.

Frodon, Jean-Michel. 2002. "Jia Zhangke Interview." *Le Monde,* 25 May. Translated by Berenice Reynaud as "Jia Zhangke Interview with *Le Monde.*"

http://www.lemonde.fr/article/0,5987,3250--277079-,00.html; http://
chinesecinemas.org

Fuchs, Christian, and Eva Horvak. 2008. "Africa and the Digital Divide."
Telematics and Informatics 25 (2): 99–116. http://dx.doi.org/10.1016/j.
tele.2006.06.004.

Gallant, Thomas W. 2001. *Modern Greece: A Brief History*. Oxford: Oxford
University Press.

Gallivant. 1996. Film. Directed by Andrew Kötting. UK: Arts Council of
England, British Film Institute (BFI), Channel Four Films.

Gama, Francisca da. 2007. "Filming the War with Sendero." *Jump Cut* 49
(Spring). http://www.ejumpcut.org/archive/jc49.2007/daGama-Sendero/
index.html

Gevgilili, Ali. 1989. *Cinema Questions the Times* [in Turkish, *Çağını Sorgulayan
Sinema*]. Istanbul: Bağlam.

Ginsberg, Terri. 2009. "Special Issue on Media and Film." *International Journal of
Contemporary Iraqi Studies* 3 (1): 3–5. http://dx.doi.org/10.1386/ijcis.3.1.3_2.

Ginsburg, Faye. 2003. "'Atanarjuat' Off-Screen: From Media Reservations to
the World Stage." *American Anthropologist* 105 (4): 827–31. http://dx.doi.
org/10.1525/aa.2003.105.4.827.

The Gold Diggers. 1983. Film. Directed by Sally Potter. UK: British Film Institute,
Channel Four.

Goldsmith, Ben. 2007. "Australian International Cinema." *Creative Economy
Online*. http://apo.org.au/research/australian-international-cinema.

Greenwald, Glenn, Ewen MacAskill, and Laura Poitras. 2013. "Edward
Snowden: The Whistleblower behind the NSA Surveillance Revelations."
The Guardian, 10 June. http://www.theguardian.com/world/2013/jun/09/
edward-snowden-nsa-whistleblower-surveillance

Gurd, G. 1998. "Canada." In *Global Media Economics; Commercialization,
Concentration, and Integration of World Media Markets*, ed. A.B. Albarran and
S.M. Chan-Olmsted, 33–50. Ames: Iowa State University Press.

Hammett-Jamart, Julia. 2005. "Context for International Coproduction." *Metro
Magazine* 140: 22–126.

Hardie, Giles. 2011. *"King's Speech* – The Little Non-Aussie That Could." *Sydney
Morning Herald Online*, 3 March. http://www.smh.com.au/entertainment/
blogs/get-flickd/kings-speech-the-littlenonaussie-that-could/20110303-1bffp.
html.

Harley, Ruth. 2009. *Keynote Speech: Melbourne International Film Festival, 24
July*. Woolloomooloo: Screen Australia.

Harrow, Kenneth W. 1999. *Postcolonial and Feminist Readings*. Trenton, Asmara:
Africa World Press.

Harry Potter and the Deadly Hallows, Part 2. 2011. Film. Directed by David
Yates. UK: Warner Bros., Heyday Films, Moving Picture Company (MPC).

Hashim, Ajami. 2007. "Festival Nyamuk?" *Bicaraskrip Blog*, 7 January. http://
bicaraskrip.blogspot.com/2007/01/festival-nyamuk.html

Hassan, Abdul Muthalib. 2011. "What Is Sought in the 24th Malaysian Film
Festival?" [in Malay, "Apakah Dicari Dalam FFM24?"]. *Utusan Online*,
18 December. http://www.utusan.com.my/utusan/info.asp?y=2011&dt=1218&
pub=Utusan_Malaysia&sec=Hiburan&pg=hi_09.htm.

Havis, Richard James. 2000. "Signs of New Life: Asia's Filmmakers Struggle
to Shake Off Old Constraints." *Asiaweek*, 29 December. http://www.
asiaweek.com/asiaweek/magazine/2000/1229/yearend_movies.html.

Haynes, Jonathan. 2007a. "Nollywood: What's in a Name?" *Film International*
5 (4): 106–8. http://dx.doi.org/10.1386/fiin.5.4.106.

Haynes, Jonathan. 2007b. "Nollywood in Lagos, Lagos in Nollywood Films."
Africa Today 54 (2): 130–50. http://dx.doi.org/10.2979/AFT.2007.54.2.130.

Haynes, Jonathan. 2012. "Reflections on Nollywood: Introduction to the
Special Issue." *Journal of African Cinemas* 4, 1: 14. http://dx.doi.org/10.1386/
jac.4.1.3_2.

Health Canada. 2013. *First Nations and Inuit Health.* http:// http://www.hc-sc.
gc.ca/fniah-spnia/promotion/mental/index-eng.php.

Heemstra, Marjolijn van. 2009. "Mobile Cinema Relief for Iraq." *The Power of
Culture*, September. http://www.krachtvancultuur.nl/en/current/2009/
september/humanfilm.

Hernandez, Eugene. 2010. "Five Sundance Films, 3 From This Year's Fest,
Coming to YouTube This Week." *Indiewire*, 20 January. http://www.
indiewire.com/article/five_sundance_films_3_from_this_years_fest_
coming_to_youtube_tomorrow.

Herold, Anna. 2004. "EU Film Policy: Between Art and Commerce." *European
Diversity and Autonomy Papers–EDAP* 3. http://www.eurac.edu/edap.

High Hopes. 1988. Film. Directed by Mike Leigh. UK: British Screen Productions,
Channel Four Films, Portman Productions.

Himpele, Jeffrey D. 1996. "Film Distribution as Media: Mapping Difference in
the Bolivian Cinemascape." *Visual Anthropology Review* 12 (1): 47–66. http://
dx.doi.org/10.1525/var.1996.12.1.47.

Hoffmann, Claudia. 2012. "Nollywood in Transit: The Globalization of Nigerian
Video Culture." In *Postcolonial Cinema Studies*, ed. Sandra Ponzanesi and
Marguerite Walker, 218–32. New York: Routledge.

Hoskins, C., A. Finn, and S. McFadyen. 1996. "Television and Film in a
Freer International Trade Environment: U.S. Dominance and Canadian
Responses." In *Mass Media and Free Trade: NAFTA and the Cultural Industries*,

ed. E.G. McAnany and K.T. Wilkinson, 63–91. Austin: University of Texas Press.

Human Film. 2013. "Iraqi Mobile Cinema Festival." Accessed 24 February. http://www.humanfilm.co.uk/about-us/projects-2/mobile-cinema-festival.

Idtnaine, Omar. 2008a. "Cinéma Amazigh au Maroc: Autre naissance artistique et importante richesse culturelle." 28 September. http://www.amazighnews. net/20080928242/Cinema-Amazigh-au-Maroc.html.

Idtnaine, Omar. 2008b. "Le Cinéma Amazigh au Maroc: Eléments d'une naissance artistique." Africultures. 20 October. http://www.africultures. com/php/index.php?nav=article&no=8117.

"Igloolik Isuma Productions Going Out of Business." 2011. CBC News. Last modified 8 July. http://www.cbc.ca/news/canada/north/ story/2011/07/08/isuma-productions-business.html.

Ikram, Ismail. 2012. "Curbing Movie Piracy a Priority." Malay Mail, 31 July. http://my.news.yahoo.com/curbing-movie-piracy-priority-083848507.html

Inbetweeners. 2011. Film. Directed by Ben Palmer. UK: Bwark Productions, Film4, Young Films.

Independent Publishers Association. 2013. Home Page. http://www.ipg. uk.com/home.

Independent Filmmaker Project (IFP). 2013. Home Page. Accessed 1 March. http://www.ifp.org/programs/international.

Indigenous Communications in Canada. 2013. "Our History." http://www. indigenousmedia.ca/indigenous-communications-in-canada-our-history.

Inland Empire. 2006. Film. Directed by David Lynch. United States: StudioCanal, Fundacja Kultury, Camerimage Festival.

Insdorf, Annette. 1981. "Ordinary People, European Style: How to Spot an Independent Feature." American Film 6 (10): 57–60.

International Film Festival Rotterdam. 2013a. "Hubert Bals Fund: Project Entry." http://www.filmfestivalrotterdam.com/professionals/hubert_bals_fund/ projectentry.

International Film Festival Rotterdam. 2013b. "Hubert Bals Fund Supports 24 Film Projects in Thirteen Countries." http://www.filmfestivalrotterdam. com/professionals/programme/news1/hbf-selection/

Internet Movie Database. 2012. "Box Office Figures for Pulp Fiction." Accessed 20 May. http://www.imdb.com/title/tt0110912/business.

Internet Movie Database. 2013. "Release Dates for sex, lies and videotape." Accessed 5 March. http://www.imdb.com/title/tt0098724/releaseinfo

Inuit Broadcasting Corporation. 2006. Notes for an Address by Debbie Brisebois. 5 October. Accessed 10 May 2010. http://www.inuitbroadcasting.ca/ Presentations/002_e.htm.

"Inuit Film Unfairly Excluded." 1998. *The Gazette* (Montreal, Quebec), 10 November, B2.

Iordanova, Dina. 2010. "Rise of the Fringe: Global Cinema's Long Tail." In *Cinema at the Periphery*, ed. Dina Iordanova, David Martin-Jones, and Belen Vidal, 23–45. Detroit, MI: Wayne State University Press.

Iordanova, Dina. 2012. "Digital Disruption: Technological Innovation and Global Film Circulation." In *Digital Disruption: Cinema Moves Online*, ed. Dina Iordanova and Stuart Cunningham, 1–31. St Andrews, UK: St Andrews Film Studies.

"The Iraqi Cinema in 1964." 1966. In *The Cinema in the Arab Countries*, ed. George Sadoul, 185–6. Beirut: Interarab Centre of Cinema and Television.

"Iraqi Film Fails to Draw in the Crowds at Cairo Film Fest." 2012. *Al Bawaba Entertainment*, 6 December. http://www.albawaba.com/entertainment/iraqi-cairo-film-festival-454849.

"Iraq Invests $4m in Film Industry." 2012. *Iraq Business News*, 9 March. http://www.iraq-businessnews.com/2012/03/09/iraq-invests-4m-in-film-industry.

Iraq Short Film Festival. 2013. "Profile of the Iraq Short Film Festival." Accessed 25 February. http://isff-iraq.org/about-3.html.

Issari, M. Ali, and Doris A. Paul. 1979. *What Is Cinema Verité?* Metuchan, NJ: Scarecrow Press.

Isuma Productions. 2013a. "About." http://www.isuma.tv/hi/en/isuma-productions/about.

Isuma Productions. 2013b. "The Art of Community-Based Filmmaking." http://www.isuma.tv/hi/en/isuma-productions/art-community-based-filmmaking.

Isuma Productions. 2013c. "Our Style." http://www.isuma.tv/hi/en/isuma-productions/our-style.

Isuma TV. 2013. *Qitdlassuaq*. http://www.isuma.tv/hi/en/taxonomy/term/3766?page=3

Jameson, Fredric. 1995. *The Geopolitical Aesthetic: Cinema and Space in the World System*. Indianapolis: Indiana University Press.

Jenkins, Henry. 2006. *Convergence Culture: Where Old and New Media Collide*. New York: New York University Press.

Jubilee. 1978. Film. Directed by Derek Jarman. UK: Megalovision, Whaley-Malin Productions.

Kami, Aseel. 2012. "After Dark Years, Lights Coming Back On for Iraqi Cinema." *Yahoo! Movies Canada*, 14 November. http://ca.movies.yahoo.com/news/dark-years-lights-coming-back-iraqi-cinema-140410225.html.

Kamin, Louise. 2012. "Swahiliwood: A Platform for Enter-Educate Feature Films: A Study about the Tanzanian Film Industry Led by Media for Development International." Paper presented at Zanzibar International Film Festival.

Karalis, Vrasidas. 2012. *A History of Greek Cinema*. London: Continuum.

Karroum, Abdellah. 2006. "Contemporary Arabic Representations, Act III (The Iraqi Equation)." *L'appartement 22*, 6 June. http://www.appartement22.com/spip.php?article13.

Kayastha, Vaskar S. 2012. "Leaving Baghdad: Review." *Cult Hub*, June. http://culthub.com/2012/06/leaving-baghdad-review/9024/.

Kelani, Tunde. 2008. "Spielberg and I: The Digital Revolution." In *Nollywood, the Video Phenomenon in Nigeria*, ed. Pierre Barrot, 90–2. Bloomington: Indiana University Press.

Kerr, Elizabeth. 2011. "Quattro Hong Kong 2: Film Review." *The Hollywood Reporter*, 22 March. http://www.hollywoodreporter.com/review/quattro-hong-kong-2-film-170019

Kettelhake, Silke. 2005. "Blinking Incredulously at the Sun." *Qantara.de*, 30 August. http://en.qantara.de/content/oday-rasheeds-underexposure-blinking-incredulously-at-the-sun

Khatchadourian, Raffi. 2010. "Julian Assange's Mission for Total Transparency." *New Yorker*, 7 June. http://www.newyorker.com/reporting/2010/06/07/100607fa_fact_khatchadourian

Khatib, Lina. 2006. *Filming the Modern Middle East: Politics in the Cinemas of Hollywood and the Arab World*. London and New York: I.B. Tauris.

Khoo, Gaik Cheng. 2004. "Just-Do-It-Yourself: Malaysian Independent Filmmaking." *Aliran Monthly* 24:9. http://aliran.com/archives/monthly/2004b/9k.html

Khoo, Gaik Cheng. 2006. "You've Come a Long Way, Baby: Erma Fatima, Film and Politics." *South East Asia Research* 14 (2): 179–209. http://dx.doi.org/10.5367/000000006778008112.

Khoo, Gaik Cheng. 2007. "Just-Do-It-(Yourself): Independent Filmmaking in Malaysia." *Inter-Asia Cultural Studies* 8 (2): 227–47. http://dx.doi.org/10.1080/13583880701238696.

King, Geoff. 2005. *American Independent Cinema*. London: I.B. Tauris.

King, Geoff. 2009. *Indiewood USA: Where Hollywood Meets American Independent Film*. London: I.B Tauris.

The King's Speech. 2010. Film. Directed by Tom Hooper. UK: Weinstein Company, UK Film Council, Momentum Pictures.

Kleinhans, Chuck. 1998. "Independent Features: Hopes and Dreams." In *The New American Cinema*, ed. Jon Lewis, 307–27. Durham, NC, and London: Duke University Press.

Knegt, Peter. 2011. "Redford, Sundance Institute, and AEG Europe Launching 'Sundance London.'" *Indiewire*. 15 March. http://www.indiewire.com/article/redford_sundance_institute_and_aeg_europe_launching_sundance_london

Knudsen, Erik. 2005. "Eyes of the Beholder." *Journal of Media Practice* 5 (3): 181–6. http://dx.doi.org/10.1386/jmpr.5.3.181/3.

Knudsen, Erik. 2010. "Cinema of Poverty." *Wide Screen* 2 (2): 1–15.

Koay, A. 2010. "Getting the Right Picture." *The Star Online*, 19 April. http://ecentral.my/services/sprinterfriendly.asp?file=/2010/4/19/movies/5653205&sec=movies

Kochan, D. 2003. "Wang Xiaoshuai." *Senses of Cinema* 28, October. http://sensesofcinema.com/ 2003/great-directors/wang.

Koestler, A. 1989. *The Act of Creation*. New York: Arkana.

Koziarski, Ed M. 2010. "From Iraq to Iowa." *Chicago Reader*, 5 August. http://www.chicagoreader.com/chicago/american-arab-usama-alshaibi-documentary/Content?oid=2193325.

Kuoshu, Harry H. 2002. *Celluloid China: Cinematic Encounters with Culture and Society*. Carbondale: Southern Illinois University Press.

Lau, Jenny Kwok Wah. 2002. "Globalization and Youthful Subculture." In *Multiple Modernities: Cinemas and Popular Media in Transcultural East Asia*, ed. Jenny Kwok Wah Lau, 13–27. Philadelphia: Temple University Press.

Lee, Joe. 2010. "A Film Fest That Lets Everyone Down." *The Malay Mail*, 28 October. http://www.mmail.com.my/content/53590-film-fest-lets-everyone-down

Lee, P. 2011. "Namewee Calls Utusan 'Trash.'" *Free Malaysia Today.com*, 28 September. http://www.freemalaysiatoday.com/2011/09/28/namewee-calls-utusan-trash/

Lequeret, Elisabeth. 2005. "Fespaco 2005: Boubacar Diallo, portrait d'un pionnier." *RFI.fr*, 23 February. http://www.rfi.fr/actufr/articles/062/article_34306.asp.

Levy, Emanuel. 1999. *Cinema of Outsiders: The Rise of American Independent Film*. New York: New York University Press.

Lewis, Jon. 2008. *American Film: A History*. New York: Norton.

"Lights, Camera, Africa." 2010. *The Economist*, 16 December. Accessed 12 January 2013. http://www.economist.com/node/17723124.

Lim, Dennis. 2001. "China's New City Symphonies." *Timeasia*, 21 February. www.villagevoice.com/film/0108,lim,22440,20.html.

Lim, Danny. 2004. "Do It Yourself " [in Malay, "Bikin Sendiri"]. *The Edge [Options]* 2, 21 (February): 8–9.

Lim, Danny. 2007. "Keeping It Reel." *The Sun*, 30 August. http://www.malaysianbar.org.my/echoes_of_the_past/danny_lim_keeping_it_reel.html?date=2010-05-01

"Lima se prepara para primer festival de cine independiente." 2011. *RPP.com*, *Cine*, 29 May. http://www.rpp.com.pe/2011-05-29-lima-se-prepara-para-primer-festival-de-cine-independiente-noticia_370198.html.

Lobato, Ramon. 2007. "Subcinema: Theorizing Marginal Film Distribution." *Limina* 13:113–20.

Lobato, Ramon. 2011. *Shadow Economies of Cinema: Mapping Informal Film Distribution*. London: Palgrave MacMillan.

Long Day Closes. 1992. Film. Directed by Terence Davies. UK: British Film Institute (BFI), Channel Four Films.

Lu, Xinyu. 2003. *Recording China: The New Documentary Movement in Contemporary China*. Beijing: Sanlian Bookstore.

Lykidis, Alexios. 2014 (forthcoming). "Crisis of Sovereignty in Recent Greek Cinema." *Journal of Greek Media and Culture* 1 (1).

Macaulay, Scott. 2011. "Five Questions for Bunohan Director Dain Said." *Filmmaker: The Magazine of Independent Film*, 10 September. http://www.filmmakermagazine.com/news/2011/09/five-questions-for-bunohan-director-dain-said/

MacCormack, Patricia. 2005. "A Cinema of Desire: Cinesexuality and Guattari's Asignifying Cinema." *Women: A Cultural Review* 16, 3 (Winter): 34.

Maddy-Weitzman, Bruce. 2001. "Contested Identities: Berbers. 'Berberism,' and the State in North Africa." *Journal of North African Studies* 6 (3): 23–47. http://dx.doi.org/10.1080/13629380108718442.

Maher, Sean. 1999. *The Internationalisation of Australian Film and Television through the 1990s*. Woolloomooloo: Australian Film Commission.

Mamat, Khalid. 2011."Bangsat Pengarah Melayu Ni Kan Mat?" *Tempurung Pecah*, 21 September. http://tempurungpecah.blogspot.com/2011/09/bangsat-pengarah-melayu-ni-kan-mat.html.

El Mariachi. 1992. Film. Directed by Robert Rodriguez. United States: Columbia Pictures Corporation, Los Hooligans Productions.

Martin, Adrian. 2010. "Ozploitation Compared to What? A Challenge to Contemporary Australian Film Studies." *Studies in Australasian Cinema* 4 (1): 9–21. http://dx.doi.org/10.1386/sac.4.1.9_1.

Martin, Catherine. 2002. "Media Release: New APTN Board Executive Elected." *APTN Official Website*. 16 December. http://www.aptn.ca.

Martínez, Gabriela. 2008. "Cinema Law in Latin America: Brazil, Peru, and Colombia." *Jump Cut*, 50 (Spring). http://www.ejumpcut.org/archive/jc50.2008/LAfilmLaw/

Mayer, G. 1999. "Genre, Post–World War II." In *The Oxford Companion to Australian Film*, ed. B. McFarlane, G. Mayer, and I. Bertrand, 177–80. Oxford: Oxford University Press.

McCall, John C. 2002. "Madness, Money, and Movies: Watching a Nigerian Popular Video with the Guidance of a Native Doctor." *Africa Today* 49 (3): 79–94. http://dx.doi.org/10.1353/at.2003.0028.

McCall, John. 2007. "The Pan-Africanism We Have: Nollywood's Invention of Africa." *Film International* 4, 4 (28): 92–7. http://dx.doi.org/10.1386/fiin.5.4.92.

McCarthy, Rory. 2002. "No More Heroes." *The Guardian*, 2 December. http:// www.guardian.co.uk/film/2002/dec/02/artsfeatures.iraq/.

McClennen, Sophia. 2008. "Theory and Practice of the Peruvian Group Chaski." *Jump Cut*, 50 (Spring). http://www.ejumpcut.org/archive/jc50.2008/Chaski/ index.html

McDonald, Paul, and Janet Wasko, eds. 2008. *The Contemporary Hollywood Film Industry*. Hoboken, NJ: Blackwell Publishing.

McFarlane, Brian. 1988. *Australian Cinema*. New York: Columbia University Press.

Media, Entertainment, and Arts Alliance. Australia. 2008. *Submission by the Media, Entertainment, and Arts Alliance to the Department of Environment, Water, Heritage, and the Arts Regarding a Proposed Bilateral Film Co-production Agreement between Australia and Malaysia*. November. http://www.alliance.org.au

"Meet the Film Producers! Malay Film Productions Ltd. (1947–1967)." 2006. *P. Ramlee – The Legend*, 31 October. http://pramlee.blogdrive.com/ archive/4.html

Meor, Shariman. 2010. "The Sad Story of Malaysia's 'Other' Films." *New Straits Times*, 16 March. https://sukaweb.penang.gov.my/pkn/Akhbar.nsf/981d6 336478572e5482575e6002c4e9f/11c1184113bde3e9482576e400287f34/$FILE/ File0428.PDF

Meyer, Birgit. 1999. "Popular Ghanaian Cinema and 'African Heritage.'" *Africa Today* 46 (2): 93–114. http://dx.doi.org/10.1353/at.1999.0007.

Meyer, Birgit. 2010a. "Ghanaian Popular Video Movies between State Film Policies and Nollywood: Discourses and Tensions." In *Viewing African Cinema in the Twenty-first Century: Art Films and the Nollywood Video Revolution*, ed. Mahir Saul and Ralph Austen, 42–62. Athens, OH: Ohio University Press.

Meyer, Birgit. 2010b. "'Tradition and Colour at Its Best': 'Tradition' and 'Heritage' in Ghanaian Video-Movies." *Journal of African Cultural Studies* 22 (1): 7–23. http://dx.doi.org/10.1080/13696810903488553.

Mhando, Martin. 2009. "Globalisation and African Cinema: Distribution and Reception in Anglophone Region." *Journal of African Cinemas* 1 (1): 19–34. http://dx.doi.org/10.1386/jac.1.1.19/1.

Mhiripiri, Nhamo. 2010. "Thematic Concerns in the Emergent Zimbabwean Short Film Genre." *Journal of African Cinemas* 2 (2): 91–109. http://dx.doi. org/10.1386/jac.2.2.91_1.

Miller, Toby, Nitin Govil, John McMurria, Richard Maxwell, and Ting Wang. 2005. *Global Hollywood 2*. London: British Film Institute.

Miller, W. 2008. "Indie Spirits Wade into Mainstream." *Weekly Variety*, 10 March: 53–4.

Mini, Panayiota. 2011. "Reflections on Pain, Loss, and Memory: Takis Kanellopoulos' Fiction Films of the 1960s." In *Greek Cinema: Texts, Histories, Identities*,
ed. Lydia Papadimitriou and Yannis Tzioumakis, 239–54. Bristol, UK: Intellect/
University of Chicago Press.

Molloy, Claire. 2010. *Memento*. Edinburgh: Edinburgh University Press.
http://dx.doi.org/10.3366/edinburgh/9780748637713.001.0001.

Montenegro, Fernando. 2010a. "¿Existe un cine independiente en el Perú?
Parte 1. Ricardo Bedoya y Fernando Montenegro." *University of Lima* video,
9:41. 8 March. http://www.youtube.com/watch?v=USCEV4lr69A.

Montenegro, Fernando. 2010b. "Forum: El cine peruano en debate; 'Peruvian
Indie,' Parte 1." *FAQTV*. 8 March. http://www.youtube.com/
watch?v=57pdCPKg_9k (accessed 14 February 2012), video 1:53–5:24.

Mosco, Vincent. 2004. *The Digital Sublime: Myth, Power, and Cyberspace*.
Cambridge, MA: MIT Press.

Motion Picture Association of America (MPAA). 1991. "The 1980s: A Reference
Guide to Motion Pictures, Television, VCR, and Cable." *Velvet Light Trap* 27
(Spring): 86–7.

Murray, D. 2006. *Defying Gravity*. Manchester, UK: North West Vision.

My Ain Folk. 1973. Film. Directed by Bill Douglas. UK: British Film Institute (BFI).

My Childhood. 1972. Film. Directed by Bill Douglas. UK: British Film Institute
(BFI).

My Way Home. 1978. Film. Directed by Bill Douglas. UK: British Film Institute
(BFI).

Naficy, Hamid. 2001. *An Accented Cinema: Exilic and Diasporic Filmmaking*.
Princeton, NJ: Princeton University Press.

Naidu, Sumisha. 2011. "Namewee Serves Up Debut Film Nasi Lemak 2.0."
Meld Magazine, 6 September. http://www.meldmagazine.com.au/2011/09/
namewee-serves-debut-film-nasi-lemak-2-0/

Nash Information Services. 2013. *The Numbers: Box Office Data*. Accessed 5
March 2013. http://www.the-numbers.com/movies/1989/0SLVT.php

National Film Development Corporation Malaysia. 2012a. *Funding:
Feature Film Loan Funds*. 8 June. http://www.finas.gov.my/index.
php?mod=dana&sub=pinjaman

National Film Development Corporation Malaysia. 2012b. *Funding: Fiction Film
Incentive*. 8 June. http://www.finas.gov.my/index.php?mod=dana&sub=itfc.

National Film Development Corporation Malaysia. 2013. *Industry: Malaysian
Film Data*. 22 May. http://www.finas.gov.my/index.php?mod=industry&su
b=filemmalaysia.

NeuCollins. Mark. 2007. "Contemporary African Cinema: The Emergence
of an Independent Cinema in Nigeria." *Speaking of Art blog*, 20 April.

Accessed 3 March 2013. http://speakingofart.wordpress.com/2007/04/20/contemporary-african-cinema-the-emergence-of-an-independent-cinema-in-nigeria/#more-8.

Newman, Michael Z. 2011. *Indie: An American Film Culture*. New York: Columbia University Press.

New York University. 2006. "CinemaEast: Underexposure." *New York University CinemaEast Fall 2006 Series*. Accessed 30 January 2013. http://www.arteeast.org/cinemaeast/fall-series-06/fall-06-films/underexposure.html.

Noorsila, Abdul Majid. 2010. "No Tax Rebate for Nasi Lemak 2.0." *The Star Online*, 10 October. http://www.thestar.com.my/story/?file=%2f2011%2f10%2f10%2fnation%2f9665958

Nouri, Shakir. 1986. *A la recherché du cinema irakien: Histoire, infrastructure, filmographie (1945–1985)*. Paris: Editions L'Harmattan.

Nowra, Louis. 2009. "Nowhere Near Hollywood." *The Monthly* (online), 52. www.themonthly.com.au.monthly-essays-louis-nowra-nowhere-near-hollywood-australian-film-2177.

"Nueva Ley de Cine aprobada en el pleno del Congreso es celebrada por actores y directores." 2010. *El Comercio*, 16 December. http://elcomercio.pe/espectaculos/685230/noticia-nueva-ley-cine-aprobada-pleno-congreso-celebrada-directores-actores.

Nu Metro Times Media Group. 2013. Accessed 1 June. http://www.timesmedia.co.za/businesses/entertainment/nu-metro/.

Nur, Aqidah Azizi. 2006. "Push to Spread Local Film Releases." *Malay Mail*, 5 October. http://www.accessmylibrary.com/article-1G1-152407849/push-spread-local-film.html

Obiaya, Ikechukwu. 2010. "Nollywood on the Internet: A Preliminary Analysis of an Online Nigerian Video-Film Audience." *Journal of African Media Studies* 2 (3): 321–38. http://dx.doi.org/10.1386/jams.2.3.321_1.

Ogundele, Wole. 2000. "From Folk Opera to Soap Opera: Improvisations and Transformations in Yoruba Popular Theater." In *Nigerian Video Films*, ed. Jonathan Haynes, 89–129. Athens, OH: Ohio University Center for International Studies.

Okome, Onookome. 2004. "Women, Religion, and the Video Film in Nigeria." *Film International* 2 (1): 4–13. http://dx.doi.org/10.1386/fiin.2.1.4.

Oladunjoye, Tunde. 2008. "Jumping on the Bandwagon." In *Nollywood, the Video Phenomenon in Nigeria*, ed. Pierre Barrot, 62–9. Bloomington: Indiana University Press.

Olesen, Alexa. 1999. "Wang Xiaoshuai's Beautifully Bleak Vision of China." *Virtual China*. http://www.virtualchina.com/archive/leisure/film/wangxiaoshuai-alo.html

Olesen, Alexa. 2001. "Chinese Dogme 2001: A New Wave Cultural Revolution." *Indiewire.com*, 16 March. www.indiewire.com/onthescene/fes_01UrbGen_010306_China.html

Olsberg, SPI. 2007. *Memorandum on Territorialisation Prepared for the European Film Agencies Directors*. London: Olsberg, SPI.

Olsberg, SPI. 2012. "Evaluation and Proposed Revisions of the European Convention on Cinematographic Co-production." A report prepared for the Council of Europe. London

Ong, Sherman. 2010. "Synopsis and Production Credits." *Memories of a Burning Tree*, 4 January. http://memoriesofaburningtree.blogspot.com.

Pachachi, Maysoon. 2004. "'Who Can Live the Way We've Had to Live and Be Normal?'" *The Guardian*, 9 April. http://www.guardian.co.uk/film/2004/apr/09/1.

Pachachi, Maysoon. 2006. "'You Can't Just Sit at Home Afraid.'" *The Guardian*, 26 August. http://www.guardian.co.uk/film/2006/aug/29/features.

Paneli, Eski Hisarlar. 2005. "Hisar Was a Center of Attraction for Us" [in Turkish, "Hisar, bizim için çekim merkeziydi"]. http://www.mafm.boun.edu.tr/files/181_Eski_Hisarlar_Paneli.pdf

Papadimitriou, Lydia. 2006. *The Greek Film Musical: A Critical and Cultural History*. Jefferson, NC: McFarland.

Papadimitriou, Lydia. 2009. "Greek Film Studies Today: In Search of Identity." *Kampos: Cambridge Papers in Modern Greek*, 17: 49–78.

Papadimitriou, Lydia. 2011. "The National and the Transnational in Contemporary Greek Cinema." *New Review of Film and Television Studies* 9 (4): 493–512. http://dx.doi.org/10.1080/17400309.2011.606535.

Parks, Stacey. 2007. *The Insider's Guide to Independent Film Distribution*. Oxford: Focus Press.

Peru. Ministry of Culture. 2012. "Dirección de Industrias Culturales." *Direccion del Audiovisual la Fonograpfia y los Nuevos Medios*. http://www.dicine.pe/?paged=5

Petersen, Rachael. 2013. *Arctic Issues On-line*. http://www.slideshare.net/RachelPeterson

Petty, Sheila J. 2008. *Contact Zones: Memory, Origin, and Discourses in Black Diasporic Cinema*. Detroit: Wayne State University.

Pickowicz, Paul. 2012. *China on Film: A Century of Exploration, Confrontation, and Controversy*. Lanham, MD: Rowman and Littlefield.

Pickowicz, Paul, and Zhang Yingjin, eds. 2006. *From Underground to Independent: Alternative Film Culture in Contemporary China*. Lanham, MD: Rowman and Littlefield.

Prospero's Books. 1991. Film. Directed by Peter Greenaway. UK: Allarts, Cinéa, Caméra One.

Psychogiopoulou, Evangelia. 2010. "The 'Cultural' Criterion in the European Commission's Assessment of State Aids to the Audio-Visual Sector." *Legal Issues of Economic Integration* 37:273–91.

Raheja, M. 2007. "Reading Nanook's Smile: Visual Sovereignty, Indigenous Revisions of Ethnography, and *Atanarjuat (The Fast Runner)*." *American Quarterly* 59 (4): 1159–85. http://dx.doi.org/10.1353/aq.2007.0083.

Rayner, Jonathan. 2000. *Contemporary Australian Cinema: An Introduction.* Manchester, UK: Manchester University Press.

Rayns, Tony. 2000. "Film Review on Xiao Wu." *Sight and Sound* 10 (3): 59.

Refiğ, Halit. 2003.: *The Adventure of a Film Movement and a Filmmaker* [in Turkish, *Bir Sinema'nın ve Sinemacının Serüveni*]. Istanbul: Dünya Kitle İletişimi Araştırma Vakfı DKIV Yayınları.

Refiğ, Halit. 2009. *Fight for a National Cinema* [in Turkish, *Ulusal Sinema Kavgası*]. Istanbul: Hareket.

Reid, Mary Anne. 1999. *More Long Shots: Australian Cinema Successes in the 90s.* Woolloomooloo: Australian Film Commission.

Reuters. 2012. "Baghdad Film Festival Ends on a Sour Note." *Al Arabiya News*, 8 October. http://english.alarabiya.net/articles/2012/10/08/242599.html.

Revengers Tragedy. 2003. Film. Directed by Alex Cox. UK: Bard Entertainments, Exterminating Angel Production, Northcroft Films.

Rheingold, Howard. 2002. *Smart Mobs: The Next Social Revolution.* Cambridge, MA: Perseus Publishing.

Rizal, Johan. 2005. "Julian Cheah on the Local Film Industry." *The Star*, 29 April. http://ecentral.my/news/story.asp?file=/2005/4/29/movies/10660736&sec=movies

Robinson, Courtney. 2011. "'Co-cultural Producing? The Definition and Role of the Australian Cultural Producer and Their Complication through International Audiovisual Coproduction." BA(Hons) thesis, University of Wollongong.

Rocchi, James. 2012. "How Sundance Got Its Edge Back." *The Guardian*, 4 February. http://www.guardian.co.uk/film/2012/feb/05/sundance-film-festival-america-Meltdown.

Rorvik, Peter. 2012. "Film and Film Development in Africa Overview and Discussion." Paper presented at the Arterial Network Conference on Creative Economy, Nairobi, December. http://www.arterialnetwork.org/uploads/2012/02/Peter_Rorviks_Presentation.doc.pdf.

Rose, Steve. 2011 "*Attenberg, Dogtooth*, and the Weird Wave of Greek Cinema." *The Guardian*, 27 August. http://www.theguardian.com/film/2011/aug/27/attenberg-dogtooth-greece-cinema.

Rosen, David, and Peter Hamilton. 1990. *Off- Hollywood: The Making and Marketing of Independent Films.* New York: Grove Weidenfeld.

Ross, Miriam. 2008. "Grupo Chaski's Microcines: Engaging the Spectator." *eSharp: Social Engagement, Empowerment, and Change* 11 (Spring). http:// www.gla.ac.uk/research/az/esharp/issues/11/

Roth, Lorna. 2002. "First Peoples' Television in Canada's North: A Case Study of the Aboriginal Peoples Television Network." In *Mediascapes: New Patterns in Canadian Communication, 2002*, ed. Paul Attallah and Leslie Regan Shade, 295–310. Scarborough, ON: Nelson.

Routt, William D. 1999. "Genre, Pre–World War II." In *The Oxford Companion to Australian Film*, ed. Brian McFarlane, Geoff Mayer, and Ina Bertrand, 180–2. Oxford: Oxford University Press.

Ryan, Mark David. 2008. "A Dark New World: Anatomy of Australian Horror Films". PhD diss., Queensland University of Technology.

Ryan, M.D. 2009. "Whither Culture? Australian Horror Films and the Limitations of Cultural Policy." *Media International Australia: Incorporating Culture and Policy* 133:43–55.

Sabine, James. 1995. *A Century of Australian Cinema*. Port Melbourne, Victoria, Australia: William Heinemann.

Sadoul, George. 1966. "Geography of the Cinema and the Arab World." In *The Cinema in the Arab Countries*, ed. George Sadoul, 135–8. Beirut: Interarab Centre of Cinema and Television.

Said, S.F. 2002. "In the Realm of the Censors." *Telegraph*, 2 July. www.arts. telegraph.co.uk.

Salman, Raheem. 2009. "Iraq Cinema Manager Flashes Back to the Boom Times." *Los Angeles Times*, 7 May. http://articles.latimes.com/2009/may/07/world/ fg-iraq-movies7.

Sama, Emmanuel. 1996. "African Films Are Foreigners in Their Own Countries." In *African Experiences of Cinema*, ed. Imruh Bakari and Mbye Cham, 148–56. London: British Film Institute.

Sanogo, Aboubakar. 2009. "Regarding Cinephilia and Africa." *Framework* 50 (1–2): 226–8. http://dx.doi.org/10.1353/frm.0.0046.

Saray, Hussam al-. 2010. "Iraq Movie Successes Betray Dire State of Industry." *Institute for War and Peace Reporting*, no. 338, 31 May. http://iwpr.net/ report-news/movie-successes-betray-dire-state-industry.

Sargeant, Jack. 2011. "Notes from the Underground: Guerrilla Filmmaking in Australia." *Metro Magazine* 168:90–2.

Saul, Mahir. 2010. "Art, Politics, and Commerce in Francophone African Cinema." In *Viewing African Cinema in the Twenty-first Century: Art Films and the Nollywood Video Revolution*, ed. Mahir Saul and Ralph Austen, 133–59. Athens, OH: Ohio University Press.

Schatz, Thomas. 2012. "Conglomerate Hollywood and American Independent Film." In *American Independent Cinema: Indie, Indiewood, and beyond,* ed. G. King, C. Molloy, and Y. Tzioumakis, 127–39. London: Routledge.

Schembri, J. 2008. "At Death's Door: An Industry Lost in the Dark." *Age* (5 December). http://blogs.theage.com.au/schembri/archives/2008/12/at_deaths_door.html.

Scognamillo, Giovanni. 2003. *History of Turkish Cinema* [in Turkish, *Türk Sinema Tarihi*]. Istanbul: Kabalcı.

Scott, A.O. 2002. "Reel Change." *New York Times,* 14 July.

Scott, A.O. 2007. "World Bank in the Docket, Charged with Africa's Woes." *New York Times,* 14 February. http://movies.nytimes.com/2007/02/14/movies/14bama.html?fta=y.

Screen Australia. 2009. *Australian Films in the Marketplace: Analysis of Release Strategies and Box Office Performance, October.* http://www.screenaustralia.gov.au/getmedia/f78eb112-340e-4760-96c0-ad4d436f8a8e/Release_boxoffice_20Nov09.pdf.

Screen Australia. 2010. *Screen Australia: Annual Report 09/10.* Woolloomooloo: Screen Australia.

Screen Australia. 2012a. *Australian Content: Box office; Share of the Australian Box Office for Australian Feature Films, 1977–2011.* Woolloomooloo: Screen Australia.

Screen Australia. 2012b. *The Drama Report 2011/12: Production of Feature Film and TV Drama in Australia.* Woolloomooloo: Screen Australia.

Screen Australia. 2013a. *Drama Report: Production of Feature Films and TV Drama in Australia 2012/13.* Ultimo: Screen Australia.

Screen Australia. 2013b. *International Co-production Program Guidelines.* http://www.screenaustralia.gov.au/getmedia/05f7de49-ac13-46fe-8840-37dab5a1b394/Glines_Copro.pdf

Screen Australia. 2013c. *Location Offset (Refundable Film Tax Offset).* http://www.screenaustralia.gov.au/research/statistics/mptax.aspx#Rao98988

Screen Australia. 2013d. *Production Industry: Drama; Proportions of Feature Films by Genre, 1993/94–2011/12.* http://www.screenaustralia.gov.au/research/statistics/mpfeaturesgenre.aspx

Screen Producers Association of Australia (SPAA). 2012. *Convergence Review Panel Interim Report, February 10: SPAA Submission to Convergence Review.* Surry Hills: Screen Producers Association of Australia.

Sea of Madness. 2005. Film. Directed by Erik Knudsen. UK: One Day Films Limited.

Secrets and Lies. 1996. Film. Directed by Mike Leigh. UK: Channel Four Films, CiBy 2000, Thin Man Films.

Shafik, Viola. 2007. *Arab Cinema: History and Cultural Identity*. Cairo and New York: American University in Cairo Press. http://dx.doi.org/10.5743/cairo/9789774160653.001.0001.

Shame. 2011. Film. Directed by Steve McQueen. UK: See-Saw Films, Film4, UK Film Council.

Shauki, Afdlin. 2008. '*Wajib Tayang*' for the Uninformed: Something You Must Know If You Love Malaysia and Malaysian Films. http://afdlinshauki.blogspot.com/2008/12/wajib-tayang-for-uninformed-something.html.

Sia, Andrew. 2004. "Local Filmmaking: Breaking the Mould." *The Star*, 9 October. http://thestar.com.my/lifestyle/story.asp?file=/2004/10/9/features/20041009081243&sec=featurs

Simon, Alissa. 2011. "Review: *In My Mother's Arms*." *Variety*, 20 September. http://variety.com/2011/film/reviews/in-my-mother-s-arms-1117946186/.

Sin City. 2005. Film. Directed by Robert Rodriguez. United States: Dimension Films, Troublemaker Studios.

Sing, Jeremy. 2010. "SIFF Production Talk: *Memories of a Burning Tree* by Sherman Ong." *SINdie*, 13 April. http://sindieonly.blogspot.com/2010/04/siff-production-talk-memories-of.html

Sivas, Ala. 2011. ""Conception of Independence in Turkish Cinema and Its Representatives" [in Turkish, "Türk Sinemasında Bağımsızlık Anlayışı ve Temsilcileri"]. In *Syntheses on Turkish and World Cinema* [in Turkish, *Türk ve Dünya Sineması Üzerine Sentezler*], ed. Serpil Kırel, 121–46. Istanbul: Parşömen Yayıncılık.

A Sketchbook for the Library Van. 2005. Film. Directed by Gideon Koppel. UK: Radical Media.

Sleep Furiously. 2008. Film. Directed by Gideon Koppel. UK: Bard Entertainments, Van Film.

Smith, Christopher J. 2000. *China in the Post-Utopian Age*. Boulder, CO: Westview Press.

Solanas, Fernando, and Octavio Getino. 1971. "Towards a Third Cinema." *Afterimage*, no. 3 (Summer): 16–30.

Sorbera, Lucia. 2009. "Dreamers without Borders." *International Journal of Contemporary Iraqi Studies* 3 (3): 321–29. http://dx.doi.org/10.1386/ijcis.3.3.321/4.

Sotiropoulou, C. 1989. *Elliniki Kinimatografia, 1965–1975: Thesmiko Plaisio – Oikonomiki Katastasi* [Greek cinema, 1965–1765: Institutional framework – Financial situation]. Athens: Themelio.

Soto, Hernando de. 2003. *The Mystery of Capital: Why Capitalism Triumphs in the West and Fails Everywhere Else*. London: Black Swan Books.

Starowicz, Mark. 1993. "Citizens of Video-America: What Happened to Canadian Television in the Satellite Age." In *Small Nations, Big Neighbour:*

Denmark and Quebec/Canada Compare Notes on American Popular Culture, 1993, ed. R. de la Garde, W. Gilsdorf, and I. Wechselmann with the collaboration of J. Lerche-Nielson, 83–102. London: John Libbey.

Stephens, Chuck. 2000. "Wet behind the Ears." *Filmmaker Magazine*. http://filmmakermagazine.com/archives/issues/fall2000/short_reports/suzhou.php.

Sterrit, David. 2002. "A Tale of Two Boys, One Bicycle, Reveals Chinese Society." *Christian Science Monitor*, 2 August. http://www.csmonitor.com/2002/0208/p15s03-almo.html

Stewart, Andrew. 2013. "Jobs Jolted by Celluloid Sayonara." *Variety*, 17 April. http://variety.com/2013/film/news/jobs-jolted-by-celluloid-sayonara-1200375848/

Sundance Institute. 2012. "First-Ever Sundance London Kicks Off at the O2 with an Evening with Robert Redford and T Bone Burnett." Accessed 5 March. http://www.sundance.org/press-center/release/first-ever-sundance-london-kicks-off-at-the-o2-with-an-evening-with-robert-/.

Suner, Asuman. 2010. *New Turkish Cinema: Belonging, Identity, and Memory*. London: I.B. Tauris.

Symposium on the Cinema and the State. 1979. *Cinema and the State: Report of the Committee on Culture and Education. Rapporteur: Joop Voogd. Documents Relating to the Lisbon Symposium on the Cinema and the State, of 14–16 June 1978*. Strasbourg: Council of Europe.

Taie, Khalid al-. 2012. "Iraq Ministry of Culture to Produce 19 New Films." *Mawtani.com*, 6 July. http://mawtani.al-shorfa.com/en_GB/articles/iii/features/2012/07/06/feature-02.

Tam, Kwok-kan, and Wimal Dissanayake. 1998. *New Chinese Cinema*. Oxford: Oxford University Press.

The Tango Lesson. 1997. Film. Directed by Sally Potter. UK: Adventure Pictures, Adventure Films, Arts Council of England.

Tarkovsky, Andrey. 1987. *Sculpting in Time: Reflections on the Cinema*. Trans. Kitty Hunter-Blair. Austin: University of Texas Press.

Tcheuyap, Alexie. 2011. *Postnationalist African Cinemas*. New York: Palgrave MacMillan.

Telefilm Canada. 1999. *Co-production Guide: Partnering with Canada*. Montreal: International Relations Division of Telefilm Canada with the collaboration of the Communications and Public Affairs Division.

Ten Thousand Waves. 2010. Film. Directed by Isaac Julien. UK: LUMA Foundation.

The Terence Davies Trilogy. 1983. Directed by Terence Davies. UK: British Film Institute (BFI), Greater London Arts Association, National Film and Television School (NFTS).

Thede, Nancy, and Alain Ambrosi, eds. 1991. *Video the Changing World*. Montreal: Black Rose Books.

This Filthy Earth. 2001. Film. Directed by Andrew Kötting. UK: East London Film Fund, Film Council, FilmFour.

Tomaselli, Keyan. 2006. *Encountering Modernity: Twentieth Century South African Cinema*. SAVUSA Series. Amsterdam: Rozenberg UNISA Press.

"Top M'sian Filmmakers Welcome Tax Rebate." 2011. *The Daily Chilli*, 31 January. http://news.asiaone.com/News/Latest+News/Showbiz/Story/A1Story20110131-261296.html.

Torino Film Lab. 2012. "In What City Does It Live?" Accessed 21 March. http://www.torinofilmlab.it/project.php?id=62.

Tribeca Film Festival. 2012. "About Us." Accessed 1 March. http://www.tribecafilm.com/about/.

Tsitsopoulou, Vassiliki. 2011. "Coloniality and Early Greek Film Culture." In *Greek Cinema: Texts, Histories, Identities*, ed. Lydia Papadimitriou and Yannis Tzioumakis, 73–95. Bristol: Intellect/University of Chicago Press.

Twixt. 2011. Film. Directed by Francis Ford Coppola. United States: Touchstone Pictures.

Tzioumakis, Yannis. 2006. *Independent American Cinema: An Introduction*. Edinburgh: Edinburgh University Press. http://dx.doi.org/10.3366/edinburgh/9780748618668.001.0001.

Tzioumakis, Yannis. 2012a. *Hollywood's Indies: Classics Divisions, Specialty Labels, and the American Film Market*. Edinburgh: Edinburgh University Press.

Tzioumakis, Yannis. 2012b. "'Independent,' 'Indie,' and 'Indiewood': Towards a Periodisation of Contemporary (Post-1980) American Independent Cinema." In *American Independent Cinema: Indie, Indiewood, and Beyond*, ed. G. King, C. Molloy, and Y. Tzioumakis, 26–38. London: Routledge.

Ukadike, N. Frank. 2002. *Questioning African Cinema: Conversations with Filmmakers*. Minneapolis: University of Minnesota Press.

"Universal's Independent Movie Operation Combines U.S. Distribution, Foreign Sales." 2003. 19 May, *Deal Memo* 10 (9): 10.

Universidad de Lima y el Cineclub P-19. 2010. "Peruvian Cinema in Debate: Is There an Independent Cinema?" [in Spanish, "El Cine Peruano en debate: ¿Existe un cine independiente?"]. *University of Lima* video, 6:46. 1 October 2013. http://www.youtube.com/watch?v=mtqjhPUS6nA

Valck, Marijke de. 2007. *Film Festivals: From European Geopolitics to Global Cinephilia*. Amsterdam: Amsterdam University Press. http://dx.doi.org/10.5117/9789053561928.

Van Couvering, Alicia. 2007. "Alicia Van Couvering Reports on the Ascending Independent Film Movement Currently Being Dubbed 'Mumblecore.'"

Filmmaker, Spring. http://www.filmmakermagazine.com/issues/
    spring2007/features/mumblecore.php.

Verhoeven, D. 2006. "Film and Video." In *The Media and Communications in
    Australia*, 2nd ed., ed. S. Cunningham and G. Turner, 154–74. Sydney: Allen
    and Unwin.

Vettath, Malavika. 2012. "After War, Iraqis Tell Their Tales through Films."
    TwoCircles.net, 22 April. http://twocircles.net/2012apr22/after_war_iraqis_
    tell_their_tales_through_films.html.

Vivarelli, Nick. 2013. "Tribeca, Doha Film Institute End Partnership."
    Variety, 30 April. http://variety.com/2013/film/international/
    tribeca-doha-film-institute-end-partnership-1200427812/.

Wasko, Janet. 2003. *How Hollywood Works*. New York: Sage.

Wiese, Michael. 1992. *Film and Video Financing*. Los Angeles: Michael Wiese
    Productions.

Wikipedia. 2013. "Internet Censorship." Accessed 29 July. http://
    en.wikipedia.org/wiki/Censorship_of_Twitter

Wright, Richard. 1995. "Technology Is the People's Friend: Computers, Class,
    and the New Cultural Politics." In *Critical Issues in Electronic Media*, ed.
    Simon Penny, 75–104. Albany: State University of New York Press.

Young, Deborah. 2010. "*Qarantina*: A Film Review." *Hollywood Reporter*,
    8 November. http://www.hollywoodreporter.com/review/
    qarantina-film-review-42932.

Young Soul Rebels. 1991. Film. Directed by Isaac Julien. UK: British Film
    Institute (BFI), Channel Four Films, Iberoamericana Films Producción.

Yow, Hong Chieh. 2011. "Census: Population Hits 27.5m Mark." *Malaysian
    Insider.com*, 22 December. http://www.themalaysianinsider.com/malaysia/
    article/census-population-hits-27.5m-mark/

Yu, Bin. 2007. "Jia Zhangke: From Movie Migrant Worker to International
    Fame" [Jia Zhangke: Cong "dianying mingong" dao guoji wenming]. *Peo-
    ple's Daily Overseas Edition*, 9 May, p. 07 [Renmin ribao haiwaiban 2007-
    05-09, 07ban]. http://paper.people.com.cn/rmrbhwb/html/2007-05/09/
    content_12854975.htm.

Yu, Bo. 2002. "The Sixth Generation Directors: The Generation That Rejects
    Generalization [in Chinese, 第六代导演:抗拒归纳的一代]. 21 May. http://
    cul.sinacom.cn/s/2002-05-21/13047.html

Yu, Sen-lun. 2002. "Director Aims Lens at China's New Generation." *Taipei Times*,
    26 May. http://www.taipeitimes.com/news/2002/05/26/story/0000137751.

Zhang, Yingjin. 2002. *Screening China: Critical Interventions, Cinematic Recon-
    figurations, and the Transnational Imaginary in Contemporary Chinese Cinema*.
    Ann Arbor: University of Michigan.

Zieman. 2012. "When Afdlin Joined UMNO." *The Star*, 5 January.
http://ecentral.my/news/story.asp?file=/2012/1/5/tvnradio/2012010514
0144&sec=tvnradio

Zion, L. 2005. "Screen Savers: Are These the Movies That Will Rescue the
Australian Film Industry?" *The Australian*, NSW Review, 2 July, 5.

Contributors

Murat Akser is a lecturer in cinematic arts at the University of Ulster. He was chair of the new-media department and founding director of the cinema and television master's program at Kadir Has University in Istanbul, Turkey. He has his master's degree in film and a doctorate in communication and culture from York University, Canada, and has published on film parody and political film in various publications including the *Canadian Journal of Film Studies* and *Film and Politics* (Cambridge Scholars Press).

Doris Baltruschat is a SSHRC Research Fellow and Instructor in the Department of Theatre and Film at the University of British Columbia. Her research focuses include globalization and culture, film and television co-production, digital cinema (3-D and virtual), interactive and alternative media, and social movements and has been featured in journals and books published in Canada, the United States, England, Australia, and China, as well as in her book *Global Media Ecologies: Networked Production in Film and Television* (Routledge, 2010). She holds a master's degree from the University of Leicester in the United Kingdom, and a doctorate from Simon Fraser University in Canada.

Mary P. Erickson is a film/media consultant and founder of the Pacific Northwest Media Research Consortium.. Her research focuses include regional audio-visual media production, global film industries, independent media, cultural policy, and communication technologies. Her studies have been published in *Film History*, *International Journal of Cultural Policy*, and *The YouTube Reader*, among other publications. She is also co-editor (with Janet Wasko) of *Cross-Border Cultural Production: Economic Runaway or Globalization?* (Cambria Press, 2008).

David Hamilton is a co-founder, with internationally acclaimed director Deepa Mehta, of the Toronto-based independent film production company Hamilton Mehta Productions. Hamilton produced Mehta's very successful films: the Elemental Trilogy *Fire, Earth, Water* (including the four years spent putting *Water* back together after it had been shut down), *Bollywood/Hollywood*, and *Heaven on Earth*. He was the executive producer on the first Hong Kong-Canada co-production, *Lunch with Charles*, directed by Michael Parker. Hamilton Mehta Productions has been internationally recognized for its powerful and politically charged films that explore the human condition. They have been the recipients of many well-respected international awards, and *Water* was nominated for a Best Foreign Film Academy Award. David Hamilton was the producer of Dilip Mehta's internationally acclaimed documentary *The Forgotten Woman*, about widows in contemporary India; he also produced a comedy about intrigue at the Canadian High Commission in New Delhi, *Cooking with Stella*, directed by Dilip Mehta.

Teresa Hoefert de Turégano is a funding adviser for international co-productions at the Medienboard Berlin-Brandenburg in Germany. She holds a doctorate from the Graduate Institute of International Studies of the University of Geneva in history and international politics. She taught cinema at the University of Lausanne, Switzerland, and has worked for Eurimages and the European Audiovisual Observatory at the Council of Europe. She regularly works as a consultant on film and cultural policy.

Gaik Cheng Khoo is an associate professor at the School of Modern Languages and Cultures at the University of Nottingham, Malaysia Campus. She has published extensively on Malaysian independent films, contributing journal articles as well as book chapters in Routledge and Cornell Southeast Asia Program. Recent publications include a book co-authored with Jean Duruz, *Eating Together: Food, Space, and Identity in Malaysia and Singapore* and a co-edited special issue, "Malaysia's New Ethnoscapes and Different Forms of Belonging" for *Citizenship Studies* (December 2014).

Erik Knudsen is a filmmaker and recently joined Bournemouth University's Media School in the UK as a professor of Visual and Digital Culture. He is a visiting professor, and the former head of the Editing Department, at the Escuela Internacional de Cine y Televisión in Cuba and at Multimedia University, Malaysia. He writes on film practice, and recent writings include co-authoring *Creative Documentary: Theory and Practice*. Erik Knudsen is a member of the editorial board of the *Journal of Media Practice* and a peer review college member for the Arts and Humanities Research Council in the United Kingdom. He currently leads the StoryLab International Research Network, funded by the UK Arts and Humanities Research Council. He also runs his own film production company, One Day Films Limited (onedayfilms.com). His films include *The Silent Accomplice, Vainilla Chip, Veil,* and *Heart of Gold*. His most recent feature film, *The Raven on the Jetty*, was produced in 2014.

Hongwei Lu is a professor in and Director of the Asian Studies Program at the University of Redlands, California. She also serves on the advisory committee of the Visual and Media Studies Program at the University of Redlands. Her teaching and research focus on modern and contemporary Chinese literature and film. Her scholarly publications have appeared in *The China Review Journal, Chinese Literature Today, Asian Cinema Journal, The Journal of Asian Studies,* and *ASIANetwork Journal*.

Gabriela Martínez is an international award-winning documentary filmmaker who has produced, directed, or edited more than ten ethnographic and social documentaries, including *Ñakaj, Textiles in the Southern Andes, Mamacoca,* and *Qoyllur Rit'i: A Woman's Journey*. She is also an associate professor at the School of Journalism and Communication at the University of Oregon. Her research interests include the global circulation of technologies and cultural products and their economic, social, cultural, and political impact on Third World countries, especially Latin America. Recent publications include *Latin American Telecommunications: Telefónica's Conquest* and articles in *Jumpcut*.

Martin Mhando is an associate professor in the School of Media, Communication, and Culture at Murdoch University in Western Australia. He is also a filmmaker with award-winning feature and documentary film credits. As well as being co-editor of the *Journal of African Cinemas*, he is the director of the Zanzibar International Film Festival (ZIFF). His areas of interest and research include documentary theory, film production praxis, African cinema, community media, world cinema, festival studies, and indigenous knowledge. His accomplishments have been acknowledged with a Lifetime Achievement Award at ZIFF 2012 and the Zeze Award 2006 in Tanzania for his contribution to the arts in that country. His Academy Award–nominated film *Maangamizi* won the Paul Robeson Award (2004) for Excellence in Independent Filmmaking.

Lydia Papadimitriou is the program leader and senior lecturer in Film Studies at Liverpool John Moores University in the United Kingdom. Her research interests include Greek cinema, popular European cinema, the films of Theo Angelopoulos, film genre, and stardom. She has published a number of books and articles on Greek cinema, including *The Greek Film Musical: A Critical and Cultural History* (also translated into Greek, 2009) and *Greek Cinema: Texts, Histories, and Identities* (co-edited with Yannis Tzioumakis). She is the principal editor of the *Journal of Greek Media and Culture* (Intellect, 2014).

Sheila Petty is a professor of Media Studies at the University of Regina, Canada. She has written extensively on issues of cultural representation, identity, and nation in African and African-diasporic screen media and has curated film, television, and digital media exhibitions for galleries across Canada. She is author of *Contact Zones: Memory, Origin, and Discourses in Black Diasporic Cinema* (Wayne State University Press, 2008). Sheila Petty is co-editor (with Blandine Stefanson) of the forthcoming *World Directory of Cinema: Africa* (Intellect Books). Her current research focuses on interpretive strategies for analysing digital creative cultural practices and real-time decision making. She is an adjunct scientist at TRLabs Regina and leader of an interdisciplinary research group, New Media Studio Laboratory, spanning computer science, engineering, and fine arts.

Mark David Ryan is a senior lecturer in film, screen, and animation for the Creative Industries Faculty at Queensland University of Technology. He is an expert in Australian horror and genre cinema and is currently working on research projects that explore emergent transmedia screen production. Mark David Ryan has written extensively on Australian horror films, genre cinema, the industry dynamics of cultural production, and cultural policy. He is an editor of the *Directory of World Cinema: Australia and New Zealand 2* published by Intellect. His research has been published in *New Review of Film & Television Studies*, *Media International Australia: Incorporating Culture and Policy*, *Continuum: Journal of Media & Cultural Studies*, and *Studies in Australasian Cinema*, and by prominent publishers such as Routledge, Sage, and University of Ottawa Press.

Yannis Tzioumakis is a senior lecturer in Communication and Media Studies at the University of Liverpool, United Kingdom. He has published widely on aspects of American cinema such as the history of Orion Pictures, film authorship in contemporary Hollywood, and film acting in independent cinema, as well as on a number of filmmakers, including John Sayles, David Mamet, Edgar G. Ulmer, and Joseph H. Lewis. He is also the author and editor of four books and numerous essays on American independent cinema, and co-edits the American Indies series for Edinburgh University Press. He is currently co-authoring a book on acting in contemporary U.S. independent films.